# KING LEAR

William Shakespeare

# KING LEAR

## William Shakespeare

Vincent F. Petronella, Editor
University of Massachusetts–Boston

J. J. M. Tobin, General Editor
University of Massachusetts–Boston

WADSWORTH
CENGAGE Learning

Australia • Brazil • Japan • Korea • Mexico • Singapore • Spain • United Kingdom • United States

## WADSWORTH
### CENGAGE Learning™

**Evans Shakespeare Editions:**
*King Lear*
**Vincent F. Petronella, Editor**
**J.J.M. Tobin, General Editor**

Senior Publisher: Lyn Uhl

Publisher: Michael Rosenberg

Development Editor:
Michell Phifer

Assistant Editor: Erin Bosco

Editorial Assistant: Rebecca
Donahue

Media Editor: Janine Tangney

Senior Marketing Manager:
Melissa Holt

Marketing Communications
Manager: Glenn McGibbon

Content Project Manager:
Aimee Chevrette Bear

Art Director: Marissa Falco

Print Buyer: Betsy Donaghey

Rights Acquisition Specialist,
Text: Katie Huha

Rights Acquisition Specialist,
Images: Jennifer Meyer Dare

Production Service: MPS Limited,
a Macmillan Company

Cover Designer: Walter Kopec

Text Designer: Maxine Ressler

Cover Image: Robert Foxworth
as King Lear and Bruce
Turk as the Fool in the 2010
Shakespeare Festival production
of *King Lear* directed by Adrian
Noble, June 12 - Sept. 23, 2010 at
The Old Globe. (© 2010 Craig
Schwartz Photography)

Compositor: MPS Limited,
a Macmillan Company

For product information and
technology assistance, contact us at **Cengage Learning
Customer & Sales Support, 1-800-354-9706**

For permission to use material from this text
or product, submit all requests online at
**www.cengage.com/permissions**
Further permissions questions can be emailed to
**permissionrequest@cengage.com**

Library of Congress Control Number: 2010942817

ISBN-13: 978-0-495-91123-4

ISBN-10: 0-495-91123-2

**Wadsworth**
20 Channel Center Street
Boston, MA 02210
USA

Cengage Learning is a leading provider of customized
learning solutions with office locations around the globe,
including Singapore, the United Kingdom, Australia,
Mexico, Brazil, and Japan. Locate your local office at:
**international.cengage.com/region**

Cengage Learning products are represented in Canada by
Nelson Education, Ltd.

For your course and learning solutions, visit
**www.cengage.com**

Purchase any of our products at your local college store
or at our preferred online store **www.cengagebrain.com**

Printed in the United States of America
1 2 3 4 5 6 7 14 13 12 11

Titles in the *Evans Shakespeare Editions*
from Cengage Learning

**As You Like It**
Heather Dubrow, Volume Editor

**Hamlet**
J. J. M. Tobin, Volume Editor

**Macbeth**
Katherine Rowe, Volume Editor

**Measure for Measure**
John Klause, Volume Editor

**A Midsummer Night's Dream**
Douglas Bruster, Volume Editor

**Richard III**
Nina Levine, Volume Editor

**The Tempest**
Grace Tiffany, Editor

**The Winter's Tale**
Lawrence F. Rhu, Volume Editor

# TABLE OF CONTENTS

Critical Essays

Classic Essays

## Modern Essays

# ACKNOWLEDGMENTS

I dedicate this volume to John J. M. Tobin and to the memory of Gwynne Evans—two scholars whose work as Shakespearean authors and teachers have been marked by a wealth of learning, intellectual illumination, exemplary encouragement, and friendship. From them springs "the true Promethean fire."

In addition, I am proud to acknowledge the assistance of two scholars I have been extremely fortunate to know and love—my wife, Mary Melvin Petronella, "She is herself a dowry," whose steadfast optimism, persevering proofreading, and astute suggestions have been invaluable—and my goddaughter, Susannah Barton Tobin, for her diligent and generous assistance in searching—even in the midst of a demanding schedule—through myriad sources for important images and adeptly managing the intricacies of typing my Excel image log. We are indebted to Susannah's legal expertise donated on behalf of the Evans Shakespeare Editions. It has been a pleasure to work with the constructive and cohesive team of Evans Editors as the series moved to fruition. I am grateful also for the expert technical assistance provided by Michell Phifer, Senior Development Editor, Cengage Wadsworth, and for her editorial skills and clarification regarding the complexities of the *King Lear* edition. For their constructive assistance, I also thank Jitendra Kumar, Sarah Bonner, Aimee Chevrette Bear, Erin Bosco, and their team. My sincere appreciation is extended to the highly commendable staff members at The Clapp Library, Wellesley College; The British Library, London; The Mugar Memorial Library, Boston University; The Goldfarb Library, Brandeis University; The Houghton Library, Harvard University; The Healey Library, University of Massachusetts Boston; and the Cary Memorial Library, Lexington, Massachusetts.

# LIST OF ILLUSTRATIONS

## Color Plates

## Illustrations in the Text

# ABOUT THIS SERIES

## J. J. M. Tobin

THE EVANS Shakespeare Editions are individual editions of essential plays by William Shakespeare, edited by leading scholars to provide college and university students, advanced high school students, and interested independent readers with a comprehensive guide to the plays and their historical and modern contexts.

The volume editor of each play has written an introduction to the play and a history of the play in performance on both stage and screen. Central sources and contexts for the play are included, and each editor also has surveyed the critical commentary on the play and selected representative influential essays to illuminate the text further. A guide to additional reading, viewing, and listening concludes the volume and will continue the reader's relationship with the play.

Each volume includes an overview of Shakespeare's life and the world of London theater that he inhabited. Our goal for these editions is that they provide the reader a window into Shakespeare and his work that reminds us all of his enduring global influence.

The text for these plays comes from *The Riverside Shakespeare*, edited with notes and textual commentary by the late Gywnne Blakemore Evans. Evans was known for his unrivaled scholarly precision, and his *Riverside* text is an essential and much-admired modern edition of Shakespeare. The Evans Shakespeare Editions preserve the *Riverside* line numbering, which is the numbering used in the invaluable *Harvard Concordance to Shakespeare* by Marvin Spevack.

Beyond his scholarly work, Evans was a generous mentor to many of the editors in this series and a tremendous influence on all of us. His kind-hearted nature made it impossible for him truly to dislike anyone. However, despite an identification with the most traditional and canonical of cultural texts, he reserved a raised eyebrow and stern words for those whose politics lacked empathy and understanding for the full diversity of human experience. In this attitude too, as in all his writing and teaching, it was evident that he was a scholar who understood Shakespeare. This series is dedicated to his memory.

# SHAKESPEARE'S LIFE

*J. J. M. Tobin*

SHAKESPEARE WAS a genius, but he was no unreachable ivory-tower poet. Instead, Shakespeare was a young man from the provinces who made good in the big city of London. Just when and how he came from the provinces remains a mystery. He was born in 1564, the eldest son of an initially quite successful father whose position as alderman and then bailiff (mayor) of the town of Stratford allowed his son to attend the local Latin Grammar School. There, Shakespeare received an education that, contrary to some critics' belief, provided him with the historical perspective and verbal flexibility that helped define his writing.

The schoolboy grew into a young man who married an older woman, Anne Hathaway, and became the father of a daughter and a set of twins, a boy and a girl, by the age of twenty-one. The boy, Hamnet, would die before his twelfth birthday. When the playwright's father, John Shakespeare, only recently recovered from two decades of legal and financial difficulties, died in 1601, having earlier secured the coat of arms of a gentleman (Duncan-Jones 90–102), Shakespeare was left in Stratford with a family of four women: his wife, his two daughters, and his mother, Mary, *née* Arden. Shakespeare's own familial experiences, from the fluctuations of his father's fortunes, to the strong influence of several female relatives, to the tragic loss of a beloved son, doubtless added heart and depth to the incisive portrayals of characters that he created in his plays and poems.

Accordingly, given the fact that all description is necessarily selective, Shakespeare often had in mind his own experiences when he chose narrative and dramatic sources for the foundation of his comedies, histories, and tragedies. The few facts of his life that survive are open to all sorts of interpretations, some of which reveal more about the interpreter than about the facts themselves, while others carry with them a greater degree of likelihood. A few critics have noted that Shakespeare was the eldest boy in a patriarchal world, the first surviving child born in a time of plague after the infant deaths of two siblings. As a child, he doubtless saw and remembered his father dressed in the furred scarlet gown of a bailiff in 1568, going about his appointed supervisory tasks, a figure both familiar as a person and strangely exalted as an

3

official, and as Stephen Greenblatt has noted, all by means of a costume (Greenblatt 30–31). He was likely to have been the indisputable favorite of his mother, acquiring a self-confidence that often leads young men with even a modicum of talent on to success.

Richard Wheeler has pointed out that Shakespeare's choice of source material in which a female is disguised as a boy, best illustrated in *Twelfth Night*, has psychological roots in the playwright's wish to have repaired the loss of his son, Hamnet, whose twin sister, Judith, remained a constant reminder of the absent boy (Wheeler 147–53). Finally, although his marriage and fatherhood indicate some clear grounds for heterosexuality, Shakespeare also wrote beautiful poems about a young man, and his plays often feature male bonding and pathetic male isolation when the bond is broken by marriage, as in the instances of Antonio and Bassanio in *The Merchant of Venice* and a second Antonio and Sebastian in *Twelfth Night*. These scenarios offer putative evidence of at least homosociability.

Of course, over-reliance on causal links between the playwright and the experiences of his creations would logically have Shakespeare a conscience-stricken killer like Claudius or Macbeth, a disoriented octogenarian like Lear, and a suicidal queen like Cleopatra—interpretative leaps that even the most imaginative critic is unwilling to make.

Between the birth of the twins in February 1585 and the writer Robert Greene's allusion to Shakespeare as an actor-turned-playwright in September 1592, there is no hard evidence of his whereabouts, although many theories abound. Perhaps he was a schoolmaster in the country; perhaps he was attached to the household of a Catholic landowner in Lancashire. Certainly one of the most plausible theories is that Shakespeare joined the traveling theatrical troupe called the Queen's Men in 1587 as it passed through Stratford and then came to London as a member of their company. If so, he joined an exciting theatrical world with competition for the entertainment dollar among several companies with plays written by both authors who were university graduates and a minority who were not. It was a world that on its stages carefully reflected the political issues and events of the moment, but did so indirectly because of restrictions created by governmental censorship and by the potential dangers posed by a personal response to criticism by the powerful men of the time.

These dramas were composed for a public audience of mixed class and gender, from work-cutting apprentices to lords of the realm and every possible class gradation in between. They were also performed occasionally for a private audience of higher status in smaller indoor venues.

The London of these plays was a fast-growing city, even in a time of plague, full of energy, color, commerce, varieties of goods, animals, and people of all social degrees. The population numbered perhaps 200,000 by the end of the sixteenth century. It was governed by a Lord Mayor and a municipal council quite concerned about issues of crowd control, the spread of disease, crime, and the fallout of all three in neighborhoods either just at the edge of their partial jurisdiction, Shoreditch in the north and Southwark, Bankside, in the south, or fully within it, like the Blackfriars. Playhouses, three-tiered amphitheaters, and the earlier open-plan inn-yards with galleries above, brought together all three of these problems and more, and they were threatened constantly with restriction by the authorities, who also had the subtle financial desire of taxing players whose performances were not protected by aristocratic patronage.

By the time he joined the newly formed Lord Chamberlain's Men in 1594, Shakespeare had already written his first four history plays (*1, 2, & 3 Henry VI* and *Richard III*), the farcical comedies *The Taming of the Shrew* and *The Comedy of Errors*, and the grotesquely interesting tragedy *Titus Andronicus*. Many, but certainly not all, of his 154 sonnets were also written in the mid-1590s. When the Lord Chamberlain's Men moved into the newly constructed Globe theatre in late 1599, having had five good years at the Theatre and the nearby Curtain in Shoreditch, Shakespeare had scripted four more history plays, *King John, Richard II*, and *1 & 2 Henry IV* (and part of a fifth play, *Edward III*), six comedies, including *The Two Gentlemen of Verona, Love's Labour's Lost*, three of the five so-called "golden comedies" (*A Midsummer Night's Dream, The Merchant of Venice,* and *Much Ado About Nothing*), and *Romeo and Juliet,* the tragic companion to *A Midsummer Night's Dream*.

The opening season at the Globe doubtless included the last of the English history plays written solely by Shakespeare, *Henry V*, the pastoral comedy both debunking and idealistic, *As You Like It*, and the most frequently taught of the plays focused on Roman history, *Julius Caesar*. Before the death of Queen Elizabeth in late March of 1603, Shakespeare had certainly written his most famous play, *Hamlet*, his most intensely claustrophobic tragedy, *Othello*, the bourgeois domestic comedy *The Merry Wives of Windsor*, the last of the "golden comedies," which we find alloyed with both satire and melancholy, *Twelfth Night*, and the uniquely powerful satirical comedy *Troilus and Cressida*, as well as the enigmatic poem about martyrdom, *The Phoenix and Turtle*.

Outbreaks of the plague affected Shakespeare both as a dramatist and as a poet, for the virulence of the disease, when deaths reached more than fifty a week in London, forced the authorities to close the theaters in order to restrict contagion. Shakespeare was thus left with added time free from the incessant pressure to produce dramatic scripts, and he then composed his two Ovidian narrative poems, *Venus and Adonis* (1593) and *The Rape of Lucrece* (1594). The most extended theater closings were from June 1592 to May 1594 and from March 1603 to April 1604, but there were other, briefer closings. The plague was an abiding and overpowering presence in the lives and imaginations of the poet and his audiences.

After the accession in 1603 of James VI of Scotland as James I of England, when the Lord Chamberlain's Men became the King's Men, and before the company activated for themselves the lease in 1608 of the Blackfriars, a smaller, indoor theater that was to draw a higher and more homogeneous class of spectator, Shakespeare created his other great tragedies, *King Lear, Macbeth, Antony and Cleopatra,* and *Coriolanus,* as well as the bitter *Timon of Athens* (although there is no record of its ever having been performed), and the two "bed-trick" plays, *All's Well That Ends Well* and *Measure for Measure,* comedies in which a lecherous man is fooled by the substitution of one woman for another in the darkness of the night. For that indoor spectacle-friendly Blackfriars theatre, Shakespeare wrote the romances *Pericles, Cymbeline, The Winter's Tale,* and *The Tempest,* with their wondrous atmospheres and radiant daughters. By 1611, Shakespeare was moving into partial retirement, co-authoring with John Fletcher, his younger colleague and successor as principal playwright of the King's Men, *Henry VIII, The Two Noble Kinsmen,* and, probably, the lost *Cardenio.*

The division of his plays into these categories—comedies, histories, tragedies, and romances—reminds us that the first step taken by the playwright (indeed any playwright) was to determine the basic genre or kind of play that he wished to write, however much he might expand its boundaries. Genre creates expectations in the mind of the audience, expectations that no dramatist of the time was willing to frustrate. Regarding kind, Polonius tells us with unconscious humor of the versatility of the players who come to Elsinore: "The best actors in the world, either for tragedy, comedy, history, pastoral, pastoral-comical, historical-pastoral, tragical-historical, tragical-comical-historical-pastoral" (2.2.396–399). In that boundary-blurring, increasingly capacious definition of genre, he also informs us of Shakespeare's own gift in all kinds of writing and the fact of his often combining many of these genres in a single work. When, at the end of Plato's *Symposium,* Socrates argues that logically, the greatest tragic writer should also be the greatest comic writer, he was prophetic of Shakespeare, even if he doesn't go on to argue that these principles of tragedy and comedy could and should be connected in the same play. And Shakespeare indirectly repays Socrates for his prophecy by alluding to the philosopher's death in Mistress Quickly's description of the dying Falstaff in *Henry V,* 2.3.

Shakespeare is Shakespeare because of a combination of philosophical tolerance, psychological profundity, and metaphoric genius; that is, he is generous-minded, aware of what makes people tick, and is able to express himself more vividly and memorably than anyone else in the language. And it is his language that truly sets him apart, while simultaneously creating some occasional static in the mind of the modern reader.

There are six areas of this problematic language worth special attention: word choice, false friends, allusions, puns, iambic rhythm, and personification. Shakespeare's vocabulary has words that are no longer part of today's language, chiefly because they refer to things and concepts no longer in use, such as "three-farthings," coins of small value, in the Bastard's metaphoric "Look where three-farthings goes" (*King John*, 1.1.143). Such terms are easily understood by looking at the footnotes, or by checking *The Oxford English Dictionary* or a Shakespearean lexicon, like that of Schmidt; C. T. Onions's *A Shakespeare Glossary;* or *Shakespeare's Words,* by David and Ben Crystal. More difficult are false friends, words spelled the same as words we use today but that have different meanings. One example of this issue is "brave," which as an adjective in the sixteenth and early seventeenth centuries meant primarily "splendid" or "glorious," as in Miranda's expression of awe and excitement in *The Tempest:* "O *brave* new world / That has such people in't" (5.1.183–84), or "virtue," which in Shakespeare's language usually means "strength or power," as in Iago's argument for personal responsibility to Roderigo and the latter's lament that "it is not in my *virtue* to amend it [being in love with Desdemona]": "*Virtue?* A fig! 'tis in ourselves that we are thus or thus" (*Othello*, 1.3.318–20).

Equally problematic, but just as easily understood by reference to footnotes, are instances of classical and biblical allusion, where Shakespeare assumes a recognition by all or some of the audience of glancing references to Greek and Roman deities, frequently to elements in that most abiding narrative in Western literature, the Trojan War, as well as historical and legendary figures, as in Hamlet's "My father's brother, but no more like my father / Than I to *Hercules*" (1.2.152–53) or his subconscious reminder in the graveyard of the fact that his father was the victim of fratricide, "How the knave jowls it to the ground, as if 'twere *Cain's* jaw-bone" (5.1.76–77).

More difficult at times are Shakespeare's puns—plays on words, sometimes comedic and sometimes intentionally non-comedic, but in each case designed to bring more than one meaning in a single word to the attention of the audience and the reader. Shakespeare's puns are almost always thematically significant, revelatory of character, or both, and attention to the possibilities of the presence of punning can only increase our understanding and pleasure in the lines. There are such simple etymological puns as "lieutenant," the military title of Cassio in *Othello*, where the word is defined as one who holds the place of the captain in the latter's absence—exactly the fear Othello has about the relationship that he imagines exists between his wife, Desdemona, and Lieutenant Cassio. There are also puns that fuse the physical and the moral, as in Falstaff's comment that his highway robbery is condoned by the goddess of the moon, "under whose *countenance* we steal" (*1 Henry IV*, 1.2.29), where the word "countenance" means both "face" and "approval." Falstaff's pun is in prose, a good example of how Shakespeare, commonly regarded as the greatest of English poets and dramatists, wrote often in prose, which itself is full of the linguistic devices of poetry.

When Shakespeare was writing in verse, he used iambic pentameter lines, ten syllable lines with five feet, or units, of two syllables each, in the sequence of short-long or unstressed-stressed. Consider, for example, Romeo's "But soft, / what light / through yond / er win /

Fig. 1. Joseph Fiennes as William Shakespeare fighting through writer's block in the film *Shakespeare in Love*: a handsome dramatist without the receding hairline of contemporary portraits and busts.

dow breaks?" (*Romeo and Juliet*, 2.2.1), or Antony's "If you / have tears / prepare / to shed / them now" (*Julius Caesar*, 3.2.169).

Scanning the rhythm of these lines is made easier by our knowledge that Shakespeare and the English language are both naturally iambic and that proof of the correct rhythm begins with marking the stress on the final syllable of the line and moving right to left. The rhythm with the emphasized syllables will lead the actor delivering the lines to stress certain words more than others, as we imagine Shakespeare to have intended, even as we know that stage delivery of lines with an unexpected stress can create fruitful tension in the ear of the audience. For example, Barnardo's "It was about to speak when the cock crew" (*Hamlet*, 1.1.147) is a pentameter line, but the expected iambic rhythm is broken in the last two feet, especially in the sequentially stressed final two syllables, which by their alliteration and double stress combine in form to underscore the moment of interruption in the play's narrative. Such playing off the expected is part of Shakespeare's arsenal of verse techniques.

In addition to these issues of unknown terms, false friends, allusions chiefly classical and biblical, meaningful puns, and verse rhythm itself, there is the metaphoric language that is the glory of Shakespeare, but each instance of this feature demands careful unpacking. Consider the early example of Romeo's personifying Death as an erotic figure keeping Juliet as his mistress, linking the commonly joined notions of love and death: "Shall I believe / That unsubstantial Death is amorous, / And that the lean abhorred monster keeps / Thee here in dark to be his paramour?" (5.3.102–05). This link already had been anticipated by the Chorus in the prologue to the play, which speaks of "The fearful passage of their death-marked love" (l.6).

More compactly, later in his career, Shakespeare will have Hamlet, in prose, combine Renaissance and medieval views in similes and metaphors, comparisons with and without "like" or "as," in order to describe the multifaceted nature of man: "...how like an angel in apprehension, how like a god! The beauty of the world; the paragon of animals; and yet to me what is this quintessence of dust?" (*Hamlet*, 2.2.306–08). Macbeth in his play will argue against his wife's view that a little water will cleanse his guilty hands: "No; this my hand will rather / The multitudinous seas incarnadine, / Making the green one red" (2.2.58–60). Here Shakespeare has been careful to combine the mouth-filling hyperbole and its Latinate terms "multitudinous" and "incarnadine" (an illustration of the technique that he had learned from Christopher Marlowe) with a crystal-clear synonymous expression, "Making the green one red," for the benefit of all in the theater, even as everyone hears the hypnotically mellifluous line that comes before it.

Sometimes Shakespeare scorned the opportunity to use high-flown language, even when one might expect it most, as in the Roman play *Antony and Cleopatra*, when the queen uses a noun as a verb in her bitter image of herself live on the Roman stage played by a child actor, "And I shall see / Some squeaking Cleopatra *boy* my greatness / I'th' posture of a whore" (*Antony and Cleopatra*, 5.2.219–221). Shakespeare gives to Cleopatra's handmaiden Charmian the least hyperbolic expression in a context linking the erotic and funereal (analogous to that situation described by Romeo), "Now boast thee, death, in thy possession lies / A *lass* unparallel'd" (5.2.315–16), where the simple pastoral monosyllable charms the audience, which all along had sensed the antithesis of the playful girl within the cunningly imperious and imperial queen.

While nothing can fully explain the development of this language, its raw material comes largely from Shakespeare's reading, as do the basic elements of plot and character. The same man who was to save and increase his money and property in London and Stratford was, as a craftsman, equally economical, preferring to alter and expand upon material given to him in the literary sources that lie behind all his compositions rather than to create from experience alone. He is the chief counter-example to Polonius's admonition "Neither a borrower nor a lender be" (*Hamlet* 1.3.75)—Shakespeare is a world-class borrower, but one who reshapes and transforms the borrowed materials.

Certainly he had a most retentive memory and could and did recall, at times subconsciously, both single expressions and rather lengthy passages from his reading. "It is often as if, at some deep level of his mind, Shakespeare thought and felt in quotation," as Emrys Jones has noted (Jones 21). Dryden's comment that Shakespeare "needed not the spectacles of books to read Nature; he looked inwards and found her there" ignores Shakespeare's conscious manipulations of his reading as a chief source for his achievement. Nevertheless, Dryden gives us the basic image useful for picturing Shakespeare's genius. The playwright's metaphorical spectacles had two lenses, one of which was focused on life as he knew it and one on the writings of his predecessors and contemporaries: historians both classical and English, proto-novelists, poets, pamphleteers, and essayists, and playwrights who had in their own ways dealt with themes that interested him.

It is by looking at what Shakespeare himself perused that we see his manipulative genius at work, omitting, adding, preserving, and qualifying those plots, motifs, and images viewed through one lens of his binoculars. An important question is just how much of the original theme and significance is brought over in the creative borrowing, a question made more difficult to answer by the fact that in the composition of his plays, Shakespeare often modified and sometimes even inverted the gender and number of the persons in the original material. See, for example, the model in the story of Cupid and Psyche from Apuleius' *The Golden Asse* (1566), where Psyche almost murders Cupid, for the description of the deaths of the little princes in *Richard III*, as well as for the presentation of the murder of Desdemona in *Othello*. The closer one looks at this source and the affected passage, the more one sees that the young man from Stratford, despite being accused by his London-educated colleague and rival Ben Jonson of having "small Latin and less Greek," was a sufficiently good Latinist to check the translation of Apuleius that he was using against the original, even as he would later check Golding's translation of the *Metamorphoses* against Ovid's Latin for use in *The Tempest*.

We don't know the workplace of Shakespeare, the desk or table where he kept his books, nor do we know for certain who provided him with these volumes, some of which were quite expensive, such as Holinshed's *Chronicles*, North's *Plutarch*, and bibles, both Bishops' and Geneva. But, if we imagine a bookshelf above his desk and envision the titles that he might have ordered there chronologically, we would first see the classics, most importantly Ovid and Virgil; then the Bible, especially Genesis, the Gospel of St. Matthew, and the Book of Revelation; medieval and Renaissance writers, including Chaucer and Erasmus; and then his own immediate predecessors and colleagues, especially Thomas Kyd, Christopher Marlowe, Robert Greene, and Thomas Nashe. Sometimes the most unlikely source can provide a motif or a character, but for more important ideas, we may note what he would have learned from four exemplary volumes on this imagined shelf.

From Seneca, the Roman philosopher, tutor to the emperor Nero and playwright of closet tragedies (that is, of plays meant to be read in the study rather than performed on stage), Shakespeare learned to balance a sensational theme—fratricide and incest—with a plot structured with care and characters subtly developed with an attitude quite fatalistic. From Plutarch, the Greek historian who wrote parallel lives of Greek and Roman leaders, he learned the importance of the nature of the private man when serving in public office and how that nature is revealed in small gestures with large significance—what James Joyce, the "spiritual son" of Shakespeare, would later refer to as "epiphanies." From Machiavelli, the notorious early-sixteenth-century political theorist, or from the image of Machiavelli, he saw what he had already known about the role of deception and amorality in political life. From Michel de Montaigne, the sixteenth-century father of the essay, he added to his already operative skepticism, a capacity to question received notions about the consistency of the "self" and the hierarchical place of human beings in creation.

Fig. 2. Later, on other writers' bookshelves, would be Shakespeare's own First Folio (1623), containing thirty-six plays, half of them appearing in print for the first time. It does not, however, include any of the longer poems or sonnets.

To enjoy Shakespeare, it is not at all necessary to understand the sources that he mined, but to study Shakespeare, the better to appreciate the depth and complexity of the work, it is extremely useful to examine the foundations upon which he has built his characters and plots. We can trace, for example, the many constituent elements that have gone into the creation of Falstaff, who, together with Hamlet, is the most discussed of Shakespeare's creations. The elements include, among still others, the Vice of the morality plays; the rogue from Nashe's *The Unfortunate Traveller;* the *miles gloriosus* or cowardly braggart warrior from the Roman comic playwright (and school text) Plautus; the cheerful toper from the Bacchus of Nashe's *Summer's Last Will and Testament;* parodically, the Protestant martyr Sir John Oldcastle from Foxe's *Book of Martyrs;* and even the dying Socrates of Plato's *Phaedo.* Not that Falstaff is at all times all these figures, but in the course of his career in four plays, alive in *1 & 2 Henry IV,* dying offstage in *Henry V,* and radically transformed in *The Merry Wives of Windsor,* he is each of them by turn and counterturn, and still so much more than the mere sum of all these literary, dramatic, and historical parts.

In terms of giving voice to multiple perspectives, to characters of different ages, genders, colors, ethnicities, religions, and social ranks, Shakespeare is unrivaled. No other playwright, then or since, makes other selves live while simultaneously concealing his own self or selves, a talent described by Keats as "negative capability." Shakespeare was also an actor; that is, a person interested in imitating imaginary persons. He was thus doubly a quite creative mimic. Some of the selves mimicked are versions of the "Other," those foreigners or aliens from around the world, including Africans (Aaron, Morocco, Othello), Jews (Shylock, Tubal, Jessica), Frenchmen and Frenchwomen (the Dauphin, Joan of Arc, Margaret of Anjou), non-English Britons (Irish: Macmorris; Scots: Jamy; Welsh: Fluellen), as well as such other continental Europeans as Spaniards (Don Armado) and Italians (including several Antonios), to say nothing of the indefinable Caliban.

Some of his topics, his subjects for dramatic treatment, came often from already set pieces at school, as Emrys Jones, among others, has shown. For example, a set question to be answered, pro and con, was, should Brutus have joined the conspiracy to assassinate Caesar, the answer to which helps create the tensions in *Julius Caesar* (Jones 16). Such an on-the-one-hand and on-the-other school exercise became part of Shakespeare's dramatic strategy, where plays provide the tension created by opposites and the consequent rich ground for multiple interpretations by readers and audiences. There were also sources in earlier stage productions, including plays about Romeo and Juliet, King John, King Lear, and Hamlet. Marlowe especially provided structures to imitate and diverge from in his plays of a weak king (*Edward II*) and of several extraordinary ambitious characters, among whom are a villainous Jew (*The Jew of Malta*), and a rhetorical conqueror (*Tamburlaine*), brilliant efforts which become in Shakespeare's hands the still more dramatic *Richard II, The Merchant of Venice*, and *Henry V*.

Shakespeare's borrowing was frequent and pervasive, but his creative adaptations of those raw materials have made him ultimately not just a borrower but in fact the world's greatest lender, giving us four hundred years of pleasure and providing countless artists, whether painters, novelists, film directors, or even comic book writers, with allusive material. Of course, we would happily surrender our knowledge of a number of these borrowings if only we could have some sense of the quality of the voice of the leading man Richard Burbage, of the facial expressions of the comic actor Will Kemp, the sounds of the groundlings' responses to both the jokes and the set soliloquies, and the reactions of both Queen Elizabeth, who allegedly after watching *1 & 2 Henry IV* wanted to see Falstaff in love, and King James, who doubtless loved the image of his ancestor Banquo in *Macbeth*.

Shakespeare's last years before his death in April 1616 were spent back in Stratford. Although little is known of that time, we are left with the enigmatic coda to his life: his will, in which he famously left to his wife, Anne Hathaway Shakespeare, "the second-best bed"—it is unclear whether it was a cruel slight or a fondly personal bequest. Care of his estate went to his elder daughter, Susannah, while a lesser inheritance went to his wayward younger daughter, Judith, and any children she might have. He died a landowner, a family man, and a once well-known playwright. His will did not cite what has become his greatest legacy—the plays and poems that we read today—but the clues that these works leave about his life, and certainly the testament to his talent that they represent, are more valuable than even the most detailed autobiography. To be sure, however, the local boy who made good, worked hard, had flaws, and lived a complicated family life has more in common with many of his readers, then and now, than does the iconic Shakespeare, who has been mistakenly portrayed as a distant genius paring his fingernails while creating many of the greatest works in world literature.

# ELIZABETHAN THEATER

*J. J. M. Tobin*

MASS ENTERTAINMENT today has become ever more frac-
tured as technology provides myriad ways to take in a film
(and myriad ways for Hollywood to try to make money).
Movie theaters now have to compete with home theaters and couches
in a way they never had to before in order to put people in the seats.
The attractions of high-definition screens and stereo surround-sound
are not the draw they once were now that individuals can access such
technology in their own homes, and stadium seating and chair-side
concessions don't make up the difference. The appeal of first-run films
is fading too, now that movies go to DVD in a matter of weeks and are
also available for immediate streaming through a Netflix subscription.
All of these technologies, however, whether enjoyed in the cinema or
at home, contribute to the moviegoer's sensation of being transported
to another time and place (a journey, moreover, that lasts not much
longer than an hour and a half). Hard to imagine, then, that a little
over four hundred years ago, when the battle for the entertainment
dollar took place on the stage rather than the screen, most members
of the Elizabethan audience gladly stood for more than two hours
without benefit of a padded seat, buttered popcorn, or Junior Mints
(although they did have dried fruit and nuts), or the pause button
in order to watch the plays of Shakespeare and his fellow dramatists
performed. The legendary plays we read today on these pages were
once the sixteenth- and early-seventeenth-century equivalents of the
*Harry Potter* series or *Avatar*—artistic creations to be sure, but first and
foremost moneymakers for their producers.

Theatrical performances in Elizabethan England took place all over
the country in a wide variety of venues. As we know from the work of
A. Gurr and others, if we put aside the sites used by touring companies
like the Queen's Men of the 1580s (to which Shakespeare himself may
have been attached), the guildhalls and marketplaces in cities and towns
like Norwich, Bristol, and Stratford, or the halls of the universities of
Oxford and Cambridge, and instead concentrate on London itself, we
see that there were five basic performance locales (Gurr, esp. 115 ff.).
There were, of course, the inns and inn-yards, in large part roofed
against the weather and useful especially during the winter months.

The most celebrated of these inns in the history of London theater were the Bel Savage, the Bull, and the Cross Keys, these latter two on the same London street. These were the locations most frequently of concern to the mayor and other municipal authorities anxious about unruly crowds and increased chances of plague contagion, until 1594, when it was declared by the Lord Chamberlain of the Queen's court that there would be only two adult companies—his own, the Lord Chamberlain's Men (Shakespeare's group), and his father-in-law's, the Lord Admiral's Men, troupes that would upon the succession of King James be called the King's Men and Prince Henry's Men—and they would not perform anymore in city inns.

Second, there were two indoor halls, one in a building abutting St. Paul's Cathedral, not too far from the Bel Savage Inn, and the other in the refectory of the old Blackfriars monastery, each used by the children's companies of boys who put on plays with adult political and moral themes. Shakespeare and his company in 1596 had hoped to use the Blackfriars because Blackfriars was a liberty—that is, a district that, for reasons of its religious history, was independent of the secular control of the sheriff—but were refused by a powerful NIMBY (not in my backyard) movement of influential residents. They then leased the building to a second generation of a children's company and had to wait until 1608 to take possession of what would turn out to be both a "tonier" and quite lucrative theatrical space.

Third were the dining halls of the Inns of Court, the London law schools or, perhaps, more accurately, legal societies, where noteworthy performances of *The Comedy of Errors* (Gray's Inn) and *Twelfth Night* (the Middle Temple) took place. There, special audiences with their appetite for contemporary satire allowed for the lampooning of particular individuals whose traits and foibles would be represented by grimace, gesture, voice imitation, and even clothing, as in the case of Dr. Pinch in *The Comedy of Errors*, Malvolio in *Twelfth Night*, and Ajax in *Troilus and Cressida*. When these plays were moved to the larger public stage, the personalized elements could be withdrawn and the characters could continue as general, non-specifically humorous figures.

Fourth was the Queen's court itself (after the death of Elizabeth in 1603, it became the King's court), where at Christmastide, the major companies would be invited to perform for the pleasure of the monarch. Indeed, throughout the long period of tension between the city authorities and the court, the justification for allowing the players to perform their craft in public was that they needed to practice in order to be ready at year's end to entertain the monarch. This argument assumed a quite disproportionate ratio of practice to performance, but it was a convenient semi-fiction that seemed to satisfy all concerned. These court performances were rewarded financially by the Master of the Revels and were less expensive than other kinds of royal entertainment, including masques with elaborate scenery and complicated production devices, the high costs of which later contributed to the downfall of Charles I, James's son and successor. Legend has it that Queen Elizabeth so enjoyed some of the performances featuring the character of Falstaff that she wished to see him in love, a comment which was allegedly the stimulus for *The Merry Wives of Windsor*, which was said to have been written in two weeks, the better to satisfy the queen's request. A close look at the multiple sources used in the creation of this middle-class comedy suggests that the legend may be well founded.

Last, there are the purpose-built amphitheaters, beginning with James Burbage's the Theatre (1576) in Shoreditch, just to the north of the city limits; and the Curtain (1578) nearby. To the south, across the Thames, were the Rose (1587), the site of the Lord Admiral's company and most notably the performances of Christopher Marlowe's plays; the Swan (1596); the Globe (1599), built with the very timbers of the Theatre transported across the river in the winter of 1598 after the twenty-one-year lease on the old property had expired and several subsequent months of renting; and, back to Shoreditch in the north, the Fortune (1600), explicitly built in imitation of the triple-tiered Globe.

There was competition for the same audience in the form of bull-baiting, bear-baiting and cockfighting, and also simple competition for attention from such activities as royal processions, municipal pageants, outdoor sermons, and public executions with hangings, eviscerations, castrations, and quarterings, not to mention the nearby temptation of the houses ("nunneries") of prostitution. Nonetheless, these theatrical structures proved that, if you build it, they will come.

And come they did, with hundreds of performances each year of thirty or more plays in repertory for each company, plays of chronicle history, romance, tragedy (especially revenge tragedy), satire, and comedy (slapstick, farcical, situational, verbal, and, from 1597, "humorous"; that is, comedy dependent upon characters moved by one dominant personality trait into behavior mechanical and predictable, almost monomaniacally focused). The two major companies could and did perform familiar plays for a week or more before adding a new play to the repertory. A successful new play would be performed at least eight times, according to Knutson, within four months to half a year (Knutson 33–34). New plays were house-fillers, and entrance fees could be doubled for openings. When sequels created a two-part play, performances were only sometimes staged in proper sequence, even as moviegoers will still watch on cable *Godfather II* or *The Empire Strikes Back* without worrying that they have not just seen *The Godfather* or *Star Wars*.

Fig. 3. Part of J. C. Visscher's view of London (c. 1616 or slightly earlier) looking north from the Bankside and showing the Beargarden theater and, to the right, the Globe theater (or possibly the Swan).

The players seemed willing to play throughout the week and throughout the year, but municipal officials repeatedly insisted that there be no performances on Sundays and holy days and holidays, nor during Lent. These demands had some effect, although their repetition by the authorities clearly suggests that there were violations, with performances on occasional Sundays, even at court, on some holidays, and on some days in Lent.

Of course, even though almost half of Shakespeare's plays had already been performed at the Theater and elsewhere, we think of the Globe, open for business probably in the late summer of 1599, as the principal venue for Shakespeare's work, perhaps with *As You Like It* the first production. The current New Globe on the Bankside in Southwark, erected in careful imitation of what we know to have been the methods and materials of the sixteenth century, allows for a twenty-first-century experience analogous to that of the Elizabethan theatergoer. It may be that the diameter of the current theater, of one hundred feet, is a bit too wide, and that seventy-two feet is rather closer to the exact diameter of not only the Globe but several of these late-sixteenth-century London theaters. If so, the judgment that such Elizabethan theaters could hold between 2,000 and 3,000 people suggests that spectators, particularly the groundlings—those who had paid a penny to stand throughout the two-to-three hour performance—were packed in cheek by jowl.

The geometry of the Globe itself is that of a polygon, but it appears circular. From a distance, one would know that a play was to be performed that day by the presence of a flag flying high above the tiring house, the dressing area for the actors. Once inside the building, the theatergoer would note the covered stage projecting from an arc of the circle almost to the center of the uncovered audience space, such that the groundlings would be on three sides of the stage, with those in the front almost able to rest their chins on the platform which was raised about five feet from the floor. This stage was not raked—that is, inclined or tilted towards the audience—as it often is in modern theaters today. Raking both creates better sightlines and potentially affects stage business, as in the case of a fallen Shylock in productions of *The Merchant of Venice*, who at one point struggled in vain to stand on a pile of slippery ducats (gold coins). This move is made even more difficult by the slight incline. However, instead of raking the stage, the Rose, and perhaps the Globe and the Fortune, had the ground on which the audience stood slightly raked (Thomson 78–79), to the great advantage of those in the back of the theater.

Behind the stage, protected by a backdrop on the first level, was the tiring house where the actors dressed and from which they came and went through two openings to the left and right. There were few surprise entrances in the Elizabethan theater, as the audience could always see before them the places of entry. Covering the upper stage and a large part of the outer stage would be the "heavens," supported by two columns or pillars behind which characters could hide in order to eavesdrop and which could serve metaphorically as trees or bushes. The underside of the "heavens" was adorned with signs of the zodiac, the better to remind the audience that all the world is a stage. At the back of the stage in the center, between the two openings of exit and entrance, was a discovery space within which, when a curtain was drawn, an additional mini-set of a study, a bed, or a cave could be revealed.

From below the stage, figures, especially ghosts, could ascend through a trapdoor, and mythological deities could be lowered from above. From the second tier of the galleries, still part of the tiring house, characters could appear as on battlements or a balcony. Music was a very great part of Elizabethan theater, and musicians would be positioned sometimes on that second level of the tiring house. Less musical but still necessary sound effects, say one indicating a storm and thunder, were achieved by such actions as the offstage rolling of a cannonball down a metal trestle or repeated drumming.

Although the groundlings were the closest to the talented actors, for those members of the audience who wished to sit in the galleries (Stern, esp. 212–13) and were willing to pay more money for the privilege, there would have been the comfort of the familiar, as V. F. Petronella has pointed out, inasmuch as these galleries included rooms not unlike those in the domestic buildings near the Globe. However, the familiar was balanced with the rare via the figures on the stage who represented kings, nymphs, fairies, and ghosts, personages not usually found in the Southwark area (Petronella, esp. 111–25). These audiences themselves came from a great range of Elizabethan society, male and female, from aristocrats to lowly apprentices, with all gradations of the social spectrum in between. The late Elizabethan and early Jacobean period is so special in theatrical history in part because of the work of a number of gifted playwrights, Shakespeare preeminent among them, but also in part because of the inclusive nature of the audiences, which were representative of the society as a whole.

When the King's Men in 1609 began to perform in the smaller, indoor Blackfriars theater while still continuing at the Globe in the summer months, they were able to charge at Blackfriars five or six times the entry fee at the Globe for productions that pleased a grander and wealthier group, but at the cost of having a more socially homogeneous audience. Although the Blackfriars was a more lucrative venue,

Shakespeare's company still profited from productions at the Globe, to the degree that when the Globe burned down during a performance of *Henry VIII* on June 29 1613, the company immediately set about rebuilding the structure so that it could reopen the very next year. One wonders whether Shakespeare came down from semi-retirement in Stratford for the new opening or was already in London working yet again in collaboration with John Fletcher, his successor as principal playwright of the King's Men.

In the more heterogeneous atmosphere at the Globe, whether the first or second version, audiences watched action taking place on a platform of about twelve hundred square feet, a stage which could be the Roman forum at one moment, the senate house at another, and a battlefield at still another. Yet the audience was never at a loss in recognizing what was what, for the dramatist provided place references in the dialogue between and among characters (and some plays may also have featured signs indicating place). The action was sometimes interrupted by informative soliloquies, speeches directed to the audience as if the character speaking on the stage were totally alone, whether or not he or she actually was. By convention, what was said in a soliloquy was understood to be the truthful indication of the character's thoughts and feelings. These soliloquies must have been in their day somewhat analogous to operatic arias—plot-useful devices, but also stand-alone bravura exercises in rhetorical display. Othello's "flaming minister" speech (5.2.1–22) is a good example of the show-stopping effect of the soliloquy, and Edmund's defense of bastardy in *King Lear* (1605; 1.2.1–22), in a passage of identical length, seldom fails to elicit applause at the last line even from today's audiences, who otherwise are accustomed not to interrupt the flow of a performance.

The actors and the audience were proximate and visible to each other during these daylight performances, putting them on more intimate terms than is the case in theaters today. Performers were dressed onstage in contemporary Elizabethan clothing, with the kings and dukes wearing specially purchased, costly garments whose fate as they grew worn and tattered was to outfit the clowns with social pretensions. There were also attempts to provide historical atmosphere when needed with helmets, shields, greaves and togas appropriate to the ancient world. Perhaps as few as ten men and four boys, who would play the women's roles in this all-male theatrical world, could perform all sixteenth-century plays. The boys would remain with the company until their voices cracked, and some then became adult members of the company when places became available. They were apprentices in a profession where the turnover was not great—a bonus to the dramatist who could visualize the actor who would be playing the character he was creating but not so advantageous for a young actor looking for a permanent place within a stable group. Because plays were very seldom performed in an uninterrupted run, actors needed powerful memories. It was a time when the aural rather than the visual understanding was much greater than in our own time, but even so, the capacity of actors to hold in their heads a large number of roles from many different plays was extraordinary, and new plays were constantly being added to the repertory.

Even as one man in his time plays many parts, so did Shakespeare's company of actors. The skills and particular strengths of these actors must have given Shakespeare a great deal of confidence about the complexity of the roles that he could ask them to create. Such an element of the familiar increased the pleasure of the audience when it could recognize the same actor behind two different characters whose similarity might now be perceived. Celebrated instances of doubling include, in *A Midsummer Night's Dream*, Theseus / Oberon and Hippolyta / Titania; and, in *Hamlet*, Polonius / First Gravedigger and, most strikingly, the Ghost / Claudius. The audience would likewise be affected by their experience with an actor in a current play having performed in a previous play that they had also seen. One example of this link between roles that allows the audience to anticipate the plot comes in *Hamlet,* when Polonius tells us of his having played Caesar. Caesar, of course, was killed by Brutus in Shakespeare's *Julius Caesar.* The actor now playing Polonius had played Caesar previously in *Julius Caesar,* and in that production, he was killed by Brutus, played by Richard Burbage (son of James). In this performance of *Hamlet*, Burbage was playing Hamlet, and he would shortly kill Polonius, in a repeat of history.

The theater is the most collaborative of enterprises. We should think of Shakespeare as a script-writer under considerable pressure to provide material for his colleagues, all of whom viewed the play to come as a fundamentally money-making project. Shakespeare had multiple advantages beyond his inherent verbal and intuitive gifts. Not only did he write for a group of actors whose individual talents he could anticipate in the composition of his characters, but the script that he was creating was often a response to recent successes by rival companies with their own revengers, weak and strong English kings, and disguised lovers.

The performances themselves relied greatly on the power of the audience's imagination to fill in what was missing because of the limitations of the Elizabethan stage, as the self-conscious Prologue in *Henry V* (1599) makes clear by appealing to the audience to imagine whole armies being transported across the sea. Other Elizabethan dramatists did attempt to be "realistic" in ways that are laughable even beyond the well-intended efforts of Quince, Bottom, and the other Mechanicals in *A Midsummer Night's Dream* (1596). Consider, as noted by G. B. Evans, Yarrington's *Two Tragedies in One* (1594–c. 1598), 2.1: "When the boy goeth in to the shop, Merry striketh six blows on his head and, with the seventh, leaves the hammer sticking in his head; the boy groaning must be heard by a maid, who must cry to her master." Three scenes later, a character "Brings him forth in a chair with a hammer sticking in his head" (Evans 71). Such grossly imperfect efforts increasingly gave way to conventional signals expressive of the limitations of the stage. Four or five men with spears and a flag could represent an army, and a single coffin could represent a whole graveyard. While the Globe stage lacked scenery as we know it, it was not lacking in props. Not only were there a trapdoor grave and a bank of flowers, but also a good number of handheld props like swords, torches, chalices, crowns, and skulls, each a real object and potentially a symbol.

Sometimes convention and symbolism gave way to nature in the case of live animals. Men in animal skins are safer, of course, but some animals, like dogs and bears, are trainable. It is certain that Crab, the dog in the *Two Gentlemen of Verona* (1595–96), was "played" by a true canine, and it is quite likely that the bear that pursues Antigonus in *The Winter's Tale* was only sometimes a disguised human being; but at other times, it was a bear, managed but real, possibly even a polar bear reared from the time of its capture as a cub. Further reflection on the known dangers associated with working with bears and our knowledge of the props listed in *Henslowe's Diary* of 'j beares skyne' (Henslowe 319) suggest that Elizabethan actors were more comfortable with artificial bears, thereby avoiding any sudden ursine aggression, revenge for all the suffering their colleagues had endured at the bear-baiting stake.

The authorities whose powers of censorship were real and forceful did not worry much about whether animals were live onstage or not, but they did care about theological issues being discussed explicitly and about urban insurrection, as we know from the strictures applied to *The Book of Sir Thomas More*, a manuscript play in which Shakespeare most probably had a hand. For all their apparent sensitivity to political issues, the government seems not to have interfered with plays that show the removal—or even the murder—of kings, although the scene of the deposing of Richard in *Richard II* (1596) was thought too delicate to be printed during the lifetime of Queen Elizabeth, who recognized Richard as a parallel figure and pointedly said: "I am Richard the Second, know ye not that?" Scholars debate whether some of these potent themes regarding right versus might, illegitimate succession, and successful usurpation were recognized imperfectly by the government and so escaped into performance if not always into print. Another theory is that the authorities allowed the audiences to be excited and then pacified by these entertaining productions, a release of energies that returned the audience at the play's end to an unchanged social and political reality.

While it is now customary to refer to this reality as part of the Early Modern Period, it is still important to remember that the two main cultural forces of the time, the Renaissance and the Reformation, came together in a perfect storm of new ideas about values. The Renaissance brought us the rebirth of classical culture and an emphasis on the dignity of human beings, and the Reformation stripped levels of interpretive authority in favor of the individual's more direct reliance on Scripture. These new ideas, sometimes in concert and sometimes in tension, have led increasingly over four hundred years to our current distant but clearly related theories of skepticism and pragmatism.

It is just as important to remember that when James Burbage built his theater in 1576, he was not so much interested in the idea of the dignity of human beings or in the proper interpretation of Scripture as in the making of money. When his son, Richard, and his son's friend and partner, William Shakespeare, and their fellow shareholders were creating and performing their scripts, they were counting the house above all else. Theater was an essential part of the entertainment industry, and for some, it was especially lucrative. If a man was an actor, he made a little bit of money; if a playwright, a little more; if a shareholder in the company that put on the play, a very great deal more; and if a householder in the building in which the plays were performed, even more still. Shakespeare was all four, and as we read his scripts, we should remember that the artist was also a businessman, interested in the box office as much as or more than any hard-to-imagine immortality. The Elizabethan theater was the forerunner of the multiplex, a collaborative, secular church in which the congregation / audience focused on the service before them, and Shakespeare and his fellows focused on both the service and the collection plate.

And yet with all the primary focus on material gain, Shakespeare and his competitors and collaborators were aware of the cultural importance and historical traditions of drama itself. Their own work continued myths and rituals that had begun in Athens and elsewhere more than two thousand years ago. It may well be true, as Dr. Samuel Johnson famously said, that no man but a blockhead ever wrote for anything but money, and Mozart might have been partially correct when he said that good health and money were the two most important elements in life. Yet we also know that just because a work has been commissioned doesn't rule out the presence of beauty and truth, as indeed Mozart's own works reveal. Michelangelo was paid by Pope Julius II to paint the Sistine Chapel, but nobody thinks of the fee the artist earned when she or he looks at the creation of Adam or the expulsion of Adam and Eve from the Garden of Eden. Shakespeare's career in the Elizabethan theatrical world turned out to be quite lucrative, but given the many profound reasons for which we read and study *A Midsummer Night's Dream, King Lear,* and *The Tempest* today (among so many other plays and poems), we see that the dramatist who created these works and gained so much material success was nevertheless grossly underpaid.

## WORKS CITED

Crystal, David and Ben Crystal. *Shakespeare's Words.* London: Penguin, 2002. Print.

Duncan-Jones, Katherine. *Ungentle Shakespeare: Scenes from His Life.* London: Arden Shakespeare-Thomson, 2001. Print.

Evans, G. Blakemore. *Elizabethan-Jacobean Drama.* London: A&C Black, 1988. Print.

Foakes, R. A., ed. *Henslowe's Diary.* 2nd ed. Cambridge: Cambridge UP, 2002. Print.

Greenblatt, Stephen. *Will in the World: How Shakespeare Became Shakespeare.* New York: Norton, 2004. Print.

Gurr, Andrew. *The Shakespearean Stage 1574–1642.* 3rd ed. Cambridge and New York: Cambridge UP, 1992. Print.

Jones, Emrys. *The Origins of Shakespeare.* Oxford: Clarendon, 1977. Print.

Knutson, Rosalyn. *The Repertory of Shakespeare's Company, 1594–1603.* Fayetteville: U of Arkansas P, 1991. Print.

Onions, C. T. *A Shakespeare Glossary.* Oxford: Clarendon, 1911. Print.

Petronella, Vincent F. "Shakespeare's Dramatic Chambers." *In the Company of Shakespeare: Essays on English Renaissance Literature in Honor of G. Blakemore Evans.* Eds. Thomas Moisan and Douglas Bruster. Madison and London: Fairleigh Dickinson and Associated UPs, 2002. 111–38. Print.

Schmidt, Alexander. *Shakespeare Lexicon.* Berlin: Georg Reimer, 1902. Print.

Stern, Tiffany. "'You that walk i' in the Galleries': Standing and Walking in the Galleries of the Globe Theater." *Shakespeare Quarterly* 51 (2000): 211–16. Print.

Thomson, Peter. *Shakespeare's Professional Career.* Cambridge: Cambridge UP, 1992. Print.

Wheeler, Richard P. "Deaths in the Family: The Loss of a Son and the Rise of Shakespearean Comedy." *Shakespeare Quarterly* 51 (2000): 127–54. Print.

# INTRODUCTION

## THE RUINED CROWN

*Vincent F. Petronella*

COMPOSED IN 1605, *King Lear* spotlights "a ruin'd piece of nature" (4.6.134), a headstrong, wrongheaded protagonist who suffers the downfall of his royal state and ends up wearing a ruined crown. Within the cultural workshop of seventeenth-century England, Shakespeare assembled his sources, developed a tragic form, and interwove structure, language, and themes to create a theatrical masterpiece that the poet Percy Bysshe Shelley in 1821 called "the most perfect specimen of the dramatic art existing in the world" (489) and about which, in 1900, playwright-critic George Bernard Shaw said that no one "will ever write a better tragedy than *Lear*" (1:80). These comments are only two examples of the way many readers and viewers have responded over the centuries to the play's majestic quality.

*King Lear* is of its own time and yet of perennial value, with a theatrical prominence corresponding to the description of Shakespeare's titular figure in *Julius Caesar* (1.2.135–6): a colossal monument towering over the small world beneath. Within the tragedy of *King Lear*, the imposing and regal central figure enjoys a short-lived eminence, which gives way to material and mental ruin and raises questions about the way this play is made, what it means, and the extent to which it unleashes its tragic power on the stage and in film or video versions.

### POLITICAL MILIEU

In the period leading up to *King Lear*, Elizabeth I's hesitation in choosing a royal successor caused a major crisis. Uncertainty about an heir to the throne weighed upon Elizabeth's courtiers and subjects, who realized all too well that for monarch and country, time was running out. One troubling concern bridging the reign of the aged queen and that of the next monarch, whoever that might be, had to do with the possible division of the kingdom. Elizabeth's successor, James VI of Scotland / James I of England (see Color Plate I), expressed his concern in cautionary remarks addressed to his son: "by dividing your kingdoms, you shall leave the seed of division and discord among your posterity" (James I quoted in Sommerville, 37). When King Lear makes a decision radically different from that which James advises, we are prompted to ask whether plays such as Shakespeare's *Henry VI* trilogy (1589–91), his *Richard III* (1592–93), *King John* (1594–96), *Richard II* (1596), *Hamlet* (1600–1601), and *King Lear*, each depicting a troublesome reign, are homiletic—sermonlike dramas in the manner of an old play like *Gorboduc* (1562), in which King Gorboduc of Britain is a negative example when he causes political chaos by dividing his kingdom between his two sons. As a consequence, a rebellious mob slays the British monarch and his queen.

## ELEMENTS OF TRAGIC FORM IN THE SOURCES

Suffering linked to human limitations—among them excessive pride or arrogance (*hubris* in Greek)—errors in judgment, political division, the workings of Nemesis (retributive justice), and the eventual fall of a high-ranking central figure are fundamental to classic tragic drama. By incorporating these fundamentals, the author of *Gorboduc* contributed unknowingly to shaping the genre of *King Lear*. Tragedy is so multifaceted that no single view of it will explain satisfactorily the complexity of Lear's particular plight. As an unequal mixture of classical, medieval, and Renaissance elements, *King Lear* is a tragic drama of Shakespeare's own devising, the result of his own inventiveness, including an imaginative use of sources. Although not usually thought of as Senecan revenge-tragedy, *King Lear* recalls the tradition with its dramatic process unfolding in five acts, ritualistic moments (the love-test and later the single-combat), violence and gore associated with Roman drama, Lear's call for vengeance (2.4.162–63), and Edgar as an avenger getting even with Edmund. A pagan context, biblical overtones, and discernible Senecan or neo-Senecan influences cover *King Lear* with an aura of "ancient" tragedy. An Aristotelian response, then, seems to make sense, especially when supported by points of similarity between Shakespeare's play and Aristotle's *Poetics*, a work rediscovered in the Renaissance and discussed in translations or commentaries.

Although Shakespeare ignores the classical dramatic "unities" of time and place emphasized in those commentaries, *King Lear* still has elements of an Aristotelian framework. It asks that we identify ourselves, through pity, with the tragic figure whose selfhood is flawed and whose errors in judgment, followed as they are by terrifying consequences, repel us, causing a conflict between that terror and our initial feelings of pity. A gradual increase in emotional intensity brings about within the spectator an easing or purging of that intensity through "catharsis," a mental process Shakespeare describes in *King*

*Lear* as "clamor-moistened" (Quarto 4.3.31): an abundance of tears lessening emotional stress and permitting inner calm to prevail.

Another of Shakespeare's derived ingredients is the concept of FORTUNE, whose inevitable role in all worldly activities fascinated various late medieval authors and inspired the writing of many narratives concerning the falls (i.e., *de casibus*) of illustrious men and women. One such narrative is a source for *King Lear: The Mirror for Magistrates*, a book that its author described as "a looking glass" reflecting one's own vice and showing how the vice of others is punished (Campbell 65–66). Many such works would plot a curve proceeding from the heights of royal or magisterial greatness to the depths of defeat, despair, and death. As with a sermon, the audience is instructed in and hence alerted to the ways of fickle Fortune.

Although Lear considers himself under the sway of Fortune (Ioppolo, Norton 104, n. 39), his dramatic trajectory is not strictly that of rise and fall, for when we first see him, he already has risen to a pinnacle. The Fool offers an incisive overview of what it is that Lear and others are facing:

> Fortune, that arrant whore,
> Ne'er turns the key to th' poor.
>
> (2.4.52–53)

Reversals or uncertainty caused by changeable Fortune turning her wheel marks the content of several works known to Shakespeare. In *Hamlet* (2.2.236), and in the passage from *Lear* just cited, Fortune is a woman in the tradition that political theorist Machiavelli made vivid in Chapter 25 of *The Prince* (1532). Fortune needs to be mastered, even violently so, in an attempt to protect oneself from her wheel-turning—that is, her unpredictable, whorish habit of distributing her favors. The Fool continues:

> . . . Let go thy hold
> when a great wheel runs down a hill, lest it
> break thy neck with following; but the great one
> that goes upward, let him draw thee after.
>
> (2.4.71–74)

The great wheels in the Fool's speech (2.3.72–73) are part of what Elton calls the "mysterious wheel of the universe" (135–36) that turns "full circle" against Edmund (5.3.175). Psychologically, Lear is tormented on a "wheel of fire" (4.7.46; see Fig. 4), making of him one who resembles not only the mythical Ixion who must, to use John Keats's phrase in his sonnet on rereading *King Lear*, "burn through" to purgation but also a "natural fool of fortune" (4.6.191). We are reminded of "nature" in the form of landscape and weather, especially the heath, and the raging tempest that Lear endures in the furious middle section of the play. Artist Benjamin West presents in Color Plate 3 the storminess in Lear's life that compels him to declare that "the rain it raineth every day" (3.2.77). Enveloped in corresponding domains (selfhood, family, state, and nature's macrocosm—wheels within wheels, as it were), Lear is a microcosm and "strives in his little world of man" (3.1.10), as discussed by Sir Walter Raleigh in his *History of the World*, a relevant selection from which is reprinted in this volume. As microcosm, Lear angrily engages macrosmic forces represented by the underside of the Globe's stage-canopy decorated with "the heavens."

By Permission of the Folger Shakespeare Library

Fig. 4. This emblem by Giovanni Ferro from his *Teatro d'imprese* (Venice, 1623) shows one who is bound to a toothed wheel enveloped in flames. Invoked here, as well as in King Lear's sense of being "bound/Upon a wheel of fire" (4.7.46), is the myth of Ixion, who, like Lear, goes mad. For misdeeds against Zeus, Ixion is chained eternally to a fiery wheel in the abyss of the underworld. For some readers, the menacing teeth in the emblem may bring to mind two important lines in King Lear: "How sharper than a serpent's tooth it is / To have a thankless child!" (1.4.288-89) and "[Goneril] hath tied / Sharp-tooth'd unkindness, like a vulture, here" (2.3.134-35). An inscription in Italian at the top of the emblem says that the solitary figure tied to the wheel revolves in perpetual suffering.

Color Plate 4 captures the open-air theater's overhanging canopy that corresponds to the actual heavens—reminders that Lear's tragic fall is personal, domestic, political, and cosmic.

Wisely if not tactfully, the knowing Kent, fully aware that a regal decline and fall are imminent, admonishes Lear:

> To plainness honor's bound
> When majesty falls to folly
> (Folio, 1.1.148–49).

Helping to make the verb "falls" in the Folio text more dramatically dynamic than its counterpart ("stoops") in the Quarto is the prepositional phrase ("to folly"), which is the equivalent of "falls into folly" and "a result of folly." Encapsulated here is the cause-and-effect relationship between foolish behavior and dire consequences. Fortune alone, one should understand, is not the basis of Lear's plight. Considering it so would diminish and even eliminate the place of individual responsibility in tragedy.

## PSYCHOMACHIA

In addition to Senecan materials and the *de casibus* literature of the Middle Ages, Shakespeare also had inherited another medieval concept: the *psychomachia*, the inner struggle for salvation with vice pitted against virtue on the battlefield of the soul in humankind's "crawl toward death" (Folio 1.1.41), to use Lear's phrase. This soul-warfare, so important in medieval sermons, paintings, engravings, and morality plays, is implied in Lear's inward drama and imaged in the mental turmoil made visible in the confrontation between villainy and virtue in the play as a whole. Reason, light, honesty, sight, and truth, pitted against passion, darkness, deception, blindness, and falsehood, toughen the fiber of *King Lear*. Each of these oppositions, to cite a phrase from the sonnet "On Sitting Down to Read *King Lear* Once Again" of John Keats (1795–1821), amounts to a "fierce dispute" largely initiated or exacerbated by Lear's destructive wrongheadedness, a fault that brings with it mistaken choices.

## TRAGIC RUIN

Foolish errors in judgment brought on by blind, arrogant presumption and outright evil precipitate Lear's fall. When he commands the storm to "Crack nature's moulds" (3.2.8), he is attempting to retaliate against all that may govern, threaten, and oppress him in nature's world and in the microcosmic world of humankind. With

a selfhood and a political state divided and crumbling into fragments, his very head becomes a bald crown of "little wit" (1.4.162–3)
prefiguring how he will end up as Gloucester says, a "ruin'd piece
of nature" (4.6.134) that Cordelia sees "Crown'd with rank [femiter]
and furrow-weeds, / With hardocks, hemlock, nettles, cuckoo-
flow'rs, / Darnel, and all the idle weeds that grow / In our sustaining corn" (4.4.3–6; see Fig. 5). Cordelia utters these lines filled with
crackling words ("hardocks, hemlock, nettles, cuckoo-flowers")
to portray for the attending doctor her father's brittle condition. By
this time, Lear has no idea where his actual crown is, but Cordelia's
descriptive account anticipates the stage direction that latter-day
editors devised for 4.6.80 (Duthie and Wilson, 94 and 246). Her
statement calls for what has become an obligatory stage prop: the
makeshift garland atop Lear's head, the headdress of twigs, stubble
and stalks—a visual signifier for "this great decay" (5.3.298); for the
splintered kingdom and mind of Lear. Once the trauma of the fall
occurs, the single most telling image of the monarch's disintegration
is the ruined crown, the material remains of a greater day.

ROBERT B. MANTELL
AS KING LEAR.

© Courtesy Harry Rousche/Emory University

Fig. 5. Scottish actor Robert
Bruce Mantell (1854–1928) as
Lear wearing a mock crown
of weeds. Mantell's production
of *King Lear* was performed in
1905–6 at New York's Garden
Theater, a part of Stanford
White's Madison Square
Garden. In 4.4.3-6, Cordelia
describes Lear's crown made
up of vegetation such as
hemlock, nettles, and cuckoo-
flowers. Later (4.6.80), mad
Lear comes in *"crowned with
weeds and flowers"* —a stage-
direction suggested by George
Ian Duthie and Dover Wilson
in the Cambridge University
Press edition of the play (1962).
The mock crown has become
a hallmark of productions of
*King Lear* ever since. It makes
dramatically emblematic the old
king's ruined crown.

## TRAGIC INSIGHT

As a tragic protagonist, who personally is largely responsible for the fray, Lear ends up suffering a devastating loss, and in the aftermath of ruin, we ask whether tragic events lead to at least some understanding as to why the suffering has occurred. Characteristically, irony courses through tragic drama and is exemplified by negatives (physical and psychological suffering, for example) moving toward positives, especially in the form of wider understanding of the perceived world and heightened self-perception. But the outcome of this pattern is not always achieved. Varying slightly the Fool's comment early in the play helps to characterize the elusive nature of answers to questions of acquiring or not acquiring wisdom in a tragedy like *King Lear*, for life often takes us to a point where, even before death, the candle may flicker and go out so that we are "left darkling" (1.4.217). Whether Lear gains any insight into himself—that is, whether he has reached, after all he has endured, a level of self-recognition in relation to the world about him—is clear at times, as in his observations on "Poor naked wretches" (3.4.28–36) but at other times ambiguous, as dramatized in Cordelia's death scene, where Lear's "Look there, look there!" (Folio, 5.3.312) remains unclear as to what it is he sees despite the suggestions of insight and revelation. His repeated imperative phrase directing one's eyes toward her face carries with it the force of a piteous, twice-asked question: "Does she live; does she live?" Terror then accompanies the anticipation of awaiting the response to the obligatory follow-up question: "Or is it that she is actually dead?" (See Fig. 13.)

Tragedy demands that the central figure interrogate who he or she is or attempt, as Lear puts it, to "take upon's the mystery of things" (5.3.16), but the reader or viewer of a play like *King Lear* should understand that tragic action ending with definitive answers is not necessarily forthcoming and may even be illusory. The point toward which tragedy proceeds may, in fact, have more indefiniteness than clarity, yet the steps toward reaching that point require a definite arrangement of characters, their interrelationships, and various dramatic events that keep us at the edge of our seats. It also requires language. All these elements combine in a tragedy like *King Lear* to vivify the process of suffering leading to the acquisition of wisdom, and as we witness that process, we respond to and take pleasure in the terrible beauty of tragic art.

## LANGUAGE, THEMES, AND THE DOUBLE PLOT

In *King Lear*, language and theme reverberate within the structural walls of two related narratives. Shakespeare fully mastered the double-plot format by the time he wrote his *Henry IV* plays (1596–98), in which two father figures (King Henry and "King" Falstaff of the Boar's Head Tavern) compete for the attention and loyalty of Prince Hal, and in so doing, character traits are compared and contrasted. A commonplace analogy applicable here is the reflective foil of a ring—the setting enhancing a gem's sparkle. Double-plotting mutually illuminates both plots through comparison and contrast with one plot acting as a reflector that highlights the other. Despite the many parallels that scholars often point out or that directors enhance through stage or film productions, the two plots do not mirror one another in lockstep fashion. Differences between the two plots, for example, often create emphasis precisely because the events of each plot are not parallel. This inequality between events and persons and language can be highly revealing (Levin, 12–15 and passim).

In *King Lear*, similarities and dissimilarities in the paternal roles of Lear and Gloucester are a central focus of interest. For example, in attempting to deal with what appears to be filial ingratitude, both men in their folly become blind to the value of a virtuous child. A loving daughter is disowned in the main plot, a devoted son in the secondary one. Edgar is not only disowned, he also assumes the guise of a "lunatic beggar . . . an escaped or released inmate of Bedlam Hospital . . . a species of actor" (Carroll, 191). Poor Tom's bizarre, theatrical demeanor, as seen at the far right in Benjamin West's painting in Color Plate 3, and his language parallel somewhat the characteristics of the court jester—Lear's Fool in this case. Furthermore, Edgar is the structural bridge between the two plots by his close relationships with his own father as well as with Lear, the father of the realm. In the BBC/Time-Life television version of the play (1982), Poor Tom wears a garland of thorny nettles similar to the crown of thorns that the character wears in Peter Brook's 1971 film (cf. Jones, 54–59). Using this stage prop conjures up the humiliation of Jesus as well as the depiction generally of suffering in the play and the ruined crown in particular. Whatever headdress Edgar chooses to wear as Poor Tom bespeaks, like Lear's garland of weeds, a drastic turnabout.

Both plots have structural turning points, scenes dramatizing a climactic moment in the overall action of the play as determined by the more particular change in an individual's fortunes. An instance is Regan's "What need one?" (2.4.263), which utterly strips Lear of his knights and drives him, mad, into the storm where he encounters "unaccommodated" Poor Tom (3.4.106–7). When Lear tears off his own clothes to reduce himself to Tom's level, he has reached the structural turning point and nadir of the main plot. In the subplot, the equivalent scene is the blinding of Gloucester, which leads to his paradoxical self-revelation: "I stumbled when I saw" (4.1.19).

Main plot/subplot linkages also recall the popular medieval-Renaissance tradition of the emblem, which sets out a graphic image followed by an instructive epigram. In Act 1, the material map that Lear consults when dividing the kingdom is a visual aid to which one may attach various epigrams pertaining to the need for geographical guideposts (political, domestic, cosmic) and the implicit admonition that to be ignorant of moral topography undermines a sense of direction—something that applies to many of the characters in *King Lear* who lose their way.

The flaws observed in characters of the play are variations upon the figurative blindness and mental drifting of King Lear himself. Disorder, discord, or what Cordelia calls "abused nature . . . untun'd and jarring senses" (4.7.14–15) is the assured outcome.

## SOURCES: THE OLD *LEIR* PLAY AND *THE MIRROR FOR MAGISTRATES*

As with ideas such as disorder and discord, Shakespeare assembled vital components of plot, motif, and image from a number of sources. He artistically transformed these features into the persons, events, and language of his tragic masterpiece. His major source, the anonymous *True Chronicle History of King Leir* (a 1605 play organized in scenes, not "acts"), was staged, it is believed, in the 1590s by the Queen's Men, a company of players with which Shakespeare was quite likely closely associated (Foakes, Arden, 90). It is even possible that he acted a role in *Leir*, perhaps that of the Kent counterpart, Perillus (Muir, xxix).

Imaginatively, Shakespeare compressed a number of scenes at the outset of *Leir* into the single, compact scene that opens *Lear*. In other places, he expanded his source material, as in the case of the storm with which Lear contends in 3.1. Where the author of *Leir* has an oncoming storm announced by a few thunderclaps and some lightning, and thunder (scenes 12 and 19, Bullough, 7:361 and 7: 377–79), Shakespeare orchestrates, as West depicts (Color Plate 3) a full-blown tempest swirling about five characters seen from left to right in the painting: Gloucester, the Fool, Lear, Kent, and a seated Poor Tom. Accompanied by similarly unfortunate comrades, Lear treads a jagged course, becoming undoubtedly central to Shakespeare's tragedy, especially when he contends with nature's furious elements. These kinds of details exemplify how much of what occurs in *Lear* is not from the older play. *Leir*, however, did provide Shakespeare with an overall format, basic character relationships, and the sequence of events.

Another source for the main plot of *King Lear* is the 1574 edition of *The Mirror for Magistrates*, which appeared in various editions from 1555 through 1587. *The Mirror* is a series of biographical verse-monologues spoken by individuals from English history. Their tragic lives are looking-glasses in which political, legal, clerical, or family leaders may see instructive examples of human error and moral frailty. Generally, humankind gazes into the mirror to be mindful of the fickle ways of Fortune in this imperfect, terrestrial world. One example of this is a forerunner of Shakespeare's Cordelia (named Cordila in *The Mirror*) whose monologue tells of her relationship with Leire and her sisters, Gonerell and Ragan, specifying how in old age, her father "had a childishe minde" (Bullough, 7: 324); how by flattery her sisters "won their fathers hart" (325) and how "they deprivde him of his crowne and right" (326). Responding favorably to matters concerning human traits, themes, diction, and genre, Shakespeare, in the light of his interest in the *de casibus* motif, could not have missed the full title of the work, which includes the "falles of the first infortunate Princes of this lande" (323). In addition, Cordila, technically France's Queen Consort, speaks of her own particular "misfortunes and mishaps" (323).

Blending invented events with derived ones, Shakespeare created *King Lear* by adding important features such as the Fool, who is based on Mumford, the comic Frenchman in *Leir*; Lear's insanity and extreme age; and a Kent figure who, unlike the equivalent character in the sources, is banished in Shakespeare's play. For his subplot—a structural masterstroke—Shakespeare recalled *The Countess of Pembroke's Arcadia* (1590), where Sir Philip Sidney narrates the tale of the Paphlagonian king and his bastard son, Plexirtus, who blinds his father and usurps the throne. By appropriating the details of blinding and a blind father's suicidal tendencies, Shakespeare intensified the tragic power of *King Lear*.

A much shorter source is in Book 2 of Spenser's *Faerie Queene* (1590 edition): the narrative of Leyr and his "three faire daughters." Leyr loses the throne, is forced out of his realm but is later welcomed by Cordelia, who helps him to regain his crown. Upon old Leyr's death, Cordelia inherits the throne, but her fortunes decline, and she hangs herself. This brief narrative provided Shakespeare with the spellings of Regan's and Cordelia's names. Spenser's account of Cordelia's death, however, is different in *King Lear*, where the villainous Edmund craftily attempts to make it appear that she hangs herself when, in fact, she is hanged by the captain whom Edmund and Goneril have ordered to do the deed (5.3.253–56).

Cornwall, the other male villain in *King Lear*, is Cornewall in Shakespeare's well-known historical source: Holinshed's *Second Booke of the Historie of England* (1587 edition), from which Shakespeare took the names of the regions over which the husbands of Lear's older daughters rule. A difference in this source, as in *Leir*, has to do with the marriage partners (Gonorilla is married to Cornewall and Regan to Albania); and a similarity is Cordeilla's "so much I love you and no more," which becomes Cordelia's "I love your Majesty / According to my bond, no more nor less" (1.1.92–93). After Cordeilla's nephews imprison her, she is overcome with grief and kills herself, which in the Holinshed edition of 1577 is the subject of a vivid illustration that Shakespeare very likely knew: Here, Cordeilla dies by her own sword on her canopy bed, with its tentlike curtains drawn aside as if revealing the deed in a theater's inner stage. (See Fig. 6.) That same illustration bears an inscription describing Cordeilla as a woman of manly courage—a characteristic that applies to all three sisters in Shakespeare. In every source, except for the action within the *Leir* play, the Cordelia figure dies by suicide. Only in *King Lear* is a planned killing (assassination or execution) the cause of her death, intensifying her plight through Shakespeare's ability to create, by slightly expanding Holinshed's account, an intense dramatic effect that involves Edmund.

Special Collections Department University of Colorado at Boulder Libraries

Fig. 6. Although the 1587 edition of Holinshed's chronicles is an acknowledged source for *King Lear*, Shakespeare very likely saw the 1577 edition that features two pictures of Cordelia, one of them (seen here) showing her committing suicide on a regal bed with a headboard, over which hangs a theatrical, tentlike canopy (a royal furnishing). An inner stage-set is suggested. The eagle or falcon head carved on the headboard (*left*) is not only a royal emblem but also an indication that in noble households one may find—as in the case of *King Lear*—political or familial birds of prey. See the reference to vulture-like behavior (2.3.134-35), the caption for Fig. 4, and Goneril as "kite" or buzzard (1.4.262). Shakespeare may have seen this picture, and if so, it should be considered an additional probable source (this one impressively iconographical) for Edmund's devious plot to make Cordelia's death by assassination look like suicide.

Shakespeare, however, did not have to depend merely on past history. One contemporary event of 1603 may have served him as a possible source for *King Lear*: the domestic and legal difficulties in the family of Sir Brian Annesley of Lee in Kent. Annesley had three daughters, the oldest of whom attempted to acquire her father's property for herself, contending that because her father was a lunatic, the will, which provided for all three daughters, was not valid (Bullough, 270-1; 309-11). Annesley's youngest daughter legally argued that her father was not insane. Three daughters, an intense family dispute, the location in Kent (recalling the name of Lear's loyal advisor), and talk of lunacy support the idea that Annesely's story is a source for *King Lear*, a viewpoint bolstered by the fact that the family's youngest daughter was named Cordell.

## SOURCES AND LANGUAGE

Shakespeare found in his sources not only ideas for dramatic plots, settings, genre, and characters, but also features of language that he shaped into blank verse—showcasing much of the play's dialogue, extended speeches, and soliloquies, as found, for example, in 1.2.1–22, 2.2.160–174, and 2.3.1–21—and into prose, rhymed verse, lyrics, nursery rhymes, or doggerel, all of which helped to create artistic variety and emotional distinctions among dramatic characters. The language of *King Lear* can be angular, knotty, playful, or plain.

Plainness, in fact, is what King James I (as James VI of Scotland) called for. Sounding like Hamlet in his advice to the players, James recommends plain, temperate usage in the *Basilicon Doron* ('The King's Gift'), his treatise of 1599 addressed to his son Henry, Prince of Wales (Sommerville, 53). If Shakespeare read this work, its impact might have had an effect on sections of *King Lear*—for example, the beginning and ending of the play, where plainness is highly effective. Kent and Gloucester's conversational prose exchange (1.1), aside from the bawdiness, is in the spirit of James's advice. Edmund's language here represents a guarded formality and is not direct; nevertheless, the scene exemplifies relative plainness in speech. Soon rhetorical directness gives way to a blank verse appropriate for court ceremony, ritual, and the context for Goneril's and Regan's crafty language in contrast with Cordelia's disturbing reticence, a "plainness" that Lear links with "pride" (1.1.129), Kent's energetic bluntness, "To plainness honor's bound," he says (1.1.148), and Lear's volcanic curses.

In the Gloucester subplot, a mixture of conversational language, deceit, and Kent-like candor echoes similar elements in the main plot. Then the Fool enters the play, with his twisted yet probing language marked by parody, doggerel, and sardonic wit that amplify the raciness and directness already associated respectively with Gloucester and Kent in the opening scene. Later, the disguised Edgar demonstrates how the play's language can be even more flexible when he mimics various dialects (see Evans and Tobin, note for 4.6.235).

## ALLUSIONS IN *KING LEAR*

In addition to various speech mannerisms, the language of *King Lear* is at times allusive. On the title page of the 1608 Quarto, such an instance occurs, announcing that the first recorded performance of *King Lear* took place on the evening of St. Stephen's Day (December 26), a festival emphasizing in part the folly and worldliness of mankind— themes important to *King Lear* (Halio, 1992, 1, n. 1). Stephen's martyrdom as told in Scripture (Acts 6.8–15 and 7.55–60) resulted from expressing in public his innermost beliefs. He spoke contrary to authority, was judged guilty, and was stoned to death. Present at the young man's execution was Saul (known later as Paul), whose subsequent conversion on the road to Damascus brought temporary blindness and spiritual insight through a vision of Jesus reprimanding him (Acts 9.3–9). Events in *Lear* parallel some of the details of these scriptural narratives centering on ruined Stephen (whose name in Greek, incidentally, means "garland" or "crown"). Cordelia's stand on personal principles in the face of authority, Gloucester's seeing-in-blindness, and the 1549 Prayer Book reading listed for St. Stephen's Day ["Behold your house is left unto you desolate" (Matthew 23.38)] are the kinds of links that explain why December 26 was selected for the play's presentation.

Another allusion—this one appearing early in the play—occurs in one of the Fool's lessons addressed to Lear: "thou bor'st thine ass on thy back ... o'er the dirt" (1.4.161–62). He refers to Aesop's fable of the old man accused of overburdening an ass. To please his critics, the man carries the animal on his back, becomes a laughingstock, grows angry, and throws the ass into the river. Like King Lear, the old man in the tale creates a topsy-turvy order by behaving foolishly wrongheaded in the face of criticism. Self-made disorder also prompts an allusion to the myth of Prometheus, who is bound to a rock for defying Zeus and having given the gift of fire to mankind and hence must endure having his liver consumed by an eagle every day. Lear, who does not possess foresight (the literal meaning of "Prometheus"), has given substantial gifts to his daughters and soon finds himself complaining to Regan, pointing toward his inwards while he says that Goneril "hath tied / Sharp-tooth' d unkindness, like a vulture, here" (2.3.134–35).

If Lear fails to anticipate the future consequences of his actions, the Fool confidently, even if confusedly, strives to envision what lies ahead. Speaking directly to the audience in Act 3, as he also does at the close of 1.5, the Fool utters an eccentric prophecy paying homage to the Arthurian wizard:

When usurers tell their gold i' th' field,
And bawds and whores do churches build;
Then comes the time, who lives to see't,
That going shall be us'd with feet.
This prophecy Merlin shall make, for I live before his time.

(Folio, 3.2.91–95)

These opaque lines, which may be related to the issue of the suspect nature of prophecy, as discussed by essayists of Shakespeare's era (see the "Sources and Contexts" section in this volume) envelop the most complex allusion in the play and exemplify the Fool's taste for parody. He fuses the ridiculous and the sublime to mock ideas not necessarily rejected even as they are being wrenched out of order. Expressing topsy-turviness with intelligent self-awareness, Lear's Fool is an actualized oxymoron, a living contradiction whose cracked mind strives through language to put the shattered world back together again.

Using an entirely different tone, Cordelia utters one of the most poignant illustrative allusions in the play. In her filial as well as maternal concern for her "lost" father, she searches for him and speaks of her quest this way: "O dear father, / It is thy business that I go about" (4. 4. 23–24). She alludes to the gospel of Luke (2.49), in which we read that during a family journey for Passover, Jesus' mother lost track of her son. After three days, he was found in the temple discussing theology among the elders, explaining his presence with a renowned question: "Knewe ye not that I must go about my father's business?" (Geneva Bible; apostrophe added).

## NOISE AND SILENCE

Another characteristic of language in the play is its ability to register an auditory impact. Pain, anger, and coarseness fill *King Lear* with words that tell of thundering anguish. Some of Shakespeare's gritty words and resounding phrases evoke the animal realm, others the world of inanimate nature or anatomical details. Lear, for example, calls Goneril a "kite" (1.4.262), Kent describes Oswald as an "heir of a mungril bitch" (2.2.22–23), Lear commands "cataracts and hurricanes" to "crack" and "rage" (3.1.1–2), and Poor Tom speaks of one's "minikin [i.e., shrill] mouth" (3.6.43). We also hear Goneril's "Pluck out" (3.7.5) preceding Cornwall's ominous command, "Bind fast his corky arms" (3.7.29), Gloucester's hard-hitting comment about the gods, "They kill us for their sport" (4.1.37), Lear's mad words about "glass eyes" and "a scurvy politician" (4.6.170–2), and his "Howl, howl, howl!" (5.3.258) followed by "Why should a dog, a horse, a rat, have life . . .?" (5.3.307). Such phrases and lines also exemplify two other qualities of the language in *King Lear*: precision and terseness.

Equal and opposite to these noisy moments in the play are references to silence or near-silence. We hear Cordelia's "Love, and be silent" (1.1.62), but her "Nothing" sets off a staggering explosion that resounds through the hall. By contrast, long after her departure from Britain, reminders of her reticence linger, as in Kent's "Few words" (3.1.52), Gloucester's "No words, no words, hush" (3.4.181), and Lear's "Make no noise, make no noise, draw the curtains" (3.6.83–84). The silences of *King Lear* form a spatial void, something like Edgar's "happy hollow of a tree" (2.3.2)—a container holding all that is sounded and heard in the natural world and in the community of speech. Climaxing the confinement or attenuation of sound is Lear's well-known line describing Cordelia's voice as "ever soft, / Gentle, and low" (5.3.273–74).

*Cordelia Disinherited*, 1850 (oil on canvas) (see 51605 for detail), Herbert, John Rogers (1810–90)/Harris Museum and Art Gallery, Preston, Lancashire, UK/The Bridgeman Art Library International

Fig. 7. Nineteenth-century artists often painted images of Cordelia, attempting to capture her quiet softness, as in this oil painting by John Rogers Herbert, *Cordelia Disinherited* (1850). This painting of Cordelia served as Herbert's study for his depiction of Cordelia seen with her father and sisters in Herbert's large fresco, *King Lear Disinheriting Cordelia* (1850) commissioned for the Upper Waiting Hall (formerly Poet's Hall) at the House of Lords in the Houses of Parliament, London/Westminster. To see a close-up magnification of the entire fresco at the Houses of Parliament, go to http://www.parliament.uk/worksofart/artwork/john-rogers-herbert/king-lear-disinheriting-cordelia--king-lear-/2884

In Act 1, her quiet "nothing" *precedes* Lear's angry roar. In Act 5, however, Lear's comment on Cordelia's usually soft voice, now silenced and uttering nothing, *follows* his high-decibel howl.

## HARSNETT AND FLORIO'S MONTAIGNE

Two important sources for much of what we read or hear in the speeches of Poor Tom, the Fool, and mad Lear are Samuel Harsnett's *A Declaration of Egregious Popish Impostures* (published 1603) and John Florio's 1603 English translation of Michel de Montaigne's essays. The absorbing content and freshness of diction in these works evidently fascinated Shakespeare. Harsnett's *Declaration*, which is discussed thoroughly in F. W. Brownlow's *Shakespeare, Harsnett, and the Devils of Denham* (1993), was based on enquiries, which got under way in 1598, investigating exorcisms of 1585–86 carried out by a Roman Catholic priest known as "Father Edmunds," a coincidental name that scholars have linked to Shakespeare's crafty Edmund in *King Lear*. Attempting to expose the illusory nature and false uses of exorcisms, Harsnett described them as theatricals "fashioned by cunning clerical dramatists and performed by actors skilled in improvisation" (Greenblatt 169). Shakespeare turned to Harsnett for various names, in particular those of Poor Tom's demons and for the language of hell. Shakespeare, moreover, found in *A Declaration* specialized concepts such as "this mother" and "[Hysterica] passio" (2.4.56–57), two terms that Edward Jorden discusses pertaining to the hysteria related to a disorder of the womb that caused, among other symptoms, the feeling of being suffocated or smothered—if a pun on "this mother" be allowed.

Upon reading Florio's translation of Montaigne, as Taylor records (58–66; cf. Salingar, 113–21), Shakespeare found over one hundred words that he did not use before 1603, many of them found in *King Lear*: "bastardizing" (1.2.133), "marble-hearted" (1.4.259), "mungril" (2.2.22), "sophisticated" (3.4.106), and "handy-dandy" (4.6.153), which, like "bo-peep" from Harsnett, refers to a child's game. Lear, the Fool explains, has receded into childhood ever since he made his daughters his mothers and started to "play bo-peep, / And go the [fools] among" (1.4.171–78). The reference is to the game of peek-a-boo or hide-and-seek. Another diversion for children, "handy-dandy" calls for guessing which concealed hand holds an object. Lear says, "see how yond justice rails upon yond simple thief. Hark in thine ear: change places, and handy-dandy, which is the justice, which is the thief?" (4.6.151–54; see "Performance History" for more). Both games, the one from Harsnett, the other from Florio's Montaigne, enrich the text of *Lear* and contribute a playful particularity to Shakespeare's play while exemplifying in a wider sense the interconnectedness of sources, language, and theme.

## WHAT DOES *KING LEAR* MEAN?

Tapping into the thematic content of language enables students to move toward discovering the play's meaning. One way of getting close to the play in this regard is to consider relationships encompassing parents, off-spring, and gender. The opening displays family dysfunction in the form of what Lear perceives as filial ingratitude, which he later portrays with a forceful image: "How sharper than a serpent's tooth it is / To have a thankless child!" (1.4.288–89). Patriarchal Lear's errors in judgment eventually drive him from power and bring about his utter physical and psychological dependence. As McLuskie argues, Lear's behavior, at first seeming to be a defense of patriarchy resulting in women's oppression, actually delivers a severe blow to patriarchy (98–105). What is more, feminine independence emerges, looking ahead to Shakespeare's strong-willed Lady Macbeth. Goneril and Regan, says Foakes, "have the courage and toughness to hold sway in a masculine world," and despite male power, *King Lear* is "dominated by its women" (215).

In allowing his daughters to play maternal roles, as emphasized in Goneril's "Old fools are babes again" (Quarto 1.3.19) and the wise Fool's lines (1.4.172–78), Lear experiences such a diminished status as patriarch and king that he reverses and confounds parent-child, father-daughter, and even husband-wife relationships (Kahn, 100). His own folly shows him falling victim to a Lear-centered version of the children's games of hide-and-seek and bo-peep.

Instead of representing what much recent scholarship has studied as widespread patriarchal villainy in Shakespeare's time, Lear brings about calamity not because his actions "fit contemporary expectations for fatherhood, but because they violate them" (Young, 46). Gradually losing (in a sense, childishly hiding) his self, he seeks security; and as his mental regression intensifies, Lear becomes more desperate to enlist the aid of his daughters, in particular that of Cordelia. Driving the quest for such assistance is the need to compensate for the fundamental cause of dysfunction in the Lear family: the absence of a mother.

An ironic parallel also occurs in the play's subplot, where a father and his two sons provide for themselves because in their "family," maternal care and security are lacking. Gloucester's world demands adherence to Edgar's aphorism, "ripeness is all" (5.2.11), with its evocation of the tradition of *ars moriendi ('the art of dying well')* but in Lear's case, ripeness— wise maturity and the readiness to accept life's limitations—remains elusive. Old Lear's world becomes the world of Cinderella and her two wicked sisters (Tobin, *Shakespeare's Favorite Novel*, 117–21), of childhood games (bo-peep and handy-dandy), and of *Jack the Giant Killer*, invoked in Poor Tom's "Child Rowland to the dark tower came" (3.4.182). Lear returns to the nursery, so to speak, and his angry responses in the play reenact "childlike rage against the absent or rejected mother as figured in his daughters" (Kahn, 100). He resentfully turns his back on them, blinding himself to them in an act of non-recognition that begins early in the play when he says to Cordelia, "avoid my sight" (1.1.124). He enacts a psychological state that Stanley Cavell has studied in detail as the avoidance of love (Cavell, 39–123). The motivation for Lear's desire to avoid love is twofold: patriarchal machismo and shame, characteristics linking him to Gloucester, the boastful yet embarrassed begetter of illegitimate Edmund in the subplot. Lear's shame arises out of two deep-seated feelings: the first that he does not deserve love, and the other that he cannot return love (Cavell, 60–63). Love ensnared in such a trap leads to a torturous existence.

As if describing the popular Elizabethan-Jacobean sport of bear-baiting, Caroline Spurgeon, in her acclaimed work of 1935, explained that the play keeps "constantly before us, chiefly by means of the verbs used, but also in metaphor, of the human body in anguished movement, tugged, wrenched, beaten, pierced, stung, scourged, dislocated, flayed, gashed, scalded, tortured and finally broken on the rack" (Spurgeon, 338). (See Fig. 4.) In recent times, the grimmer aspects of the human drama have been enacted on the world stage and reflected in art, but no more powerfully than in Shakespeare's play.

## EXISTENTIAL CONCERNS AND
### *THEATRUM MUNDI*

Lear asks two fundamental existential questions: "Who is it that can tell me who I am?" (1.4.230) and 'Is man no more than this?' (3.4.102–3). In the crucial scene at Dover (4.6), he contemplates the mutilated, raggedly dressed Gloucester and articulates the insight that the blind wretch he sees before him is no more than an unaccommodated Tom of Bedlam—a projection of Lear himself. Climactically, recognition follows:

If thou wilt weep my fortunes, take my eyes.
I know thee well enough, thy name is Gloucester.
Thou must be patient; we came crying hither.
Thou know'st, the first time that we smell the air
We wawl and cry. I will preach to thee. Mark.
[*Lear takes off his crown of weeds and flowers.*]
(4.6.176–80)

But when in the concluding moments of the play, the dying Lear asks a third existential question, it is directed at Kent and the whole of humanity, including the audience: "Who are you?" (5.3.279). As a verbal bridge between his world and ours, the question draws us into Lear's realm by cutting across timelines and the margins of the apron stage of Shakespeare's theater. Linking the imagined world with the real one is a timeless process, one form of which has classical origins: the world as a stage. Resonating through history, the metaphor of *theatrum mundi*, "the theater of the world," was applied, as tradition tells us, to Shakespeare's playhouse, the Globe, and inspired its motto: "*totus mundus agit histrionem*" ("the entire world plays the actor"). Jaques may be referring to this motto, and hence to the great Globe itself (Color Plate 4), in his "All the world's a stage" speech in *As You Like It* (2.7.139–66). Although that is indeed the best-known use of the metaphor, an important application also occurs in *King Lear*. Just after he removes from his head the garland of weeds and flowers that symbolize both his ruined crown and the pattern of divestiture that is his fate, demented Lear offers this maxim to blind Gloucester:

When we are born, we cry that we are come
To this great stage of fools.

(4.6.182–3)

Universal folly, according to Elton (304), reveals itself as (1) sinfulness—the theme of Sebastian Brant's *Das Narrenschiff / The Ship of Fools* (1494)—and (2) a constant presence in human life—the central point of Desiderius Erasmus's *Moriae Encomium / In Praise of Folly* (1509).

*King Lear* addresses issues that resonated in the past and that still resound today. Dramatizing vital, tough issues still confronting us, this play is a sounding board for the theme of the world-as-stage—the stage upon which mankind frequently plays the fool.

## JUSTICE AND INJUSTICE

The collective anguish of Lear, Gloucester, Cordelia, Kent, Edgar, and the Fool tells not only of the damage that folly causes but also what motivates us to identify ourselves with suffering humanity. *King Lear* stages the struggle between the value of love, service, and loyalty against characteristics of evil—bestial behavior, futility, isolation, enslavement, the violation of the bodies and souls of others, the arrogance of patriarchy, and other manifestations of hubris or smug pride. All these issues are involved within the endless combat between reason and passion, nature and the unnatural, justice and injustice. In a play filled with images of eyes, Lear proceeds toward achieving some insight regarding justice even as it becomes glaringly clear to other characters in the play (as well as to the audience) how "all ruinous disorders" (Folio, 1.2.113) surrounding the ruined king have been fueled tragically by the king himself. Frank Kermode's indispensable essay on *King Lear* in *The Riverside Shakespeare* considers at length the theme of justice. For Dr. Samuel Johnson (1709–84), the brilliant critic and sixth editor of Shakespeare's works, justice comes up not so much as a theme but as a literary obligation. Johnson called for literary standards based upon classical examples, emphasizing "poetic justice," the eighteenth-century critical view demanding that the good be rewarded and the evil punished. Johnson judged Nahum Tate's version of *Lear*, *The History of King Lear* (1681), more acceptable than Shakespeare's play, primarily because the adaptation includes poetic justice, ending as it does with villainous Edmund slain, Lear restored, and Cordelia alive and headed toward marriage with Edgar. For Kermode, poetic justice is of historical interest but not the necessary literary ingredient that it is for Johnson.

A rich variety of statements evoking justice mark Shakespeare's play. Albany, for example, states his belief that the heavens are not indifferent when he learns of the death of vicious Cornwall: "This shows you are above, / You [justicers], that these our nether crimes / So speedily venge!" (4.2.78–80). And Edgar, who has just triumphed over Edmund in single combat, declares confidently, "The gods are just" (5.3.171). The context finds Edmund attempting to right a wrong, to act justly ["Some good I mean to do" (5.3.244)], but his effort is too late to prevent Cordelia's being hanged at the order that he himself gave in an earlier scene. (See Fig. 6.) Although the theme of justice fills the air of *King Lear*, justice itself never comes to earth as a practical corrective to injustice. The gods themselves may not intervene in *King Lear*, but an equivalent of such intervention does materialize when "the wicked bring destruction upon themselves" (Evans and Tobin, 1300).

### INJUSTICE AND APOCALYPSE

Usually the belief that evil will destroy itself is an idle dream. In the meantime, perverted justice, mockeries of justice, and cruel injustice thrive. These forces dominate the play, and in such a setting, men and women, like Job and Lear, are "More sinn'd against than sinning" (3.2.60), and justice is ineffectual, especially vis-à-vis poverty:

> [Plate sin] with gold
> And the strong lance of justice hurtless breaks;
> Arm it in rags, a pigmy's straw does pierce it.
> None does offend, none, I say none . . .
>
> (4.6.165–68)

The defenseless poor can easily be found to offend, but those who can buy off the law, says Lear, are not found guilty of offenses because where the law is corrupt, all things are lawful—or at least seem to be lawful. Boundaries in such situations barely differentiate fair from foul, so that the distinctions between good and evil are smudged or blurred. Individuals who offend and who are not called to account enjoy the insidious privilege of unaccountability. Theirs is a no-fault existence. The demented Lear, capable of uttering commonsense truths about "lances of justice" that are powerless against offenders, creates a tragic irony so electrifying that Edgar must respond with an aside commenting on what to him is a revelation of almost scriptural proportions: "O matter and impertinency mix'd, / Reason in madness!" (4.6.174–75). Lear's madness is paradoxically interfused with his reason.

Although usually thought of as a secular play, *King Lear* recalls the urgent cry of Isaiah: "Howl ye; for the day of the Lord is at hand; it shall come as a destruction from the Almighty" (13.6). Early on, Gloucester enumerated destructive disorders relevant to Shakespeare's tragedy: "Love cools, friendship falls off, brothers divide: in cities, mutinies; in countries, discord; in places treason; and the bond crack'd 'twixt son and father: the king falls from bias of nature; there's father against child" (1.2.106–12). The play just about pleads for final judgments, for Apocalypse to come here and now in this world of uncertain geometries. "Fall and cease!" cries Albany (5.3.265). The line epitomizes the way the Book of Revelation is for *King Lear* a frame of reference. Similarly, Thomas Nashe's *Christ's Tears over Jerusalem* (1593), which Shakespeare knew well and from which he drew specific instances of diction and tone (Tobin, 1998, 324), was inspired by the Gospel of Luke 19.41–42. Isaiah's warning and Lear's homily are of a piece with what Nashe writes: "Comfort us, Lord; we mourn, our bread is mingled with ashes and our drink with tears. With so many funerals are we oppressed that we have no leisure to weep for our sins, for howling for our sons and daughters. Oh, hear the voice of our howling" (Tobin 1998, 174–75).

## TRAGIC RESOLUTION

No matter how much the suffering intensifies in *King Lear*, a miracle is not imminent unless Cordelia herself is envisioned as such. Earlier, we noted the straightforward allusion to Scripture when Cordelia speaks of going about her father's business; soon afterward, we hear that she "redeems nature from the general curse" (4.6.206). One school of thought contends that Cordelia directs the plot toward resolution through redemption. Although no longer an academically fashionable view, it remains a possible understanding of the play. Cordelia's

Spenserian name incorporates the much-used Elizabethan anagram linking the name "Delia" with "Ideal" and also contains the Latin word for heart (*cor* or *cordis*) which, when combined with the anagrammatic *delia*, associates her with the "ideal heart" and love. That she refuses to heave her heart into her mouth (1.1.91–92) manifests her very nature. She is not "empty-hearted" (153) and rejects being forced to regurgitate a declaration of love that is devoid of truth. Being compelled to do so leads to falsehood and division, as we see at the opening of the play when her sisters strive to outdo one another. In contrast, Cordelia stands for union and, as her name suggests, accord—a binding principle which has the power to tie people together and which underlies the importance that she places on the "bond" with her father (1.1.93), to whom she attempts to explain that her decision not to participate in the love test is heartfelt (104–5), an act of love in itself. (See Fig. 13.)

In their misery, Lear and the realm of Britain are ready to accept whatever hope, miraculous or otherwise, Cordelia can offer. However, Kent cautions that the relationship between misery and miracle is a double-edged possibility fraught with irony when he says that "Nothing almost sees miracles / But misery" (2.2.165–6). In beginning the line with "Nothing"—the crucial negative term in the play—Shakespeare anticipates Søren Kierkegaard's view that in our sad human journey, "No miracle occurs. The whole of life is a trial" (63). In *King Lear*, it may be said, humanity is on trial, the verdict is yet to be handed down, and a miraculous exoneration is not likely to occur. Edgar tells us that "the worst is not / So long as we can say, 'This is the worst'" (4.1.27–28), which Frank Kermode in the *Riverside* glosses as "no man can even *say* his trials are at an end" (1302).

As the drama closes, Cordelia assists Lear as a devoted daughter as well as a military hope, an emblem of virtue wearing the armor of France. Like a Joan of Arc figure, Cordelia is committed to a spiritual mission and nobly does battle with the forces of vice in an externalized *psychomachia*. But tragic irony wins the day: Neither her father nor her father's realm is ever restored.

The nightmare goes on, and when Kent asks, "Is this the promis'd end?" (5.3.264), we realize that the final verdict hangs in the air. In the course of his trial, Lear gathers unto himself, albeit in inadequate measure, the faint glow of an inner life. His self-illumination is the culmination of several powerful moments generated artistically and psychologically in Shakespeare's play. Fascinatingly, we hear as well as see Lear responding with compassion to poverty around him, admitting to his own folly, and declaring in mad triumph that he is the very essence of a king (4.6.107). However, the remaining, persistent image is that of a ruined Lear wearing a ruined crown.

# PERFORMANCE HISTORY

*Vincent F. Petronella*

PRODUCTIONS OF *King Lear* have managed to grow in number and quality over the centuries despite those who believe that any attempt to perform the play is tantamount to creating what Lear himself calls a "great stage of fools" (4.6.182–3). In 1811, essayist Charles Lamb (1775–1834) made his well-known declaration: "the Lear of Shakespeare cannot be acted" (237). Almost one hundred years after the publication of Lamb's essay, A. C. Bradley announced that *King Lear* is "too huge for the stage" (211), implying that the work is a narrative poem rather than a script upon which to base a theater production. The views of Lamb and Bradley influenced the theatergoing public and tended to limit interest in *King Lear* as a stage play until the outbreak of (and anguish caused by) two world wars in Europe.

## EARLIEST PRODUCTIONS

Although *King Lear* was performed shortly after its composition in 1605, the play's early performance history, as R. A. Foakes puts it, "is a blank" (Foakes, Arden, 90). Richard Burbage very likely played Lear at the Globe with Robert Armin as the Fool, but much more certain is the recorded fact, as discussed in the Introduction, that Shakespeare's company staged *King Lear* in the presence of King James (Color Plate 1) at the palace of Whitehall during the Christmas season of 1606. *King Lear* continued to be staged until the closing of the theaters in 1642.

The old anonymous ballad of "King Lear and His Three Daughters" (in circulation before 1620) may be based on descriptive details of a very early performance. The ballad tells how the old king grows faint and collapses in the presence of Cordela, whose name, like Cordelia's, has the identical first syllable ("cor") referring to matters of the heart. We also read that Lear "never parted" from his daughter and that on her "bosom left his life, / That was so truly-hearted" (Wells, 173–76). The compound adjective that concludes the lines follows an important word that Shakespeare's Lear repeats at the close of the play: "never" (5.3.309). We may be glimpsing in the ballad, as Stanley Wells observes, the way that, in a stage performance, "Burbage himself expired over the body of the boy actor playing Cordelia" (279). It is quite possible, then, that the ballad includes an account of a stage production that occurred near or during Shakespeare's lifetime.

## RESTORATION AND EIGHTEENTH CENTURY

With the restoration of the English monarchy in 1660, Shakespeare's plays had an added attraction: actresses appeared in female roles. In 1664 and 1675, women played Cordelia in productions of Thomas Betterton (c. 1635–1710). Another development was Betterton's choice for performances of a text similar to the original Quarto or Folio. Playing Lear in the robust and yet stylized and artificial acting style of Burbage, Betterton's stage successes continued into the early eighteenth century until his death eight years prior to that of playwright Nicholas Rowe (1674–1718), who in 1709 published the first critical edition of Shakespeare's plays.

### FROM TATE'S LOVE-STORY *LEAR* TO GARRICK'S REALISM

In the same era, Nahum Tate (1625–1715), from Trinity College in Dublin, became England's poet laureate (1692–1715); and in 1681, he published his love-story/happy-ending version of *King Lear*. The public strongly preferred Tate's version, with its redemptive love match between Cordelia and Edgar. In this adaptation, Lear is restored to sanity, which was considered quite suitable for the stage in the light of King George III's actual madness that prompted the official ban on performances of Shakespeare's play. For reading purposes, however, "informed taste," as Brian Gibbons tells us, returned to Shakespeare's text (317).

After Tate and Rowe came David Garrick (1717–79), who was at the Drury Lane Theatre both as spectacular actor and joint manager. From the age of twenty-four, he began acting in *King Lear*, using the Tate version while incorporating poetry closer to that of Shakespeare. Pursuing realism, Garrick shaped his role by visiting mental hospitals to study the behavior of patients. The theatrical impact of these experiences combined with his ability to project volcanic passions that "dissolved his audience in tears and froze them with horror" (Stone and Kahrl, 260). Between his powerful, even explosive, voice and his animated facial features, Garrick assumed titanic proportions onstage. He preferred natural acting and generally avoided spectacular dramatic effects so common during the eighteenth century. Although he retained Tate's happy ending, he offered a Lear that was closer to the original than any that had been seen and heard for decades.

### A LEAR FOR THE ROMANTIC AGE

For his *King Lear* of 1823, Edmund Kean (1787–1833) reinserted the tragic scenes that Tate left out. Although he valiantly tried to reinstate Shakespeare's ending for the play, audiences demanded, after several performances, that the Tate version be restored (Halio, 1992, 114, n.6).

William Hazlitt (1778–1830) saw Kean's Lear in London in 1820. He disliked the traces of Tate in the production and bluntly asserted that "perhaps the genius of no living actor can be expected to cope with Lear" (quoted in White, 1996, 219). In the United States, Kean's Lear was successful except for his appearance at the Boston Theatre in 1821, where he discontinued his engagement because of the small audiences. Bostonians were angered by what they took as a display of arrogance. Nevertheless, between his inflection and a commanding, often thunderous, voice, he portrayed for audiences an intense, memorable Lear that made him a favorite of various Romantic writers of his day. Like Garrick, Kean prepared for the role by studying the characteristics of actual insanity, visiting St. Luke's and Bethlehem hospitals regularly before appearing as Lear (Furness, 442). Samuel Taylor Coleridge (1772–1834) created a Romantic image for Kean: "To see him act is like reading Shakespeare by flashes of lightning" (qtd. in Foakes, *Hamlet* 184).

## *LEAR* AND SHAKESPEARE'S "NEGATIVE CAPABILITY"

John Keats (1795–1821), who had a high regard for Kean's ability, hoped to emulate the actor's dramatic intensity: "One of my ambitions is to make a great revolution in modern dramatic writing as Kean has done in acting . . ." (Rollins, 2:139). In a review of Kean dated December 21, 1817, Keats –anticipating his own letter of October 27, 1818, to Richard Woodhouse, in which he says that "the poetical Character . . . lives in gusto" (Cook, 418) –characterizes Kean's voice as possessing "an indescribable gusto"—i.e., a forceful vitality (Cook, 346), using the critical term associated with William Hazlitt, whom Keats knew, admired, and from whom he learned much about Shakespeare (White, 1987, 31–55; Bate, 1963, 233–50). In the context of Kean's theatrical practice and the example of Shakespeare's dramatic words, especially in connection with *King Lear* (Letter of December 21, ?27 1817; Cook, 370), Keats formulated his theory of "Negative Capability," the ability to suspend one's need for definite or precise conclusions—a suspension related to Keats's view, stated in his letter to Richard Woodhouse (October 27, 1818) that the poet's own identity or ego is deemphasized (negated) by "filling some other Body"—that is, an entity separate from oneself. In this way, the poet achieves objectivity, as Hazlitt explains, through the projection out of oneself of one's imagination (Willis, 76–77). Keats responded to the play not only with his sonnet, "On Sitting Down to Read *King Lear* Once Again," but also with perceptive marginal comments in his personal copy of a Facsimile First Folio Shakespeare (Bate, 1989, 168). Lear within the play and Keats as poet / audience "burn through" the tragic experience and will be "consumed in the fire" that brings psychological purgation and the possibility of Phoenix-like renewal. (See p. 304 and Fig. 8.)

That *Rofincrance* and *Guildenſterne* are dead :
Where ſhould we haue our thankes ?
  *Hor.* Not from his mouth,
Had it th'abilitie of life to thanke you :
He neuer gaue command'ment for their death.
But ſince ſo iumpe vpon this bloodie queſtion,
You from the Polake warres, and you from England
Are heere arriued. Giue order that theſe bodies
High on a ſtage be placed to the view,
And let me ſpeake to th'yet vnknowing world,
How theſe things came about. So ſhall you heare
Of carnall, bloudie, and vnnaturall acts,
Of accidentall iudgements, caſuall ſlaughters
Of death's put on by cunning, and forc'd cauſe,
And in this vpſhot, purpoſes miſtooke,
Falne on the Inuentors heads. All this can I
Truly deliuer.
  *For.* Let vs haſt to heare it,
And call the Nobleſt to the Audience.
For me, with ſorrow, I embrace my Fortune,
I haue ſome Rites of memory in this Kingdome,

Which are ro claime, my vantage doth
Inuite me,
  *Hor.* Of that I ſhall haue alwayes cauſe to ſpeake,
And from his mouth
Whoſe voyce will draw on more :
But let this fame be preſently perform'd,
Euen whiles mens mindes are wilde,
Leſt more miſchance
On plots, and errors happen.
  *For.* Let foure Captaines
Beare *Hamlet* like a Soldier to the Stage,
For he was likely, had he beene put on
To haue prou'd moſt royally : '
And for his paſſage,
The Souldiours Muſicke, and the rites of Warre
Speake lowdly for him.
Take vp the body ; Such a ſight as this
Becomes the Field, but heere ſhewes much amis.
Go, bid the Souldiers ſhoote.
    *Exeunt Marching : after the which, a Peale of*
      *Ordenance are ſhot off.*

# FINIS.

On sitting down to read King Lear once again.

O Golden-tongued Romance, with serene lute!
  Fair plumed Syren, Queen of far-away!
  Leave melodizing on this wintry day,
Shut up thine olden Pages, and be mute.
Adieu! for, once again, the fierce dispute,
  Betwixt Damnation and impassion'd clay
  Must I burn through; once more humbly assay
The bitter-sweet of this Shakspherean fruit.

Chief Poet! and ye Clouds of Albion,
  Begetters of our deep eternal theme!
When through the old oak forest I am gone,
  Let me not wander in a barren dream:
But when I am consumed in the fire,
  Give me new Phœnix wings to fly at my desire.
          Jan. 22. 1818.

Fig. 8. The title-page of *King Lear* in Keats's Folio facsimile (page *right*) reveals a few of the many markings in Keats's own hand found throughout Shakespeare's text. A strong sense of mortality prompted the young Romantic poet, who would die only a few years later, to underline Lear's verbal enactment of the art of dying as he crawls disburdened "toward death" (1.1.41). Keats wrote in his own hand the poem on *King Lear* (See the reproduction of the holograph *above.* Also see a modern printing of the poem in the "Classic Essays" section of this Evans Edition.

# THE TRAGEDIE OF

## KING LEAR.

*Actus Primus. Scæna Prima.*

*Enter Kent, Gloucester, and Edmond.*

*Kent.*

I Thought the King had more affeƈted the Duke of *Albany*, then *Cornwall*.

*Glou.* It did alwayes feeme fo to vs : But now in the diuiſion of the Kingdome, it appeares not which the Dukes hee valewes moſt, for qualities are fo weigh'd, that curioſity in neither, can make choiſe of others moity.

*Kent.* Is not this your Son, my Lord ?

*Glou.* His breeding Sir, hath bin at my charge. I haue ſo often bluſh'd to acknowledge him, that now I am braz'd too't.

*Kent.* I cannot conceiue you.

*Glou.* Sir, this yong Fellowes mother could ; whereupon ſhe grew round womb'd, and had indeede (Sir) a ſonne for her Cradle, ere ſhe had a husband for her bed. Do you ſmell a fault ?

*Kent.* I cannot wiſh the fault vndone, the iſſue of it, being fo proper.

*Glou.* But I haue a Sonne, Sir, by order of Law, fome yeere elder then this ; who, yet is no deerer in my account, though this Knaue came fomthing fawcily to the world before he was ſent for : yet was his Mother fayre, there was good fport at his making, and the horfon muſt be acknowledged. Doe you know this Noble Gentleman, *Edmond* ?

*Edm.* No, my Lord.

*Glou.* My Lord of Kent : Remember him heereafter, as my Honourable Friend.

*Edm.* My feruices to your Lordſhip.

*Kent.* I muſt loue you, and fue to know you better.

*Edm.* Sir, I ſhall ſtudy deferuing.

*Glou.* He hath bin out nine yeares, and away he ſhall againe. The King is comming.

*Sonnet. Enter King Lear, Cornwall, Albany, Gonerill, Regan, Cordelia, and attendants.*

*Lear.* Attend the Lords of France & Burgundy, Gloſter.

*Glou.* I ſhall, my Lord. *Exit.*

*Lear.* Meane time we ſhal expreſſe our darker purpoſe. Giue me the Map there. Know, that we haue diuided In three our Kingdome : and 'tis our faſt intent, To ſhake all Cares and Buſineſſe from our Age, Conferring them on yonger ſtrengths, while we Vnburthen'd crawle toward death. Our ſon of *Cornwal*, And you our no leſſe louing Sonne of *Albany*,

We haue this houre a conſtant will to publiſh Our daughters feuerall Dowers, that future ſtrife May be preuented now. The Princes, *France* & *Burgundy*, Great Riuals in our yongeſt daughters loue, Long in our Court, haue made their amorous foiourne, And heere are to be anſwer'd. Tell me my daughters (Since now we will dineſt vs both of Rule, Intereſt of Territory, Cares of State) Which of you ſhall we ſay doth loue vs moſt, That we, our largeſt bountie may extend Where Nature doth with merit challenge. *Gonerill*, Our eldeſt borne, ſpeake firſt.

*Gon.* Sir, I loue you more then word can weild $\tilde{y}$ matter, Deerer then eye-ſight, ſpace, and libertie, Beyond what can be valewed, rich or rare, No leſſe then life, with grace, health, beauty, honor : As much as Childe ere lou'd, or Father found. A loue that makes breath poore, and ſpeech vnable, Beyond all manner of fo much I loue you.

*Cor.* What ſhall *Cordelia* ſpeake ? Loue, and be ſilent.

*Lear.* Of all theſe bounds euen from this Line, to this, With ſhadowie Forreſts, and with Champains rich'd With plenteous Riuers, and wide-skirted Meades We make thee Lady. To thine and *Albanies* iſſues Be this perpetuall. What ſayes our ſecond Daughter ? Our deereſt *Regan*, wife of *Cornwall* ?

*Reg.* I am made of that felfe-mettle as my Siſter, And prize me at her worth. In my true heart, I finde ſhe names my very deede of loue : Onely ſhe comes too ſhort, that I profeſſe My felfe an enemy to all other ioyes, Which the moſt precious ſquare of ſenſe profeſſes, And finde I am alone felicitate In your deere Highneſſe loue.

*Cor.* Then poore *Cordelia*, And yet not fo, ſince I am ſure my loue's More ponderous then my tongue.

*Lear.* To thee, and thine hereditarie euer, Remaine this ample third of our faire Kingdome, No leſſe in ſpace, validitie, and pleaſure Then that conferr'd on *Gonerill*. Now our Ioy, Although our laſt and leaſt ; to whoſe yong loue, The Vines of France, and Milke of Burgundie, Striue to be intereſt. What can you ſay, to draw A third, more opilent then your Siſters ? ſpeake.

*Cor.* Nothing my Lord.

*Lear.* Nothing ?

## MACREADY AND THE MID-NINETEENTH CENTURY

What Kean was to the Romantic era and Keats's "On Sitting Down to Read *King Lear* Once Again" (1818), William Charles Macready (1793–1873) was to the early Victorian period and Robert Browning's dramatic monologue, "Childe Roland to the Dark Tower Came" (1853) inspired by Poor Tom's song in *King Lear* (3.4.182). Although Macready's *Lear* of 1838, staged a year after Victoria became Queen, usually receives more discussion than his *Lear* of 1834, both are indications that, after a century and a half of Tate's version, Macready changed the course of *Lear* productions. Even though he used in 1834 a severely cut text, Macready is still credited with the theatrical restoration of *King Lear*. In 1844 Macready presented *King Lear* at New York's Park Street Theatre and then traveled north to do the same at Boston's Melodeon Theatre. Charlotte Cushman (1816–1876), who played Lady Macbeth to Macready's Macbeth, was Goneril to his Lear. Given her imposing physique, prominent facial features, and powers of vocal projection, Cushman, if she had been called upon to do so, would have succeeded in performing convincingly and memorably the role of Lear. She was perhaps the only American actress of her time capable of such an achievement.

When Queen Victoria attended Macready's performance, royal opinion hung precariously in the balance. He addressed the "poor naked wretches" speech directly at Her Majesty, and she quickly sensed that the actor was lecturing her on the plight of the poor. She was not amused. Macready's bold statement could easily have brought an official reprimand, but the play went on, and the theater remained open.

An actor who could have upset any monarch or democratic leader he chose with a scolding that roared from the stage was the American Edwin Forrest (1806–72), a forceful actor with leonine energy. When enacting anger, Forrest, "a massive man," had a "voice [that] could shake theater walls," and yet that same voice could murmur softly if need be (Shattuck, 1997, 1914). King Lear was Forrest's masterwork, about which the commanding actor declared, "I *play* Hamlet, Richard, Shylock . . . but, by God, sir! I *am* Lear" (1914).

### EDWIN BOOTH

Edwin Booth (1833–93), brother of John Wilkes Booth, President Lincoln's assassin, performed the role of Lear in the United States, as well as in England and Germany. His script was a modified Tate version. At the final curtain calls in San Francisco (1856), the twenty-three-year-old Booth removed his white wig and beard to reveal his youth, much to the delight and surprise of the audience (Ruggles, 77). Realizing that the part was too large for him, Booth waited ten years before performing Lear again. During the hiatus, he studied the play closely. Following the incubation period, his performance "attained a stature that made some people consider his Lear the most wonderful of all his roles" (Ruggles, 252). Then, in 1875, came his "restored" version—"the first Lear-without-Tate to be performed by any important American actor" (Shattuck, 1976, 2:33). Booth's next Lear performance, at London's Princess Theatre in 1881, enjoyed a definite critical success. Poet Laureate Alfred Lord Tennyson, who never came to the theater unless a free box was arranged for him, responded well to Booth's Lear and invited the actor to dine with him the next day (Ruggles, 277).

## HENRY IRVING

Actor-manager Henry Irving (1838–1905) presented his *King Lear* in 1892 at London's Lyceum Theatre and elicited an interesting response from novelist Henry James: "Mr. Irving has several points in common with Edwin Booth," who "comes nearer to being a man of genius," but Irving is "more comfortable to see" (James, 37). James had in mind the visual appeal of Irving's productions. Irving even produced a *King Lear* souvenir program that told how his version incorporated designs by artist Ford Madox Brown (1821–93). Contending that Irving cut too much of Shakespeare's texts and used too much scenery, George Bernard Shaw wrote in 1896 that Sir Henry Irving "was smashed" when he tried "to interpolate a most singular and fantastic notion of an old man between the lines of a fearfully mutilated acting version of King Lear . . ." (1932, 2: 199). Irving, said Shaw, tended to play versions of Irving rather than playing Shakespeare's characters and often foundered (Shattuck, 1997, 1916).

## BEYOND IRVING: GIELGUD AND OLIVIER

In a production of 1931 at the Old Vic, John Gielgud (1904–2000) first undertook Lear. Nine years later, he enacted Lear again, but now with the directorial guidance of Harley Granville-Barker (1877–1946), who sought to achieve, as he records in *Prefaces to Shakespeare* (1946, 1:271), the "megalithic grandeur" of Lear. In 1950, at Stratford-on-Avon, John Gielgud enjoyed another great success with the play. In 1955, however, his portrayal ran into difficulties. Isamu Noguchi's costume designs reflected those of the classical Noh drama. According to Gielgud, however, "the costumes looked like shower curtains," and the innovative sets, with their blocks of contrasting shapes and colors, tended to dominate the stage and obstruct the actors' movements (Barnet, 308). Gielgud's vision of the play was thwarted, so the production was disappointing. But some forty years later, he starred in the commendable BBC Radio broadcast of *King Lear* directed by Kenneth Branagh. The performance is now available on CD. Gielgud at the age of ninety—older, that is, than Lear himself—performed in this BBC version his fifth and final Lear.

Laurence Olivier (1907–89) presented his final Lear in collaboration with Michael Elliott for Granada TV in 1983 (see Fig. 9), but earlier in his career—in 1946 at the Old Vic—he performed Lear during a time when the play was "no longer dismissed as unactable or treated as endurable only in a completely garbled text" (Brown, 3). Goneril (Pamela Brown) and Regan (Margaret Leighton) became intense "studies in evil," and Alec Guinness played the Fool magnificently (Brown, 3, 14). Olivier's Lear was "an old testy curmudgeon ... breaking and wounding himself on the flints of his own folly"—humanized to the point that he was "infinitely pathetic in his collapse" (Brown, 15).

Fig. 9. Sir Laurence Olivier as Lear and John Hunt as the Fool (Granada Television, 1983). The Fool, having just referred to a cleft egg (1.4.155–62), the basis of a parable explaining how Lear brought on his own ruin by dividing his kingdom, says, "Thou hadst little wit in thy bald crown when thou gav'st thy golden one away" (162–63). For a discussion of this poignant yet amusing moment in the play, see Petronella, "The Cleft Egg in *King Lear*" in "Works Cited." See also Wells, Oxford *Lear*, 152, n. 147.

Olivier's realistic acting style was capable of transforming the actor into madness itself (Warren, 260; David, 127), a characteristic of his work in 1946 and still noticeable in 1983.

## DONALD WOLFIT AND *THE DRESSER*

Like Gielgud and Olivier, Donald Wolfit (1902–68) enjoyed theatrical successes from the 1930s into the 1960s. His manner of presenting Lear was in part captured in the 1961 audio recording for the Living Shakespeare series, as well as in Ronald Harwood's *The Dresser* (1980), in which Wolfit (who was knighted in 1957 to honor his distinguished accomplishments in the theater) is known simply as "Sir." The setting is London during the Blitz of 1940–41, the period during which Wolfit was touring the provinces with *King Lear* and the world was cracking up, as Harwood's play shows. Sir repeatedly whines that he does not remember the opening line of *King Lear* and that he has neither the will nor strength to perform the role. With a line epitomizing the twentieth-century context of *King Lear*, Norman, Sir's costume dresser (for whom the play is named), scolds the aging actor: "The whole world's struggling for bloody survival, so why can't you?" (Harwood, 1980, 29). Both the play itself and the film version of 1983 starring Albert Finney as Sir and Tom Courtney as Norman are insightful. Harwood's work reflects theater critic James Agate's observation that Lear "must be a man, and what is more, *a king in ruins*" (Harwood, 1971, 166; emphasis added) and that Wolfit's Lear is "the greatest tragic performance . . . seen on the British stage since the death of Irving" (Halio, 1992, 49).

## ORSON WELLES'S LEAR

Actors such as Gielgud, Olivier, and Wolfit secured the permanent status of *King Lear* in the Shakespeare repertory as a work with theatrical viability. Thirty years before Olivier's production for Granada TV, a television audience saw its first *King Lear* when Orson Welles appeared in Peter Brook's production for CBS's *Omnibus* in 1953. Telecasts were then "live" and hence captured the spontaneity found in the theater, but since camera work and production values were not what they would be in later decades, the ninety-minute *King Lear*, which opens with Lear violently tearing a large map of Britain into three parts, looks stilted and stagy today. And yet, to see and hear Welles as Lear is to witness the forceful presentations that the popular American actor Edwin Forrest and the internationally acclaimed Italian actor Tommaso Salvini (1829–1916) were known for.

## CHARLES LAUGHTON: CLARITY OF
## THE SPOKEN WORD

A highly successful *Lear* was Byam Shaw's production for the Royal Shakespeare Company at Stratford-on-Avon in 1959. Charles Laughton, who in the 1934 film, *The Barretts of Wimpole Street*, had portrayed the tyrannical father of three daughters, one of them poet Elizabeth Barrett, was now King Lear in confrontation with *his* three daughters. The emphasis of this Stratford production was upon the clarity of the spoken word and a realism that ran counter to what Granville-Barker called "megalithic grandeur." Following the Folio, this staging of the play omitted the mock trial (as does the 1623 Folio), but this and other cuts did not detract from Laughton's mastery of the role and the impact of the production. According to one seasoned reviewer, this was a Lear "for our time and of our time," which did not hesitate to highlight Shakespeare's language so pointedly and brilliantly that she found herself listening "to the *words* as if [she] had never heard the play before" (Byrne, 193).

## MORRIS CARNOVSKY: THE PATRIARCHAL
## TRADITION

Morris Carnovsky (1897–1992) "brought the real pathos of the Cold War age to Lear's suffering" (Ioppolo, 2003, 70), exhibiting "a massive nobility of his own" and making effective use of the patriarchal tradition that has distinguished the great Jewish actors' performances of *King Lear*" (Houseman, 39). His successful 1963 Lear was followed in 1965 by an even greater success. Using a virtually uncut text, Allen Fletcher directed a version in which Carnovsky's Lear suffered a loss of mental powers while holding on to his kingly stature.

## ROYAL SHAKESPEARE COMPANY 1968

Three years after Carnovsky's Lear in the United States, Eric Porter was an imposing Lear at Stratford-on-Avon. Trevor Nunn's 1968 version also had Patrick Stewart as a terrifying Cornwall and Michael Williams, who played a filial Fool to Porter's grandfatherly Lear (Color Plate 2). After a sonorous fanfare played by a brass choir offstage, a regally attired Lear with a magnificent crown and flowing patriarchal beard entered to preside over his court wearing handsome costumes of fabric resembling chain mail, which signified the martial strain in the play. With the entrance of Burgundy and France, the total effect was one of ancient grandeur.

## FILMS OF KOZINTSEV AND BROOK

Russian director Grigori Kozintsev's compelling film version of *King Lear* (*Korol Lir*) of 1969 / 1970 also possesses grandeur. Here, the orchestral and vocal compositions of Dimitri Shostakovich contribute to the film's epic sweep, with its emphasis upon the plight of a wounded society requiring ritual healing. Yuri Yarvet's Lear develops into a haunting emblem of tormented humanity, accompanied by Oleg Dal as an impish, childlike Fool who sings his songs with playful mischievousness. Bells adorning Dal's costume ring as he moves, so that when he sings (in Russian translation) "That lord that counseled thee / To give away thy land" (1608 Quarto 1.4.140–41) to the tune of "Jingle Bells," the melodic anachronism projects the drama closer to our own era; it suggests minds "jangled out of time" (*Hamlet*, 3.1.158) and afflicted with "untun'd and jarring senses" (*King Lear*, 4.7.15). With its masterful interplay of landscape, crowd scenes, animal imagery, and thoroughly natural-looking individuals, Kotzinsev's *Lear* is a masterpiece offering us a "Christian-Marxist story of redemption and social renewal" (Jorgens, 237). Convincing acting, brilliant cinematography, the sound of Boris

Copyright © Courtesy Everett Collection

Fig. 10. Gloucester (played by Alan Webb, *left*) and King Lear (Paul Scofield, *right*) confer in 2.4 at Gloucester's Castle. In this image from Peter Brook's 1970 film, Lear is on the threshold of his crucial dark night of the soul, especially when he sees that his servant, Caius (Kent), is placed in the stocks. In this scene Goneril and Regan will strip Lear of all his knights.

Pasternak's Russian translation, and the Shakespearean subtitles enable the film to capture an imaginary medieval world with real people in it. A year later, Peter Brook's *King Lear* (1971), a film made after his successful stage production, tells "a bleak tale of meaningless violence in a cold, empty universe" (Jorgens, 236–37). Shakespeare's text is so heavily cut here that one may see it as a revision of the play, an adaptation reversing Nahum Tate's sentimental approach of 1681. Sentimentality is banished from Brook's *Lear*. (See Fig. 10). What is left is "the thing itself" after having been artistically stripped down like Poor Tom and the old king. Brook sacrifices language to the point of its being absent, which lends more weight and value to each uttered word when heard. This is particularly true when Lear (Paul Scofield) and Gloucester (Alan Webb) enact their powerful apocalyptic scene on the strand at Dover, which is the heart of the film. Barrenness often marks the landscape—a wasteland shrouded in gloom. It is a flickering void in which humanity, almost erased, is trapped as an absurd plaything of the gods. Presented as an Absurdist drama in the school of Samuel Beckett, Brook's *King Lear* would go on to influence productions of *King Lear* over the next forty years.

## AFRICAN-AMERICAN, JEWISH, AND JAPANESE LEARS

Kotzinsev and Brook enhanced the legacy of *King Lear* performed, as did James Earl Jones, who at the same time contributed to another legacy, the one started by Ira Aldridge (c.1805–67) when, as the first African American to play Lear, he appeared in a London production of 1858. Over a century later, Jones played Lear at the Delacorte Theater in New York. Directed by Joseph Papp and Edwin Sherin, the 1973 production featured a racially mixed cast, with Puerto Rican–born Raul Julia as a craftily charismatic Edmund and Lear's three daughters portrayed by African-American actresses: Rosalind Cash as Goneril, Ellen Holly as Regan, and Lee Chamberlin as Cordelia. Televised in 1974 at Central Park's outdoor theater during an actual performance, the Papp / Sherwin *King Lear* with James Earl Jones has been distributed as a video recording. As a result, present-day audiences can still experience the spontaneity of the production led by Jones, who brings his compelling acting skills and sonorous voice to the role.

A contrasting atmosphere, but one in which ethnic diversity is a feature similar to the Delacorte production, is that of *Der Yidisher Kenig Lir* (1892), written by Russian-born Jacob Gordin (1853–1909). Harry Thomashefsky's 1934 film visualization of Gordin's play opens with a seder. A father inadvertently causes disorder when he reveals his decision to retire to Jerusalem after distributing his wealth among his three daughters. He turns a deaf ear toward his virtuous but defiant daughter, who strongly advises him not to carry out his retirement scheme. As a result, family tensions develop and become fierce. Such domestic strife is central to Gordin's play, as it is to the drama of a sixteenth-century Japanese family in Akira Kurosawa's film called *Ran* (i.e., "Chaos"). Here, Lord Hidetora deals with three sons rather than three daughters and decides to relinquish political power to his eldest. When the youngest son calls Hidetora's plan foolish and describes his father as a senile old man, tension mounts to the point that the young man and his defender, the counterpart of Kent, are banished. The central villain of Kurosawa's film is Mieko Harada as the vengeful Lady Kaede, a horrendous mixture of Goneril, Regan, and Edmund; like Lady Macbeth, she violently hews her way toward power in a production not at all lacking in blood and gore.

## HOLM, PLUMMER, MCKELLEN, AND FOXWORTH

Ian Holm performed Lear at the National Theatre in 1997 and in a BBC-TV production as well. Vocal inflection, a wonderfully expressive face, and energetic projection make Holm's Lear a tempestuous force to contend with. The indoor sets tend to be lurid, especially with an oily Edmund delighting in his decentering schemes. One very striking scene is the discovery of Poor Tom (played by Paul Rhys), who emerges from and stands atop the hovel to be scrutinized by Lear. Before stripping almost naked, Holm's Lear directs the Fool and the disguised Kent to "Consider [Tom] well." He then declares that the mad beggar is "the thing itself" (3.4.103, 106) as the Christlike Tom stands on the sarcophagus-womb-hovel in the manner of the *Ecce Homo* tradition of religious art or the iconographic staging of a medieval mystery play (Jones, 57–59).

Ian Holm's Lear was indeed good, but in another production—this one at Ontario's 2002 Stratford Festival—Christopher Plummer was "too good," for his naturalness and ease in performing a difficult part exceeded the efforts of the rest of the cast: therefore, when he was on-stage, the audience hung upon his every word and gesture, but when he was not, the mood among the spectators dwindled into relative boredom: "We sat there wondering when Lear was coming back," said one member of the audience (Macdonald, 89). By contrast, Trevor Nunn's 2007 production of *King Lear* had Ian McKellen at its center and a strong supporting cast that held its own confidently when Lear was offstage (see Fig. 11).

Richard Price TV Associates

Fig. 11. Ian McKellen as King Lear, with his crown resting on the map of Britain before him, is accompanied by Cordelia (Romola Garai), *left*, Goneril (Frances Barber) and Regan (Monica Dolan), Royal Shakespeare Company, Stratford-upon-Avon, 2007. Directed by Trevor Nunn. A telefilm version was produced in the U.K. by Television Four on December 25, 2008. See Color Plate 2 for the 1968 Trevor Nunn *King Lear*.

In a *New York Times* review, Ben Brantley captured the power of McKellen's Lear: "By tortured degrees . . . this Lear arrives with a clarity that I've never seen before into a state of cosmic empathy and humility, a pained resignation that comes with facing the nothingness into which all men descend." But as if metaphysical "nothingness" is too abstract, too mysterious, and not palpable enough, McKellen's Lear, in the "Off, off you lendings" scene (3.4.108), strips himself to the level of frontal nudity in a literal exhibition of physical selfhood, with its suggestion that fleshly revelation in our cynically materialistic age is often seen as the way to the naked truth.

McKellen's commanding Lear is hard to match, but directors and casts are dauntless in striving to produce, direct, and act the next memorable Lear. Adrian Noble, the former artistic director of England's Royal Shakespeare Theatre, succeeded in doing just that during the summer of 2010 with his production of *King Lear* at the Old Globe Theatre in San Diego. As reviewer Jenny Sandman writes, "the ensemble at the Old Globe did its homework (as one would expect under Noble's tutelage)" and understood "every word and nuance of Shakespeare's elevated language." Robert Foxworth played Lear with energy and conviction, and as the Fool, Bruce Turk, blended very well word and gesture. Noble allowed Shakespeare's language to prevail even in the midst of eye-catching visual effects. "Moments of beauty offset the violence, like the splendid opening scene, with fallen leaves heaped around the stage (Lear in the autumn of his years?)," wrote Pat Launer. The observation reminds us that Lear's life falls, as Macbeth says of himself, "into the sear, the yellow leaf" (Launer, 5.3.23). Noble brilliantly directed the storm scene, which had snow falling (suggestion of a tragic fall in Lear's winter of discontent) upon the stage already coated with the gold of autumn leaves. The Craig Schwartz photograph of Foxworth as Lear and Turk as Fool that is featured in the cover of the present Evans Edition of the play captures the visual—indeed visionary—power of Shakespeare's tragedy, which is, among other things, about seeing and not seeing. Adding much to the production's theatrical beauty was Ralph Funicello's set design, which was understated and yet at times dazzling—another instance of what we do not see and what we do. All in all, then, Noble's 2010 *King Lear*, was a quest to seek and to illuminate, in theater critic Charles McNulty's words, "the hidden layers of this inexhaustible parable."

## OUR WORLD AND *KING LEAR*

As the last two centuries slogged through two world wars, risings and revolution in Ireland and Russia; the Great Depression; genocide (including the Holocaust); wars on the Korean peninsula, in Vietnam, and in the Middle East; assassinations; and vicious terrorist assaults throughout the world, notably the 9/11 attack on the World Trade Center in New York, *King Lear* was evaluated less and less as a barbaric drama belonging strictly to the violence-ridden Middle Ages and the bear-baiting milieu of the Elizabethan-Jacobean era. For ill or for good, the play holds up a mirror to all ages as a reflection of humanity through whose hands civilization is rapidly slipping.

Generally the inherent murkiness of *King Lear* has been intensified by directors hoping to inject into the drama something of overwhelming anxiety growing out of the realities of the human lot and its institutions. To trace the erratic waves of destabilizing and dehumanizing forces, innovative stagings of *King Lear* have occurred repeatedly. Whether these "new" techniques yield a measure of theatrical progress or merely result in an array of flitting novelties or gratuitous violence is pertinent to the assessment of *King Lear* performed. Through creative and / or controversial additions and deletions, loose adaptation, and provocative experiment, the play has lent itself to a theatrical modernity, implying an open future and infinite possibilities that propel our age toward new insights into the tragedy that is *King Lear*.

## WORKS CITED FOR INTRODUCTION AND PERFORMANCE HISTORY

Barnet, Sylvan. "*King Lear* on Stage and Screen." In *King Lear*, ed. Russell Fraser. New York: New American Library, 1986: 301–12.

Bate, Jonathan. *Shakespeare and the English Romantic Imagination*. Oxford: Clarendon P, 1989.

——, and Eric Rasmussen, eds. *William Shakespeare: Complete Works*. New York: Modern Library, 2007.

Bate, Walter Jackson. *John Keats*. Cambridge, MA: Harvard UP, 1963.

Bradley, A. C. *Shakespearean Tragedy*. Macmillan: London, 1904.

Brantley, Ben. "*King Lear* and *The Seagull*: Lear Stripped Bare." 14 September, 2007, Theater Reviews. *New York Times*. Web. September 28, 2008; http://www.mckellen.com/stage/lear07/.

Brown, Ivor. "The Old Vic *King Lear*." *The Masque* 1 (1946): 3, 14–15.

Brownlow, Frank W. *Shakespeare, Harsnett, and the Devils of Denham*. Associated University Presses: London, 1993.

Byrne, Muriel St. Clare. "*King Lear* at Stratford-on-Avon, 1959." *Shakespeare Quarterly* 11 (1960): 189–206.

Bullough, Geoffrey, ed. *Narrative and Dramatic Sources of Shakespeare*. 7 vols. New York: Columbia UP, 1975.

Campbell, Lily B., ed. *The Mirror for Magistrates*. 1938. New York: Barnes and Noble, 1960.

Carroll, William C. *Fat King, Lean Beggar: Representation of Poverty in the Age of Shakespeare*. Ithaca: Cornell UP, 1996.

Cavell, Stanley. "The Avoidance of Love." *Disowning Knowledge in Six Plays of Shakespeare*. 1987. Updated ed. Cambridge, UK: Cambridge UP, 2003.

Cook, Elizabeth, ed. *John Keats*. The Oxford Authors. Oxford: Oxford UP, 1990.

David, Richard. "Drams of Eale: A Review of Recent Productions." *Shakespeare Survey* 10 (1957): 126–34.

Duthie, George Ian, and John Dover Wilson, eds. *King Lear*. Cambridge, UK: Cambridge UP, 1962.

Elton, William R. "*King Lear*" *and the Gods*. San Marino: Huntington Library, 1968.

Evans, G. Blakemore and John J. M. Tobin, eds. *The Riverside Shakespeare*. 2d ed. Boston: Houghton, 1997.

Foakes, R. A. *Hamlet versus Lear: Cultural Politics and Shakespeare's Art*. Cambridge, UK: Cambridge UP, 1993.

——. "Introduction." *King Lear*. Arden Edition. Walton-on-Thames, UK: Thomas Nelson, 1997.

Furness, Horace Howard, ed. "*King Lear*": *A New Variorum Edition of Shakespeare*. New York: Lippincott, 1880.

*The Geneva Bible: A Facsimile of the 1560 Edition*. Introduction by Lloyd E. Berry. Madison: U of Wisconsin, 1969.

Gibbons, Brian. "*The Madness of George III*: Shakespeare, the History Play, and Alan Bennett." In *In the Company of Shakespeare: Essays in English Renaissance Literature in Honor of G. Blakemore Evans*. Eds. Thomas Moisan and Douglas Bruster. Madison: Fairleigh Dickinson UP, 2002: 314–30.

Granville-Barker, Harley. *Prefaces to Shakespeare*. 4 vols. Princeton: Princeton UP, 1946.

Greenblatt, Stephen. "Shakespeare and the Exorcists." In *Shakespeare and the Question of Theory*. Eds. Patricia Parker and Geoffrey Hartman, 1985.

Halio, Jay L., "Introduction." *King Lear*. New Cambridge Edition. Cambridge: Cambridge UP, 1992.

——. "*King Lear*": *A Guide to the Play*. Westport: Greenwood, 2001.

Harwood, Ronald. *Sir Donald Wolfit, C. B. E.: His Life and Work in the Unfashionable Theater*. New York: St. Martin's, 1971.

——. *The Dresser*. New York: Grove, 1980.

Hazlitt, William. *Complete Works*. 21 vols. Ed. P. P. Howe after the edition of A. R. Waller and Arnold Glover. London: Dent, 1930–34.

Houseman, John. "King Lears I've Known." *WGBH/PBS Magazine* (October 1982): 33, 39.

Ioppolo, Grace, ed. *A Routledge Literary Sourcebook on William Shakespeare's "King Lear."* London: Routledge, 2003.

——, ed. *King Lear*. Norton Critical Edition. W. W Norton: New York, 2008.

James, Henry. *The Scenic Art, Notes on Acting and the Drama: 1872–1901*. Ed. Allan Wade. New Brunswick: Rutgers UP, 1948.

Jones, Emrys. *The Origins of Shakespeare*. Oxford: Clarendon P, 1977.

Jorgens, Jack J. *Shakespeare on Film*. Bloomington: Indiana UP, 1977.

Kahn, Coppélia. "The Absent Mother in *King Lear*." In *Rewriting the Renaissance: The Discourses of Sexual Difference in Early Modern Europe*. Eds. Margaret Ferguson, Maureen Quilligan, and Nancy Vickers. Chicago: U of Chicago P, 1986: 33–49.

Kermode, Frank. "Introduction" to *King Lear*. In *The Riverside Shakespeare*, eds. G. Blakemore Evans and John J. M. Tobin. Boston: Houghton, 1997.

Kierkegaard, Søren. *Fear and Trembling* and *The Sickness Unto Death*. Trans. Walter Lowrie. Princeton: Princeton UP, 1941.

Lamb, Charles. "On the Tragedies of Shakespeare, Considered with Reference to Their Fitness for Stage Representation" (1818 text). In *Prose of the Romantic Period*. Riverside Edition. Ed. Carl R. Woodring. Boston: Houghton, 1961: 229–40.

Launer, Pat. "*King Lear*: Surf Report plus More Theater Reviews." Web. June 30, 2010; http://www.sdnn.com/sandiego/2010-06-30/things-to-do/theater-things-to-do/'king-lear'-'surf-report'-plus-more-theater-reviews.

Levin, Richard L. *The Multiple Plot in English Renaissance Drama.* Chicago: U of Chicago P: 1971.

MacDonald, Robert. "Christopher Plummer in Jonathan Miller's Production of *King Lear* at Stratford, Ontario." *Shakespeare Newsletter* (Fall 2002): 89–90.

McLuskie, Kathleen. "The Patriarchal Bard: Feminist Criticism and Shakespeare: *King Lear* and *Measure for Measure*." In *Political Shakespeare.* 1985, eds. Jonathan Dollimore and Alan Sinfield. Ithaca: Cornell UP, 1994: 88–108.

McNulty, Charles. "Theater Review: *King Lear* 3 Times." Culture Monster. Web. June 28, 2010; http://latimesblogs.latimes.com/culturemonster/2010/06/theater-review-king-lear-times-three.html.

Muir, Kenneth. "Introduction." *King Lear.* Arden Edition. London: Methuen, 1972.

Petronella, Vincent F. "The Cleft Egg in *King Lear. Die Neueren Sprachen* Issue 5 (1971): 269-72.

Rollins, Hyder E., ed. *The Keats Circle: Letters and Papers, 1816–1878,* 2d ed. 2 vols. Cambridge: Harvard UP, 1965.

——, ed. *The Letters of John Keats, 1814-1821.* 2 vols. Cambridge MA: Harvard UP, 1958.

Ruggles, Eleanor. *Prince of Players: Edwin Booth.* New York: Norton, 1953.

Salingar, Leo. *Dramatic Form in Shakespeare and the Jacobeans.* Cambridge, UK: Cambridge UP, 1986.

Sandman, Jenny. "A *CurtainUp* San Diego Review: *King Lear.*" *The Internet Theater Magazine of Reviews, Features, Annotated Listings.* Web. June 26, 2010; http://www.curtainup.com/kinglearsandiego.html.

Shattuck, Charles. *Shakespeare in America.* 2 vols. Washington, DC: Folger Shakespeare Library, 1976.

——. "Shakespeare's Plays in Performance: From 1660–1971." Appendix A. *The Riverside Shakespeare,* eds. G. Blakemore Evans and John J. M. Tobin. Boston: Houghton, 1997: 1905–31.

Shaw, George Bernard. *Our Theaters in the Nineties,* 3 vols. London: Constable, 1932.

——. *The Complete Prefaces.* 3 vols. Eds. Dan H. Laurence and Daniel J. Leary. London: Penguin, 1993.

Shelley, Percy Bysshe. *Shelley's Poetry and Prose.* Eds. Donald H. Reiman and Sharon B. Powers. New York: Norton, 1977.

Sommerville, Johann P., ed. *King James VI and I: Political Writings.* Cambridge, UK: Cambridge UP, 1994.

Spurgeon, Caroline. *Shakespeare's Imagery and What It Tells Us.* New York: Macmillan, 1935.

Stone, George Winchester, Jr., and George M. Kahrl. *David Garrick: A Critical Biography.* Carbondale: Southern Illinois UP, 1979.

Taylor, George Coffin. *Shakespeare's Debt to Montaigne.* Cambridge, MA: Harvard UP, 1925.

Tobin, John J. M. *Shakespeare's Favorite Novel: A Study of* The Golden Asse *as Prime Source*. London: UP of America, 1984.

——. "Antony, Brutus, and *Christ's Tears over Jerusalem*." *Notes & Queries* New Series 45 (September 1998): 324–31.

——. "Lear's Howling Again." *Notes & Queries* New Series 51 (September 2004): 287–91.

Warren, Roger. "Shakespeare on the Twentieth-Century Stage." *The Cambridge Companion to Shakespeare Studies*. Ed. Stanley Wells. Cambridge, UK: Cambridge UP, 1986: 257–72.

Wells, Stanley, ed. "The Ballad of King Lear and His Three Daughters." *King Lear*. Oxford Shakespeare. Oxford: Oxford UP, 2000: 277–80.

White, R. S. *Keats as a Reader of Shakespeare*. Norman: Oklahoma UP, 1987.

——, ed. *Hazlitt's Criticism of Shakespeare: A Selection*. Queenston, Ontario: Edwin Mellen, 1996.

Willis, Brian. *Lectures on the English Poets*. New York: Dutton, 1908.

Young, Bruce W. "*King Lear* and the Calamity of Fatherhood." In *In the Company of Shakespeare: Essays in English Renaissance Literature in Honor of G. Blakemore Evans*. Eds. Thomas Moisan and Douglas Bruster. Madison: Fairleigh Dickinson UP, 2002: 43–64.

# ABBREVIATIONS

F1, F2, etc. First Folio, Second Folio, etc.
Q1, Q2, etc. First Quarto, Second Quarto, etc.
(c) corrected state
(u) uncorrected state
conj. conjecture
ed. editor; edition
eds. editors, editions
l(l). line(s)
n.pag. no pagination, no page-numbers
n.s. new series
om. omit(s), omitted
o.s.d. opening stage direction
s.d(d). stage direction(s)
ser. series
s.p(p). speech-prefix(es)
subs. substantially

# KEY TO WORKS CITED IN EXPLANATORY AND TEXTUAL NOTES

Reference in explanatory and textual notes is in general by last name of editor or author. Not included in the following list of works so cited are editions of individual plays or special studies referred to in the selected bibliographies appended to the "Note on the Text" following each of the plays and poems.

ALEXANDER, Peter, ed., *Works*, 1951
CAMBRIDGE, *Works*, eds. W. G. Clark and W. A. Wright, 1863–66 (9 vols.); ed. W. A. Wright, 1891-93 (9 vols.)
CAPELL, Edward, ed., *Works*, [1768] (10 vols.)
COLLIER, John P., ed., *Works*, 1842–44 (8 vols.); 1853; 1858 (6 vols.)
CRAIG, William J., ed., *Works*, 1891
DANIEL, P. A., *Notes and Conjectural Emendations*, 1870
DAVENPORT, A., "Notes on *King Lear*," *N & Q*, n.s., CXCVIII (1953), 20–22
DELIUS, Nicolaus, ed., *Works*, 1854–60 (7 vols.); 1872 (2 vols.)
DUTHIE, George Ian and John Dover Wilson, eds. *King Lear*. Cambridge, UK: Cambridge UP, 1960.
DYCE, Alexander, ed., *Works*, 1857 (6 vols.); 1864–67 (9 vols.); 1875–76 (9 vols.) *Works of Beaumont and Fletcher*, 1843–46 (11 vols.)
EDWARDS, Thomas, *The Canons of Criticism*, 1748
FURNESS, H. H., ed., *New Variorum Edition*, 1871–1928 (vols. 1–15; vols. 16–21 by H. H. Furness, Jr.)
GENTLEMAN, Francis, ed., *Poems Written by Shakespeare*, 1774
GLOBE, eds. William G. Clark and W. A. Wright, *Works*, 1864
HANMER, Thomas, ed., *Works*, 1743–44 (6 vols.); 1745; 1770–71 (6 vols.)
HART, H. C., ed., *Love's Labour's Lost* (Arden), 1906
HEATH, Benjamin, *Revisal of Shakespeare's Text*, 1765
JENNENS, Charles, ed., *Hamlet* (1773), *Julius Caesar* (1773, 1774), *King Lear* (1770), *Macbeth* (1773), *Othello* (1773)
JOHNSON, Samuel, ed. *Works*, 1765 (2 eds. 8 vols.); 1768 (8 vols.)
KELLNER, Leon, *Restoring Shakespeare*, 1925
KITTREDGE, George L., ed., *Works*, 1936
KNIGHT, Charles, ed., *Works*, 1838–43 (8 vols.); 1842–44 (12 vols.)
MALONE, Edmond, ed., *Works*, 1790 (10 vols.)
McEACHERN, Claire, ed. *King Lear*. New York: Longman, 2005.
MUIR, Kenneth, ed., New Arden *King Lear* (London, rev. ed., 1963)
NEILSON, William A., ed., *Works*, 1906
PELICAN, *Works*, general ed. Alfred Harbage (rev. 1-vol. ed.), 1969
POPE, Alexander, ed., *Works*, 1723–25 (6 vols.); 1728 (8 vols.)
RIDLEY, M. R., ed., *Works* (New Temple), 1935–36 (40 vols.)
RINGLER, William, "Exit Kent," *SQ*, XI (1960), 311–17

SCHMIDT, Alexander, *Shakespeare-Lexicon* (2 vols., 4th ed., rev. G. Sarrazin), 1923

SINGER, S. W., ed., *Works*, 1826 (10 vols.); 1855–56 (10 vols.)

SISSON, Charles, ed., *Works*, [1954]

SKEAT, Walter W., ed., *The Two Noble Kinsmen*, 1875

STAUNTON, Howard, ed., *Works*, 1858–60 (3 vols.)

STEEVENS, George, ed., *Works*, 1773 (with Samuel Johnson, 10 vols.); 1778 (10 vols.); 1793 (15 vols.)

THEOBALD, Lewis, ed., *Works*, 1733 (7 vols.); 1740 (8 vols.); 1757 (8 vols.) (with Thomas Seward and J. Sympson), *Works of Beaumont and Fletcher*, 1750 (vol. X: *The Two Noble Kinsmen*)

WALKER, William S., *Critical Examination of the Text of Shakespeare*, 1860 (3 vols.)

WARBURTON, William, ed., *Works*, 1747 (8 vols.)

WHITE, Richard Grant, ed. *Works*, 1857–66 (12 vols.); 1883 (6 vols.)

WILSON, John Dover (with A. Quiller-Couch et al.), eds., *Works* (New Shakespeare), 1921–66 (39 vols.)

# THE TRAGEDY OF

# KING LEAR

# DRAMATIS PERSONAE

LEAR, *King of Britain*
KING OF FRANCE
DUKE OF BURGUNDY
DUKE OF CORNWALL, *husband to Regan*
DUKE OF ALBANY, *husband to Goneril*
EARL OF KENT
EARL OF GLOUCESTER
EDGAR, son *to Gloucester*
EDMUND, *bastard son to Gloucester*
CURAN, *a courtier*
OSWALD, *steward to Goneril*
OLD MAN, *tenant to Gloucester*
DOCTOR
FOOL, *to Lear*
CAPTAIN *employed by Edmund*
GENTLEMAN *attendant on Cordelia*
HERALD
SERVANTS *to Cornwall*
GONERIL ⎫
REGAN ⎬ *daughters to Lear*
CORDELIA ⎭
KNIGHTS *of Lear's train*, GENTLEMEN, OFFICERS,
MESSENGERS, SOLDIERS, *and* ATTENDANTS

SCENE: *Britain*

# Act I

SCENE I

*Enter* KENT, GLOUCESTER, *and* EDMUND.

KENT I thought the King had more affected the
Duke of Albany than Cornwall.

GLOUCESTER It did always seem so to us; but now in the
division of the kingdom, it appears not which of the
Dukes he values most, for [equalities] are so                          5
Weigh'd, that curiosity in neither can make choice of
either's moi'ty.

KENT Is not this your son, my lord?

GLOUCESTER His breeding, sir, hath been at my charge.          10
I have so often blush'd to acknowledge him, that now
I am braz'd to 't.

KENT I cannot conceive you.

GLOUCESTER Sir, this young fellow's mother could;
whereupon she grew round-womb'd, and had indeed,
sir, a son for her cradle ere she had a husband for her          15
bed. Do you smell a fault?

KENT I cannot wish the fault undone, the issue of it
being so proper.

GLOUCESTER But I have a son, sir, by order of law, some
year elder than this, who yet is no dearer in my               20
account. Though this knave came something saucily

*Words and passages enclosed in square brackets in the text above are either emendations of the
copy-text or additions to it. The Textual Notes immediately following the play cite the earliest
authority for every such change or insertion and supply the reading of the copy-text wher-
ever it is emended in this edition. Notes within square brackets below are by Evans Editor,
V. F. Petronella.*

1.1 Location: **Britain. King Lear's palace.   1. affected:** liked.   **2. Albany:**
northern Britain.   **6. weigh'd:** precisely balanced. **curiosity:** meticulous scrutiny.
**7. moi'ty:** portion.   **9. breeding:** rearing.   **charge:** expense.   **11. braz'd:** bra-
zened, hardened.   **12. conceive:** understand (with following quibble).   **17. issue:**
(1) outcome; (2) offspring.   **18. proper:** (1) excellent; (2) handsome.   **19. by . . .
law:** legitimate.   **21. account:** estimation.   **knave:** young fellow (not derogatory).
**something:** somewhat.

to the world before he was sent for, yet was his
mother fair, there was good sport at his making, and
the whoreson must be acknowledg'd. Do you know
this noble gentleman, Edmund?                                    25
EDMUND  No, my lord.
GLOUCESTER  My Lord of Kent. Remember him hereafter
as my honorable friend.
EDMUND  My services to your lordship.
KENT  I must love you, and sue to know you better.          30
EDMUND  Sir, I shall study deserving.
GLOUCESTER  He hath been out nine years, and away he
shall again. ([*Sound a*] *sennet.*) The King is coming.

*Enter* [*one bearing a coronet, then*] KING LEAR, CORNWALL,
ALBANY, GONERIL, REGAN, CORDELIA, *and* ATTENDANTS.

LEAR  Attend the lords of France and Burgundy, Gloucester.
GLOUCESTER  I shall, my lord.                    *Exit* [*with Edmund*]. 35
LEAR  Mean time we shall express our darker purpose.
Give me the map there. Know that we have divided
In three our kingdom; and 'tis our fast intent
To shake all cares and business from our age,
Conferring them on younger strengths, while we       40
Unburthen'd crawl toward death. Our son of Cornwall,
And you, our no less loving son of Albany,
We have this hour a constant will to publish
Our daughters' several dowers, that future strife
May be prevented now. The princes, France and Burgundy,    45
Great rivals in our youngest daughter's love,
Long in our court have made their amorous sojourn,
And here are to be answer'd. Tell me, my daughters
(Since now we will divest us both of rule,
Interest of territory, cares of state),                    50
Which of you shall we say doth love us most,
That we our largest bounty may extend
Where nature doth with merit challenge? Goneril,
Our eldest-born, speak first.
GONERIL  Sir, I love you more than [words] can wield the matter,    55
Dearer than eyesight, space, and liberty,
Beyond what can be valued, rich or rare,

---

**32. out:** abroad.  **33** s.d. **sennet:** trumpet call signalling the arrival or departure of
a procession.  **36. darker:** more secret.  **38. fast:** firm.  **43. publish:** announce
publicly.  **44. several:** individual.  **50. Interest:** possession.  **53. Where ... challenge:** where natural affection in addition to (other) merit claims it.

No less than life, with grace, health, beauty, honor;
As much as child e'er lov'd, or father found;
A love that makes breath poor, and speech unable: 60
Beyond all manner of so much I love you.
CORDELIA [*Aside.*] What shall Cordelia speak? Love, and be silent.
LEAR Of all these bounds, even from this line to this,
With shadowy forests and with champains rich'd,
With plenteous rivers and wide-skirted meads, 65
We make thee lady. To thine and Albany's [issue]
Be this perpetual. What says our second daughter,
Our dearest Regan, wife of Cornwall? [Speak.]
REGAN I am made of that self metal as my sister,
And prize me at her worth. In my true heart 70
I find she names my very deed of love;
Only she comes too short, that I profess
Myself an enemy to all other joys
Which the most precious square of sense [possesses],
And find I am alone felicitate 75
In your dear Highness' love.
CORDELIA [*Aside.*] Then poor Cordelia!
And yet not so, since I am sure my love's
More ponderous than my tongue.
LEAR To thee and thine hereditary ever
Remain this ample third of our fair kingdom, 80
No less in space, validity, and pleasure,
Than that conferr'd on Goneril.—Now, our joy,
Although our last and least, to whose young love
The vines of France and milk of Burgundy
Strive to be interess'd, what can you say to draw 85
A third more opulent than your sisters'? Speak.
CORDELIA Nothing, my lord.
LEAR Nothing?
CORDELIA Nothing.

---

**60. breath:** voice. **64. champains:** unwooded plains. **rich'd:** made rich.
**65. wide-skirted:** extensive. **69. self:** same. **metal:** With some of the sense
of modern *mettle.* **70. prize . . . worth:** esteem myself her equal (in love
for you). **71. she . . . love:** she exactly describes my love. **72. that:** in that.
**74. square:** Usually glossed as "region" or "criterion," but more probably *square
of sense* is figurative for the human body or human life. See *The Faerie Queene*,
2.9.22, "a quadrate was the base" (the lower part of the soul, which works through
sense). **75. felicitate:** made happy. **78. ponderous:** weighty. **81. validity:**
value. **pleasure:** pleasing features. **83. last and least:** Cordelia is the youngest
child and therefore ranks below her sisters. **84. milk:** pasture lands (?). **85. be
interess'd:** establish a claim. **draw:** win.

LEAR  Nothing will come of nothing, speak again.                    90
CORDELIA  Unhappy that I am, I cannot heave
 My heart into my mouth. I love your Majesty
 According to my bond, no more nor less.
LEAR  How, how, Cordelia? Mend your speech a little,
 Lest you may mar your fortunes.
CORDELIA      Good my lord,                    95
 You have begot me, bred me, lov'd me: I
 Return those duties back as are right fit,
 Obey you, love you, and most honor you.
 Why have my sisters husbands, if they say
 They love you all? Happily, when I shall wed,                    100
 That lord whose hand must take my plight shall carry
 Half my love with him, half my care and duty.
 Sure I shall never marry like my sisters,
 [To love my father all].
LEAR  But goes thy heart with this?
CORDELIA      Ay, my good lord.                    105
LEAR  So young, and so untender?
CORDELIA  So young, my lord, and true.
LEAR  Let it be so: thy truth then be thy dow'r!
 For by the sacred radiance of the sun,
 The [mysteries] of Hecat and the night;                    110
 By all the operation of the orbs,
 From whom we do exist and cease to be;
 Here I disclaim all my paternal care,
 Propinquity and property of blood,
 And as a stranger to my heart and me                    115
 Hold thee from this for ever. The barbarous Scythian,
 Or he that makes his generation messes
 To gorge his appetite, shall to my bosom
 Be as well neighbor'd, pitied, and reliev'd,
 As thou my sometime daughter.
KENT      Good my liege—                    120

---

**90. Nothing . . . nothing:** Echoing the famous Aristotelian doctrine *Ex nihilo nihil fit* (denied by Christian philosophers in respect of the Creation). **93. bond:** duty. **97. Return . . . fit:** am properly dutiful in return. **100. Happily:** haply, perhaps. **101. plight:** marriage pledge. **110. Hecat:** Hecate, goddess of witchcraft and of the moon. **111. operation:** influence. **orbs:** stars. **112. From whom:** by the effect of which. **114. Propinquity:** closeness. **property:** identity. **116. from this:** from this time forth. **Scythian.** The Scythians' reputation for barbarity extended back to classical times. **117. makes . . . messes:** makes meals of his progeny. **120. liege:** sovereign.

LEAR  Peace, Kent!
Come not between the dragon and his wrath;
I lov'd her most, and thought to set my rest
On her kind nursery. [*To Cordelia.*] Hence, and avoid my sight!—
So be my grave my peace, as here I give                               125
Her father's heart from her. Call France. Who stirs?
Call Burgundy. Cornwall and Albany,
With my two daughters' dow'rs digest the third;
Let pride, which she calls plainness, marry her.
I do invest you jointly with my power,                                130
Pre-eminence, and all the large effects
That troop with majesty. Ourself, by monthly course,
With reservation of an hundred knights
By you to be sustain'd, shall our abode
Make with you by due turn. Only we shall retain                      135
The name, and all th' addition to a king;
The sway, revenue, execution of the rest,
Beloved sons, be yours, which to confirm,
This coronet part between you.
KENT                                      Royal Lear,
Whom I have ever honor'd as my king,                                 140
Lov'd as my father, as my master follow'd,
As my great patron thought on in my prayers—
LEAR  The bow is bent and drawn, make from the shaft.
KENT  Let it fall rather, though the fork invade
The region of my heart; be Kent unmannerly                           145
When Lear is mad. What wouldest thou do, old man?
Think'st thou that duty shall have dread to speak
When power to flattery bows? To plainness honor's bound,
When majesty falls to folly. Reserve thy state,
And in thy best consideration check                                  150
This hideous rashness. Answer my life my judgment,
Thy youngest daughter does not love thee least,
Nor are those empty-hearted whose low sounds
Reverb no hollowness.

---

122. **his wrath:** the object of its wrath.  123. **set my rest:** (1) stake my all (a term
from the card game primero); (2) depend for my repose.  124. **kind nursery:**
loving care.  **avoid:** leave.  128. **digest:** assimilate.  136. **addition:** honors and
prerogatives.  143. **make from:** get out of range of.  144. **fall:** strike. **fork:**
two-pronged head.  149. **Reserve thy state:** retain control of your kingdom.
151. **Answer . . . judgment:** i.e. I'll stake my life on my opinion.  154. **Reverb
no hollowness:** do not reverberate hollowly. *Hollowness* means both "emptiness"
and "insincerity."

LEAR                    Kent, on thy life, no more.
KENT  My life I never held but as [a] pawn                           155
  To wage against thine enemies, ne'er [fear'd] to lose it,
  Thy safety being motive.
LEAR                    Out of my sight!
KENT  See better, Lear, and let me still remain
  The true blank of thine eye.
LEAR  Now, by Apollo—
KENT                    Now, by Apollo, King,                        160
  Thou swear'st thy gods in vain.
LEAR                    O vassal! miscreant!
                              [*Starts to draw his sword.*]
ALBANY, CORNWALL  Dear sir, forbear.
KENT  Kill thy physician, and [the] fee bestow
  Upon the foul disease. Revoke thy gift,
  Or whilst I can vent clamor from my throat,                        165
  I'll tell thee thou dost evil.
LEAR                    Hear me, recreant,
  On thine allegiance, hear me!
  That thou hast sought to make us break our [vow]—
  Which we durst never yet—and with strain'd pride
  To come betwixt our sentence and our power,                        170
  Which nor our nature nor our place can bear,
  Our potency made good, take thy reward.
  Five days we do allot thee, for provision
  To shield thee from disasters of the world,
  And on the sixt to turn thy hated back                             175
  Upon our kingdom. If, on the tenth day following,
  Thy banish'd trunk be found in our dominions,
  The moment is thy death. Away! By Jupiter,
  This shall not be revok'd.
KENT  Fare thee well, King; sith thus thou wilt appear,              180
  Freedom lives hence, and banishment is here.
  [*To Cordelia.*] The gods to their dear shelter take thee, maid,
  That justly think'st and hast most rightly said!
  [*To Regan and Goneril.*] And your large speeches may
          your deeds approve,
  That good effects may spring from words of love.                   185

---

**155. pawn:** stake.  **156. wage:** wager.  **159. blank:** centre of the target.  **161. miscreant:** villain (literally, misbeliever).  **166. recreant:** traitor.  **168. That:** since.  **169. strain'd:** excessive.  **171. Which . . . place:** which neither my temperament nor my dignity as king.  **172. Our . . . good:** to prove my authority.  **174. disasters:** misfortunes.  **175. sixt:** sixth.  **180. sith:** since.  **184. approve:** validate.

Thus Kent, O princes, bids you all adieu,
He'll shape his old course in a country new.            *Exit.*

*Flourish. Enter* GLOUCESTER *with* FRANCE *and*
BURGUNDY, ATTENDANTS.

[GLOUCESTER  Here's France and Burgundy, my noble lord.
LEAR  My Lord of Burgundy,
    We first address toward you, who with this king            190
    Hath rivall'd for our daughter. What, in the least,
    Will you require in present dower with her,
    Or cease your quest of love?
BURGUNDY                            Most royal Majesty,
    I crave no more than hath your Highness offer'd,
    Nor will you tender less.
LEAR                            Right noble Burgundy,            195
    When she was dear to us, we did hold her so,
    But now her price is fallen. Sir, there she stands:
    If aught within that little seeming substance,
    Or all of it, with our displeasure piec'd,
    And nothing more, may fitly like your Grace,            200
    She's there, and she is yours.
BURGUNDY                            I know no answer.
LEAR  Will you, with those infirmities she owes,
    Unfriended, new adopted to our hate,
    Dow'r'd with our curse, and stranger'd with our oath,
    Take her, or leave her?
BURGUNDY                            Pardon me, royal sir,            205
    Election makes not up in such conditions.
LEAR  Then leave her, sir, for by the pow'r that made me,
    I tell you all her wealth. [*To France.*] For you, great King,
    I would not from your love make such a stray
    To match you where I hate; therefore beseech you            210
    T' avert your liking a more worthier way
    Than on a wretch whom Nature is asham'd
    Almost t' acknowledge hers.
FRANCE                            This is most strange,
    That she, whom even but now was your [best] object,

---

**187.** s.d. **Flourish:** trumpet fanfare.  **195. tender:** offer.  **198. seeming substance:** deceptive appearance of reality; creature who seems substantial but is nothing. **199. piec'd:** joined. **200. like:** please. **202. owes:** possesses. **204. stranger'd with:** made a stranger by. **206. Election . . . conditions:** it is impossible to choose on these terms.  [**208. I tell:** I'll reveal. ~ *Evans Editor*]  **209. make . . . stray:** deviate so far. **210. To:** as to.

The argument of your praise, balm of your age, 215
The best, the dearest, should in this trice of time
Commit a thing so monstrous, to dismantle
So many folds of favor. Sure her offense
Must be of such unnatural degree
That monsters it, or your fore-vouch'd affection 220
Fall into taint; which to believe of her
Must be a faith that reason without miracle
Should never plant in me.

CORDELIA                              I yet beseech your Majesty—
If for I want that glib and oily art 224
To speak and purpose not, since what I [well] intend,
I'll do't before I speak—that you make known
It is no vicious blot, murther, or foulness,
No unchaste action, or dishonored step,
That hath depriv'd me of your grace and favor,
But even for want of that for which I am richer— 230
A still-soliciting eye, and such a tongue
That I am glad I have not, though not to have it
Hath lost me in your liking.

LEAR                              Better thou
Hadst not been born than not t' have pleas'd me better.

FRANCE Is it but this—a tardiness in nature 235
Which often leaves the history unspoke
That it intends to do? My Lord of Burgundy,
What say you to the lady? Love's not love
When it is mingled with regards that stands
Aloof from th' entire point. Will you have her? 240
She is herself a dowry.

BURGUNDY                              Royal King,
Give but that portion which yourself propos'd,
And here I take Cordelia by the hand,
Duchess of Burgundy.

LEAR Nothing. I have sworn, I am firm. 245

BURGUNDY I am sorry then you have so lost a father
That you must lose a husband.

---

**215. argument:** theme.  [**216. this trice:** an instant. ~ *Evans Editor*] **217. dismantle:** strip off.  **218. folds of favor.** The image is of Cordelia wrapped in garments signifying the royal favor.  **220. That monsters it:** as makes it monstrous. **or:** before.  **221. Fall into taint:** decay.  **223. Should:** could.  **224. for I want:** because I lack.  **225. and purpose not:** without intending to make good what I say.  **228. dishonored:** dishonorable.  **231. still-soliciting:** continually begging. [**238.** Cf. Shakespeare's Sonnet 116, line 2. ~ *Evans Editor*]  **239–40. regards . . . point:** totally irrelevant considerations.

CORDELIA                    Peace be with Burgundy!
Since that [respects of fortune] are his love, I shall not be his wife.
FRANCE  Fairest Cordelia, that art most rich being poor,                    250
    Most choice forsaken, and most lov'd despis'd,
    Thee and thy virtues here I seize upon,
    Be it lawful I take up what's cast away.
    Gods, gods! 'tis strange that from their cold'st neglect
    My love should kindle to inflam'd respect.                    255
    Thy dow'rless daughter, King, thrown to my chance,
    Is queen of us, of ours, and our fair France.
    Not all the dukes of wat'rish Burgundy
    Can buy this unpriz'd precious maid of me.
    Bid them farewell, Cordelia, though unkind,                    260
    Thou losest here, a better where to find.
LEAR  Thou hast her, France, let her be thine, for we
    Have no such daughter, nor shall ever see
    That face of hers again. [*To Cordelia.*] Therefore be gone,
    Without our grace, our love, our benison.—                    265
    Come, noble Burgundy.
        *Flourish. Exeunt [all but FRANCE, GONERIL, REGAN, and CORDELIA].*
FRANCE  Bid farewell to your sisters.
CORDELIA  The jewels of our father, with wash'd eyes
    Cordelia leaves you. I know you what you are,
    And like a sister am most loath to call                    270
    Your faults as they are named. Love well our father;
    To your professed bosoms I commit him,
    But yet, alas, stood I within his grace,
    I would prefer him to a better place.
    So farewell to you both.                    275
REGAN  Prescribe not us our duty.
GONERIL                    Let your study
    Be to content your lord, who hath receiv'd you
    At fortune's alms. You have obedience scanted,
    And well are worth the want that you have wanted.
CORDELIA  Time shall unfold what plighted cunning hides,                    280

---

**248. respects:** considerations.  **255. inflam'd respect:** impassioned regard.
**258. wat'rish:** (1) well-watered; (2) watery, feeble.  **259. unpriz'd:** not valued (by Lear).  **261. here:** this place.  **where:** place elsewhere.  **265. grace:**
favor.  **benison:** blessing.  **268. wash'd:** tear-washed.  **271. as . . . named:**
by their true names.  **272. professed:** love-professing.  **274. prefer:** recommend.  **278. At fortune's alms:** as a small handout from fortune.  **scanted:** come
short in.  **279. are . . . wanted:** deserve to suffer the same lack of affection (from
your husband) that you have shown (to your father).  **280. what . . . hides:** what
is concealed under cunning folds (*plighted* = pleated).

Who covers faults, at last with shame derides.
Well may you prosper!
FRANCE                    Come, my fair Cordelia.

*Exeunt France and Cordelia.*

GONERIL  Sister, it is not little I have to say of what
most nearly appertains to us both. I think our father
will hence to-night.                                                    285
REGAN  That's most certain, and with you; next month with us.
GONERIL  You see how full of changes his age is; the
observation we have made of it hath [not] been little.
He always lov'd our sister most, and with what          290
poor judgment he hath now cast her off appears too grossly.
REGAN  'Tis the infirmity of his age, yet he hath ever
but slenderly known himself.
GONERIL  The best and soundest of his time hath been         295
but rash; then must we look from his age to receive not
alone the imperfections of long-ingraff'd condition,
but therewithal the unruly waywardness that infirm
and choleric years bring with them.
REGAN  Such unconstant starts are we like to have          300
from him as this of Kent's banishment.
GONERIL  There is further compliment of leave-taking
between France and him. Pray you let us [hit] together; if our father carry authority with such disposition as he bears, this last surrender of his will but     305
offend us.
REGAN  We shall further think of it.
GONERIL  We must do something, and i' th' heat.

*Exeunt.*

### SCENE 2

*Enter [EDMUND the] Bastard [with a letter].*

EDMUND  Thou, Nature, art my goddess, to thy law
My services are bound. Wherefore should I
Stand in the plague of custom, and permit

281. **Who:** i.e. time. 292. **grossly:** obviously. 295–96. **The best . . . rash:** even in the prime of life he was impetuous and irascible. 297. **long-ingraff'd:** deep-rooted. 298. **therewithal:** along with that. 300. **starts:** ill-considered actions. 302. **compliment:** ceremony. 303–4. **hit together:** agree on our course of action. 305. **last surrender:** latest action of giving up rule. 306. **offend:** injure. 308. **i' th' heat:** while the iron is hot. 1.2. **Location: The Earl of Gloucester's castle.** 3. **Stand . . . custom:** undergo the trials imposed by convention (on bastards). Custom is opposed to Nature.

Pl. 1. James I of England, wearing an emblem of the Order of the Garter and the "Mirror of Great Britain," a jewel on his hat celebrating the union of the Scottish and English crowns in 1603, by the Anglo-Flemish-Dutch painter, John de Critz. When James was an infant of thirteen months, his mother, Mary Stuart, Queen of Scots, abdicated in 1567, and he became James VI of Scotland. In 1603, the Elizabethan Age ended when Elizabeth I died. James Stuart then assumed his second royal title: King of England. Just about the same time he was honored with a third regal identity: King of England and Ireland. That he was associated with three royal crowns tells us much about the complicated and precarious age James lived in.

The Latin form of the king's name (*Jacobus*) explains why the era of James I in England (1603-25) is called the "Jacobean Age." During this time much of Shakespeare's greatest work was produced, meaning that Shakespeare was as much or more a Jacobean artist than an Elizabethan one.

In 1603, Shakespeare's company became the official play-acting company for James I and changed its name from the Queen's Men to the King's Men. In 1604 the king, who supported the idea of a fresh translation of the Bible, called for a conference of experts to implement such an effort. The result, in 1611, was a great work of literature: the Authorized or King James Version of the Bible. In the "Sources and Contexts" section of this Evans Edition, see James I's *Basilicon Doron* ('The King's Gift'), which contains instructions to his son, Prince Henry. To see the details of this portrait with a magnifier/zoom go to: http://www.nmm.ac.uk/collections/displayRepro.cfm?reproID=BHC2796&picture=1#content

Pl. 2. King Lear (Eric Porter) and the Fool (Michael Williams) as they appeared in the 1968 Royal Shakespeare Company production at Stratford-on-Avon. See Evans Editor's discussion of "Royal Shakespeare Company 1968" in "Performance History."

Sitting on the floor with his head resting against Lear's knee, the Fool is childlike. The Lear-Fool relationship in this production resembled that of grandfather and grandson. Trevor Nunn, who directed this Royal Shakespeare Company version, directed the same company's production of *King Lear* in 2007/8 featuring Ian McKellen (see Fig. 11).

Pl. 3. *King Lear in the Storm*, by the American artist Benjamin West (1738-1820), illustrates Act 3. scene 4. West captures the storm's correspondence to the tempestuous insanity welling up within Lear and to the apocalyptic rumblings in Lear's world. As Shakespeare captures, in words, the microcosmic nature of Lear's tragedy and its cosmic overtones, West uses melodramatic action and *chiaroscuro* (contrasts of light and dark) to dramatize microcosmic man being subjected to what Lear himself calls a "contentious storm" (3.4.6.).

Gloucester, the "walking fire" (3.4.114), *left*, illuminates the unsettled and unsettling scene in which Lear is exposed to the "tyrannous night" (3.4.151). Edgar, not recognized by his father, is disguised as Poor Tom, a demented beggar who sits cowering to the right. It is during this scene that Gloucester, with irony, asks, "What, hath your Grace no better company?" (3.4.141).

This huge, highly dramatic oil painting (dated 1788 and retouched by West in 1806) may be seen at the Museum of Fine Arts/Art of the Americas Wing, Boston, MA. West was appointed history painter to King George III (reigned 1760–1820), whose mental difficulties led to the banning of performances of *King Lear* in the king's lifetime. Alan Bennett's play, *The Madness of George III* (1991), the basis of the film, *The Madness of King George* (1994), incorporates key lines from *King Lear*.

Pl. 4. John Tramper, using a fish-eye lens, captures the cosmic sweep of the present-day Shakespeare's Globe Theatre on Bankside in London by making visually palpable the important relationship between the heavens on high and the "Heavens" (sun, moon, astrological symbols) painted on the underside of the stage canopy. An actor playing Lear may point to the canopy or the sky itself when speaking of "heaven's vault" (5.3.260).

Tramper's image offers a compelling view of the theater of the world where all men and women are players. It is easy to imagine how the design of Shakespeare's three-tier open-air theater would powerfully express the venue in Act 2. scene 3 of *King Lear* when the disguised Kent, whose legs have been place in the stocks, looks skyward toward the moon (the "beacon"), which may have been visible—in actuality or pictorially—to some members of the audience. Wishing to read a crucial letter from Cordelia, Kent addresses the light-giving moon with an appropriate line: "Approach, thou beacon to this under globe."

The curiosity of nations to deprive me,
For that I am some twelve or fourteen moonshines          5
Lag of a brother? Why bastard? Wherefore base?
When my dimensions are as well compact,
My mind as generous, and my shape as true,
As honest madam's issue? Why brand they us
With base? with baseness? bastardy? base, base?          10
Who, in the lusty stealth of nature, take
More composition, and fierce quality,
Than doth within a dull, stale, tired bed
Go to th' creating a whole tribe of fops,
Got 'tween asleep and wake? Well then,                   15
Legitimate Edgar, I must have your land.
Our father's love is to the bastard Edmund
As to th' legitimate. Fine word, "legitimate"!
Well, my legitimate, if this letter speed
And my invention thrive, Edmund the base                 20
Shall [top] th' legitimate. I grow, I prosper:
Now, gods, stand up for bastards!

*Enter* GLOUCESTER.

GLOUCESTER  Kent banish'd thus? and France in choler parted?
And the King gone to-night? Prescrib'd his pow'r,
Confin'd to exhibition? All this done                    25
Upon the gad? Edmund, how now? what news?
EDMUND  So please your lordship, none.
                                    [*Putting up the letter.*]
GLOUCESTER  Why so earnestly seek you to put up that letter?
EDMUND  I know no news, my lord.
GLOUCESTER  What paper were you reading?                 30
EDMUND  Nothing, my lord.
GLOUCESTER  No? What needed then that terrible dis-
patch of it into your pocket? The quality of nothing
hath not such need to hide itself. Let's see. Come, if it
be nothing, I shall not need spectacles.                 35
EDMUND  I beseech you, sir, pardon me. It is a letter

---

**4. curiosity of nations:** finicking distinctions of society (with reference to the expression "the law of nations"). **5. For that:** because. **6. Lag of:** behind, younger than. **7. compact:** composed, framed. **8. generous:** befitting one who is well-born. **9. honest:** chaste. **11. lusty . . . nature:** stealthy enjoyment of natural sexual appetite. **12. composition:** strength of constitution. **fierce:** vigorous. **14. fops:** fools. **15. Got:** begotten. **19. speed:** succeed. **20. invention thrive:** scheme go well. **24. Prescrib'd:** limited. **25. exhibition:** an allowance of money. **26. gad:** spur of the moment. **32. terrible:** terrified.

from my brother that I have not all o'er-read; and for
so much as I have perus'd, I find it not fit for your o'erlooking.
GLOUCESTER Give me the letter, sir.                               40
EDMUND I shall offend either to detain or give it: the
contents, as in part I understand them, are to blame.
GLOUCESTER Let's see, let's see.
EDMUND I hope, for my brother's justification, he
wrote this but as an essay or taste of my virtue.               45
GLOUCESTER (*Reads.*) "This policy and reverence of age
makes the world bitter to the best of our times; keeps
our fortunes from us till our oldness cannot relish them.
I begin to find an idle and fond bondage in the oppression of aged tyranny, who sways, not as it hath              50
power, but as it is suffer'd. Come to me, that of this I
may speak more. If our father would sleep till I wak'd
him, you should enjoy half his revenue for ever, and
live the belov'd of your brother.        Edgar."
Hum? conspiracy? "Sleep till I wake him, you            55
should enjoy half his revenue." My son Edgar! had
he a hand to write this? a heart and brain to breed it in?
—When came you to this? Who brought it?
EDMUND It was not brought me, my lord; there's the
cunning of it. I found it thrown in at the casement of        60
my closet.
GLOUCESTER You know the character to be your brother's?
EDMUND If the matter were good, my lord, I durst
swear it were his; but in respect of that, I would fain
think it were not.                                          65
GLOUCESTER It is his.
EDMUND It is his hand, my lord; but I hope his heart is
not in the contents.
GLOUCESTER Has he never before sounded you in this
business?                                                   70

---

**39. o'erlooking:** perusal.    **42. to blame:** blameworthy.    **45. essay or taste:** trial or
test.    **46. policy . . . of:** policy of revering. In Elizabethan English, *policy* regularly
connotes craftiness; here the implication is that deference to age has been imposed
upon society by old men.    **47. best . . . times:** best part of our lives (i.e. youth, when
fathers are still alive, to the inconvenience of their heirs).    **49. idle and fond:** useless
and foolish.    **50–51. who . . . suffer'd:** which rules not by reason of its own power
but because we put up with it.    [**54. your brother:** Adding a comma after the word
"brother" would normalize the close of the letter for many readers and writers.  In
her edition of *Lear* for Longman (2005), Claire McEachern adds such a comma. Both
Q1 and Q2 drop the period after "brother." ~ *Evans Editor*]    **61. closet:** private room.
**62. character:** handwriting.    **64. fain:** gladly.

EDMUND  Never, my lord. But I have heard him oft
maintain it to be fit that, sons at perfect age and fathers
declin'd, the father should be as ward to the son, and
the son manage his revenue.
GLOUCESTER  O villain, villain! his very opinion in the          75
letter. Abhorred villain! unnatural, detested, brutish
villain! worse than brutish! Go, sirrah, seek him; I'll
apprehend him. Abominable villain! Where is he?
EDMUND  I do not well know, my lord. If it shall
please you to suspend your indignation against my          80
brother till you can derive from him better testimony of
his intent, you should run a certain course; where, if
you violently proceed against him, mistaking his purpose, it would make a great gap in your own honor and
shake in pieces the heart of his obedience. I dare          85
pawn down my life for him that he hath writ this to feel
my affection to your honor, and to no other pretense
of danger.
GLOUCESTER  Think you so?
EDMUND  If your honor judge it meet, I will place you          90
where you shall hear us confer of this, and by an
auricular assurance have your satisfaction, and that
without any further delay than this very evening.
GLOUCESTER  He cannot be such a monster—
[EDMUND  Nor is not, sure.          95
GLOUCESTER  To his father, that so tenderly and entirely
loves him. Heaven and earth!] Edmund, seek him out;
wind me into him, I pray you. Frame the business after
your own wisdom. I would unstate myself to be in a
due resolution.          100
EDMUND  I will seek him, sir, presently; convey the
business as I shall find means, and acquaint you withal.
GLOUCESTER  These late eclipses in the sun and moon
portend no good to us. Though the wisdom of nature
can reason it thus and thus, yet nature finds itself          105
scourg'd by the sequent effects. Love cools, friendship

72. **perfect age:** full maturity. 76. **Abhorred:** abhorrent. **detested:** detestable.
77. **sirrah:** familiar form of address used by parents to children or by masters to
servants. 82. **certain:** safe. **where:** whereas. 86. **feel:** test, sound out. 87–88.
**pretense of danger:** dangerous intention. 98. **wind ... him:** worm your way into
his confidence (*me* is the so-called "ethical dative"). 99–100. **unstate ... resolution:**
give all I own to have my uncertainty resolved. 101. **presently:** at once. **convey:**
manage. 103. **late:** recent. 104. **wisdom of nature:** natural philosophy, i.e. science. 105. **reason ... and thus:** i.e. give explanations of the occurrence of eclipses.

falls off, brothers divide: in cities, mutinies; in countries,
discord; in palaces, treason; and the bond crack'd
'twixt son and father. This villain of mine comes under
the prediction; there's son against father: the                               110
King falls from bias of nature; there's father against
child. We have seen the best of our time. Machina-
tions, hollowness, treachery, and all ruinous disorders
follow us disquietly to our graves. Find out this villain,
Edmund, it shall lose thee nothing, do it carefully.                          115
And the noble and true-hearted Kent banish'd! his
offense, honesty! 'Tis strange.                                    *Exit.*

EDMUND This is the excellent foppery of the world,
that when we are sick in fortune—often the surfeits of
our own behavior—we make guilty of our dis-                                    120
asters the sun, the moon, and stars, as if we were
villains on necessity, fools by heavenly compulsion,
knaves, thieves, and treachers by spherical predominance; drunkards, liars, and adulterers by an enforc'd
obedience of planetary influence; and all that we                             125
are evil in, by a divine thrusting on. An admirable
evasion of whoremaster man, to lay his goatish disposition on the charge of a star! My father compounded
with my mother under the Dragon's tail, and my
nativity was under Ursa Major, so that it follows,                            130
I am rough and lecherous. [Fut,] I should have been
that I am, had the maidenl'est star in the firmament
twinkled on my bastardizing.    [Edgar—]

*Enter* EDGAR.

Pat! he comes like the catastrophe of the old comedy.
My cue is villainous melancholy, with a sigh like                             135
Tom o' Bedlam.—O, these eclipses do portend these
divisions! *fa, sol, la, mi.*                      [*Humming these notes.*]
EDGAR How now, brother Edmund, what serious
contemplation are you in?

---

**107. mutinies:** insurrection riots.  **111. falls . . . nature:** acts contrary to the natural tendencies of a father. In the game of bowls, *bias* = the curving course of
the bowl, which in Shakespeare's day was weighted on one side.  **118. foppery:**
foolishness.  **119. surfeits:** diseased effects.  **123. treachers:** traitors.  **spherical
predominance:** ascendancy of some one of the planets (each of which was thought
to be fixed in a revolving sphere).  **126. divine:** supernatural.  **127. goatish:**
lecherous.  **129, 130. Dragon, Ursa Major:** names of constellations. [See note on the
Pleiades, 1.5.35. ~ *Evans Editor*]  **131. Fut:** contemptuous exclamation (from "God's
foot").  **134. catastrophe:** the event that resolves the plot.  **136. Tom o' Bedlam:**
lunatic beggar, so called from Bethlehem Hospital, the London madhouse.

EDMUND I am thinking, brother, of a prediction I read 140
this other day, what should follow these eclipses.
EDGAR Do you busy yourself with that?
EDMUND I promise you, the effects he writes of succeed
unhappily, [as of unnaturalness between the child and
the parent, death, dearth, dissolutions of ancient 145
amities, divisions in state, menaces and maledictions
against king and nobles, needless diffidences, banishment of friends, dissipation of cohorts, nuptial breaches,
and I know not what.
EDGAR How long have you been a sectary astronomical? 150
EDMUND Come, come,] when saw you my father last?
EDGAR The night gone by.
EDMUND Spake you with him?
EDGAR Ay, two hours together. 155
EDMUND Parted you in good terms? Found you no
displeasure in him by word nor countenance?
EDGAR None at all.
EDMUND Bethink yourself wherein you may have
offended him; and at my entreaty forbear his 160
presence until some little time hath qualified the heat of
his displeasure, which at this instant so rageth in him,
that with the mischief of your person it would scarcely
allay.
EDGAR Some villain hath done me wrong. 165
EDMUND That's my fear. I pray you have a continent
forbearance till the speed of his rage goes slower; and
as I say, retire with me to my lodging, from whence
I will fitly bring you to hear my lord speak. Pray ye
go, there's my key. If you do stir abroad, go arm'd. 170
EDGAR Arm'd, brother?
EDMUND Brother, I advise you to the best; I am no
honest man if there be any good meaning toward you.
I have told you what I have seen and heard; but faintly,
nothing like the image and horror of it. Pray you 175
away.

---

**143. succeed:** follow.   **144. unnaturalness:** disaffection.   **145. dearth:** famine.
**147. needless diffidences:** groundless suspicions.   **148. dissipation of cohorts:**
dissolution of troops, i.e. large-scale desertion.   **150–51. sectary astronomical:**
devotee of astrology.   **157. countenance:** demeanor.   **161. qualified:** moderated.
**163. mischief:** injury.   **164. allay:** be abated.   **166–67. have . . . forbearance:**
keep discreetly out of his way (*continent* = self-restrained).   **169. fitly:** at the proper
moment.   **175. image and horror:** horrible actuality (*image* = true likeness).

EDGAR  Shall I hear from you anon?
EDMUND  I do serve you in this business.

*Exit [Edgar].*

A credulous father and a brother noble,
Whose nature is so far from doing harms                               180
That he suspects none; on whose foolish honesty
My practices ride easy. I see the business.
Let me, if not by birth, have lands by wit:
All with me's meet that I can fashion fit.                          *Exit.*

### SCENE 3

*Enter GONERIL and Steward [OSWALD].*

GONERIL  Did my father strike my gentleman for chiding of his Fool?
OSWALD  Ay, madam.
GONERIL  By day and night he wrongs me, every hour
He flashes into one gross crime or other
That sets us all at odds. I'll not endure it.                          5
His knights grow riotous, and himself upbraids us
On every trifle. When he returns from hunting,
I will not speak with him; say I am sick.
If you come slack of former services,
You shall do well; the fault of it I'll answer.                       10

*[Horns within.]*

OSWALD  He's coming, madam, I hear him.
GONERIL  Put on what weary negligence you please,
You and your fellows; I'd have it come to question.
If he distaste it, let him to my sister,
Whose mind and mine I know in that are one,                           15
[Not to be overrul'd. Idle old man,
That still would manage those authorities
That he hath given away! Now by my life
Old fools are babes again, and must be us'd
With checks as flatteries, when they are seen abus'd.]                20
Remember what I have said.
OSWALD                              Well, madam.
GONERIL  And let his knights have colder looks among you;
What grows of it, no matter. Advise your fellows so.
[I would breed from hence occasions, and I shall,
That I may speak.] I'll write straight to my sister                   25

---

**182. practices:** plots.  **184. fashion fit:** manipulate to serve my purpose.
**1.3. Location: The Duke of Albany's palace.  3. By . . . night.** Possibly an
oath.  **4. crime:** offense (milder than in modern usage).  **9. come slack:** fall
short.  **13. question:** discussion, issue.  **14. distaste:** be displeased by.  **16. Idle:**
foolish.  **20. as:** for, in place of.  **abus'd:** deluded.

To hold my [very] course. Prepare for dinner.

*Exeunt.*

SCENE 4

*Enter* KENT *[disguised as Caius].*

KENT If but as [well] I other accents borrow,
That can my speech defuse, my good intent
May carry through itself to that full issue
For which I raz'd my likeness. Now, banish'd Kent,
If thou canst serve where thou dost stand condemn'd,    5
So may it come, thy master, whom thou lov'st,
Shall find thee full of labors.

*Horns within. Enter* LEAR, [KNIGHTS,] *and*
ATTENDANTS *[from hunting].*

LEAR Let me not stay a jot for dinner, go get it
ready. [*Exit an Attendant.*] How now, what art thou?
KENT A man, sir.    10
LEAR What dost thou profess? What wouldst thou
with us?
KENT I do profess to be no less than I seem, to
serve him truly that will put me in trust, to love him
that is honest, to converse with him that is wise    15
and says little, to fear judgment, to fight when I cannot
choose, and to eat no fish.
LEAR What art thou?
KENT A very honest-hearted fellow, and as poor
as the King.    20
LEAR If thou be'st as poor for a subject as he's for a
king, [th'] art poor enough. What wouldst thou?
KENT Service.

---

**25. straight:** straightway.    **1.4. Location: Scene continues.** [o.s.d. Why Kent
assumes the name Caius invites speculation. Pertinent details may provide clarification: Plutarch (North translation, 1579), the main source for Shakespeare's
Roman plays, tells of Caius Gracchus, a man praised for his service, compassion, verbal boldness, and defending a citizen being unjustly banished. Caius's
mother, Cornelia—like Cordelia— lost her portion of family wealth (specifically
her dowry) and possessed fortitude and stoic nobility. ~ *Evans Editor*] **1. as well:**
i.e. as well as I have disguised my person.    **2. defuse:** disguise.    **4. raz'd my
likeness:** destroyed my identity. ['changed my appearance by shaving off (raz-
ing) my facial hair.' ~ *Evans Editor*]    **7. full of labors:** excellent in service.    **11.
What . . . profess:** what's your skill.    **13. profess:** avow myself, claim.    **14. put
. . . trust:** give me his confidence.    **15. honest:** honorable.    **converse:** associate.
**16. judgment:** i.e. God's judgment.    **16–17. cannot choose:** have no alternative.    **17.
eat no fish:** be a Protestant (?) or be a hearty fellow, a meat-eater (?).

LEAR  Who wouldst thou serve?

KENT  You.                                                    25

LEAR  Dost thou know me, fellow?

KENT  No, sir, but you have that in your countenance which I would fain call master.

LEAR  What's that?

KENT  Authority.                                             30

LEAR  What services canst do?

KENT  I can keep honest counsel, ride, run, mar a
curious tale in telling it, and deliver a plain message
bluntly. That which ordinary men are fit for, I am
qualified in, and the best of me is diligence.               35

LEAR  How old art thou?

KENT  Not so young, sir, to love a woman for singing,
nor so old to dote on her for any thing. I have
years on my back forty-eight.

LEAR  Follow me, thou shalt serve me. If I like thee         40
no worse after dinner, I will not part from thee yet.
Dinner, ho, dinner! Where's my knave? my Fool?
Go you and call my Fool hither.           [*Exit an Attendant.*]

*Enter Steward* [OSWALD].

You, you, sirrah, where's my daughter?

OSWALD  So please you—                          *Exit.* 45

LEAR  What says the fellow there? Call the clotpole
back. [*Exit a Knight.*] Where's my Fool? Ho!
I think the world's asleep.

[*Enter* KNIGHT.]

How now? where's that mungrel?

KNIGHT  He says, my lord, your [daughter] is not            50
well.

LEAR  Why came not the slave back to me when I
call'd him?

KNIGHT  Sir, he answer'd me in the roundest manner, he would not.                                          55

LEAR  He would not?

KNIGHT  My lord, I know not what the matter is,
but to my judgment your Highness is not entertain'd
with that ceremonious affection as you were wont.

---

**32. keep honest counsel:** respect confidences.   **33. curious:** elaborate, intri-
cate.   **45. So please you:** i.e. sorry, I'm busy.   **46. clotpole:** clotpoll, blockhead.   **49. mungrel:** mongrel.   **54. roundest:** bluntest.

There's a great abatement of kindness appears as    60
well in the general dependants as in the Duke himself
also, and your daughter.
LEAR  Ha? say'st thou so?
KNIGHT  I beseech you pardon me, my lord, if I be
mistaken, for my duty cannot be silent when I think    65
your Highness wrong'd.
LEAR  Thou but rememb'rest me of mine own conception. I have perceiv'd a most faint neglect of late,
which I have rather blam'd as mine own jealous
curiosity than as a very pretense and purpose of    70
unkindness. I will look further into't. But where's my
Fool? I have not seen him this two days.
KNIGHT  Since my young lady's going into France,
sir, the Fool hath much pin'd away.
LEAR  No more of that, I have noted it well. Go    75
you and tell my daughter I would speak with her.
[*Exit an Attendant.*] Go you call hither my Fool.
                              [*Exit another Attendant.*]

*Enter Steward* [OSWALD].

O, you, sir, you, come you hither, sir. Who am I, sir?
OSWALD  My lady's father.
LEAR  "My lady's father"? My lord's knave!    80
You whoreson dog, you slave, you cur!
OSWALD  I am none of these, my lord, I beseech your
pardon.
LEAR  Do you bandy looks with me, you rascal?
                                        [*Striking him.*]
OSWALD  I'll not be strucken, my lord.    85
KENT  Nor tripp'd neither, you base football player.
                                  [*Tripping up his heels.*]
LEAR  I thank thee, fellow. Thou serv'st me, and I'll love thee.
KENT  Come, sir, arise, away! I'll teach you
differences. Away, away! If you will measure your    90
lubber's length again, tarry; but away! Go to, have
you wisdom? So.              [*Pushes Oswald out.*]
LEAR  Now, my friendly knave, I thank thee,
there's earnest of thy service.      [*Giving Kent money.*]

---

67. **rememb'rest:** remindest.    68. **faint:** indolent.    70. **very pretense:** deliberate
intention.    86. **football player.** Football was a lower-class diversion in Shakespeare's day.    90. **differences:** distinctions of rank.    94. **earnest:** down payment.

*Enter* FOOL.

FOOL  Let me hire him too, here's my coxcomb.                    95
                                    [*Offering Kent his cap.*]
LEAR  How now, my pretty knave, how dost thou?
FOOL  Sirrah, you were best take my coxcomb.
[KENT]  Why, [Fool]?
FOOL  Why? for taking one's part that's out of
    favor. Nay, and thou canst not smile as the wind sits,    100
    thou'lt catch cold shortly. There, take my coxcomb.
    Why, this fellow has banish'd two on 's daughters, and
    did the third a blessing against his will; if thou follow
    him, thou must needs wear my coxcomb.—How now,
    nuncle? Would I had two coxcombs and two daughters!    105
LEAR  Why, my boy?
FOOL  If I gave them all my living, I'ld keep my
    coxcombs myself. There's mine, beg another of thy
    daughters.
LEAR  Take heed, sirrah—the whip.                             110
FOOL  Truth's a dog must to kennel, he must be
    whipt out, when the Lady Brach may stand by th' fire
    and stink.
LEAR  A pestilent gall to me!
FOOL  Sirrah, I'll teach thee a speech.                       115
LEAR  Do.
FOOL  Mark it, nuncle:
                Have more than thou showest,
                Speak less than thou knowest,
                Lend less than thou owest,                    120
                Ride more than thou goest,
                Learn more than thou trowest,
                Set less than thou throwest;
                Leave thy drink and thy whore,
                And keep in a' door,                          125

---

**100. and:** if. **smile . . . sits:** i.e. ingratiate yourself with the party in power.
**101. catch cold:** i.e. find yourself out in the cold.   **102–3. banish'd . . . blessing.**
This reverses the situation as Lear sees it—the more fool he, the Fool implies.
**102. on 's:** of his.   **105. nuncle:** mine uncle; familiar form of address from Fool
to master.   **107. living:** property.   **107–8. keep my coxcombs:** i.e. to show
that I was a double fool.   **112. Brach:** hound bitch (here apparently symbol-
izing flattering falsehood).   **114. gall:** source of irritation.   **120. owest:** ownest.
**121. goest:** walkest.   **122. Learn:** i.e. hear.  **trowest:** believest.   **123. Set . . .
throwest:** (presumably) stake less than your all on a throw of the dice.   **125. in
a' door:** indoors.

> And thou shalt have more
> Than two tens to a score.

KENT That is nothing, Fool.

FOOL Then 'tis like the breath of an unfee'd law-
yer, you gave me nothing for't. Can you make no                    130
use of nothing, nuncle?

LEAR Why, no, boy, nothing can be made out of
nothing.

FOOL [*To Kent.*] Prithee tell him, so much the rent
of his land comes to. He will not believe a fool.                   135

LEAR A bitter fool!

FOOL Dost know the difference, my boy, between
a bitter fool and a sweet one?

LEAR No, lad, teach me.

FOOL                [That lord that counsell'd thee                 140
                To give away thy land,
                Come place him here by me,
                Do thou for him stand.
                The sweet and bitter fool
                Will presently appear:                             145
                The one in motley here,
                The other found out there.

LEAR Dost thou call me fool, boy?

FOOL All thy other titles thou hast given away,
that thou wast born with.                                          150

KENT This is not altogether fool, my lord.

FOOL No, faith, lords and great men will not let me;
if I had a monopoly out, they would have part an't.
And ladies too, they will not let me have all the
fool to myself, they'll be snatching.] Nuncle, give me             155
an egg, and I'll give thee two crowns.

LEAR What two crowns shall they be?

FOOL Why, after I have cut the egg i' th' middle
and eat up the meat, the two crowns of the egg.

---

**126–27. thou . . . score:** i.e. you will grow richer.   **136. bitter:** vexatious.
**140. That lord:** i.e. Lear himself, as the Fool comes close to saying in line 143.
**147. there.** Pointing at Lear, the "bitter fool."   **152. No . . . me.** The Fool quibbles
on Kent's *altogether fool* in the sense "the sum total of folly."   **153. monopoly.**
Both Elizabeth and James granted monopolies in various commodities to favorite
courtiers. There was much complaint; Dover Wilson suggests that the satire here
may have caused the censor to excise this passage from the manuscript that was
the basis of the F1 text.   **an't:** on it, i.e. of it.   **154–55. ladies . . . snatching:**
Probably alluding to the Fool's traditional bauble, of phallic shape.   [**155–64:** See
Fig. 9 (cleft-egg scene) in "Introduction." ~ *Evans Editor*]

95

When thou clovest thy [crown] i' th' middle and                         160
gav'st away both parts, thou bor'st thine ass on thy
back o'er the dirt. Thou hadst little wit in thy bald
crown when thou gav'st thy golden one away. If I
speak like myself in this, let him be whipt that first
finds it so.                                                           165
[*Sings.*]    "Fools had ne'er less grace in a year,
                     For wise men are grown foppish,
               And know not how their wits to wear,
                     Their manners are so apish."
LEAR  When were you wont to be so full of songs, sirrah?              170
FOOL  I have us'd it, nuncle, e'er since thou mad'st
thy daughters thy mothers, for when thou gav'st them
the rod, and put'st down thine own breeches,
[*Sings.*]    "Then they for sudden joy did weep,                     175
                     And I for sorrow sung,
               That such a king should play bo-peep,
                     And go the [fools] among."
Prithee, nuncle, keep a schoolmaster that can teach thy
Fool to lie—I would fain learn to lie.                                180
LEAR  And you lie, sirrah, we'll have you whipt.
FOOL  I marvel what kin thou and thy daughters are.
They'll have me whipt for speaking true; thou'lt
have me whipt for lying; and sometimes I am
whipt for holding my peace. I had rather be any       185
kind o' thing than a Fool, and yet I would not be thee,
nuncle: thou hast par'd thy wit o' both sides, and left
nothing i' th' middle. Here comes one o' the parings.

*Enter* GONERIL.

LEAR  How now, daughter? what makes that frontlet on? You are too much of late i' th' frown.          190
FOOL  Thou wast a pretty fellow when thou hadst
no need to care for her frowning, now thou art an O
without a figure. I am better than thou art now, I am

---

**161–62. bor'st . . . dirt:** i.e. foolishly reversed the order of nature. The allusion
is to one of Aesop's fables.  **164. like myself:** i.e. like a fool.  **165. finds it so:**
learns from experience that it is true.  **166–69. Fools . . . apish.** The point is that
fools are no longer in demand since wise men now do their work.  **166. grace:**
favor.  **in a year:** in any year, i.e. ever.  **168. wear:** use.  **172. us'd it:** made it
my practice.  **175–78. Then . . . among.** These verses parody the "Ballad of John
Carelesse."  **177. bo-peep:** a children's game.  **181. And:** if.  **189–90. frontlet:**
band worn on the forehead; here, frown.  **192–93. an O . . . figure:** a zero without
another digit in front of it.

a Fool, thou art nothing. [*To Goneril.*] Yes, for-
sooth, I will hold my tongue; so your face bids me,                    195
thou you say nothing.
Mum, mum:
    He that keeps nor crust [nor] crumb,
    Weary of all, shall want some.
[*Pointing to Lear.*] That's a sheal'd peascod.                        200
GONERIL  Not only, sir, this your all-licens'd Fool,
But other of your insolent retinue
Do hourly carp and quarrel, breaking forth
In rank and not-to-be-endur'd riots. Sir,
I had thought, by making this well known unto you,                     205
To have found a safe redress, but now grow fearful,
By what yourself too late have spoke and done,
That you protect this course and put it on
By your allowance; which if you should, the fault
Would not scape censure, nor the redresses sleep,                      210
Which, in the tender of a wholesome weal,
Might in their working do you that offense,
Which else were shame, that then necessity
Will call discreet proceeding.
FOOL                        For you know, nuncle,
    "The hedge-sparrow fed the cuckoo so long,                         215
    That [it] had it head bit off by it young."
So out went the candle, and we were left darkling.
LEAR  Are you our daughter?
GONERIL  I would you would make use of your good wisdom
(Whereof I know you are fraught) and put away                          220
These dispositions which of late transport you
From what you rightly are.
FOOL  May not an ass know when the cart draws
the horse?
[*Sings.*]  "Whoop, Jug! I love thee."                                 225

---

**198–99. He . . . some:** i.e. he who gives everything away because he's tired of it
will later need some part of what he has lost.   **198. crumb:** the part of the loaf that
is not crust; "crust and crumb" = the whole loaf.   **200. sheal'd:** shelled, empty.
**peascod:** pea pod.   **201. all-licens'd:** privileged to do and say anything he likes.
**207. too late:** all too recently.   **208. put it on:** encourage it.   **209. allowance:**
permission.   **211. tender of:** care for.   **weal:** commonweal, state.   **213. else
were:** under other circumstances would be.   **215. cuckoo.** The cuckoo laid its
eggs in other birds' nests.   **216. it head it young:** its head . . . its nestling, i.e. the
cuckoo.   **217. darkling:** in the dark.   **220. fraught:** freighted, amply provided.
**221. dispositions:** capricious moods.

LEAR  Does any here know me? This is not Lear.
Does Lear walk thus? speak thus? Where are his eyes?
Either his notion weakens, his discernings
Are lethargied—Ha! waking? 'Tis not so.
Who is it that can tell me who I am?                          230
FOOL  Lear's shadow.
[LEAR  I would learn that, for by the marks of sovereignty,
Knowledge, and reason, I should be false persuaded
I had daughters.
FOOL  Which they will make an obedient father.]            235
LEAR  Your name, fair gentlewoman?
GONERIL  This admiration, sir, is much o' th' savor
Of other your new pranks. I do beseech you
To understand my purposes aright,
As you are old and reverend, should be wise.              240
Here do you keep a hundred knights and squires,
Men so disorder'd, so debosh'd and bold,
That this our court, infected with their manners,
Shows like a riotous inn. Epicurism and lust
Makes it more like a tavern or a brothel                     245
Than a grac'd palace. The shame itself doth speak
For instant remedy. Be then desir'd
By her, that else will take the thing she begs,
A little to disquantity your train,
And the remainders that shall still depend,                 250
To be such men as may besort your age,
Which know themselves and you.
LEAR                              Darkness and devils!
Saddle my horses; call my train together!
Degenerate bastard, I'll not trouble thee;
Yet have I left a daughter.
GONERIL                         You strike my people,     255
And your disorder'd rabble make servants of their betters.

---

**225. Whoop . . . thee:** Origin unknown; *Jug* is a nickname for *Joan*, and *jug* sometimes means "whore." **228. notion:** mental power. **discernings:** senses. **232–33.
by . . . reason:** i.e. everything—the outward signs that I am king, my memory, my
common sense—suggests (falsely) that I am the man who had daughters. **235.
Which:** whom. **237. admiration:** i.e. pretended wonderment. **242. disorder'd:**
disorderly. **debosh'd:** debauched. **244. Epicurism:** sensuality; perhaps specifically
"gluttony" in view of *tavern* in line 245. **246. grac'd:** honored. **249. disquantity:** reduce the size of. **250. still depend:** continue to be your dependents.
**251. besort:** befit.

*Enter* ALBANY.

LEAR  Woe, that too late repents!—[O, sir, are you come?]
Is it your will? Speak, sir.—Prepare my horses.—
Ingratitude! thou marble-hearted fiend,
More hideous when thou show'st thee in a child          260
Than the sea-monster.
ALBANY                    Pray, sir, be patient.
LEAR  [*To Goneril.*] Detested kite, thou liest.
My train are men of choice and rarest parts,
That all particulars of duty know,
And in the most exact regard support                    265
The worships of their name. O most small fault,
How ugly didst thou in Cordelia show!
Which, like an engine, wrench'd my frame of nature
From the fix'd place; drew from my heart all love,
And added to the gall. O Lear, Lear, Lear!              270
Beat at this gate, that let thy folly in
                                      [*Striking his head.*]
And thy dear judgment out! Go, go, my people.
                                  [*Exeunt Knights and Kent.*]
ALBANY  My lord, I am guiltless as I am ignorant
Of what hath moved you.
LEAR                      It may be so, my lord.
Hear, Nature, hear, dear goddess, hear!                 275
Suspend thy purpose, if thou didst intend
To make this creature fruitful.
Into her womb convey sterility,
Dry up in her the organs of increase,
And from her derogate body never spring                 280
A babe to honor her! If she must teem,
Create her child of spleen, that it may live
And be a thwart disnatur'd torment to her.
Let it stamp wrinkles in her brow of youth,
With cadent tears fret channels in her cheeks,          285

---

**257. Woe, that:** woe to him who.   **261. patient:** calm.   [**262. kite:** bird of prey,
buzzard, hawk.   ~ *Evans Editor*]   **263. parts:** qualities, accomplishments.   **266.
worships . . . name:** their honorable reputation.   **268. engine:** mechanical device.   **frame of nature:** natural frame, normal being.   **269. the fix'd place:** its firm
base.   **272. dear:** precious.   **274. moved:** angered.   **280. derogate:** debased.   **281.
teem:** breed.   **282. spleen:** malice, spitefulness.   **283. thwart:** perverse. **disnatur'd:**
unnatural, unfilial.   **285. cadent:** falling.

Turn all her mother's pains and benefits
To laughter and contempt, that she may feel
How sharper than a serpent's tooth it is
To have a thankless child!—Away, away!                    *Exit.*
ALBANY  Now, gods that we adore, whereof comes this?       290
GONERIL  Never afflict yourself to know more of it,
But let his disposition have that scope
As dotage gives it.

*Enter* LEAR.

LEAR  What, fifty of my followers at a clap
Within a fortnight?
ALBANY                    What's the matter, sir?            295
LEAR  I'll tell thee. [*To Goneril.*] Life and death! I am asham'd
That thou hast power to shake my manhood thus,
That these hot tears, which break from me perforce,
Should make thee worth them. Blasts and fogs upon thee!
Th' untented woundings of a father's curse                 300
Pierce every sense about thee! Old fond eyes,
Beweep this cause again, I'll pluck ye out,
And cast you, with the waters that you loose,
To temper clay. [Yea, is't come to this?]
Ha? let it be so: I have another daughter,                 305
Who I am sure is kind and comfortable.
When she shall hear this of thee, with her nails
She'll flea thy wolvish visage. Thou shalt find
That I'll resume the shape which thou dost think
I have cast off for ever.                             *Exit.*
GONERIL                    Do you mark that?                 310
ALBANY  I cannot be so partial, Goneril,
To the great love I bear you—
GONERIL  Pray you, content.—What, Oswald, ho!
[*To the Fool.*] You, sir, more knave than fool, after your master.
FOOL  Nuncle Lear, nuncle Lear, tarry, take the             315
Fool with thee.

---

**286. mother's:** maternal.   **pains and benefits:** beneficent care.   **287. laughter:** mockery.   **293. As:** which.   **299. Blasts:** blights. **fogs:** Supposed to breed infection.
**300. untented:** too deep to be probed, i.e. incurable.   **301. fond:** foolish.
**304. temper:** soften.   **306. comfortable:** ready to offer comfort.   **308. flea:**
flay.   **315–16. take . . . thee:** (1) take me with you; (2) take the name "fool" with
you, i.e. goodbye, fool (a stock phrase).

A fox, when one has caught her,
And such a daughter,
Should sure to the slaughter,
If my cap would buy a halter,                                        320
So the Fool follows after.                              *Exit.*
GONERIL  This man hath had good counsel—a hundred knights!
'Tis politic and safe to let him keep
At point a hundred knights; yes, that on every dream,
Each buzz, each fancy, each complaint, dislike,                      325
He may enguard his dotage with their pow'rs,
And hold our lives in mercy.—Oswald, I say!
ALBANY  Well, you may fear too far.
GONERIL                          Safer than trust too far.
Let me still take away the harms I fear,
Not fear still to be taken. I know his heart.                        330
What he hath utter'd I have writ my sister;
If she sustain him and his hundred knights,
When I have show'd th' unfitness—

                    *Enter Steward* [OSWALD].

                              How now, Oswald?
What, have you writ that letter to my sister?
OSWALD  Ay, madam.                                                   335
GONERIL  Take you some company, and away to horse.
Inform her full of my particular fear,
And thereto add such reasons of your own
As may compact it more. Get you gone,
And hasten your return. [*Exit Oswald.*] No, no, my lord,            340
This milky gentleness and course of yours
Though I condemn not, yet, under pardon,
[You] are much more [attax'd] for want of wisdom
Than prais'd for harmful mildness.
ALBANY  How far your eyes may pierce I cannot tell:                  345
Striving to better, oft we mar what's well.
GONERIL  Nay then—
ALBANY  Well, well, th' event.                        *Exeunt.*

---

**324. At point:** armed.   **325. buzz:** rumor.   **327. in mercy:** at his mercy.   **329.
still:** always.   **330. Not . . . taken:** not always be in fear of danger from those
harms.   **337. particular:** own.   **339. compact:** confirm.   **341. milky . . . course:**
mildly gentle course of action.   **342. under pardon:** if you will allow me to say
so.   **343. attax'd:** to be censured.   **344. harmful mildness:** mildness that may well
have harmful consequences.   **348. th' event:** we'll see what happens.   1.5. Location: **The court before Albany's palace.**

## SCENE 5

*Enter* LEAR, KENT [*disguised as Caius*], *and* FOOL.

LEAR  Go you before to Gloucester with these
letters.  Acquaint my daughter no further with any
thing you know than comes from her demand out of the
letter.  If your diligence be not speedy, I shall be there
afore you.                                                                    5
KENT  I will not sleep, my lord, till I have deliver'd
your letter.                                                       *Exit.*
FOOL  If a man's brains were in 's heels, were't not
in danger of kibes?
LEAR  Ay, boy.                                                         10
FOOL  Then I prithee be merry, thy wit shall not
go slip-shod.
LEAR  Ha, ha, ha!
FOOL  Shalt see thy other daughter will use thee
kindly, for though she's as like this as a crab's like an       15
apple, yet I can tell what I can tell.
LEAR  What canst tell, boy?
FOOL  She will taste as like this as a crab does to a
crab.  Thou canst tell why one's nose stands i' th'
middle on 's face?                                                  20
LEAR  No.
FOOL  Why, to keep one's eyes of either side 's nose,
that what a man cannot smell out, he may spy into.
LEAR  I did her wrong.
FOOL  Canst tell how an oyster makes his shell?           25
LEAR  No.
FOOL  Nor I neither; but I can tell why a snail has
a house.
LEAR  Why?

---

**1. Gloucester.** The city, not the Earl. Some editors prefer to read *Cornwall.*
[See, for example, Duthie and Wilson, who emend Gloucester to Cornwall. ~ *Evans
Editor*]  **1–2. these letters:** this letter (Latin *litterae*).  **3. demand out of:** question arising from.  [**9. kibes:** chilblains. A kibe is an ulcerated chilblain (i.e., an
inflammatory swelling produced by exposure to cold affecting hands and feet)
that develops especially on the heel. ~ *Evans Editor*]  **11–12. thy . . . slip-shod:**
your wits won't get chilblains, because they aren't in your heels, i.e. there is
no sense in your proposed journey. *Go slip-shod* = wear slippers (because of
chilblains).  **15. kindly:** according to her nature (i.e. just the same as Goneril,
but the sense "with natural affection" is ironically present).  **crab:** crab apple.
**20. on 's:** of his.  **22. of:** on.

FOOL  Why, to put 's head in, not to give it away to  30
his daughters, and leave his horns without a case.
LEAR  I will forget my nature. So kind a father! Be
my horses ready?
FOOL  Thy asses are gone about 'em. The reason
why the seven stars are no moe than seven is a pretty  35
reason.
LEAR  Because they are not eight.
FOOL  Yes indeed, thou wouldst make a good Fool.
LEAR  To take't again perforce! Monster ingratitude!  40
FOOL  If thou wert my Fool, nuncle, I'ld have thee
beaten for being old before thy time.
LEAR  How's that?
FOOL  Thou shouldst not have been old till thou
hadst been wise.  45
LEAR  O, let me not be mad, not mad, sweet heaven!
Keep me in temper, I would not be mad!

[*Enter* GENTLEMAN.]

How now, are the horses ready?
GENTLEMAN  Ready, my lord.
LEAR  Come, boy.                          [*Exeunt Lear and Gentleman.*]  50
FOOL  She that's a maid now, and laughs at my departure,
Shall not be a maid long, unless things be cut shorter.

*Exit.*

---

**35. seven stars:** Pleiades. [Daughters and sisters are on the Fool's mind. Seven stars suggest the the constellation of Ursa Major and the myth of a king's young daughter (Callisto) as well as the Pleiades and the myth of the seven sisters. See note and reference to Ursa Major in 1.2.130. ~ *Evans Editor*]  **moe:** more.  **39. again:** back.  **47. temper:** mental balance.  **51–52. She . . . shorter:** a girl who would laugh at the Fool's departure is so simple or trusting as not to see its serious implications. She's the type who couldn't long preserve her virginity. [At the very close of 1.4, then, painful difficulties in Lear's life do not thwart the Fool's impish bawdiness. ~ *Evans Editor*]

# Act 2

*Enter Bastard* [EDMUND] *and* CURAN *severally.*

EDMUND  'Save thee, Curan.

CURAN  And [you,] sir. I have been with your father,
and given him notice that the Duke of Cornwall and
Regan his duchess will be here with him this night.

EDMUND  How comes that?                                    5

CURAN  Nay, I know not. You have heard of the news
abroad, I mean the whisper'd ones, for they are yet but
ear-[bussing] arguments?

EDMUND  Not I. Pray you, what are they?

CURAN  Have you heard of no likely wars toward,          10
'twixt the Dukes of Cornwall and Albany?

EDMUND  Not a word.

CURAN  You may do then in time. Fare you well, sir.

                                                        *Exit.*

EDMUND  The Duke be here to-night? The better! best!
This weaves itself perforce into my business.            15
My father hath set guard to take my brother,
And I have one thing, of a queasy question,
Which I must act. Briefness and fortune, work!
Brother, a word! Descend. Brother, I say!

                    *Enter* EDGAR.

My father watches: O sir, fly this place,                20
Intelligence is given where you are hid;
You have now the good advantage of the night.
Have you not spoken 'gainst the Duke of Cornwall?
He's coming hither, now i' th' night, i' th' haste,
And Regan with him. Have you nothing said              25

2.1. Location: **Gloucester's castle.** **1.** **'Save:** God save. **8. ear-bussing:**
ear-kissing, whispered (with pun on *bussing/buzzing*). **arguments:** topics of
conversation. **10. toward:** imminent. **17. of . . . question:** needing delicate
handling. **18. Briefness . . . work:** may expedition and good luck be with me.

Upon his party 'gainst the Duke of Albany?
Advise yourself.
EDGAR            I am sure on't, not a word.
EDMUND  I hear my father coming. Pardon me:
In cunning I must draw my sword upon you.
Draw, seem to defend yourself; now quit you well.—       30
Yield! Come before my father. Light ho, here!—
Fly, brother.—Torches, torches!—So farewell.
                                      *Exit Edgar.*
Some blood drawn on me would beget opinion.
                                  *[Wounds his arm.]*
Of my more fierce endeavor. I have seen drunkards
Do more than this in sport.—Father, father!       35
Stop, stop! No help?

      *Enter* GLOUCESTER, *and* SERVANTS *with torches.*

GLOUCESTER  Now, Edmund, where's the villain?
EDMUND  Here stood he in the dark, his sharp sword out,
Mumbling of wicked charms, conjuring the moon
To stand ['s] auspicious mistress.                 40
GLOUCESTER            But where is he?
EDMUND  Look, sir, I bleed.
GLOUCESTER            Where is the villain, Edmund?
EDMUND  Fled this way, sir, when by no means he could—
GLOUCESTER  Pursue him, ho! Go after.     *[Exeunt some Servants.]*
                            By no means what?
EDMUND  Persuade me to the murther of your lordship,
But that I told him, the [revengive] gods       45
'Gainst parricides did all the thunder bend,
Spoke, with how manifold and strong a bond
The child was bound to th' father; sir, in fine,
Seeing how loathly opposite I stood
To his unnatural purpose, in fell motion       50
With his prepared sword he charges home
My unprovided body, latch'd mine arm;
And when he saw my best alarum'd spirits,

26. Upon . . . 'gainst: having to do with his enmity toward.   27. Advise yourself:
consider carefully.   30. quit you: acquit yourself.   33–34. beget . . . endeavor:
create an impression that I had fought fiercely.   40. stand . . . mistress: shed fa-
vorable influence upon him ('s = his).   45. that: when.  revengive: revenging.
48. in fine: finally.   49. loathly opposite: abhorringly opposed.   50. in fell motion: with a deadly thrust.   52. unprovided: unarmed.  latch'd: caught. Many
editors follow Q1 in reading *lanch'd* = lanced, pierced.   53. alarum'd: called to
arms, aroused to action.

Bold in the quarrel's right, rous'd to th' encounter,
Or whether gasted by the noise I made,                    55
Full suddenly he fled.
GLOUCESTER                    Let him fly far.
Not in this land shall he remain uncaught;
And found—dispatch. The noble Duke my master,
My worthy arch and patron, comes to-night.
By his authority I will proclaim it,                    60
That he which finds him shall deserve our thanks,
Bringing the murderous coward to the stake;
He that conceals him, death.
EDMUND  When I dissuaded him from his intent,
And found him pight to do it, with curst speech          65
I threaten'd to discover him; he replied,
"Thou unpossessing bastard, dost thou think,
If I would stand against thee, would the reposal
Of any trust, virtue, or worth in thee
Make thy words faith'd? No. What [I should] deny         70
(As this I would, [ay,] though thou didst produce
My very character), I'ld turn it all
To thy suggestion, plot, and damned practice;
And thou must make a dullard of the world
If they not thought the profits of my death             75
Were very pregnant and potential spirits
To make thee seek it."
GLOUCESTER                    O strange and fast'ned villain!
Would he deny his letter, said he? [I never got him.]
                                        *Tucket within.*
Hark, the Duke's trumpets! I know not [why] he comes.
All ports I'll bar, the villain shall not scape;         80
The Duke must grant me that. Besides, his picture
I will send far and near, that all the kingdom
May have due note of him, and of my land,
Loyal and natural boy, I'll work the means
To make thee capable.                    85

54. **quarrel's right:** justice of the cause. **55. gasted:** scared. **59. arch:** chief.
65. **pight:** pitched, determined. **curst:** angry. **66. discover:** reveal. [**68. reposal:** reposure (Q1), placing; cf. repository. ~ *Evans Editor*]  **70. faith'd:** believed.
72. **My very character:** i.e. incriminating evidence in my own handwriting.
73. **suggestion:** instigation.  **practice:** plot.  **74. make . . . world:** think people
very stupid.  **76. pregnant and potential:** ready and powerful. **spirits:** i.e. tempt-
ers (like devils). Many editors adopt the Q1 reading *spurs*.  **77. fast'ned:** confirmed.
78. **got:** begot. s.d. **Tucket:** flourish on a trumpet.  **85. capable:** legally able to
inherit.

*Enter* CORNWALL, REGAN, *and* ATTENDANTS.

CORNWALL  How now, my noble friend? since I came hither
(Which I can call but now) I have heard [strange news].
REGAN  If it be true, all vengeance comes too short
Which can pursue th' offender. How dost, my lord?
GLOUCSTER  O madam, my old heart is crack'd, it's crack'd!  90
REGAN  What, did my father's godson seek your life?
He whom my father nam'd, your Edgar?
GLOUCESTER  O lady, lady, shame would have it hid!
REGAN  Was he not companion with the riotous knights
That tended upon my father?  95
GLOUCESTER  I know not, madam. 'Tis too bad, too bad.
EDMUND  Yes, madam, he was of that consort.
REGAN  No marvel then, though he were ill affected:
'Tis they have put him on the old man's death,
To have th' expense and waste of his revenues.  100
I have this present evening from my sister
Been well inform'd of them, and with such cautions,
That if they come to sojourn at my house,
I'll not be there.
CORNWALL             Nor I, assure thee, Regan.
Edmund, I hear that you have shown your father  105
A child-like office.
EDMUND             It was my duty, sir.
GLOUCESTER  He did bewray his practice, and receiv'd
This hurt you see, striving to apprehend him.
CORNWALL  Is he pursued?
GLOUCESTER.             Ay, my good lord.
CORNWALL  If he be taken, he shall never more  110
Be fear'd of doing harm. Make your own purpose,
How in my strength you please. For you, Edmund,
Whose virtue and obedience doth this instant
So much commend itself, you shall be ours.
Natures of such deep trust we shall much need;  115
You we first seize on.
EDMUND             I shall serve you, sir,
Truly, however else.

---

**97. consort:** band, company.  **98. aspir'd . . . affected:** that he became ill-disposed.
**99. put him on:** incited him to plan.  **100. expense . . . of:** power to spend
wastefully.  **106. child-like:** filial.  **107. bewray his practice:** reveal his (Edgar's)
plot.  **111. of doing:** lest he do.  **112. strength:** authority, power.  **115. trust:**
trustworthiness.  **117. however else:** i.e. whether ably or not.

GLOUCESTER               For him I thank your Grace.
CORNWALL  You know not why we came to visit you?
REGAN  Thus out of season, threading dark-ey'd night:
     Occasions, noble Gloucester, of some poise,                    120
     Wherein we must have use of your advice.
     Our father he hath writ, so hath our sister,
     Of differences, which I best [thought] it fit
     To answer from our home; the several messengers
     From hence attend dispatch. Our good old friend,               125
     Lay comforts to your bosom, and bestow
     Your needful counsel to our businesses,
     Which craves the instant use.
GLOUCESTER                    I serve you, madam.
     Your Graces are right welcome.            *Flourish, Exeunt.*


SCENE 2

*Enter* KENT *[disguised as Caius] and
Steward* [OSWALD] *severally.*

OSWALD  Good dawning to thee, friend. Art of this
     house?
KENT  Ay.
OSWALD  Where may we set out horses?
KENT  I' th' mire.                                                    5
OSWALD  Prithee, if thou lov'st me, tell me.
KENT  I love thee not.
OSWALD  Why then I care not for thee.
KENT  If I had thee in Lipsbury pinfold, I would
     make thee care for me.                                         10
OSWALD  Why dost thou use me thus? I know thee
     not.
KENT  Fellow, I know thee.
OSWALD  What dost thou know me for?
KENT  A knave, a rascal, an eater of broken meats;                 15
     a base, proud, shallow, beggarly, three-suited, hundred-

---

120. **poise:** importance, [weight. ~ *Evans Editor*]   124. **from:** away from.   125. **attend dispatch:** are waiting to be sent back.   127. **needful:** needed   128. **craves . . .
use:** require immediate attention.   2.2. Location: **Before Gloucester's castle.**   6. **if
. . . me:** a conventional phrase equivalent to "of your good will"; but Kent quibbles
on the literal sense.   9. **In . . . pinfold:** A pinfold is a pound (i.e., a pen) for stray animals; Lipsbury is an invented place-name (Lipville) presumably meaning "mouth";
i.e. if I had you between my teeth.   15. **broken meats:** kitchen scraps.   16. **three-
suited:** having three suits (a servant's annual allowance).

pound, filthy worsted-stocking knave; a lily-liver'd,
action-taking, whoreson, glass-gazing, superserviceable, finical rogue; one-trunk-inheriting slave; one that
wouldst be a bawd in way of good service, and art                    20
nothing but the composition of a knave, beggar,
coward, pandar, and the son and heir of a mungril
bitch; one whom I will beat into [clamorous] whining,
if thou deni'st the least syllable of thy addition.
OSWALD Why, what a monstrous fellow art thou, thus                   25
to rail on one that is neither known of thee nor knows thee?
KENT What a brazen-fac'd varlet art thou, to deny
thou knowest me? Is it two days since I tripp'd up thy
heels, and beat thee before the King? Draw, you                      30
rogue, for though it be night, yet the moon shines;
[drawing his sword] I'll make a sop o' th' moonshine of
you, you whoreson cullionly barber-monger, draw!
OSWALD Away, I have nothing to do with thee.
KENT Draw, you rascal! You come with letters                         35
against the King, and take Vanity the puppet's part
against the royalty of her father. Draw, you rogue, or
I'll so carbonado your shanks! Draw, you rascal!
Come your ways.
OSWALD Help ho! murther, help!                                       40
KENT Strike, you slave! Stand, rogue, stand, you
neat slave! Strike!                                        [Beating him.]
OSWALD Help ho! murther, murther!

*Enter Bastard* [EDMUND, *with his rapier drawn*].

EDMUND How now, what's the matter? Part!
KENT With you, goodman boy, [and] you please!                        45
Come, I'll flesh ye, come on, young master.

**16–17. hundred-pound:** Perhaps a sneer at the small amount of wealth underlying
Oswald's pretensions.   **17. worsted-stocking:** wearing woollen stockings (gentlemen
wore silk).   **lily-liver'd:** white-livered, i.e. cowardly.   **18. action-taking:** preferring
litigation to fighting.   **glass-gazing:** mirror-gazing, i.e. vain or effeminate.   **18–19.
superserviceable:** officious.   **19. finical:** foppish.   **one-trunk-inheriting:** own-
ing no more than will fit into a single trunk (*inherit* = possess).   **19–20. one . . .
service:** one willing to regard pandering as part of his duties.   **21. composition:**
combination.   **24. thy addition:** the titles I have given you.   **32–33. make . . . you:**
pierce your body so that it can soak up moonlight as a sop (a piece of toast floating
in a drink) soaks up liquor.   **33. cullionly:** rascally.   **barber-monger:** frequenter
of barber-shops, fop.   **36. Vanity the puppet:** i.e. Goneril, abstract Vanity (like a
character in a morality puppet-show) opposed to abstract Royalty in Kent's figure.
**38. carbonado:** slash.   **39. Come your ways:** come on.   **42. neat:** foppish.
**44. matter:** cause of the quarrel (so also *difference* in line 51).   **45. goodman boy:** a
form of address intended to deflate a presumptuous youth.   **and:** if.

[*Enter*] CORNWALL, REGAN, GLOUCESTER, SERVANTS.

GLOUCESTER  Weapons? arms? What's the matter here?
CORNWALL  Keep peace, upon your lives!
He dies that strikes again. What is the matter?
REGAN  The messengers from our sister and the King.                50
CORNWALL  What is your difference? speak.
OSWALD  I am scarce in breath, my lord.
KENT  No marvel, you have so bestirr'd your valor.
You cowardly rascal, Nature disclaims in thee: a
tailor made thee.                                               55
CORNWALL  Thou art a strange fellow. A tailor make a
man?
KENT  A tailor, sir; a stone-cutter or a painter
could not have made him so ill, though they had been
but two years o' th' trade.                                     60
CORNWALL  Speak yet, how grew your quarrel?
OSWALD  This ancient ruffian, sir, whose life I have
spar'd at suit of his grey beard—
KENT  Thou whoreson zed, thou unnecessary letter!
My lord, if you['ll] give me leave, I will tread          65
this unbolted villain into mortar, and daub the wall of a
jakes with him. Spare my grey beard, you wagtail?
CORNWALL  Peace, sirrah!
You beastly knave, know you no reverence?
KENT  Yes, sir, but anger hath a privilege.                     70
CORNWALL  Why art thou angry?
KENT  That such a slave as this should wear a sword,
Who wears no honesty. Such smiling rogues as these,
Like rats, oft bite the holy cords a-twain
Which are t' intrinse t' unloose; smooth every passion        75
That in the natures of their lords rebel,
Being oil to fire, snow to the colder moods;
[Renege,] affirm, and turn their halcyon beaks

---

**46. flesh:** initiate into fighting.  **54. disclaims in thee:** denies that she had any hand in creating you.  **64. zed:** the letter *z*, unnecessary because its sound could usually be represented by *s*.  **66. unbolted:** unsifted, i.e. coarse.  **67. jakes:** privy.  **wagtail.** The image is of a bird waggling or fluttering its tail feathers.  **69. beastly:** beastlike (because he shows no proper respect for rank).  **73. honesty:** honorable character.  **74. holy cords:** i.e. bonds of natural affection.  **75. t' intrinse:** too intricately knotted.  **smooth:** humor, flatter.  **78. Renege:** deny.  **halcyon:** kingfisher; its body, when hung up, supposedly behaved like a weathervane.

With every [gale] and vary of their masters,
Knowing nought (like dogs) but following.                          80
A plague upon your epileptic visage!
Smile you my speeches, as I were a fool?
Goose, [and] I had you upon Sarum plain,
I'ld drive ye cackling home to Camelot.
CORNWALL  What, art thou mad, old fellow?                          85
GLOUCESTER  How fell you out? say that.
KENT  No contraries hold more antipathy
Than I and such a knave.
CORNWALL  Why dost thou call him knave? What is his fault?
KENT  His countenance likes me not.                                90
CORNWALL  No more, perchance, does mine, nor his, nor hers.
KENT  Sir, 'tis my occupation to be plain:
I have seen better faces in my time
Than stands on any shoulder that I see
Before me at this instant.
CORNWALL                    This is some fellow                    95
Who, having been prais'd for bluntness, doth affect
A saucy roughness, and constrains the garb
Quite from his nature. He cannot flatter, he,
An honest mind and plain, he must speak truth!
And they will take['t], so; if not, he's plain.                   100
These kind of knaves I know, which in this plainness
Harbor more craft and more corrupter ends
Than twenty silly-ducking observants
That stretch their duties nicely.
KENT  Sir, in good faith, in sincere verity,                      105
Under th' allowance of your great aspect,
Whose influence, like the wreath of radiant fire
On [flick'ring] Phoebus' front—
CORNWALL                    What mean'st by this?
KENT  To go out of my dialect, which you discom-

---

**79. gale and vary:** changing wind.  **81. epileptic:** grimacing.  **82. Smile:** smile
at. **as:** as if.  **83. Sarum:** Salisbury.  **84. Camelot:** the site of King Arthur's court,
variously identified; perhaps Winchester is intended here.  **90. likes:** pleases.
**97. constrains the garb:** assumes the plain manner.  **98. from . . . nature:** contrary to his own nature, i.e. hypocritically (?) or (if *his* = its) apart from the real
nature of plainness (which is courageous speaking of the truth).  **100. And:** if.
**so:** well and good.  **103. observants:** obsequious attendants.  **104. nicely:** with
excessive concern for every detail.  **105. faith:** truth.  **106. aspect:** (1) countenance; (2) astrological position of a planet.  **107. influence.** Another astrological
term; Cornwall is being likened to a heavenly body.  **108. Phoebus' front:** the
sun-god's forehead.  **109. dialect:** manner of speech.

mend so much. I know, sir, I am no flatterer. 110
He that beguil'd you in a plain accent was a plain
knave, which for my part I will not be, though I should
win your displeasure to entreat me to't.

CORNWALL What was th' offense you gave him?

OSWALD I never gave him any. 115
It pleas'd the King his master very late
To strike at me upon his misconstruction,
When he, compact, and flattering his displeasure,
Tripp'd me behind; being down, insulted, rail'd,
And put upon him such a deal of man 120
That worthied him, got praises of the King
For him attempting who was self-subdued,
And in the fleshment of this [dread] exploit,
Drew on me here again.

KENT                                     None of these rogues and cowards
But Ajax is their fool.

CORNWALL                        Fetch forth the stocks! 125
Your stubborn ancient knave, you reverent braggart,
We'll teach you.

KENT                        Sir, I am too old to learn.
Call not your stocks for me, I serve the King,
On whose employment I was sent to you.
You shall do small respects, show too bold malice 130
Against the grace and person of my master,
Stocking his messenger.

CORNWALL Fetch forth the stocks! As I have life and honor,
There shall he sit till noon.

REGAN                        Till noon? Till night, my lord, and all night too. 135

KENT Why, madam, if I were your father's dog,
You should not use me so.

REGAN                        Sir, being his knave, I will.

CORNWALL This is a fellow of the self-same color

---

**111. He . . . accent:** the plain-speaking man who misled you into your estimate of plain-speakers. **113. your displeasure.** Ironically analogous with such expressions as "your Grace" (?). Or perhaps, as Sisson suggests, *to entreat me to't* means "if you requested me to be a plain knave, i.e. to flatter you." **116. very late:** recently. **118. compact:** leagued (with the King), i.e. taking the King's side. **120. put . . . man:** struck such heroic attitudes. **121. That worthied him:** as caused him to be esteemed worthy. **122. For . . . self-subdued:** for his courage in taking on a man who offered no resistance. **123. fleshment of:** wild excitement engendered by. **124–25. None . . . fool:** villains of this kind are always willing to boast that they are braver than Ajax. **126. reverent:** reverend, i.e. aged. **130. malice:** ill will. **131. grace and person:** honor as king and personal honor.

Our sister speaks of. Come, bring away the stocks!
                                                    *Stocks brought out.*
GLOUCESTER  Let me beseech your Grace not to do so.                    140
[His fault is much, and the good King his master
Will check him for't. Your purpos'd low correction
Is such as basest and [contemned'st] wretches
For pilf'rings and most common trespasses
Are punish'd with.] The King must take it ill                         145
That he, so slightly valued in his messenger,
Should have him thus restrained.
CORNWALL                          I'll answer that.
REGAN  My sister may receive it much more worse
To have her gentleman abus'd, assaulted,
[For following her affairs. Put in his legs.]                         150
                          [*Kent is put in the stocks.*]
Come, my [good] lord, away.
                  *Exit [with all but Gloucester and Kent].*
GLOUCESTER  I am sorry for thee, friend, 'tis the Duke['s] pleasure,
Whose disposition, all the world well knows,
Will not be rubb'd nor stopp'd. I'll entreat for thee.
KENT  Pray do not, sir. I have watch'd and travell'd hard:            155
Some time I shall sleep out, the rest I'll whistle.
A good man's fortune may grow out at heels.
Give you good morrow!
GLOUCESTER  The Duke's to blame in this, 'twill be ill taken.   *Exit.*
KENT  Good King, that must approve the common saw,                    160
Thou out of heaven's benediction com'st
To the warm sun!
Approach, thou beacon to this under globe,
That by thy comfortable beams I may
Peruse this letter. Nothing almost sees miracles                      165
But misery. I know 'tis from Cordelia,
Who hath most fortunately been inform'd
Of my obscured course; [*reads*] "—and shall find time
From this enormous state—seeking to give

**139. away:** along.  **142. check:** rebuke.  **147. answer:** answer for.  **154. be
rubb'd:** tolerate any obstacle (a term from the game of bowls).  **155. watch'd:**
gone without sleep.  **157. A good . . . heels:** i.e. one must not repine at misfortune, since it befalls even good men.  **160. approve . . . saw:** prove the proverb
true.  **161–62. out . . . sun:** i.e. go from better to worse.  **163. beacon . . .
globe:** i.e. the moon.  **164. comfortable:** aiding.  **165–66. Nothing . . . misery:**
there's hardly anything like misery for putting one in the way of miracles (since
then any change for the better seems miraculous [?]).  **168. obscured:** disguised.
**169. enormous:** abnormal, monstrous.  **state:** state of affairs.

Losses their remedies."—All weary and o'erwatch'd,                    170
Take vantage, heavy eyes, not to behold
This shameful lodging.
Fortune, good night; smile once more, turn thy wheel.

                                                            [*Sleeps.*]


                        SCENE 3

                      *Enter* EDGAR.

EDGAR  I heard myself proclaim'd,
And by the happy hollow of a tree
Escap'd the hunt. No port is free, no place
That guard and most unusual vigilance
Does not attend my taking. Whiles I may scape          5
I will preserve myself, and am bethought
To take the basest and most poorest shape
That ever penury, in contempt of man,
Brought near to beast. My face I'll grime with filth,
Blanket my loins, elf all my hairs in knots,           10
And with presented nakedness outface
The winds and persecutions of the sky.
The country gives me proof and president
Of Bedlam beggars, who, with roaring voices,
Strike in their numb'd and mortified arms              15
Pins, wooden pricks, nails, sprigs of rosemary;
And with this horrible object, from low farms,
Poor pelting villages, sheep-cotes, and mills,
Sometimes with lunatic bans, sometime with prayers,
Enforce their charity. Poor Turlygod! poor Tom!        20
That's something yet: Edgar I nothing am.              *Exit.*

**170. o'erwatch'd:** exhausted from lack of sleep.  **171. Take vantage:** take advantage (of sleep).  **172. shameful lodging:** i.e. the stocks.  **2.3.** Location: **Scene continues. (The sleeping Kent remains on stage.)  2. happy:** opportune. **4. That:** in which.  **5. attend my taking:** wait to take me prisoner.  **6. am bethought:** have in mind, intend.  **10. elf:** tangle, as in elf-locks.  **11. presented:** exposed.  **13. proof:** example. **president:** precedent.  **14. Bedlam beggars.** See note on 1.2.136.  **15. mortified:** deadened to feeling.  **17. object:** sight. **18. pelting:** paltry.  **19. bans:** curses.  **20. Turlygod.** Unexplained. ["Turlygod" (sometimes "Tuelygod") is "seemingly a name given to bedlam beggars" (Schmidt); it may simply be another name for a beggar. ~ *Evans Editor*]  **poor Tom.** Catch phrase of the Bedlam beggars, who became known as "poor Toms."  **21. That's . . . am:** there's that much left for me; as Edgar I am nothing at all.

# SCENE 4

*Enter* LEAR, FOOL, *and* GENTLEMAN.
[KENT, *disguised as Caius, in the stocks.*]

LEAR 'Tis strange that they should so depart from home,
And not send back my [messenger].
GENTLEMAN                    As I learn'd,
The night before there was no purpose in them
Of this remove.
KENT                    Hail to thee, noble master!
LEAR  Ha?                                                    5
Mak'st thou this shame thy pastime?
KENT                    No, my lord.
FOOL  Hah, ha, he wears cruel garters.  Horses
are tied by the heads, dogs and bears by th' neck,
monkeys by th' loins, and men by th' legs. When a
man['s] overlusty at legs, then he wears wooden        10
nether-stocks.
LEAR  What's he that hath so much thy place mistook
To set thee here?
KENT                    It is both he and she,
Your son and daughter.
LEAR  No.                                                   15
KENT  Yes.
LEAR  No, I say.
KENT  I say yea.
[LEAR  No, no, they would not.
KENT  Yes, they have.]                                       20
LEAR  By Jupiter, I swear no.
KENT  By Juno, I swear ay.
LEAR                    They durst not do't;
They could not, would not do't. 'Tis worse than murther
To do upon respect such violent outrage.
Resolve me with all modest haste which way        25
Thou mightst deserve, or they impose, this usage,
Coming from us.
KENT                    My lord, when at their home

---

2.4. Location: **Scene continues.**  **6. Mak'st . . . pastime:** are you undergoing
this humiliation for a joke.  **7. cruel garters:** i.e. the stocks (with pun on *crewel*,
"worsted").  **10. 's . . . legs:** i.e. has run away from service.  **11. nether-stocks:**
stockings.  **12. place:** position (as the King's messenger).  **24. upon respect:**
against the respect due to the King in his messenger (?), or against the whole principle of subordination (?).  **25. Resolve:** inform.  **modest:** moderate, reasonable.

I did commend your Highness' letters to them,
Ere I was risen from the place that showed
My duty kneeling, came there a reeking post,                              30
Stew'd in his haste, half breathless, [panting] forth
From Goneril his mistress salutations;
Deliver'd letters, spite of intermission,
Which presently they read; on those contents
They summon'd up their meiny, straight took horse,                       35
Commanded me to follow, and attend
The leisure of their answer, gave me cold looks:
And meeting here the other messenger,
Whose welcome I perceiv'd had poison'd mine—
Being the very fellow which of late                                      40
Display'd so saucily against your Highness—
Having more man than wit about me, drew.
He rais'd the house with loud and coward cries.
Your son and daughter found this trespass worth
The shame which here it suffers.                                         45
FOOL   Winter's not gone yet, if the wild geese fly
   that way.
      Fathers that wear rags
         Do make their children blind,
      But fathers that bear bags                                         50
         Shall see their children kind.
      Fortune, that arrant whore,
      Ne'er turns the key to th' poor.
   But for all this, thou shalt have as many dolors for
   thy daughters as thou canst tell in a year.                          55
LEAR   O how this mother swells up toward my heart!
   [Hysterica] passio, down, thou climbing sorrow,
   Thy element's below.—Where is this daughter?
KENT   With the Earl, sir, here within.

28. commend: deliver.   30. reeking: steaming.   33. spite of intermission: careless of interrupting me.   34. on: in consequence of.   35. meiny: household servants.   41. Display'd so saucily: showed himself so insolent.   46–47. Winter's . . .
way: i.e. this behavior is a sure sign that your troubles aren't over.   49. blind:
i.e. blind to their fathers' needs and comforts.   50. bags: i.e. money bags.
53. turns the key: unlocks the door.   54. dolors: sorrows (with pun on *dol-
lars*).   for: because of.   55. tell: relate (with quibble on the sense "count").
56. mother: hysteria.   57. Hysterica passio: hysteria, thought to be the result
of the ascent of vapors from abdomen to head. [See, in "Sources and Contexts,"
Edward Jorden's treatise, *A Brief Discourse of a Disease Called the Suffocation of the
Mother* (1603), which discusses "hysterica passio" or "the mother" as a physiological
disorder involving a sense of suffocation within the womb and not not having to
do with a woman's being possessed demonically. ~ *Evans Editor*]

LEAR                  Follow me not,
  Stay here.                                        *Exit.*

GENTLEMAN Made you no more offense but what you      60
  speak of?
KENT None.
  How chance the King comes with so small a number?
FOOL And thou hadst been set i' th' stocks for that
  question, thou'dst well deserv'd it.                  65
KENT Why, Fool?
FOOL We'll set thee to school to an ant, to
  teach thee there's no laboring i' th' winter. All
  that follow their noses are led by their eyes but
  blind men, and there's not a nose among twenty      70
  but can smell him that's stinking. Let go thy
  hold when a great wheel runs down a hill, lest it
  break thy neck with following; but the great one
  that goes upward, let him draw thee after. When
  a wise man gives thee better counsel, give me       75
  mine again, I would have none but knaves follow it,
  since a fool gives it.
    That sir which serves and seeks for gain,
      And follows but for form,
    Will pack when it begins to rain,                  80
      And leave thee in the storm.
    But I will tarry, the Fool will stay,
      And let the wise man fly.
    The knave turns fool that runs away,
      The Fool no knave, perdie.                     85
KENT Where learn'd you this, Fool?
FOOL Not i' th' stocks, fool.

             *Enter* LEAR *and* GLOUCESTER.

LEAR Deny to speak with me? They are sick? they are weary?
  They have travell'd all the night? Mere fetches,
  The images of revolt and flying off.                90
  Fetch me a better answer.

---

**67–68. We'll . . . winter:** i.e. the wise ant knows that labor in winter is unprofitable; Lear in his "winter" is bound to be deserted by the shrewd. **68–71. All . . . stinking:** i.e. if they couldn't see that he was out of Fortune's favor, they could smell it. **76. knaves.** Expressing the Fool's opinion of those who deserted Lear. **80. pack:** be off. **84. The knave . . . away.** Again, the Fool's true opinion; those who run away are the actual fools. **85. perdie:** assuredly (a weakened oath, like French *pardieu*, originally "by God"). **89. fetches:** deceptive excuses. **90. images:** signs. **flying off.** Synonymous with *revolt*.

GLOUCESTER          My dear lord,
You know the fiery quality of the Duke,
How unremovable and fix'd he is
In his own course.
LEAR                Vengeance! plague! death! confusion!                    95
Fiery? What quality? Why, Gloucester, Gloucester,
I'ld speak with the Duke of Cornwall and his wife.
GLOUCESTER  Well, my good lord, I have inform'd them so.
LEAR  Inform'd them? Dost thou understand me, man?
GLOUCESTER  Ay, my good lord.                                             100
LEAR  The King would speak with Cornwall, the dear father
Would with his daughter speak, commands, tends service.
Are they inform'd of this? My breath and blood!
Fiery? the fiery Duke? Tell the hot Duke that—
No, but not yet, may be he is not well:                                  105
Infirmity doth still neglect all office
Whereto our health is bound; we are not ourselves
When nature, being oppress'd, commands the mind
To suffer with the body. I'll forbear,
And am fallen out with my more headier will,                             110
To take the indispos'd and sickly fit
For the sound man. [Looking on Kent.] Death on my state! wherefore
Should he sit here? This act persuades me
That this remotion of the Duke and her
Is practice only. Give me my servant forth.                              115
Go tell the Duke, and 's wife, I'ld speak with them—
Now, presently. Bid them come forth and hear me,
Or at their chamber-door I'll beat the drum
Till it cry sleep to death.
GLOUCESTER  I would have all well betwixt you.            *Exit.* 120
LEAR  O me, my heart! my rising heart! But down!
FOOL  Cry to it, nuncle, as the cockney did to the
eels when she put 'em i' th' paste alive; she knapp'd 'em
o' th' coxcombs with a stick, and cried, "Down,
wantons, down!" 'Twas her brother that, in pure            125
kindness to his horse, butter'd his hay.

---

**92. quality:** nature. **95. confusion:** destruction. **102. tends:** attends, awaits. **106. office:** duty. **107. bound:** obligated. **110. am . . . will:** chide my impetuous disposition. **111. To take:** for taking. **112. state:** royal power. **114. remotion:** keeping apart, aloofness. **115. practice:** trickery. **119. cry . . . death:** make sleep impossible with the din. **122. it:** i.e. your heart. **cockney:** city woman (ignorant of the ways of eels). [**123. paste:** pastry dough; cf. pie, pasty, turnover. ~ *Evans Editor*] **knapp'd:** knocked. **124–25. Down, wantons:** lie down, you lively creatures. The Fool implies that Lear's cry to his heart will be just as effectual.

*Enter* CORNWALL, REGAN, GLOUCESTER, SERVANTS.

LEAR  Good morrow to you both.
CORNWALL                    Hail to your Grace!
                                    *Kent here set at liberty.*
REGAN  I am glad to see your Highness.
LEAR  Regan, I think [you] are;  I know what reason
  I have to think so. If thou shouldst not be glad,                    130
  I would divorce me from thy [mother's] tomb,
  Sepulchring an adult'ress. [*To Kent.*] O, are you free?
  Some other time for that. [*Exit Kent.*] Beloved Regan,
  Thy sister's naught. O Regan, she hath tied
  Sharp-tooth'd unkindness, like a vulture, here.                    135
                                    [*Points to his heart.*]
  I can scarce speak to thee; thou'lt not believe
  With now deprav'd a quality—O Regan!
REGAN  I pray you, sir, take patience. I have hope
  You less know how to value her desert
  Than she to scant her duty.
LEAR                    Say? How is that?                    140
REGAN  I cannot think my sister in the least
  Would fail her obligation.  If, sir, perchance
  She have restrain'd the riots of your followers,
  'Tis on such ground and to such wholesome end
  As clears her from all blame.                    145
LEAR  My curses on her!
REGAN                    O sir, you are old,
  Nature in you stands on the very verge
  Of his confine.  You should be rul'd and led
  By some discretion that discerns your state
  Better than you yourself.  Therefore I pray you                    150
  That to our sister you do make return.
  Say you have wrong'd her.
LEAR                    Ask her forgiveness?
  Do you but mark how this becomes the house!
  "Dear daughter, I confess that I am old;                    [*Kneeling.*]
  Age is unnecessary.  On my knees I beg                    155
  That you'll vouchsafe me raiment, bed, and food."
REGAN  Good sir, no more; these are unsightly tricks.
  Return you to my sister.

---

**132. Sepulchring:** in the certainty that it sepulchred.   **134. naught:** wicked.
**138. take patience:** control yourself.   **140. scant.** Modern idiom would require
*do* or *fulfill*.   **148. his confine:** its extreme limit.   **153. becomes the house:** befits
family decorum.   **155. Age is unnecessary:** old people are useless.

LEAR    [*Rising.*]    Never, Regan:
She hath abated me of half my train;
Look'd black upon me, strook me with her tongue,                    160
Most serpent-like, upon the very heart.
All the stor'd vengeances of heaven fall
On her ingrateful top! Strike her young bones,
You taking airs, with lameness!
CORNWALL                    Fie, sir, fie!
LEAR  You nimble lightnings, dart your blinding flames              165
Into her scornful eyes!  Infect her beauty,
You fen-suck'd fogs, drawn by the pow'rful sun,
To fall and blister!
REGAN                  O the blest gods! so
Will you wish on me, when the rash mood is on.
LEAR  No, Regan, thou shalt never have my curse.                   170
Thy tender-hefted nature shall not give
Thee o'er to harshness.  Her eyes are fierce, but thine
Do comfort, and not burn.  'Tis not in thee
To grudge my pleasures, to cut off my train,
To bandy hasty words, to scant my sizes,                           175
And in conclusion to oppose the bolt
Against my coming in.  Thou better know'st
The offices of nature, bond of childhood,
Effects of courtesy, dues of gratitude:
Thy half o' th' kingdom hast thou not forgot,                      180
Wherein I thee endow'd.
REGAN                    Good sir, to th' purpose.
LEAR  Who put my man i' th' stocks?

                                        *Tucket within.*

              *Enter Steward* [OSWALD].

CORNWALL                    What trumpet's that?
REGAN  I know't, my sister's.  This approves her letter,
   That she would soon be here.  [*To Oswald.*] Is your lady come?
LEAR  This is a slave whose easy-borrowed pride                    185
   Dwells in the [fickle] grace of her he follows.

---

160. **strook:** struck.   163. **top:** head.   **young bones.** It has been argued that the
reference is to an unborn child of Goneril's.   164. **taking:** infectious.   168. **fall:**
strike.   171. **tender-hefted:** moved by a tender nature, lovingly inclined.
175. **sizes:** allowances.   176. **oppose the bolt:** lock the door.   178. **offices of nature:** natural duties.   179. **Effects of courtesy:** courteous actions.   183. **approves:**
confirms.   185. **easy-borrowed:** borrowed from his betters, without charge to
himself.

Out, varlet, from my sight!
CORNWALL                    What means your Grace?

*Enter* GONERIL.

LEAR Who stock'd my servant? Regan, I have good hope
Thou didst not know on't.   Who comes here? O heavens!
If you do love old men, if your sweet sway           190
Allow obedience, if you yourselves are old,
Make it your cause; send down, and take my part.
[*To Goneril.*] Art not asham'd to look upon this beard?
O Regan, will you take her by the hand?
GONERIL Why not by th' hand, sir?   How have I offended?   195
All's not offense that indiscretion finds
And dotage terms so.
LEAR                    O sides, you are too tough!
Will you yet hold?   How came my man i' th' stocks?
CORNWALL I set him there, sir; but his own disorders
Deserv'd much less advancement.
LEAR                    You? Did you?           200
REGAN I pray you, father, being weak, seem so.
If till the expiration of your month
You will return and sojourn with my sister,
Dismissing half your train, come then to me.
I am now from home, and out of that provision           205
Which shall be needful for your entertainment.
LEAR Return to her? and fifty men dismiss'd?
No, rather I abjure all roofs, and choose
To wage against the enmity o' th' air,
To be a comrade with the wolf and owl—           210
Necessity's sharp pinch. Return with her?
Why, the hot-bloodied France, that dowerless took
Our youngest born, I could as well be brought
To knee his throne, and squire-like, pension beg
To keep base life afoot.   Return with her?           215
Persuade me rather to be slave and sumpter
To this detested groom.           [*Pointing at Oswald.*]
GONERIL                    At your choice, sir.
LEAR I prithee, daughter, do not make me mad.
I will not trouble thee, my child; farewell:

**191. Allow:** approve.   **200. much less advancement:** i.e. far worse treatment.   **201. seem so:** do not pretend to be otherwise.   **209. wage:** contend.   **212. hot-bloodied:** hot-blooded, choleric (cf. 1.2.23).   **216. sumpter:** pack-horse, drudge.

We'll no more meet, no more see one another.                220
But yet thou art my flesh, my blood, my daughter—
Or rather a disease that's in my flesh,
Which I must needs call mine. Thou art a bile,
A plague-sore, or embossed carbuncle,
In my corrupted blood. But I'll not chide thee,          225
Let shame come when it will, I do not call it.
I do not bid the thunder-bearer shoot,
Nor tell tales of thee to high-judging Jove.
Mend when thou canst, be better at thy leisure,
I can be patient, I can stay with Regan,                 230
I and my hundred knights.
REGAN                          Not altogether so,
I look'd not for you yet, nor am provided
For your fit welcome. Give ear, sir, to my sister,
For those that mingle reason with your passion
Must be content to think you old, and so—               235
But she knows what she does.
LEAR                          Is this well spoken?
REGAN I dare avouch it, sir. What, fifty followers?
Is it not well? What should you need of more?
Yea, or so many? sith that both charge and danger
Speak 'gainst so great a number? How in one house        240
Should many people under two commands
Hold amity? 'Tis hard, almost impossible.
GONERIL Why might not you, my lord, receive attendance
From those that she calls servants or from mine?
REGAN Why not, my lord? If then they chanc'd to slack ye,  245
We could control them. If you will come to me
(For now I spy a danger), I entreat you
To bring but five and twenty; to no more
Will I give place or notice.
LEAR I gave you all—
REGAN          And in good time you gave it.              250
LEAR Made you my guardians, my depositaries,
But kept a reservation to be followed

223. bile: boil. 224. embossed: swollen, risen to a head. 226. call: summon.
228. high-judging: judging from on high. 232. look'd not for: did not
expect. 234. mingle . . . passion: bring reason to the consideration of your passion. 237. avouch: vouch for. 239. charge: expense. 245. slack: be negligent
toward. 246. control: correct. 249. notice: recognition. 251. my guardians,
my depositaries: the protectors and trustees of my kingdom. 252. kept a reservation: reserved the right.

With such a number. What, must I come to you
With five and twenty? Regan, said you so?
REGAN  And speak't again, my lord, no more with me.      255
LEAR  Those wicked creatures yet do look well-favor'd
When others are more wicked; not being the worst
Stands in some rank of praise. [*To Goneril.*] I'll go with thee,
Thy fifty yet doth double five and twenty,
And thou art twice her love.
GONERIL                    Hear me, my lord:      260
What need you five and twenty? ten? or five?
To follow in a house where twice so many
Have a command to tend you?
REGAN                    What need one?
LEAR  O, reason not the need! our basest beggars
Are in the poorest thing superfluous.      265
Allow not nature more than nature needs,
Man's life is cheap as beast's. Thou art a lady;
If only to go warm were gorgeous,
Why, nature needs not what thou gorgeous wear'st,
Which scarcely keeps thee warm. But for true need—      270
You heavens, give me that patience, patience I need!
You see me here, you gods, a poor old man,
As full of grief as age, wretched in both.
If it be you that stirs these daughters' hearts
Against their father, fool me not so much      275
To bear it tamely; touch me with noble anger,
And let not women's weapons, water-drops,
Stain my man's cheeks! No, you unnatural hags,
I will have such revenges on you both
That all the world shall—I will do such things—      280
What they are yet I know not, but they shall be
The terrors of the earth! You think I'll weep:
No, I'll not weep.
I have full cause of weeping, but this heart

                                   *Storm and tempest.*
Shall break into a hundred thousand flaws      285
Or ere I'll weep. O Fool, I shall go mad!
           *Exeunt* [*Lear, Gloucester, Gentleman, and Fool*].

---

**265. Are . . . superfluous:** have some wretched things they could manage without.  **266. Allow not:** if you don't allow.  [**269. gorgeous:** splendidly adorned.
~ *Evans Editor*]  **271. patience:** endurance, fortitude.  **275–76. fool . . . To:** do not
make me such a fool as to.  **285. flaws:** fragments.  **286. Or ere:** before.

CORN  Let us withdraw, 'twill be a storm.

REGAN  This house is little, the old man and 's people
Cannot be well bestow'd.

GONERIL  'Tis his own blame hath put himself from rest,      290
And must needs taste his folly.

REGAN  For his particular, I'll receive him gladly,
But not one follower.

GONERIL          So am I purpos'd.
Where is my Lord of Gloucester?

CORNWALL  Followed the old man forth.

*Enter* GLOUCESTER.

            He is return'd.

GLOUCESTER  The King is in high rage.      295

CORNWALL          Whither is he going?

GLOUCESTER  He calls to horse, but will I know not whither.

CORNWALL  'Tis best to give him way, he leads himself.

GONERIL  My lord, entreat him by no means to stay.

GLOUCESTER  Alack, the night comes on, and the [bleak] winds      300
Do sorely ruffle; for many miles about
There's scarce a bush.

REGAN          O sir, to willful men,
The injuries that they themselves procure
Must be their schoolmasters. Shut up your doors.
He is attended with a desperate train,      305
And what they may incense him to, being apt
To have his ear abus'd, wisdom bids fear.

CORNWALL  Shut up your doors, my lord, 'tis a wild night,
My Regan counsels well. Come out o' th' storm.

            *Exeunt.*

---

**289. bestow'd:** lodged. **292. For his particular:** as far as he himself is concerned. **301. ruffle:** bluster. [**306–07. being apt . . . bids fear:** being in a frame of mind to be deceived or provoked, wisdom asks that we be fearful of retaliation. ~ *Evans Editor*] **307. abus'd:** deceived.

# Act 3

## SCENE I

*Storm still. Enter* KENT *[disguised as Caius] and a*
GENTLEMAN *severally.*

KENT Who's there, besides foul weather?
GENTLEMAN One minded like the weather, most unquietly.
KENT I know you. Where's the King?
GENTLEMAN Contending with the fretful elements;
Bids the wind blow the earth into the sea,                    5
Or swell the curled waters 'bove the main,
That things might change or cease, [tears his white hair,
Which the impetuous blasts with eyeless rage
Catch in their fury, and make nothing of,
Strives in his little world of man to outscorn              10
The to-and-fro-conflicting wind and rain.
This night, wherein the cub-drawn bear would couch,
The lion and the belly-pinched wolf
Keep their fur dry, unbonneted he runs,
And bids what will take all.]
KENT                          But who is with him?           15
GENTLEMAN None but the Fool, who labors to outjest
His heart-strook injuries.
KENT                          Sir, I do know you,
And dare upon the warrant of my note
Commend a dear thing to you. There is division
(Although as yet the face of it is cover'd                  20
With mutual cunning) 'twixt Albany and Cornwall;
Who have—as who have not, that their great stars

---

3.1. Location: **A heath near Gloucester's castle.**   **6. main:** mainland.   **9. make
nothing of:** handle irreverently.   **10. little . . . man.** Alluding to the idea of man
as a microcosm, image of the macrocosm or universe.   **12. cub-drawn:** sucked
dry, therefore hungry.   **couch:** remain in her den.   **16. outjest:** relieve by his
jests.   **18. note:** observation, i.e. knowledge (of you).   **19. Commend:** entrust.
**dear:** important.

Thron'd and set high?—servants, who seem no less,
Which are to France the spies and speculations
Intelligent of our state. What hath been seen,      25
Either in snuffs and packings of the Dukes,
Or the hard rein which both of them hath borne
Against the old kind King; or something deeper,
Whereof (perchance) these are but furnishings—
[But true it is, from France there comes a power      30
Into this scattered kingdom, who already
Wise in our negligence, have secret feet
In some of our best ports, and are at point
To show their open banner. Now to you:
If on my credit you dare build so far      35
To make your speed to Dover, you shall find
Some that will thank you, making just report
Of how unnatural and bemadding sorrow
The King hath cause to plain.
I am a gentleman of blood and breeding,      40
And from some knowledge and assurance, offer
This office to you.]
GENTLEMAN  I will talk further with you.
KENT                      No, do not.
For confirmation that I am much more
Than my out-wall, open this purse and take      45
What it contains. If you shall see Cordelia
(As fear not but you shall), show her this ring,
And she will tell you who that fellow is
That yet you do not know. Fie on this storm!
I will go seek the King.      50
GENTLEMAN      Give me your hand. Have you no more to say?
KENT  Few words, but to effect, more than all yet:
That when we have found the King—in which your pain
That way, I'll this—he that first lights on him
Holla the other.              *Exeunt [severally].*  55

---

23. **no less:** no other.   24. **speculations:** secret observers.   25. **Intelligent of:** who furnish intelligence relating to.   26. **snuffs:** quarrels.  **packings:** plots.   29. **furnishings:** superficial additions, i.e. pretexts.   30. **power:** army.   31. **scattered:** divided.   32. **Wise in:** profiting by.   33. **at point:** ready.   35. **credit:** trustworthiness.   39. **plain:** complain of.   41. **knowledge and assurance:** assured knowledge.   45. **out-wall:** exterior.   48. **fellow:** companion.   52. **to effect:** in importance.   53. **pain:** effort, i.e. search.

## SCENE 2

*Storm still. Enter* LEAR *and* FOOL.

LEAR  Blow, winds, and crack your cheeks! rage, blow!
You cataracts and hurricanoes, spout
Till you have drench'd our steeples, [drown'd] the cocks!
You sulph'rous and thought-executing fires,
Vaunt-couriers of oak-cleaving thunderbolts,                    5
Singe my white head! And thou, all-shaking thunder,
Strike flat the thick rotundity o' th' world!
Crack nature's moulds, all germains spill at once
That makes ingrateful man!
FOOL  O nuncle, court holy-water in a dry house is             10
better than this rain-water out o' door. Good nuncle,
in, ask thy daughters blessing. Here's a night pities
neither wise men nor fools.
LEAR  Rumble thy bellyful! Spit, fire! Spout, rain!
Nor rain, wind, thunder, fire are my daughters.               15
I tax not you, you elements, with unkindness;
I never gave you kingdom, call'd you children;
You owe me no subscription. Then let fall
Your horrible pleasure. Here I stand your slave,
A poor, infirm, weak, and despis'd old man;                   20
But yet I call you servile ministers,
That will with two pernicious daughters join
Your high-engender'd battles 'gainst a head
So old and white as this. O, ho! 'tis foul.                   25
FOOL  He that has a house to put 's head in has a
good head-piece.
    The codpiece that will house
    Before the head has any,
    The head and he shall louse:

---

3.2. Location: **The heath.**  2. hurricanoes: waterspouts.  3. drench'd: drowned, submerged.  cocks: weathercocks.  4. thought-executing: acting as quick as thought.  5. Vaunt-couriers: precursors. oak-cleaving thunderbolts. The damage caused by lightning was formerly thought to be due to a stone projectile discharged from the clouds during a storm.  8. germains: germens, seeds; the *semina* existing in nature from which all, including man, is created.  spill: destroy.  10. court holy-water: flattery.  12. ask ... blessing: ask a blessing of your daughters, i.e. submit to their authority (since the normal procedure would be for them to ask a blessing of him).  18. subscription: submission, deference.  21. ministers: agents.  23. high-engender'd: bred in the heavens.  battles: battalions, forces.  26. head-piece: (1) head-covering; (2) brain.  27–30. The cod-piece ... many: he who engages in sexual intercourse before he can afford to keep up a house ends in beggary.

So beggars marry many.                                    30
The man that makes his toe
What he his heart should make,
Shall of a corn cry woe,
And turn his sleep to wake.
For there was never yet fair woman but she made          35
mouths in a glass.

*Enter* KENT [*disguised as Caius*].

LEAR  No, I will be the pattern of all patience,
I will say nothing.
KENT  Who's there?
FOOL  Marry, here's grace and a codpiece—that's          40
a wise man and a fool.
KENT  Alas, sir, are you here? Things that love night
Love not such nights as these. The wrathful skies
Gallow the very wanderers of the dark,
And make them keep their caves. Since I was man,         45
Such sheets of fire, such bursts of horrid thunder,
Such groans of roaring wind and rain, I never
Remember to have heard. Man's nature cannot carry
Th' affliction nor the fear.
LEAR                          Let the great gods,
That keep this dreadful pudder o'er our heads,           50
Find out their enemies now. Tremble, thou wretch
That hast within thee undivulged crimes
Unwhipt of justice! Hide thee, thou bloody hand;
Thou perjur'd, and thou simular of virtue
That art incestuous! Caitiff, to pieces shake,          55
That under covert and convenient seeming
Has practic'd on man's life! Close pent-up guilts,
Rive your concealing continents, and cry
These dreadful summoners grace. I am a man
More sinn'd against than sinning.

---

**31–34. The man . . . wake:** he who cherishes his toe as he should cherish his heart (as Lear has favored Goneril and Regan rather than Cordelia) will be caused such suffering by his toe that he will be unable to sleep.  **35–36. made . . . glass:** practiced facial expressions in front of a mirror.  **40. Marry:** indeed (originally, the name of the Virgin Mary used as an oath).  **44. Gallow:** terrify.  **45. keep:** stay inside.  **48. carry:** hold out against.  **49. affliction:** i.e. physical impact.  **50. pudder:** pother (i.e., turmoil, disturbance).  **54. simular:** dissembler.  **55. Caitiff:** wretch.  **56. covert . . . seeming:** i.e. a concealing pretense of virtue.  **57. practic'd on:** plotted against.  **58. Rive:** burst. **continents:** containers, bounds.  **58–59. cry . . . grace:** ask . . . for mercy.

KENT                              Alack, bare-headed?                    60
Gracious my lord, hard by here is a hovel,
Some friendship will it lend you 'gainst the tempest.
Repose you there, while I to this hard house
(More harder than the stones whereof 'tis rais'd,
Which even but now, demanding after you,                              65
Denied me to come in) return, and force
Their scanted courtesy.
LEAR                              My wits begin to turn.
Come on, my boy. How dost, my boy? Art cold?
I am cold myself. Where is this straw, my fellow?
The art of our necessities is strange                                 70
And can make vild things precious. Come, your hovel.
Poor Fool and knave, I have one part in my heart
That's sorry yet for thee.
FOOL  [Sings.]
           "He that has and a little tine wit—
                With heigh-ho, the wind and the rain—          75
              Must make content with his fortunes fit,
                Though the rain it raineth every day."
LEAR  True, boy. Come bring us to this hovel.
                                              Exit [with Kent].

FOOL  This is a brave night to cool a courtezan.
I'll speak a prophecy ere I go:                                       80
    When priests are more in word than matter;
    When brewers mar their malt with water;
    When nobles are their tailors' tutors;
    No heretics burn'd, but wenches' suitors;
    Then shall the realm of Albion                                   85
    Come to great confusion.
    When every case in law is right;
    No squire in debt, nor no poor knight;
    When slanders do not live in tongues;

61. **hovel:** shed for animals or for storing grain or tools. 65. **demanding:** inquiring (modifies *me* in the next line). 70. **art:** skill. 71. **vild:** vile, worthless. 74. **tine:** tiny (a variant spelling). [74–77: Cf. Feste's song in *Twelfth Night*, 5.1.389–408. ~ *Evans Editor*] 81–94. **When . . . feet.** Lines 81–86 are "a satirical description of the present manners as future," with "its proper inference or deduction"; lines 87–94 are "a satirical description of future manners, which the corruption of the present would prevent from ever happening," with "its proper inference or deduction" (Warburton). In F1 lines 85–86 follow line 92. The whole is a parody of a pseudo-Chaucerian "Merlin's Prophecy." 83. **nobles . . . tutors:** i.e. pay so much attention to clothes that they can instruct their tailors. 84. **burn'd.** The suitors are "burned" by venereal disease. 87. **right:** just.

Nor cutpurses come not to throngs; 90
When usurers tell their gold i' th' field,
And bawds and whores do churches build;
Then comes the time, who lives to see't,
That going shall be us'd with feet.
This prophecy Merlin shall make, for I live before his time. 95

*Exit.*


## SCENE 3

*Enter* GLOUCESTER *and* EDMUND [*with lights*].

GLOUCESTER  Alack, alack, Edmund, I like not this unnatural dealing. When I desir'd their leave that I
might pity him, they took from me the use of mine
own house, charg'd me on pain of perpetual displeasure
neither to speak of him, entreat for him, or any way
sustain him. 5
EDMUND  Most savage and unnatural!
GLOUCESTER  Go to; say you nothing. There is division
between the Dukes, and a worse matter than that. I
have receiv'd a letter this night—'tis dangerous to 10
be spoken; I have lock'd the letter in my closet. These
injuries the King now bears will be reveng'd home;
there is part of a power already footed: we must
incline to the King. I will look him and privily relieve
him. Go you and maintain talk with the Duke, that 15
my charity be not of him perceiv'd. If he ask for me,
I am ill and gone to bed. If I die for['t] (as no less is
threat'ned me), the King my old master must be reliev'd. There is strange things toward, Edmund,
pray you be careful. *Exit.* 20
EDMUND  This courtesy, forbid thee, shall the Duke
Instantly know, and of that letter too.
This seems a fair deserving, and must draw me
That which my father loses: no less than all.
The younger rises when the old doth fall. *Exit.* 25


91. tell . . . field: count their money openly.  92. churches build: endow churches
(as penance for their sins).  94. going . . . feet: walking will be done on foot.
3.3. Location: Gloucester's castle.  3. pity: i.e. aid, relieve.  12. home: fully.
13. footed: landed.  14. incline to: side with.  look: seek.  21. forbid: which is
forbidden.  23. fair deserving: action to make me deserving of reward.

## SCENE 4

*Enter* LEAR, KENT [*disguised as Caius*], *and* FOOL.

KENT  Here is the place, my lord; good my lord, enter,
The tyranny of the open night's too rough
For nature to endure.                          *Storm still.*
LEAR                    Let me alone.
KENT  Good my lord, enter here.
LEAR                    Wilt break my heart?
KENT  I had rather break mine own. Good my lord, enter.      5
LEAR  Thou think'st 'tis much that this contentious storm
Invades us to the skin; so 'tis to thee;
But where the greater malady is fix'd,
The lesser is scarce felt. Thou'dst shun a bear,
But if [thy] flight lay toward the roaring sea,          10
Thou'dst meet the bear i' th' mouth. When the mind's free,
The body's delicate; [this] tempest in my mind
Doth from my senses take all feeling else,
Save what beats there—filial ingratitude!
Is it not as this mouth should tear this hand          15
For lifting food to't? But I will punish home.
No, I will weep no more. In such a night
To shut me out? Pour on, I will endure.
In such a night as this? O Regan, Goneril!
Your old kind father, whose frank heart gave all—          20
O, that way madness lies, let me shun that!
No more of that.
KENT                    Good my lord, enter here.
LEAR  Prithee go in thyself, seek thine own ease.
This tempest will not give me leave to ponder
On things would hurt me more. But I'll go in.          25
[*To the Fool.*] In, boy, go first.—You houseless poverty—
Nay, get thee in; I'll pray, and then I'll sleep.

                                              *Exit [Fool].*

Poor naked wretches, wheresoe'er you are,
That bide the pelting of this pitiless storm,
How shall your houseless heads and unfed sides,          30
Your [loop'd] and window'd raggedness, defend you

---

3.4. Location: **The heath. Before a hovel. 4. break my heart:** i.e. by freeing
my mind for thought. **8. fix'd:** entrenched, deep-rooted. **11. free:** at ease. **12.
delicate:** sensitive. **14. there:** i.e. in my mind. **15. as:** as if. **20. frank:** generous. **29. bide:** endure. **31. loop'd:** full of holes (synonymous with *window'd*).

From seasons such as these? O, I have ta'en
Too little care of this! Take physic, pomp,
Expose thyself to feel what wretches feel,
That thou mayst shake the superflux to them,                    35
And show the heavens more just.
EDGAR  [*Within.*] Fathom and half, fathom and half!
Poor Tom!

> [*Enter*] *Fool* [*from the hovel*].

FOOL  Come not in here, nuncle, here's a spirit.
Help me, help me!                                               40
KENT  Give me thy hand. Who's there?
FOOL  A spirit, a spirit! he says his name's poor
Tom.
KENT  What art thou that dost grumble there i' th'
straw? Come forth.                                             45

> *Enter* EDGAR [*disguised as a madman*].

EDGAR  Away, the foul fiend follows me! Through
the sharp hawthorn blow the [cold] winds. Humh,
go to thy bed and warm thee.
LEAR  Didst thou give all to thy daughters? And
art thou come to this?                                         50
EDGAR  Who gives any thing to poor Tom? whom the
foul fiend hath led through fire and through flame,
through [ford] and whirlpool, o'er bog and quagmire;
that hath laid knives under his pillow, and halters in
his pew, set ratsbane by his porridge, made him               55
proud of heart, to ride on a bay trotting-horse over
four-inch'd bridges, to course his own shadow for a
traitor. Bless thy five wits! Tom's a-cold—O do de,
do de, do de. Bless thee from whirlwinds, star-blasting,
and taking! Do poor Tom some charity, whom             60

---

**33. pomp:** i.e. men who live in splendor.  **35. superflux:** superfluity, wealth above
one's needs.  **37. Fathom and half:** Sailor's cry. The hovel is shipping water.
**46. Away:** keep away.  **follows:** attends (cf. line 140).  **46–47. Through . . .
winds:** Possibly a ballad fragment. It reappears in "The Friar of Orders Grey," an
eighteenth-century pastiche.  **Humh.** Perhaps he imitates the sound of the wind.
**54–55. knives, halters, ratsbane:** Inducements to suicide and so to damnation.
**55. porridge:** soup.  **57. four-inch'd:** i.e. very narrow. Such riding would
require diabolic help.  **course:** hunt.  **59. star-blasting:** malign astrological
influence.  **60. taking:** being bewitched (?) or pestilence (?).

the foul fiend vexes. There could I have him now—
and there—and there again—and there.          *Storm still.*
LEAR  Has his daughters brought him to this pass?
Couldst thou save nothing? Wouldst thou give 'em all?
FOOL  Nay, he reserv'd a blanket, else we had been          65
all sham'd.
LEAR  Now all the plagues that in the pendulous air
Hang fated o'er men's faults light on thy daughters!
KENT  He hath no daughters, sir.
LEAR  Death, traitor! nothing could have subdu'd nature          70
To such a lowness but his unkind daughters.
Is it the fashion, that discarded fathers
Should have thus little mercy on their flesh?
Judicious punishment! 'twas this flesh begot
Those pelican daughters.          75
EDGAR  Pillicock sat on Pillicock-Hill, alow! alow,
loo, loo!
FOOL  This cold night will turn us all to fools and
madmen.
EDGAR  Take heed o' th' foul fiend. Obey thy par-          80
ents, keep thy word's justice, swear not, commit not
with man's sworn spouse, set not thy sweet heart on
proud array. Tom's a-cold.
LEAR  What hast thou been?
EDGAR  A servingman! proud in heart and mind; that          85
curl'd my hair; wore gloves in my cap; serv'd the lust
of my mistress' heart, and did the act of darkness with
her; swore as many oaths as I spake words, and broke
them in the sweet face of heaven: one that slept in the
contriving of lust, and wak'd to do it. Wine lov'd I          90
[deeply], dice dearly; and in woman out-paramour'd
the Turk. False of heart, light of ear, bloody of hand;
hog in sloth, fox in stealth, wolf in greediness, dog in
madness, lion in prey. Let not the creaking of shoes

---

**61–62. There . . . there:** He slaps vermin on his body.     **67. pendulous:** overhanging.     **68. fated:** as agencies of fate.     **74. Judicious:** befitting the offense.
**75. pelican:** The young pelican was believed to feed upon its mother's blood.
**76. Pillicock . . . Pillicock-Hill:** Perhaps from some song or rhyme, but in any
case suggested by the phonetic similarity of *pelican* and *Pillicock*, which would
commend itself to a madman.     **80–83. Obey . . . array:** Apparently poor Tom's
recollection of the Ten Commandments. *Justice* = integrity.     **86. gloves:** As favors
from his mistress.     **91–92. out-paramour'd the Turk:** had more mistresses than
the Sultan.     **92. light of ear:** credulous (of evil) (?) or attentive to levity and falsehood (?).     **94. prey:** preying.

nor the rustling of silks betray thy poor heart to                    95
woman. Keep thy foot out of brothels, thy hand out of
plackets, thy pen from lenders' books, and defy the
foul fiend. Still through the hawthorn blows the cold
wind: says suum, mun, nonny. Dolphin my boy, boy,
sessa! let him trot by.                                    *Storm still.*  100
LEAR  Thou wert better in a grave than to answer
with thy uncover'd body this extremity of the skies. Is
man no more than this? Consider him well. Thou
ow'st the worm no silk, the beast no hide, the sheep no
wool, the cat no perfume. Ha? here's three on 's           105
are sophisticated. Thou art the thing itself: unaccommodated man is no more but such a poor, bare, fork'd
animal as thou art. Off, off, you lendings! Come,
unbutton here.                         [*Tearing off his clothes.*]
FOOL  Prithee, nuncle, be contented, 'tis a naughty        110
night to swim in. Now a little fire in a wild field were
like an old lecher's heart, a small spark, all the rest
on 's body cold.

*Enter* GLOUCESTER *with a torch.*

Look, here comes a walking fire.
EDGAR  This is the foul [fiend] Flibbertigibbet; he        115
begins at curfew, and walks [till the] first cock; he
gives the web and the pin, [squinies] the eye, and
makes the hare-lip; mildews the white wheat, and
hurts the poor creature of earth.
    Swithold footed thrice the 'old,                       120
    He met the night-mare and her nine-fold;

**97. plackets:** openings in petticoats.  **leaders' books:** moneylenders' account-
books (in which borrowers signed statements of their debts).  **99. Dolphin my
boy, boy.** Perhaps another quotation (which possibly should extend to the end of
the sentence).  **100. sessa.** Unexplained; perhaps equivalent to "let it (him, them)
go." Cf. 3.6.74, where it follows a reference to dogs running, and *The Taming of the
Shrew*, Ind.1.6, where it follows the words "let the world slide."  **102. extremity:**
extreme violence.  **105. cat:** civet cat.  **on 's:** of us.  **106. sophisticated:** adulter-
ated.  **106–7. unaccommodated:** unfurnished, without additions.  **108. lendings:**
i.e. garments, borrowed from animals.  **110–11. be . . . swim in:** i.e. don't take
off your clothes; it's a very bad night to go swimming.  **111. wild:** unculti-
vated, barren.  **113. on 's:** of his.  **115. Flibbertigibbet.** A devil's name (from
Harsnett).  **116. curfew:** 9 p.m.  **first cock:** midnight.  **117. web . . . pin:** cata-
ract.  **squinies:** causes to squint.  **118. white:** i.e. ripe.  **120. Swithold:** St. With-
old, who protects suppliants from disaster.  **footed:** walked over.  **'old:** wold,
upland plain.  **121. night-mare:** demon thought to afflict people while they slept.
**nine-fold:** nine offspring (?).

Bid her alight,
And her troth plight,
And aroint thee, witch, aroint thee!
KENT  How fares your Grace?                                          125
LEAR  What's he?
KENT  Who's there? What is't you seek?
GLOUCESTER  What are you there? Your names?
EDGAR  Poor Tom, that eats the swimming frog, the
    toad, the todpole, the wall-newt, and the water;               130
    that in the fury of his heart, when the foul fiend rages,
    eats cow-dung for sallets; swallows the old rat and the
    ditch-dog; drinks the green mantle of the standing
    pool; who is whipt from tithing to tithing, and
    [stock-]punish'd and imprison'd; who hath [had] three          135
    suits to his back, six shirts to his body—
        Horse to ride, and weapon to wear;
        But mice and rats, and such small deer,
        Have been Tom's food for seven long year.
    Beware my follower. Peace, Smulkin, peace, thou fiend!         140
GLOUCESTER  What, hath your Grace no better company?
EDGAR  The prince of darkness is a gentleman. Modo he's call'd,
    and Mahu.
GLOUCESTER  Our flesh and blood, my lord, is grown so vild          145
    That it doth hate what gets it.
EDGAR  Poor Tom's a-cold.
GLOUCESTER  Go in with me; my duty cannot suffer
    T' obey in all your daughters' hard commands.
    Though their injunction be to bar my doors,                    150
    And let this tyrannous night take hold upon you,
    Yet have I ventured to come seek you out,
    And bring you where both fire and food is ready.
LEAR  First let me talk with this philosopher.
    What is the cause of thunder?                                  155

---

**122. alight:** i.e. leave the person she was afflicting (?).   **123. her troth plight:**
i.e. promise to do no harm.   **124. aroint thee:** begone.   **130. todpole:** tad-
pole.   **water:** i.e. water-newt.   **132. sallets:** salads, savories.   **133. mantle:**
scum.   **standing:** stagnant.   **134. tithing:** district.   **138. deer:** animals. (Lines
137–39 are adapted from the romance *Bevis of Hampton*.)   **140. follower:** attendant
devil.   **Smulkin.** The name comes from Harsnett, like *Modo* and *Mahu* in lines
143, 144.   **146. gets:** begets.   **148. my . . . suffer:** i.e. as a dutiful subject I cannot
endure.   **154. philosopher:** natural philosopher, scientist. Lear's appropriate question is of the type answered in contemporary encyclopedias.

KENT  Good my lord, take his offer, go into th' house.
LEAR  I'll talk a word with this same learned Theban.
What is your study?
EDGAR  How to prevent the fiend, and to kill vermin.
LEAR  Let me ask you one word in private.                          160
KENT  Importune him once more to go, my lord,
His wits begin t' unsettle.
GLOUCESTER              Canst thou blame him?     *Storm still.*
His daughters seek his death. Ah, that good Kent!
He said it would be thus, poor banish'd man.
Thou sayest the King grows mad, I'll tell thee, friend,           165
I am almost mad myself. I had a son,
Now outlaw'd from my blood; he sought my life,
But lately, very late. I lov'd him, friend,
No father his son dearer; true to tell thee,
The grief hath craz'd my wits. What a night's this!              170
I do beseech your Grace—
LEAR                          O, cry you mercy, sir.
Noble philosopher, your company.
EDGAR                     Tom's a-cold.
GLOUCESTER  In, fellow, there, into th' hovel; keep thee warm.
LEAR  Come, let's in all.
KENT                     This way, my lord.
LEAR                              With him;                        175
I will keep still with my philosopher.
KENT  Good my lord, soothe him; let him take the fellow.
GLOUCESTER  Take him you on.
KENT  Sirrah, come on; go along with us.
LEAR  Come, good Athenian.                                        180
GLOUCESTER  No words, no words, hush.
EDGAR  Child Rowland to the dark tower came,
His word was still, "Fie, foh, and fum,
I smell the blood of a British man."
                                              *Exeunt.*

**157. Theban:** i.e. scholar.  **158. study:** special field of knowledge. Edgar quibbles
on the sense "preoccupation."  **159. prevent the fiend:** thwart the devil, i.e. avoid
damnation.  **171. cry you mercy:** I beg your pardon.  **176. will . . . with:** refuse to be separated from.  **177. soothe:** humor.  **180. Athenian:** i.e. philosopher.
**182. Child . . . came.** Perhaps from some lost ballad dealing with Roland, hero
of the French *Chanson de Roland.* "*Child*" means an aspirant to knighthood. [The
opening line of Edgar's/Poor Tom's lyric inspired Robert Browning's nightmarish
poem, "Childe Roland to the Dark Tower Came" (1853), a dramatic monologue
that derives its title from *Lear* along with elements of tone and atmosphere. ~ *Evans
Editor*]  **183. word:** watchword.  **still:** always.  **183–84. Fie . . . man.** Traditional,
with *English* for *British.*

## SCENE 5

*Enter* CORNWALL *and* EDMUND.

CORNWALL  I will have my revenge ere I depart his house.

EDMUND  How, my lord, I may be censur'd, that nature
thus gives way to loyalty, something fears me to think of.

CORNWALL  I now perceive, it was not altogether your          5
brother's evil disposition made him seek his death; but
a provoking merit, set a-work by a reprovable badness
in himself.

EDMUND  How malicious is my fortune, that I must
repent to be just! This is the letter which he spoke          10
of, which approves him an intelligent party to the
advantages of France. O heavens! that this treason
were not; or not I the detector!

CORNWALL  Go with me to the Duchess.

EDMUND  If the matter of this paper be certain, you          15
have mighty business in hand.

CORNWALL  True or false, it hath made thee Earl of GLOUCESTER
Seek out where thy father is, that he may
be ready for our apprehension.

EDMUND  [*Aside.*] If I find him comforting the King,          20
it will stuff his suspicion more fully.—I will persever
in my course of loyalty, though the conflict be sore
between that and my blood.

CORNWALL  I will lay trust upon thee; and thou shalt find
a [dearer] father in my love.                                *Exeunt.* 25

## SCENE 6

*Enter* KENT [*disguised as Caius*] *and* GLOUCESTER.

GLOUCESTER  Here is better than the open air, take it
thankfully. I will piece out the comfort with what
addition I can. I will not be long from you.

---

3.5. Location: **Gloucester's castle.**   2. censur'd: judged.   3. something fears:
somewhat frightens.   6. his: i.e. Gloucester's.   7–8. a provoking . . . himself: i.e.
a deserving (on Gloucester's part) to be killed, which provoked Edgar to plot his father's death, though he was also moved by an evil propensity in himself which must
be condemned.   11. approves: proves.   intelligent . . . to: informed . . . of (?) or
supplying information . . . for (?).   party: partisan.   19. ready . . . apprehension:
available for arrest.   20. comforting: helping.   21. his suspicion: suspicion of
him. 3.6. Location: **An outbuilding of Gloucester's castle.**   2. piece: eke
[(as in 'eking it out'). ~ *Evans Editor*]

KENT  All the pow'r of his wits have given way to
his impatience. The gods reward your kindness!  5

*Exit [Gloucester].*

*Enter* LEAR, EDGAR, *and* FOOL.

EDGAR  Frateretto calls me, and tells me Nero is an
angler in the lake of darkness. Pray, innocent, and
beware the foul fiend.

FOOL  Prithee, nuncle, tell me whether a madman
be a gentleman or a yeoman?  10

LEAR  A king, a king!

FOOL  No, he's a yeoman that has a gentleman to
his son; for he's a mad yeoman that sees his son a
gentleman before him.

LEAR  To have a thousand with red burning spits  15
Come hizzing in upon 'em—

[EDGAR  The foul fiend bites my back.

FOOL  He's mad that trusts in the tameness of a
wolf, a horse's health, a boy's love, or a whore's oath.

LEAR  It shall be done, I will arraign them straight.  20
[*To Edgar.*] Come sit thou here, most learned [justicer];
[*To the Fool.*] Thou, sapient sir, sit here. [Now], you she-foxes—

EDGAR  Look where he stands and glares! Want'st
thou eyes at trial, madam? [*Sings.*]
"Come o'er the [bourn], Bessy, to me"—  25

FOOL  [*Sings.*]
  Her boat hath a leak,
  And she must not speak
Why she dares not come over to thee.

---

**5. impatience:** inability to endure more.  **6. Frateretto:** Another Harsnett devil.
[Cf. Italian *fratelletto*, 'little or younger brother.' The suggestion here is twofold:
(1) Frateretto is associated with a fraternity of devils and (2) Edmund, Edgar's
younger brother, is diabolical. ~ *Evans Editor*]  **6–7. Nero . . . angler:** A legend from
Chaucer's "Monk's Tale," lines 485–86, suggested by passages in Harsnett immediately following his mention of Frateretto. [Chaucer's "Monk's Tale" is a narrative
concerning the falls (*de casibus*) of various personages toppled by Fortune, including
Nero, who, among his many devilish deeds, committed matricide. In *King Lear*,
Edmund (a type of Frateretto) is figuratively a victim of Fortune. ~ *Evans Editor*]
**7. innocent.** He addresses the Fool.  **23. he:** i.e. the fiend that Edgar pretends to
see.  **24. eyes at trial:** spectators at your trial.  **25. Come . . . me:** A line from an
old song. Lines 26–28 are the Fool's own indecent addition.  **bourn:** burn, brook.
[**26.** The Fool may be referring to the medieval tradition of the Ship of Fools
(*Das Narrenschiff*) made renowned by the Alsatian satirist Sebastian Brant in 1494.
~ *Evans Editor*]

EDGAR  The foul fiend haunts poor Tom in the voice
of a nightingale. Hoppedance cries in Tom's belly       30
for two white herring. Croak not, black angel, I have
no food for thee.
KENT  How do you, sir? Stand you not so amaz'd.
Will you lie down and rest upon the cushions?
LEAR  I'll see their trial first, bring in their evidence.      35
[*To Edgar.*] Thou robed man of justice, take thy place,
[*To the Fool.*] And thou, his yoke-fellow of equity,
Bench by his side. [*To Kent.*] You are o' th' commission,
Sit you too.
EDGAR  [*Sings.*] Let us deal justly.       40
Sleepest or wakest thou, jolly shepherd?
Thy sheep be in the corn,
And for one blast of thy minikin mouth,
Thy sheep shall take no harm.
Purr the cat is grey.       45
LEAR  Arraign her first, 'tis Goneril. I here take
my oath before this honorable assembly, [she] kick'd
the poor king her father.
FOOL  Come hither, mistress. Is your name
Goneril?       50
LEAR  She cannot deny it.
FOOL  Cry you mercy, I took you for a join-stool.
LEAR  And here's another, whose warp'd looks proclaim
What store her heart is made an. Stop her there!

---

**30. Hoppedance:** Harsnett has *Hoberdidance.* His cries are the rumbling of Tom's
empty stomach.   **31. white:** fresh, unsmoked (with following play on *black* =
smoked, i.e. blackened by the smoke of hell).   **33. amaz'd:** bewildered.   **35. their
evidence:** the witnesses against them.   **36. robed:** Referring to Tom's blanket.
[**37. yokefellow of equity:** referring to the Courts of Equity (presided over by the
Lord Chancellor, portrayed by Poor Tom), which are associated with judicial fair-
ness. Here presides the Lord Chief Justice whose "yokefellow" or associate in the
mock trial scene (Quarto 3.6) is the Fool. ~ *Evans Editor*]   **38. o' th' commission:**
appointed one of the judges.   **41–44. Sleepest . . . harm:** If this is a quoted stanza, its
source has not been found.   **42. corn:** wheatfield.   **43–44. And . . . harm:** if you
call back your sheep we will let them off without putting them in the pound (?) or we
will consider a song from you compensation for the damage done by the sheep (?).
**43. blast:** blowing, strain.   **minikin:** dainty.   **45. Purr the cat:** A devil in Harsnett; witches' familiars often took the form of cats.   **52. join-stool:** joint-stool,
stool expertly made by a joiner. The Fool's words are a jocular formula of apology
for overlooking the presence of a person.   **54. store:** material.   **an:** on (= of)

Arms, arms, sword, fire! Corruption in the place! 55
False justicer, why hast thou let her scape?]
EDGAR  Bless thy five wits!
KENT  O pity! Sir, where is the patience now
That you so oft have boasted to retain?
EDGAR  [*Aside.*] My tears begin to take his part so much, 60
They mar my counterfeiting.
LEAR  The little dogs and all,
Trey, Blanch, and Sweetheart, see, they bark at me.
EDGAR  Tom will throw his head at them. Avaunt,
EDGAR  Tom will throw his head at them. Avaunt, you curs! 65
Be thy mouth or black or white,
Tooth that poisons if it bite;
Mastiff, greyhound, mongril grim,
Hound or spaniel, brach or [lym],
Or bobtail [tike] or trundle-tail, 70
Tom will make him weep and wail,
For with throwing thus my head,
Dogs leapt the hatch, and all are fled.
Do de, de, de. Sessa! Come, march to wakes and fairs
and market towns. Poor Tom, thy horn is dry. 75
LEAR  Then let them anatomize Regan; see what
breeds about her heart. Is there any cause in nature
that make these hard hearts? [*To Edgar.*] You, sir, I
entertain for one of my hundred; only I do not like the
fashion of your garments. You will say they are 80
Persian, but let them be chang'd.
KENT  Now, good my lord, lie here and rest awhile.
LEAR  Make no noise, make no noise, draw the
curtains. So, so; we'll go to supper i' th' morning.
FOOL  And I'll go to bed at noon. 85

**55. Corruption . . . place:** bribery in the court.  **64. throw . . . them:** stare them down (?).  **68. mongril:** mongrel.  **69. lym:** bloodhound.  **70. bobtail tike:** short-tailed cur. **trundle-tail:** long-tailed dog.  **73. hatch:** lower half of a divided or "Dutch" door.  **74. wakes:** parish merrymakings.  **75. thy . . . dry:** Beggars carried animal horns to hold drink given as alms. Edgar is repeating a begging formula; perhaps he is also implying that he cannot maintain his impersonation much longer.  **76. anatomize:** dissect.  **79. entertain:** engage.  **80–81. You . . . Persian:** you will tell me that they are the fashion in Persia (where dress was reputed to be elaborate). Perhaps there is an echo of Horace's famous line, *Odes,* 1.38: *Persicos odi, puer, apparatus* (My boy, I detest Persian pomp).  **84. curtains:** bed-curtains. Lear supposes he is in his usual bed.

*Enter* GLOUCESTER.

GLOUCESTER Come hither, friend; where is the King my master?
KENT Here, sir, but trouble him not—his wits are gone.
GLOUCESTER Good friend, I prithee take him in thy arms;
I have o'erheard a plot of death upon him.
There is a litter ready, lay him in't,                                    90
And drive toward Dover, friend, where thou shalt meet
Both welcome and protection. Take up thy master;
If thou shouldst dally half an hour, his life,
With thine and all that offer to defend him,
Stand in assured loss. Take up, take up,                              95
And follow me, that will to some provision
Give thee quick conduct.
[KENT                                       Oppressed nature sleeps.
This rest might yet have balm'd thy broken sinews,
Which, if convenience will not allow,
Stand in hard cure. [*To the Fool.*] Come help to bear thy master;  100
Thou must not stay behind.]
[GLOUCESTER]                            Come, come, away.
                                                    *Exeunt [all but Edgar].*
[EDGAR When we our betters see bearing our woes,
We scarcely think our miseries our foes.
Who alone suffers, suffers most i' th' mind,
Leaving free things and happy shows behind,                          105
But then the mind much sufferance doth o'erskip,
When grief hath mates, and bearing fellowship.
How light and portable my pain seems now,
When that which makes me bend makes the King bow:
He childed as I fathered! Tom, away!                                  110
Mark the high noises, and thyself bewray
When false opinion, whose wrong thoughts defile thee,
In thy just proof repeals and reconciles thee.
What will hap more to-night, safe scape the King!
Lurk, lurk.]                                           [*Exit.*] 115

---

**85. I'll . . . noon:** i.e. I'll play the fool (proverbial).   **89. upon:** against.
**95. Stand . . . loss:** will certainly be lost.   **98. balm'd:** soothed, healed.   **sinews:**
nerves (serving the brain).   **100. Stand . . . cure:** will be hard to cure.   **102. bearing
our woes:** suffering woes like ours.   **103. We . . . foes:** i.e. we almost forget our own
misery.   **104. suffers . . . mind:** has the greatest mental suffering.   **105. free:** care-
free.   **107. bearing fellowship:** suffering (has) company.   **111. high noises:** rumors
of great events.   **bewray:** disclose.   **113. In . . . proof:** upon your being proved
guiltless.   **repeals:** recalls.   **reconciles thee:** restores you to favor.   **114. What:**
whatever.   **3.7. Location: Gloucester's castle.**

## SCENE 7

*Enter* CORNWALL, REGAN, GONERIL, *Bastard*
[EDMUND], *and* SERVANTS.

CORNWALL [*To Goneril.*] Post speedily to my lord your
husband, show him this letter. The army of France is
landed.—Seek out the traitor Gloucester.
[*Exeunt some of the Servants.*]

REGAN Hang him instantly.

GONERIL Pluck out his eyes.                                         5

CORN Leave him to my displeasure. Edmund, keep
you our sister company; the revenges we are bound to
take upon your traitorous father are not fit for your
beholding. Advise the Duke, where you are going, to a
most [festinate] preparation; we are bound to the         10
like. Our posts shall be swift and intelligent betwixt
us. Farewell, dear sister, farewell, my Lord of
Gloucester.

*Enter Steward* [OSWALD].

How now? where's the King?

OSWALD My Lord of Gloucester hath convey'd him hence.  15
Some five or six and thirty of his knights,
Hot questrists after him, met him at gate,
Who, with some other of the lord's dependants,
Are gone with him toward Dover, where they boast
To have well-armed friends.

CORNWALL                     Get horses for your mistress.       20

GONERIL Farewell, sweet lord, and sister.

CORN Edmund, farewell.
*Exeunt* [*Goneril, Edmund, and Oswald*].
Go seek the traitor Gloucester,
Pinion him like a thief, bring him before us.
[*Exeunt other Servants.*]
Though well we may not pass upon his life
Without the form of justice, yet our power              25
Shall do a court'sy to our wrath, which men
May blame, but not control.

---

**7. bound:** required.   **10. festinate:** speedy. **are bound to:** intend (?) or are committed to (?).   **11. be . . . intelligent:** carry information swiftly.   **17. questrists:**
seekers.   **24. pass . . . life:** sentence him to death.   **26. do a court'sy:** be indul-
gent, make a concession.   **29. corky:** withered.

*Enter* GLOUCESTER *[brought in by two or three]* SERVANTS.

                Who's there?   The traitor?

REGAN  Ingrateful fox, 'tis he.

CORNWALL  Bind fast his corky arms.

GLOUCESTER  What means your Graces? Good my
    friends, consider                            30
  You are my guests. Do me no foul play, friends.

CORNWALL  Bind him, I say.        *[Servants bind him.]*

REGAN              Hard, hard. O filthy traitor!

GLOUCESTER  Unmerciful lady as you are, I'm none.

CORNWALL  To this chair bind him. Villain, thou shalt
    find—                   *Regan plucks his beard.]*

GLOUCESTER  By the kind gods, 'tis most ignobly done     35
  To pluck me by the beard.

REGAN           So white, and such a traitor?

GLOUCESTER           Naughty lady,
  These hairs which thou dost ravish from my chin
  Will quicken and accuse thee. I am your host,
  With robber's hands my hospitable favors        40
  You should not ruffle thus. What will you do?

CORNWALL  Come, sir, what letters had you late from France?

REGAN  Be simple-answer'd, for we know the truth.

CORNWALL  And what confederacy have you with the traitors
  Late footed in the kingdom?                  45

REGAN  To whose hands you have sent the lunatic King—
  Speak.

GLOUCESTER     I have a letter guessingly set down,
  Which came from one that's of a neutral heart,
  And not from one oppos'd.

CORNWALL            Cunning.

REGAN               And false.

CORNWALL  Where hast thou sent the King?         50

GLOUCESTER  To Dover.

REGAN  Wherefore to Dover? Wast thou not charg'd at peril—

CORNWALL  Wherefore to Dover? Let him answer that.

GLOUCESTER  I am tied to th' stake, and I must stand the course.

---

**34.** s.d. **plucks his beard.** An act of extreme contempt.   **37. Naughty:** wicked.
**39. quicken:** assume life.   **40. hospitable favors:** features of your host.   **41. ruffle:**
snatch at roughly.   **42. late:** lately.   **43. Be simple-answer'd:** give straightforward
answers.   **54. course:** attack of the dogs (figure from bear-baiting).   **58. anointed:**
consecrated with holy oil (as king).   **rash:** strike violently, as a boar with its tusks.
**60. buoy'd:** risen up.   **61. stelled fires:** fires of the stars.   **62. holp:** helped.

REGAN  Wherefore to Dover?                                           55
GLOUCESTER  Because I would not see thy cruel nails
  Pluck out his poor old eyes, nor thy fierce sister
  In his anointed flesh [rash] boarish fangs.
  The sea, with such a storm as his bare head
  In hell-black night endur'd, would have buoy'd up          60
  And quench'd the stelled fires;
  Yet, poor old heart, he holp the heavens to rain.
  If wolves had at thy gate howl'd that [dearn] time,
  Thou shouldst have said, "Good porter, turn the key."
  All cruels else subscribe; but I shall see                  65
  The winged vengeance overtake such children.
CORNWALL  See't shalt thou never. Fellows, hold the chair,
  Upon these eyes of thine I'll set my foot.
GLOUCESTER  He that will think to live till he be old,
  Give me some help! O cruel! O you gods!                      70
REGAN  One side will mock another; th' other too.
CORNWALL  If you see vengeance—
[1.] SERVANT                      Hold your hand, my lord!
  I have serv'd you ever since I was a child;
  But better service have I never done you
  Than now to bid you hold.
REGAN                        How now, you dog?                        75
[1.] SERVANT  If you did wear a beard upon your chin,
  I'ld shake it on this quarrel. What do you mean?
CORNWALL  My villain!                         [Draw and fight.]
[1.] SERVANT  Nay then come on, and take the chance of anger.
                                          [Cornwall is wounded.]
REGAN  Give me thy sword. A peasant stand up thus?                    80
  [She takes a sword and runs at him behind; kills him.
[1.] SERVANT  O, I am slain! My lord, you have one eye left
  To see some mischief on him. O!                   [He dies.]
CORNWALL  Lest it see more, prevent it. Out, vild jelly!
  Where is thy lustre now?
GLOUCESTER  All dark and comfortless! Where's my son Edmund?         85

---

**63. dearn:** dire, dread.  **64. turn the key:** i.e. open the door and let them in.
**65. All . . . subscribe:** all other cruel beings would yield thus to pity (though
you do not).  **66. winged:** (1) swooping down from heaven; (2) swift.  **69. will
think:** hopes.  **77. on this quarrel:** in this cause. **What . . . mean:** how dare you.
Many editors give this sentence to Regan.  **78. villain:** serf.  **82. mischief:** injury.
**86. nature:** filial feeling.  **87. quit:** requite.  **Out:** an exclamation of anger.
**89. overture:** disclosure.  **91. abus'd:** wronged.

Edmund, enkindle all the sparks of nature,
To quit this horrid act.
REGAN                              Out, treacherous villain!
Thou call'st on him that hates thee. It was he
That made the overture of thy treasons to us,
Who is too good to pity thee.                                    90
GLOUCESTER O my follies! then Edgar was abus'd.
Kind gods, forgive me that, and prosper him!
REGAN Go thrust him out at gates, and let him smell
His way to Dover.                         *Exit [one] with Gloucester.*
How is't, my lord? How look you?
CORNWALL I have receiv'd a hurt; follow me, lady.—              95
Turn out that eyeless villain; throw this slave
Upon the dunghill. Regan, I bleed apace,
Untimely comes this hurt. Give me your arm.
                                              *Exit [led by Regan].*
[[2.] SERVANT I'll never care what wickedness I do,
If this man come to good.
[3.] SERVANT                         If she live long,          100
And in the end meet the old course of death,
Women will all turn monsters.
[2.] SERVANT Let's follow the old Earl, and get the Bedlam
To lead him where he would; his roguish madness
Allows itself to any thing.                                    105
[3.] SERVANT Go thou. I'll fetch some flax and whites of eggs
To apply to his bleeding face. Now heaven help him!
                                              *Exeunt [severally].]*

---

**94. How look you:** how is it with you.   **101. old:** usual, natural.   **102. Women ...
monsters:** Because they will not fear divine punishment for crimes.   **104–5. his ...
thing:** the fact that he is a madman and a vagabond allows him to do anything
with impunity.

# Act 4

## SCENE I

*Enter* EDGAR.

EDGAR  Yet better thus, and known to be contemn'd,
Than still contemn'd and flatter'd. To be worst,
The lowest and most dejected thing of fortune,
Stands still in esperance, lives not in fear.
The lamentable change is from the best,                                    5
The worst returns to laughter. Welcome then,
Thou unsubstantial air that I embrace:
The wretch that thou hast blown unto the worst
Owes nothing to thy blasts.

        *Enter* GLOUCESTER *[led by]* an OLD MAN.

                  But who comes here?
My father, [parti-ey'd]? World, world, O world!                           10
But that thy strange mutations make us hate thee,
Life would not yield to age.
OLD MAN                        O my good lord,
I have been your tenant, and your father's tenant,
These fourscore years.
GLOUCESTER  Away, get thee away! Good friend, be gone,                    15
Thy comforts can do me no good at all;
Thee they may hurt.
OLD MAN                        You cannot see your way.
GLOUCESTER  I have no way, and therefore want no eyes;
I stumbled when I saw. Full oft 'tis seen,

---

4.1. Location: **The heath.**  **1. known . . . contemn'd:** to know that one is despised.  **3. most . . . fortune:** thing most cast down by fortune.  **4. Stands . . . esperance:** can always hope.  **6. The worst . . . laughter:** i.e. any change from the worst must be for the better.  **9. Owes nothing:** cannot be called on to pay anything more.  **10. parti-ey'd:** with his eyes "motley" or parti-colored, i.e. bleeding. (On this reading see the Textual Notes. Most editors read *poorly led*.)  **11–12. But . . . age:** if the strange changes of fortune didn't make us hate life, we should never be reconciled to old age and death.  **16. comforts:** attempts to help me.

Our means secure us, and our mere defects                              20
Prove our commodities. O dear son Edgar,
The food of thy abused father's wrath!
Might I but live to see thee in my touch,
I'ld say I had eyes again.
OLD MAN                          How now? who's there?
EDGAR [*Aside.*] O gods! Who is't can say, "I am at the worst"?        25
I am worse than e'er I was.
OLD MAN                              'Tis poor mad Tom.
EDGAR [*Aside.*] And worse I may be yet: the worst is not
So long as we can say, "This is the worst."
OLD MAN Fellow, where goest?
GLOUCESTER                          Is it a beggar-man?
OLD MAN Madman and beggar too.                                         30
GLOUCESTER He has some reason, else he could not beg.
I' th' last night's storm I such a fellow saw,
Which made me think a man a worm. My son
Came then into my mind, and yet my mind
Was then scarce friends with him. I have heard more since.            35
As flies to wanton boys are we to th' gods,
They kill us for their sport.
EDGAR                          [*Aside.*] How should this be?
Bad is the trade that must play fool to sorrow,
Ang'ring itself and others.—Bless thee, master!
GLOUCESTER Is that the naked fellow?
OLD MAN                          Ay, my lord.                          40
GLOUCESTER [Then prithee] get thee away. If for my sake
Thou wilt o'ertake us hence a mile or twain
I' th' way toward Dover, do it for ancient love,
And bring some covering for this naked soul,
Which I'll entreat to lead me.
OLD MAN                          Alack, sir, he is mad.               45
GLOUCESTER 'Tis the time's plague, when madmen lead the blind.
Do as I bid thee, or rather do thy pleasure;
Above the rest, be gone.
OLD MAN I'll bring him the best 'parel that I have,
Come on't what will.                               *Exit.* 50
GLOUCESTER Sirrah, naked fellow—
EDGAR Poor Tom's a-cold. [*Aside.*] I cannot daub it further.

**20. Our . . . us:** prosperity makes us careless.  **20–21. our . . . commodities:**
our utter disadvantages prove benefits.  **22. food of:** object fed upon by. **abused:**
deceived.  **23. in:** by means of.  **36. wanton:** playful.  **39. Ang'ring:** distressing.
**52. daub it further:** continue this dissembling.

GLOUCESTER Come hither, fellow.
EDGAR [*Aside.*] And yet I must.—Bless thy sweet eyes, they bleed.
GLOUCESTER Know'st thou the way to Dover?                                55
EDGAR Both stile and gate, horse-way and foot-path
Poor Tom hath been scar'd out of his good wits. Bless
thee, good man's son, from the foul fiend! [Five fiends
have been in poor Tom at once: of lust, as Obidicut;
Hobbididence, prince of dumbness; Mahu, of               60
stealing; Modo, of murder; Flibbertigibbet, of [mop-
ping] and mowing, who since possesses chambermaids
and waiting-women. So, bless thee, master!]
GLOUCESTER Here, take this purse, thou whom the heav'ns' plagues
Have humbled to all strokes. That I am wretched       65
Makes thee the happier; heavens, deal so still!
Let the superfluous and lust-dieted man,
That slaves your ordinance, that will not see
Because he does not feel, feel your pow'r quickly;
So distribution should undo excess,                           70
And each man have enough. Dost thou know Dover?
EDGAR Ay, master.
GLOUCESTER There is a cliff, whose high and bending head
Looks fearfully in the confined deep.
Bring me but to the very brim of it,                           75
And I'll repair the misery thou dost bear
With something rich about me.   From that place
I shall no leading need.
EDGAR Give me thy arm;
Poor Tom shall lead thee.                          *Exeunt.*


SCENE 2

*Enter* GONERIL, *Bastard* [EDMUND].

GONERIL Welcome, my lord. I marvel our mild husband
Not met us on the way.

59–61. Obidicut . . . Flibbertigibbet: The names of the five devils are derived,
sometimes with changed spelling, from Harsnett. 61–62. mopping and mowing: making faces, 66. happier: i.e. less wretched. 67. superfluous: having
too much. lust-dieted: having provision for indulging his appetites. 68. slaves
your ordinance: makes your law subservient to his own desires. 73. bending:
overhanging. 74. the confined deep: the sea held in on both sides (probably the
Straits of Dover). 4.2. Location: Before Albany's palace.

[*Enter* OSWALD, *the Steward.*]

            Now, where's your master?
OSWALD  Madam, within, but never man so chang'd.
I told him of the army that was landed;
He smil'd at it. I told him you were coming;      5
His answer was, "The worse." Of Gloucester's treachery,
And of the loyal service of his son,
When I inform'd him, then he call'd me sot,
And told me I had turn'd the wrong side out.
What most he should dislike seems pleasant to him;   10
What like, offensive.
GONERIL        [*To Edmund.*] Then shall you go no further.
It is the cowish terror of his spirit
That dares not undertake; he'll not feel wrongs
Which tie him to an answer. Our wishes on the way
May prove effects. Back, Edmund, to my brother,   15
Hasten his musters and conduct his pow'rs.
I must change names at home, and give the distaff
Into my husband's hands. This trusty servant
Shall pass between us. Ere long you are like to hear
(If you dare venture in your own behalf)   20
A mistress's command. Wear this; spare speech.
Decline your head: this kiss, if it durst speak,
Would stretch thy spirits up into the air.
Conceive, and fare thee well.
EDMUND  Yours in the ranks of death.        *Exit.*
GONERIL           My most dear Gloucester!  25
O, the difference of man and man!
To thee a woman's services are due,
[A] fool usurps my [bed].
OSWALD         Madam, here comes my lord.  [*Exit.*]

        *Enter* ALBANY.

GONERIL  I have been worth the [whistling].

---

**8. sot:** fool.  **9. turn'd . . . out:** reversed things (since the loyal service was Gloucester's and the treachery Edmund's).  **12. cowish:** cowardly.  **13–14. he'll . . . answer:** he'll ignore such insults as require in honor to be answered.  **15. prove effects:** be realized.  **16. musters:** assembling of forces.  **17. change names:** exchange names, i.e. assume the responsibilities that should be my husband's and hand over my wifely duties to him.  **22. Decline your head:** i.e. for a kiss.  **24. Conceive:** (1) take my meaning; (2) let the seed I have planted in your mind quicken and bear fruit.  **29. I . . . whistling:** i.e. there was a time when you would have thought me worth the trouble of coming to meet me (alluding to the proverb "It is a poor dog that is not worth the whistling").

ALBANY                       O Goneril,
You are not worth the dust which the rude wind      30
Blows in your face. [I fear your disposition;
That nature which contemns it origin
Cannot be bordered certain in itself.
She that herself will sliver and disbranch
From her material sap, perforce must wither,      35
And come to deadly use.
GONERIL    No more, the text is foolish.
ALBANY Wisdom and goodness to the vild seem vild,
Filths savor but themselves. What have you done?
Tigers, not daughters, what have you perform'd?    40
A father, and a gracious aged man,
Whose reverence even the head-lugg'd bear would lick,
Most barbarous, most degenerate, have you madded.
Could my good brother suffer you to do it?
A man, a prince, by him so benefited!      45
If that the heavens do not their visible spirits
Send quickly down to tame [these] vild offenses,
It will come,
Humanity must perforce prey on itself,
Like monsters of the deep.]
GONERIL                Milk-liver'd man,    50
That bear'st a cheek for blows, a head for wrongs,
Who hast not in thy brows an eye discerning
Thine honor from thy suffering, [that not know'st
Fools do those villains pity who are punish'd
Ere they have done their mischief, where's thy drum?    55
France spreads his banners in our noiseless land,
With plumed helm thy state begins [to threat],
Whilst thou, a moral fool, sits still and cries,
"Alack, why does he so?"]
ALBANY              See thyself, devil!

---

**31. fear your disposition:** have fears concerning your nature. **32. it:** its. **33. bordered certain:** kept safely within bounds. **34. sliver and disbranch:** Both verbs mean "cut off." **35. material sap:** vital sustenance. **36. to deadly use:** to destruction (as branches are destroyed by use as firewood). **37. text:** She implies that he has been preaching a sermon. **39. Filths . . . themselves:** to the filthy everything seems filthy. **42. head-lugg'd:** dragged by the head. **46. visible:** in visible form. **50. Milk-liver'd:** white-livered, cowardly. **52–53. discerning . . . suffering:** able to distinguish what should be borne from what should be resented. **54. Fools:** i.e. only fools. **56. noiseless:** not yet aroused; without military preparation. **58. moral:** moralizing.

Proper deformity [shows] not in the fiend                    60
So horrid as in woman.
GONERIL                    O vain fool!
[ALBANY Thou changed and self-cover'd thing, for shame
Bemonster not thy feature. Were't my fitness
To let these hands obey my blood,
They are apt enough to dislocate and tear              65
Thy flesh and bones. Howe'er thou art a fiend,
A woman's shape doth shield thee.
GONERIL Marry, your manhood mew!]

*Enter a* MESSENGER.

[ALBANY What news?]
MESSENGER O my good lord, the Duke of Cornwall's dead,    70
Slain by his servant, going to put out
The other eye of Gloucester.
ALBANY                    Gloucester's eyes?
MESSENGER A servant that he bred, thrill'd with remorse,
Oppos'd against the act, bending his sword
To his great master, who, [thereat] enraged,          75
Flew on him, and amongst them fell'd him dead,
But not without that harmful stroke which since
Hath pluck'd him after.
ALBANY                    This shows you are above,
You [justicers], that these our nether crimes
So speedily can venge! But, O poor Gloucester,        80
Lost he his other eye?
MESSENGER                    Both, both, my lord.
This letter, madam, craves a speedy answer;
'Tis from your sister.
GONERIL [*Aside.*]          One way I like this well,
But being widow, and my Gloucester with her,
May all the building in my fancy pluck                85

---

**60–61. Proper . . . woman:** deformity can show itself more horribly in a woman than in the devil himself, because it is appropriate to him.   **62. changed:** transformed (into a monster). **self-cover'd:** whose true nature is concealed.   **63. feature:** (human) appearance. **my fitness:** suitable for me.   **64. blood:** impulse. **68. mew:** mew up, keep under restraint (a term from falconry). Many editors insert a comma or a dash after *manhood* and interpret *mew* as a derisive exclamation.   **73. thrill'd:** pierced. **remorse:** pity.   **74. bending:** directing. **75. To:** against.   **76. amongst them:** together with the others.   **79. nether:** i.e. committed on earth.   **85. all . . . pluck:** pull down all that I have constructed in my imagination.

Upon my hateful life. Another way,
The news is not so tart.—I'll read, and answer.        [*Exit.*]
ALBANY  Where was his son when they did take his eyes?
MESSENGER  Come with my lady hither.
ALBANY                                He is not here.
MESSENGER          No, my good lord, I met him back again.        90
ALBANY  Knows he the wickedness?
MESSENGER  Ay, my good lord; 'twas he inform'd against him,
    And quit the house on purpose that their punishment
    Might have the freer course.
ALBANY                                Gloucester, I live
    To thank thee for the love thou show'dst the King,        95
    And to revenge thine eyes. Come hither, friend,
    Tell me what more thou know'st.            *Exeunt.*


SCENE 3

*Enter* KENT *and a* GENTLEMAN.

KENT  Why the King of France is so suddenly gone
    back, know you no reason?
GENTLEMAN  Something he left imperfect in the state,
    which since his coming forth is thought of, which im-
    ports to the kingdom so much fear and danger that his        5
    personal return was most requir'd and necessary.
KENT  Who hath he left behind him general?
GENTLEMAN  The Marshal of France, Monsieur La Far.
KENT  Did your letters pierce the Queen to any
    demonstration of grief?        10
GENTLEMAN  Ay, [sir], she took them, read them in my presence,
    And now and then an ample tear trill'd down
    Her delicate cheek. It seem'd she was a queen
    Over her passion, who, most rebel-like,
    Sought to be king o'er her.
KENT                                O then it mov'd her.        15
GENTLEMAN  Not to a rage, patience and sorrow [strove]
    Who should express her goodliest. You have seen
    Sunshine and rain at once; her smiles and tears
    Were like a better way: those happy smilets

---

**86. my hateful life:** my life, which would then become hateful.   **90. back:** on
his way back.   4.3. Location: **The French camp near Dover.**   **12. trill'd:** trick-
led.   **19. like . . . way:** similar, but after a better fashion.

That play'd on her ripe lip [seem'd] not to know 20
What guests were in her eyes, which, parted thence,
As pearls from diamonds dropp'd. In brief,
Sorrow would be a rarity most beloved,
If all could so become it.

KENT                         Made she no verbal question?

GENTLEMAN  Faith, once or twice she heav'd the name of "father"  25
Pantingly forth, as if it press'd her heart;
Cried, "Sisters, sisters! Shame of ladies, sisters!
Kent! father! sisters! What, i' th' storm? i' th' night?
Let pity not be believ'd!"  There she shook
The holy water from her heavenly eyes,                    30
And, clamor-moistened, then away she started
To deal with grief alone.

KENT                         It is the stars,
The stars above us, govern our conditions,
Else one self mate and make could not beget
Such different issues. You spoke not with her since?       35

GENTLEMAN  No.

KENT  Was this before the King return'd?

GENTLEMAN                         No, since.

KENT  Well, sir, the poor distressed Lear's i' th' town,
Who sometime, in his better tune, remembers
What we are come about, and by no means                   40
Will yield to see his daughter.

GENTLEMAN                         Why, good sir?

KENT  A sovereign shame so elbows him: his own unkindness,
That stripp'd her from his benediction, turn'd her
To foreign casualties, gave her dear rights
To his dog-hearted daughters—these things sting           45
His mind so venomously, that burning shame
Detains him from Cordelia.

GENTLEMAN                         Alack, poor gentleman!

KENT  Of Albany's and Cornwall's powers you heard not?

GENTLEMAN  'Tis so, they are afoot.

KENT  Well, sir, I'll bring you to our master Lear,          50

---

**23. rarity:** precious thing.   **24. If . . . it:** if it were as becoming to all as it is to
her.   **verbal question:** comment in words.   **29. believ'd:** i.e. believed to exist.
**31. clamor-moistened:** "having her emotion calmed by a flood of tears, as the
storm is assuaged by a shower of rain" (Craig).   **33. conditions:** characters.
**34. one . . . make:** one and the same husband and wife.   **39. better tune:** saner
moments.   **41. yield:** consent.   **42. sovereign:** overruling.   **elbows:** pushes
away.   **44. foreign casualties:** chances in a foreign land.

And leave you to attend him. Some dear cause
Will in concealment wrap me up awhile;
When I am known aright, you shall not grieve
Lending me this acquaintance. I pray you go
Along with me.                                            *Exeunt.*] 55

SCENE [4]

*Enter, with Drum and Colors,* CORDELIA,
[DOCTOR], *and* SOLDIERS.

CORDELIA  Alack, 'tis he! Why, he was met even now
As mad as the vex'd sea, singing aloud,
Crown'd with rank [femiter] and furrow-weeds,
With hardocks, hemlock, nettles, cuckoo-flow'rs,
Darnel, and all the idle weeds that grow                          5
In our sustaining corn. A [century] send forth;
Search every acre in the high-grown field,
And bring him to our eye. [*Exit an Officer.*] What can man's wisdom
In the restoring his bereaved sense?
He that helps him take all my outward worth.                     10
[DOCTOR]  There is means, madam.
Our foster-nurse of nature is repose,
The which he lacks; that to provoke in him
Are many simples operative, whose power
Will close the eye of anguish.
CORDELIA                          All blest secrets,             15
All you unpublish'd virtues of the earth,
Spring with my tears; be aidant and remediate
In the good man's [distress]! Seek, seek for him,
Lest his ungovern'd rage dissolve the life
That wants the means to lead it.                                 20

*Enter* MESSENGER.

MESSENGER                          News, madam!
The British pow'rs are marching hitherward.

---

**51. dear cause:** important reason.  **53. grieve:** repent.  **4.4.** Location: **The French camp.**  **3. rank:** luxuriant. **femiter:** fumitory, an herb.  **4. hardocks:** burdocks, or harlock (wild mustard).  **5. Darnel:** a weedy grass. **6. sustaining corn:** life-supporting wheat. **A century:** a hundred soldiers. **8. can man's wisdom:** i.e. can medical knowledge accomplish.  **12. Our . . . nature:** the fostering nurse of our nature.  **14. simples:** medicinal herbs. **operative:** effective.  **16. unpublish'd:** not generally known. **virtues:** i.e. beneficial herbs.  **17. Spring:** grow (as her tears water them). **aidant:** helpful. **remediate:** healing.  **19. rage:** frenzy.  **20. wants:** lacks. **the means:** i.e. his reason.

CORDELIA 'Tis known before; our preparation stands
In expectation of them. O dear father,
It is thy business that I go about;
Therefore great France                                    25
My mourning and importun'd tears hath pitied.
No blown ambition doth our arms incite,
But love, dear love, and our ag'd father's right.
Soon may I hear and see him!                 *Exeunt.*

### SCENE [5]

*Enter* REGAN *and Steward* [OSWALD].

REGAN But are my brother's pow'rs set forth?
OSWALD                                    Ay, madam.
REGAN Himself in person there?
OSWALD                      Madam, with much ado;
Your sister is the better soldier.
REGAN Lord Edmund spake not with your lord at home?
OSWALD No, madam.                                        5
REGAN What might import my sister's letter to him?
OSWALD I know not, lady.
REGAN Faith, he is posted hence on serious matter.
It was great ignorance, Gloucester's eyes being out,
To let him live; where he arrives he moves             10
All hearts against us. Edmund, I think, is gone,
In pity of his misery, to dispatch
His nighted life; moreover to descry
The strength o' th' enemy.
OSWALD I must needs after him, madam, with my letter.  15
REGAN Our troops set forth to-morrow, stay with us;
The ways are dangerous.
OSWALD                   I may not, madam;
My lady charg'd my duty in this business.
REGAN Why should she write to Edmund? Might not you
Transport her purposes by word? Belike               20

---

**22. our preparation:** the troops we have ready. [**24.** Cordelia (ll. 23–24) alludes to Jesus's response to his anxious mother from whom he had been separated after a family Passover journey to Jerusalem. His parents found their 12 yr. old son in the temple discussing theology among the elders. The Geneva Bible (1560) reads: "knewe ye not that I must go about my father's business" (Luke 2.49; apostrophe added). ~ *Evans Editor*] **26. importun'd:** importunate. **27. blown:** puffed-up. **4.5.** Location: **Gloucester's castle. 2. with much ado:** after much persuasion. **9. ignorance:** folly. **18. charg'd my duty:** i.e. gave me strict orders to carry out my instructions.

Some things—I know not what. I'll love thee much—
Let me unseal the letter.
OSWALD                    Madam, I had rather—
REGAN   I know your lady does not love her husband,
I am sure of that; and at her late being here
She gave strange eliads and most speaking looks        25
To noble Edmund. I know you are of her bosom.
OSWALD   I, madam?
REGAN   I speak in understanding: y' are; I know't.
Therefore I do advise you take this note:
My lord is dead; Edmund and I have talk'd,         30
And more convenient is he for my hand
Than for your lady's. You may gather more.
If you do find him, pray you give him this;
And when your mistress hears thus much from you,
I pray desire her call her wisdom to her.            35
So fare you well.
If you do chance to hear of that blind traitor,
Preferment falls on him that cuts him off.
OSWALD   Would I could meet [him,] madam! I should show
What party I do follow.
REGAN                Fare thee well.           *Exeunt.* 40

## SCENE [6]

*Enter* GLOUCESTER *and* EDGAR [*dressed like a peasant*].

GLOUCESTER   When shall I come to th' top of that same hill?
EDGAR   You do climb up it now.   Look how we labor.
GLOUCESTER   Methinks the ground is even.
EDGAR                           Horrible steep.
Hark, do you hear the sea?
GLOUCESTER               No, truly.
EDGAR   Why then your other senses grow imperfect       5
By your eyes' anguish.
GLOUCESTER            So may it be indeed.
Methinks thy voice is alter'd, and thou speak'st
In better phrase and matter than thou didst.
EDGAR   Y' are much deceiv'd.   In nothing am I chang'd
But in my garments.

**21. love thee much:** i.e. make it worth your while.    **25. eliads:** oeillades, amorous glances.    **26. of her bosom:** in her confidence.    **29. take this note:** to take note of what I say.    **31. convenient:** fitting.    **32. gather more:** i.e. make your own inferences.    4.6. Location: **The country near Dover.**

| | | |
|---|---|---|
| GLOUCESTER | Methinks y' are better spoken. | 10 |

EDGAR Come on, sir, here's the place; stand still. How fearful
And dizzy 'tis, to cast one's eyes so low!
The crows and choughs that wing the midway air
Show scarce so gross as beetles. Half way down
Hangs one that gathers sampire, dreadful trade!     15
Methinks he seems no bigger than his head.
The fishermen that [walk] upon the beach
Appear like mice; and yond tall anchoring bark,
Diminish'd to her cock; her cock, a buoy
Almost too small for sight. The murmuring surge,     20
That on th' unnumb'red idle pebble chafes,
Cannot be heard so high. I'll look no more,
Lest my brain turn, and the deficient sight
Topple down headlong.

GLOUCESTER                 Set me where you stand.

EDGAR Give me your hand. You are now within a foot     25
Of th' extreme verge. For all beneath the moon
Would I not leap upright.

GLOUCESTER                 Let go my hand.
Here, friend, 's another purse; in it a jewel
Well worth a poor man's taking. Fairies and gods
Prosper it with thee! Go thou further off:     30
Bid me farewell, and let me hear thee going.

EDGAR Now fare ye well, good sir.

GLOUCESTER                 With all my heart.

EDGAR [*Aside.*] Why I do trifle thus with his despair
Is done to cure it.

GLOUCESTER       O you mighty gods!         [*He kneels.*]
This world I do renounce, and in your sights     35
Shake patiently my great affliction off.
If I could bear it longer, and not fall
To quarrel with your great opposeless wills,
My snuff and loathed part of nature should
Burn itself out. If Edgar live, O bless him!     40
Now, fellow, fare thee well.           [*He falls.*]

---

**13. choughs:** jackdaws.   **14. gross:** large.   **15. sampire:** samphire, an aromatic plant eaten pickled.   **19. cock:** cockboat, small ship's boat.   **23. the deficient sight:** i.e. I, my sight failing.   **29. Fairies.** Thought to guard and multiply hidden treasure.   **33. Why . . . trifle:** i.e. what I do, trifling.   **38. To quarrel with:** into rebellion against.   **opposeless:** not to be opposed (because opposition is both sinful and futile).   **39. My . . . nature:** the smouldering wick and hateful remnant of my life.

EDGAR                         Gone, sir; farewell!
And yet I know not how conceit may rob
The treasury of life, when life itself
Yields to the theft. Had he been where he thought,
By this had thought been past. Alive or dead?—                45
Ho, you, sir! friend! Hear you, sir! speak!—
Thus might he pass indeed; yet he revives.—
What are you, sir?
GLOUCESTER          Away, and let me die.
EDGAR  Hadst thou been aught but goss'mer, feathers, air
(So many fathom down precipitating),                          50
Thou'dst shiver'd like an egg: but thou dost breathe,
Hast heavy substance, bleed'st not, speak'st, art sound.
Ten masts at each make not the altitude
Which thou hast perpendicularly fell.
Thy life's a miracle. Speak yet again.                        55
GLOUCESTER  But have I fall'n, or no?
EDGAR  From the dread summit of this chalky bourn.
Look up a-height, the shrill-gorg'd lark so far
Cannot be seen or heard. Do but look up.
GLOUCESTER  Alack, I have no eyes.                            60
Is wretchedness depriv'd that benefit,
To end itself by death? 'Twas yet some comfort,
When misery could beguile the tyrant's rage,
And frustrate his proud will.
EDGAR                         Give me your arm.
Up—so. How is't? Feel you your legs? You stand.              65
GLOUCESTER  Too well, too well.
EDGAR                    This is above all strangeness.
Upon the crown o' th' cliff, what thing was that
Which parted from you?
GLOUCESTER          A poor unfortunate beggar.
EDGAR  As I stood here below, methought his eyes
Were two full moons; he had a thousand noses,               70
Horns welk'd and waved like the [enridged] sea.
It was some fiend; therefore, thou happy father,

---

42. **conceit:** imagination.  44. **Yields:** consents.  47. **pass:** die.  49. **goss'mer:**
gossamer, floating thread spun by a spider.  53. **at each:** end to end.  57. **chalky**
**bourn:** i.e. chalk cliff bounding the sea.  58. **a-height:** on high.  **shrill-gorg'd:**
shrill-throated.  63. **beguile:** cheat.  71. **welk'd:** convoluted.  **enridged:** furrowed.  72. **happy father:** fortunate old man. Edgar's use of *father* here and later
does not betray his identity.

Think that the clearest gods, who make them honors
Of men's impossibilities, have preserved thee.
GLOUCESTER I do remember now. Henceforth I'll bear          75
Affliction till it do cry out itself
"Enough, enough," and die. That thing you speak of,
I took it for a man; often 'twould say,
"The fiend, the fiend!"—he led me to that place.
EDGAR Bear free and patient thoughts.

*Enter* LEAR [*mad, crowned with weeds and flowers*].

                         But who comes here?          80
The safer sense will ne'er accommodate
His master thus.
LEAR No, they cannot touch me for [coining,] I am
the King himself.
EDGAR O thou side-piercing sight!          85
LEAR Nature's above art in that respect. There's
your press-money. That fellow handles his bow like a
crow-keeper; draw me a clothier's yard. Look, look,
a mouse! Peace, peace, this piece of toasted cheese will
do't. There's my gauntlet, I'll prove it on a giant.          90
Bring up the brown bills. O, well flown, bird! i' th'
clout, i' th' clout—hewgh! Give the word.
EDGAR Sweet marjorum.
LEAR Pass.
GLOUCESTER I know that voice.          95
LEAR Ha! Goneril with a white beard? They
flatter'd me like a dog, and told me I had the white
hairs in my beard ere the black ones were there. To
say "ay" and "no" to every thing that I said! "Ay,"
and "no" too, was no good divinity. When the          100
rain came to wet me once, and the wind to make me

---

**73–74. who . . . impossibilities:** who acquire our reverence by doing deeds impossible
to men. **80. free:** serene. [See "Textual Notes" for s.d. 4.6.80.~ *Evans Editor*] **81. The
safer sense:** a sane mind. **86. Nature's . . . respect:** "a king who coins by divine
right standing for Nature and a forger for Art" (Dover Wilson). **87. press-money:**
money paid to a conscript. **88. crow-keeper:** boy hired to drive crows away. **me:**
for me. **clothier's yard:** arrow a cloth-yard long. **90. There's my gauntlet:** He
issues a challenge. **prove it on:** maintain my cause against. **91. brown bills:** men
carrying pikes painted brown to prevent rusting. **bird:** i.e. arrow. **92. clout:** centre of target. **hewgh.** He imitates the sound of an arrow in flight. **word:** password. **93. Sweet marjorum:** Offered as password. The herb marjoram was used to
treat mental disease. **97. like a dog:** i.e. fawningly. **97–98. had . . . beard:** i.e. had
wisdom. **99. say . . . said:** i.e. contradict me in nothing. **100. no good divinity:**
bad theology. James 5.12 says, ". . . let your yea be yea; and your nay, nay."

chatter, when the thunder would not peace at my
bidding, there I found 'em, there I smelt 'em out. Go
to, they are not men o' their words: they told me I was
every thing. 'Tis a lie, I am not ague-proof.                    105
GLOUCESTER  The trick of that voice I do well remember;
Is't not the King?
LEAR                    Ay, every inch a king!
When I do stare, see how the subject quakes.
I pardon that man's life. What was thy cause?
Adultery?                                                        110
Thou shalt not die. Die for adultery? No,
The wren goes to't, and the small gilded fly
Does lecher in my sight.
Let copulation thrive; for Gloucester's bastard son
Was kinder to his father than my daughters              115
Got 'tween the lawful sheets.
To't, luxury, pell-mell, for I lack soldiers.
Behold yond simp'ring dame,
Whose face between her forks presages snow;
That minces virtue, and does shake the head             120
To hear of pleasure's name—
The fitchew nor the soiled horse goes to't
With a more riotous appetite.
Down from the waist they are Centaurs,
Though women all above;                                     125
But to the girdle do the gods inherit,
Beneath is all the fiends': there's hell, there's darkness,
There is the sulphurous pit, burning, scalding,
Stench, consumption. Fie, fie, fie! pah, pah!
Give me an ounce of civet; good apothecary,              130
Sweeten my imagination. There's money for thee.
GLOUCESTER  O, let me kiss that hand!
LEAR  Let me wipe it first, it smells of mortality.
GLOUCESTER  O ruin'd piece of nature! This great world
Shall so wear out to nought. Dost thou know me?          135

---

**103. found 'em:** found them out.  **106. trick:** characteristic quality.  **108. the
subject:** my subjects.  **109. cause:** offense.  **117. luxury:** lust.  **pell-mell:** pro-
miscuously.  **119. Whose . . . snow:** who seems icily chaste.  **forks:** legs (*between
her forks* modifies *snow*).  **120. minces:** coyly affects.  **121. pleasure's name:** the
very name of sexual pleasure.  **122. The fitchew:** (neither) the polecat.  **soiled:**
high-spirited from feeding on fresh grass in spring.  **124. Centaurs:** i.e. beasts (like
the horse of line 122).  **126. inherit:** possess.  **127. hell:** Traditional slang for the
female genitals.  **130. civet:** perfume.  **134. piece:** masterpiece, i.e. man; the little
world.  **135. so:** in the same way.

LEAR I remember thine eyes well enough. Dost thou
squiny at me? No, do thy worst, blind Cupid, I'll not love.
Read thou this challenge; mark but the penning of it.
GLOUCESTER Were all thy letters suns, I could not see.          140
EDGAR [Aside.] I would not take this from report; it is,
And my heart breaks at it.
LEAR Read.
GLOUCESTER What, with the case of eyes?
LEAR O ho, are you there with me? No eyes in          145
your head, nor no money in your purse? Your eyes are
in a heavy case, your purse in a light, yet you see how
this world goes.
GLOUCSTER I see it feelingly.
LEAR What, art mad? A man may see how this          150
world goes with no eyes. Look with thine ears; see
how yond justice rails upon yond simple thief. Hark
in thine ear: change places, and handy-dandy, which is
the justice, which is the thief? Thou hast seen a
farmer's dog bark at a beggar?          155
GLOUCESTER Ay, sir.
LEAR And the creature run from the cur? There
thou mightst behold the great image of authority: a
dog's obey'd in office.
Thou rascal beadle, hold thy bloody hand!          160
Why dost thou lash that whore? Strip thy own back,
Thou hotly lusts to use her in that kind
For which thou whip'st her. The usurer hangs the cozener.
Thorough tatter'd clothes [small] vices do appear;
Robes and furr'd gowns hide all. [Plate sin] with gold,          165
And the strong lance of justice hurtless breaks;
Arm it in rags, a pigmy's straw does pierce it.
None does offend, none, I say none, I'll able 'em.
Take that of me, my friend, who have the power
To seal th' accuser's lips. Get thee glass eyes,          170

---

**137. squiny:** squint. **blind.** As Cupid traditionally was; hence he was sometimes used as a brothel-sign. **141. take:** believe. **144. case:** sockets. **145. are . . . me:** is that the way things are. **147. heavy case:** sad condition. **149. feelingly:** (1) by means of my sense of touch; (2) with keen emotion. **153. handy-dandy:** i.e. take your choice. **157. creature:** human being. **160. beadle:** parish officer who administered corporal punishment. **162. kind:** way. **163. The usurer . . . cozener:** the justice guilty of usury sentences the petty cheat to be hanged. **165. Plate . . . gold:** clothe sin in gold armor. **166. hurtless:** without doing any harm. **168. able 'em:** authorize them, i.e. exempt everyone from legal guilt.

And like a scurvy politician, seem
To see the things thou dost not. Now, now, now, now.
Pull off my boots; harder, harder—so.
EDGAR [*Aside.*] O, matter and impertinency mix'd,
Reason in madness!                                        175
LEAR If thou wilt weep my fortunes, take my eyes.
I know thee well enough, thy name is Gloucester.
Thou must be patient; we came crying hither.
Thou know'st, the first time that we smell the air
We wawl and cry. I will preach to thee. Mark.           180
                    [*Lear takes off his crown of weeds and flowers.*]
GLOUCESTER Alack, alack the day!
LEAR When we are born, we cry that we are come
To this great stage of fools.—This' a good block.
It were a delicate stratagem, to shoe
A troop of horse with felt. I'll put't in proof,       185
And when I have stol'n upon these son-in-laws,
Then kill, kill, kill, kill, kill, kill!

                    *Enter a* GENTLEMAN [*with* ATTENDANTS].

GENTLEMAN O, here he is: lay hand upon him.—Sir,
Your most dear daughter—
LEAR No rescue? What, a prisoner? I am even             190
The natural fool of fortune. Use me well,
You shall have ransom. Let me have surgeons,
I am cut to th' brains.
GENTLEMAN                    You shall have any thing.
LEAR No seconds? All myself?
Why, this would make a man a man of salt                195
To use his eyes for garden water-pots,
[Ay, and laying autumn's dust.
GENTLEMAN                    Good sir—]
LEAR I will die bravely, like a smug bridegroom.
        What?
I will be jovial. Come, come, I am a king,
Masters, know you that?                                 200
GENTLEMAN You are a royal one, and we obey you.

---

**171. scurvy:** vile. **politician:** trickster. **174. impertinency:** irrelevance, inco-
herence. **183. This':** this is. **block:** style of hat (here the weeds and flowers from
his hair—which he has taken off to preach his sermon). **185. in proof:** to the
test. **191. natural:** born. **fool:** plaything. **194. seconds:** supporters. **195. salt:**
tears. **198. smug:** trimly dressed. The simile of the "smug bridegroom." arises
from quibbles on the sexual sense of *die* and on *bravely* in the sense "finely attired."

LEAR  Then there's life in't. Come, and you get it,
  you shall get it by running. Sa, sa, sa, sa.
                    *Exit [running; Attendants follow].*
GENTLEMAN  A sight most pitiful in the meanest wretch,
  Past speaking of in a king! Thou hast [one] daughter          205
  Who redeems nature from the general curse
  Which twain have brought her to.
EDGAR  Hail, gentle sir.
GENTLEMAN  Sir, speed you: what's your will?
EDGAR  Do you hear aught, sir, of a battle toward?
GENTLEMAN  Most sure and vulgar; every one hears that,
  Which can distinguish sound.                                  210
EDGAR                          But by your favor,
  How near's the other army?
GENTLMAN  Near and on speedy foot; the main descry
  Stands on the hourly thought.
EDGAR                          I thank you, sir, that's all.
GENTLEMAN  Though that the Queen on special cause is here,     215
  Her army is mov'd on.
EDGAR            I thank you, sir.        *Exit [Gentleman].*
GLOUCESTER  You ever-gentle gods, take my breath from me,
  Let not my worser spirit tempt me again
  To die before you please!
EDGAR                      Well pray you, father.
GLOUCESTER  Now, good sir, what are you?                        220
EDGAR  A most poor man, made tame to fortune's blows,
  Who, by the art of known and feeling sorrows,
  Am pregnant to good pity. Give me your hand,
  I'll lead you to some biding.
GLOUCESTER                    Hearty thanks;
  The bounty and the benison of heaven                          225
  To boot, and boot!
              *Enter Steward [OSWALD].*
OSWALD              A proclaim'd prize! Most happy!
  That eyeless head of thine was first fram'd flesh

---

202. **there's life in't:** the situation isn't hopeless. **and:** if. **203. Sa . . . sa:** A hunting cry. **206. general:** universal. **208. gentle:** noble. **209. toward:** imminent. **210. vulgar:** of common knowledge. **213–14. the main . . . thought:** any hour now we expect to catch sight of the main body. **215. on special cause:** for special reason. **218. worser spirit:** evil angel. **221. tame:** submissive. **222. by . . . sorrows:** i.e. by virtue of the heartfelt sorrows I have experienced. **223. pregnant:** readily disposed. **224. biding:** lodging. **226. To boot:** in addition. **A proclaim'd prize:** i.e. a man with a price on his head.

To raise my fortunes. Thou old unhappy traitor,
Briefly thyself remember; the sword is out
That must destroy thee.
GLOUCESTER          Now let thy friendly hand
Put strength enough to't.                    [*Edgar interposes.*] 230
OSWALD          Wherefore, bold peasant,
[Durst] thou support a publish'd traitor? Hence,
Lest that th' infection of his fortune take
Like hold on thee. Let go his arm.
EDGAR  Chill not let go, zir, without vurther [cagion].          235
OSWALD  Let go, slave, or thou di'st!
EDGAR  Good gentleman, go your gait, and let poor
voke pass. And chud ha' bin zwagger'd out of my life,
'twould not ha' bin zo long as 'tis by a vortnight. Nay,
come not near th' old man; keep out, che vor' ye,          240
or Ice try whither your costard or my ballow be the
harder. Chill be plain with you.
OSWALD  Out, dunghill!                          [*They fight.*]
EDGAR  Chill pick your teeth, zir. Come, no matter
vor your foins.                                       245
OSWALD  Slave, thou hast slain me. Villain, take my purse:
If ever thou wilt thrive, bury my body,
And give the letters which thou find'st about me
To Edmund Earl of Gloucester; seek him out
Upon the English party. O untimely death!          250
Death!                                          [*He dies.*]
EDGAR  I know thee well; a serviceable villain,
As duteous to the vices of thy mistress
As badness would desire.
GLOUCESTER          What, is he dead?
EDGAR  Sit you down, father; rest you.                 255
Let's see these pockets; the letters that he speaks of
May be my friends. He's dead; I am only sorry
He had no other deathsman. Let us see.
Leave, gentle wax, and, manners, blame us not:

---

**229. thyself remember:** i.e. think on your soul's welfare.   **232. publish'd:** proclaimed.   **235. Chill:** I will. (Edgar takes the part of a peasant and uses Somerset dialect.) **cagion:** occasion.   **237. gait:** way.   **238. voke:** folk. **And chud:** if I could.   **240. che vor' ye:** I warrant you.   **241. Ice:** I shall.   **whither:** whether. **costard:** head (from the name of a kind of apple.)   **ballow:** cudgel.   **245. foins:** thrusts.   **250. Upon . . . party:** on the English side.   **258. deathsman:** executioner.   **259. Leave:** by your leave.

To know our enemies' minds, we rip their hearts, 260
Their papers is more lawful.
[*Reads the letter.*] "Let our reciprocal vows be rememb'red. You have many opportunities to cut him
off; if your will want not, time and place will be
fruitfully offer'd. There is nothing done, if he return 265
the conqueror; then am I the prisoner, and his bed my
jail; from the loath'd warmth whereof deliver me, and
supply the place for your labor.
    Your (wife, so I would say) affectionate servant, Goneril." 270
O indistinguish'd space of woman's will!
A plot upon her virtuous husband's life,
And the exchange my brother! Here, in the sands,
Thee I'll rake up, the post unsanctified
Of murtherous lechers; and in the mature time 275
With this ungracious paper strike the sight
Of the death-practic'd Duke. For him 'tis well
That of thy death and business I can tell.
GLOUCESTER The King is mad; how stiff is my vild sense
That I stand up, and have ingenious feeling 280
Of my huge sorrows! Better I were distract,
So should my thoughts be sever'd from my griefs,
And woes by wrong imaginations lose
The knowledge of themselves.     *Drum afar off.*
EDGAR            Give me your hand;
Far off methinks I hear the beaten drum. 285
Come, father, I'll bestow you with a friend.     *Exeunt.*

## SCENE 7

*Enter* CORDELIA, KENT [*still dressed as Caius*], *and* [DOCTOR].

CODELIA O thou good Kent, how shall I live and work
To match thy goodness? My life will be too short,
And every measure fail me.

---

**264. want:** be lacking. **265. fruitfully:** plentifully. **There . . . done:** i.e. we shall have achieved nothing. **268. for your labor:** With obvious double meaning. **269. servant:** lover. **271. indistinguish'd space:** boundless range. **will:** lust. **274. rake:** cover. **post unsanctified:** damnable messenger. **275. in . . . time:** when the time is ripe. **276. ungracious:** wicked. **277. death-practic'd:** whose death is plotted. **279. stiff:** stubborn. **sense:** mental powers. **280. ingenious feeling:** keen consciousness. **281. distract:** mad. **283. wrong imaginations:** delusions. **286. bestow:** lodge. **4.7. Location: A tent in the French camp. 3. measure:** i.e. attempt to measure out an adequate recompense.

KENT  To be acknowledg'd, madam, is o'erpaid.
All my reports go with the modest truth,                         5
Nor more nor clipt, but so.
CORDELIA                        Be better suited,
These weeds are memories of those worser hours;
I prithee put them off.
KENT                        Pardon, dear madam,
Yet to be known shortens my made intent.
My boon I make it, that you know me not               10
Till time and I think meet.
CORDELIA  Then be't so, my good lord. [*To the Doctor.*]
How does the King?
[DOCTOR]  Madam, sleeps still.
CORDELIA                        O you kind gods!
Cure this great breach in his abused nature,
Th' untun'd and jarring senses, O, wind up          15
Of this child-changed father!
[DOCTOR]                        So please your Majesty
That we may wake the King? he hath slept long.
CORDELIA  Be govern'd by your knowledge, and proceed
I' th' sway of your own will. Is he array'd?
GENTLEMAN  Ay, madam; in the heaviness of sleep      20
We put fresh garments on him.
[DOCTOR]  Be by, good madam, when we do awake him,
I doubt [not] of his temperance.
[CORDELIA                        Very well.]

*Enter* LEAR *in a chair carried by* SERVANTS.
[GENTLEMAN *in attendance. Soft music.*]

[DOCTOR  Please you draw near.—Louder the music there!]
CORDELIA  O my dear father, restoration hang          25
Thy medicine on my lips, and let this kiss
Repair those violent harms that my two sisters
Have in thy reverence made.
KENT                        Kind and dear princess!
CORDELIA  Had you not been their father, these white flakes
Did challenge pity of them. Was this a face           30

5. go: accord.  modest: moderate, i.e. strictly accurate.  9. Yet . . . intent: to
reveal my identity at this point would cause the purpose I have formed to fall
short of its mark.  10. My . . . it: I beg it as a special favor.  15. jarring: discord-
ant.  wind up: tune (figure from stringed instrument).  16. child-changed:
changed by his children.  19. I' th' sway: under the direction.  23. temperance:
self-control.  29. Had you: even if you had.  white flakes: snowy locks.
30. Did challenge: would have demanded.

To be oppos'd against the [warring] winds?
[To stand against the deep dread-bolted thunder?
In the most terrible and nimble stroke
Of quick cross lightning? to watch—poor perdu!—
With this thin helm?] Mine enemy's dog,                                    35
Though he had bit me, should have stood that night
Against my fire, and wast thou fain, poor father,
To hovel thee with swine and rogues forlorn
In short and musty straw? Alack, alack,
'Tis wonder that thy life and wits at once                                 40
Had not concluded all. He wakes, speak to him.
[DOCTOR]  Madam, do you, 'tis fittest.
CORDELIA  How does my royal lord? How fares your Majesty?
LEAR  You do me wrong to take me out o' th' grave:
Thou art a soul in bliss, but I am bound                                    45
Upon a wheel of fire, that mine own tears
Do scald like molten lead.
CORDELIA                          Sir, do you know me?
LEAR  You are a spirit, I know; [when] did you die?
CORDELIA  Still, still, far wide!
[DOCTOR]  He's scarce awake, let him alone a while.
LEAR  Where have I been? Where am I? Fair daylight?                        50
I am mightily abus'd; I should ev'n die with pity
To see another thus. I know not what to say.
I will not swear these are my hands. Let's see,
I feel this pin prick. Would I were assur'd                                55
Of my condition!
CORDELIA                          O, look upon me, sir,
And hold your hand in benediction o'er me.
[No, sir,] you must not kneel.
LEAR                          Pray do not mock me.
I am a very foolish fond old man,
Fourscore and upward, not an hour more nor less;                          60
And to deal plainly,
I fear I am not in my perfect mind.
Methinks I should know you, and know this man,

---

**32. deep:** deep-toned. **dread-bolted:** accompanied by the dread thunderbolt.
**34. cross:** zigzag. **perdu:** sentinel at a dangerous post. **35. thin helm:** light hel-
met, i.e. his hair. **37. fain:** glad, i.e. forced. **38. rogues:** vagabonds. **39. short:**
scanty (?) or broken up by earlier use as bedding (?). **41. all:** altogether.
**46. wheel of fire:** One of the punishments associated with both hell and purgatory
in medieval accounts. **that:** so that. **49. wide:** astray. **52. abus'd:** confused.

Yet I am doubtful: for I am mainly ignorant
What place this is, and all the skill I have                     65
Remembers not these garments; nor I know not
Where I did lodge last night. Do not laugh at me,
For (as I am a man) I think this lady
To be my child Cordelia.
CORDELIA                 And so I am; I am.
LEAR  Be your tears wet? Yes, faith. I pray weep not.          70
If you have poison for me, I will drink it.
I know you do not love me, for your sisters
Have (as I do remember) done me wrong:
You have some cause, they have not.
CORDELIA                 No cause, no cause.
LEAR  Am I in France?
KENT                 In your own kingdom, sir.                  75
LEAR  Do not abuse me.
[DOCTOR]  Be comforted, good madam, the great rage,
You see, is kill'd in him, [and yet it is danger
To make him even o'er the time he has lost.]
Desire him to go in, trouble him no more                        80
Till further settling.
CORDELIA  Will't please your Highness walk?
LEAR                 You must bear with me.
Pray you now forget, and forgive; I am old and foolish.
                 Exeunt. [Manent Kent and Gentleman.]
[GENTLEMAN.  Holds it true, sir, that the Duke of Cornwall
was so slain?                                                   85
KENT  Most certain, sir.
GENTLEMAN  Who is conductor of his people?
KENT  As 'tis said, the bastard son of Gloucester.
GENTLEMAN  They say Edgar, his banish'd son, is with the
Earl of Kent in Germany.                                        90
KENT  Report is changeable. 'Tis time to look
about, the powers of the kingdom approach apace.
GENTLEMAN  The arbiterment is like to be bloody. Fare
you well, sir.                                        [Exit.]
KENT  My point and period will be thoroughly wrought,          95
Or well or ill, as this day's battle's fought.        Exit.]

---

**64. mainly:** completely.   **76. abuse:** deceive.   **79. even o'er:** fill in.   **[83.** s.d. Manent: 'they remain' 'they stay put'. ~ *Evans Editor*]   **87. conductor:** leader.   **91–92. look about:** be on guard.   **93. arbiterment:** decisive encounter.   **95–96. My . . . fought:** this battle will decide for good or ill the outcome of my life.

# Act 5

SCENE I

*Enter, with Drum and Colors,* EDMUND, REGAN,
GENTLEMEN, *and* SOLDIERS.

EDMUND  Know of the Duke if his last purpose hold,
Or whether since he is advis'd by aught
To change the course. He's full of alteration
And self-reproving—bring his constant pleasure.
                    [*To a Gentleman, who goes out.*]
REGAN  Our sister's man is certainly miscarried.                    5
EDMUND  'Tis to be doubted, madam.
REGAN                    Now, sweet lord,
You know the goodness I intend upon you:
Tell me but truly, but then speak the truth,
Do you not love my sister?
EDMUND                    In honor'd love.
REGAN  But have you never found my brother's way
To the forfended place?                    10
[EDMUND                    That thought abuses you.
REGAN  I am doubtful that you have been conjunct
And bosom'd with her—as far as we call hers.]
EDMUND  No, by mine honor, madam.
REGAN  I never shall endure her. Dear my lord,
Be not familiar with her.                    15
EDMUND                    Fear [me] not.
She and the Duke her husband!

---

5.1. Location: **The British camp near Dover.** [**1. Know . . . hold:** Learn
whether the Duke will hold to his most recent plan. ~ *Evans Editor*]  **2. advis'd
by aught:** persuaded by any consideration.  **4. constant pleasure:** firm decision.  **5. is . . . miscarried:** has met with some accident.  **6. doubted:** feared.
**9. honor'd:** honorable.  **11. forfended:** forbidden.  **abuses:** wrongs.  **12. doubtful:** suspicious.  **12–13. conjunct And bosom'd.** Regan uses words that might
be used of a traitor—"in league with her and admitted to her private counsel"—
but intends them in their primary physical sense, as her following words show.
**16. Fear me not:** have no such fears about me.

*Enter with Drum and Colors,* ALBANY, GONERIL, SOLDIERS.

[GONERIL *[Aside.]* I had rather lose the battle than that sister
    Should loosen him and me.]
ALBANY  Our very loving sister, well bemet.              20
    Sir, this I heard: the King is come to his daughter,
    With others whom the rigor of our state
    Forc'd to cry out. [Where I could not be honest,
    I never yet was valiant. For this business,
    It touches us as France invades our land,        25
    Not bolds the King, with others whom, I fear,
    Most just and heavy causes make oppose.
EDMUND  Sir, you speak nobly.]
REGAN                    Why is this reason'd?
GONERIL  Combine together 'gainst the enemy;
    For these domestic and particular broils        30
    Are not the question here.
ALBANY              Let's then determine
    With th' ancient of war on our proceeding.
[EDMUND  I shall attend you presently at your tent.]
REGAN  Sister, you'll go with us?
GONERIL  No.                           35
REGAN  'Tis most convenient, pray go with us.
GONERIL  *[Aside.]* O ho, I know the riddle.—I will go.
                        *Exeunt both the armies.*

[*As they are going out,*] *enter* EDGAR [*disguised.  Albany remains*].
EDGAR  If e'er your Grace had speech with man so poor,
    Hear me one word.
ALBANY             I'll overtake you.—Speak.
EDGAR  Before you fight the battle, ope this letter.     40
    If you have victory, let the trumpet sound
    For him that brought it. Wretched though I seem,
    I can produce a champion that will prove
    What is avouched there. If you miscarry,
    Your business of the world hath so an end,       45
    And machination ceases. Fortune [love] you!

---

**22. rigor . . . state:** harshness of our rule.  **23. honest:** honorable.  **25. touches us as:** concerns us in so far as.  **26. Not bolds:** i.e. not in so far as he supports.  **28. reason'd:** discussed.  **30. domestic and particular:** family and personal.  **32. ancient of war:** experienced officers.  **37. know the riddle:** know why you say so (Regan wants to keep Goneril and Edmund apart).  **43. prove:** i.e. in trial by combat.  **44. avouched:** maintained.

ALBANY  Stay till I have read the letter.
EDGAR                                              I was forbid it.
   When time shall serve, let but the herald cry,
   And I'll appear again.
ALBANY  Why, fare thee well, I will o'erlook thy
   paper.                                    *Exit [Edgar].* 50

*Enter* EDMUND.

EDMUND  The enemy's in view, draw up your powers.
   Here is the guess of their true strength and forces,
   By diligent discovery, but your haste
   Is now urg'd on you.
ALBANY                          We will greet the time.          *Exit.*
EDMUND  To both these sisters have I sworn my love;          55
   Each jealous of the other, as the stung
   Are of the adder. Which of them shall I take?
   Both? one? or neither? Neither can be enjoy'd
   If both remain alive: to take the widow
   Exasperates, makes mad her sister Goneril,          60
   And hardly shall I carry out my side,
   Her husband being alive. Now then, we'll use
   His countenance for the battle, which being done,
   Let her who would be rid of him devise
   His speedy taking off.    As for the mercy          65
   Which he intends to Lear and to Cordelia,
   The battle done, and they within our power,
   Shall never see his pardon; for my state
   Stands on me to defend, not to debate.          *Exit.*

SCENE 2

*Alarum within. Enter, with Drum and Colors,*
*[the* POWERS *of France] over the stage,* CORDELIA
*[with her* FATHER *in her hand,] and exeunt.*

*Enter* EDGAR *and* GLOUCESTER.

EDGAR  Here, father, take the shadow of this tree
   For your good host; pray that the right may thrive.

50. **o'erlook:** read over.   53. **discovery:** scouting.   54. **greet the time:** meet the
occasion.   56. **jealous:** suspicious.   61. **hardly:** with difficulty.   **carry . . . side:**
win my game.   63. **His countenance:** the authority of his name.   68. **Shall:**
they shall.   69. **Stands on:** requires.   5.2. Location: **A field between the two**
**camps.**   o.s.d. **Alarum:** trumpet signal to advance.   2. **host:** shelterer.

If ever I return to you again,
I'll bring you comfort.
GLOUCESTER.                Grace go with you, sir!        *Exit [Edgar].*

*Alarum and retreat within. Enter* EDGAR.

EDGAR  Away, old man, give me thy hand, away!                5
King Lear hath lost, he and his daughter ta'en.
Give me thy hand; come on.
GLOUCESTER  No further, sir, a man may rot even here.
EDGAR  What, in ill thoughts again? Men must endure
Their going hence even as their coming hither,            10
Ripeness is all. Come on.
GLOUCESTER                And that's true too.        *Exeunt.*


SCENE 3

*Enter in conquest, with Drum and Colors,* EDMUND, LEAR
*and* CORDELIA *as prisoners,* SOLDIERS, CAPTAIN.

EDMUND  Some officers take them away. Good guard,
Until their greater pleasures first be known
That are to censure them.
CORDELIA                    We are not the first
Who with best meaning have incurr'd the worst.
For thee, oppressed king, I am cast down,                 5
Myself could else out-frown false Fortune's frown.
Shall we not see these daughters and these sisters?
LEAR  No, no, no, no! Come let's away to prison:
We two alone will sing like birds i' th' cage;
When thou dost ask me blessing, I'll kneel down          10
And ask of thee forgiveness. So we'll live,
And pray, and sing, and tell old tales, and laugh
At gilded butterflies, and hear poor rogues
Talk of court news; and we'll talk with them too—
Who loses and who wins; who's in, who's out—             15
And take upon 's the mystery of things
As if we were God's spies; and we'll wear out,

---

**4.** s.d. **retreat:** trumpet signal to withdraw.    **11. Ripeness is all:** the only thing that
matters with regard to death is to be ready for it when it comes.    5.3. Location:
**Scene continues.    2. their greater pleasures:** the desires of those greater
persons.    **3. censure:** pass judgment on.    **13. gilded butterflies:** trivial and
ephemeral people.    **17. God's spies:** beings sent from heaven to watch men's
doings, i.e. detached observers with special insight.    **wear out:** outlast.

In a wall'd prison, packs and sects of great ones,
That ebb and flow by th' moon.
EDMUND                                Take them away.
LEAR Upon such sacrifices, my Cordelia,                      20
The gods themselves throw incense. Have I caught thee?
He that parts us shall bring a brand from heaven,
And fire us hence like foxes.    Wipe thine eyes;
The good-years shall devour them, flesh and fell,
Ere they shall make us weep!    We'll see 'em starv'd first.    25
Come.                              *Exit [with Cordelia, guarded].*
EDMUND    Come hither, captain; hark.
Take thou this note [*giving a paper*]; go follow them to prison.
One step I have advanc'd thee; if thou dost
As this instructs thee, thou dost make thy way
To noble fortunes. Know thou this, that men          30
Are as the time is: to be tender-minded
Does not become a sword. Thy great employment
Will not bear question; either say thou'lt do't,
Or thrive by other means.
CAPTAIN                          I'll do't, my lord.
EDMUND About it, and write happy when th' hast done.    35
Mark, I say instantly, and carry it so
As I have set it down.
[CAPTAIN I cannot draw a cart, nor eat dried oats,
If it be man's work, I'll do't.]                  *Exit Captain.*

*Flourish. Enter* ALBANY, GONERIL, REGAN,
[*another Captain,*] *Soldiers.*

ALBANY Sir, you have show'd to-day your valiant strain,    40
And fortune led you well. You have the captives
Who were the opposites of this day's strife;
I do require them of you, so to use them
As we shall find their merits and our safety
May equally determine.
EDMUND                        Sir, I thought it fit              45

18. **packs and sects:** groups of intriguers and partisans.  20. **such sacrifices:** i.e.
as Cordelia's for her father (?) or as their giving up the world (?).  [**21. Have I
caught thee?:** Cf. the opening of Sir Philip Sidney's second song in *Astrophil and
Stella* (1581): "Have I caught my heav'nly jewel?" ~ *Evans Editor*]  22–23. **He ...
foxes:** i.e. it would take a torch from heaven, not an earthly one, to smoke us out
of our prison refuge (as foxes were smoked out of their holes).  22. **shall:** must.
24. **good-years:** Obviously referring to some evil force, but not satisfactorily explained. **flesh and fell:** both flesh and skin, i.e. altogether.  33. **question:** discussion.
35. **write happy:** call yourself lucky (because I shall reward you well).  38. **I ...
oats:** I can't do a horse's work.  40. **strain:** lineage.  42. **opposites:** opponents.

To send the old and miserable King
To some retention [and appointed guard],
Whose age had charms in it, whose title more,
To pluck the common bosom on his side,
And turn our impress'd lances in our eyes          50
Which do command them. With him I sent the Queen,
My reason all the same, and they are ready
To-morrow, or at further space, t' appear
Where you shall hold your session. [At this time
We sweat and bleed: the friend hath lost his friend,          55
And the best quarrels, in the heat, are curs'd
By those that feel their sharpness.
The question of Cordelia and her father
Requires a fitter place.]
ALBANY                    Sir, by your patience,
I hold you but a subject of this war,          60
Not as a brother.
REGAN                    That's as we list to grace him.
Methinks our pleasure might have been demanded
Ere you had spoke so far. He led our powers,
Bore the commission of my place and person,
The which immediacy may well stand up,          65
And call itself your brother.
GONERIL                    Not so hot.
In his own grace he doth exalt himself,
More than in your addition.
REGAN                    In my rights,
By me invested, he compeers the best.
[GONERIL] That were the most, if he should husband you.          70
REGAN Jesters do oft prove prophets.
GONERIL                    Holla, holla!
That eye that told you so look'd but a-squint.
REGAN Lady, I am not well, else I should answer
From a full-flowing stomach. General,
Take thou my soldiers, prisoners, patrimony;          75
Dispose of them, of me; the walls is thine.

---

**47. retention:** confinement.     **49. common bosom:** sympathy of the multitude.     **50–51. turn . . . Which:** i.e. turn our conscript soldiers against us who.     **54.
session:** trial     [**56. quarrels:** causes. ~ *Evans Editor*]     **61. list:** wish, choose.
**62. demanded:** ascertained.     **65. immediacy:** close connection.     **67. grace:**
meritorious qualities.     **68. your addition:** the honors you have conferred on him.
**69. compeers:** equals.     **70. That . . . most:** he would be most fully invested in
your rights.     **74. stomach:** anger.     **76. the walls:** i.e. the citadel of my heart.

Witness the world, that I create thee here
My lord and master.
GONERIL          Mean you to enjoy him?
ALBANY  The let-alone lies not in your good will.
EDMUND  Nor in thine, lord.
ALBANY           Half-blooded fellow, yes.       80
REGAN  [*To Edmund.*] Let the drum strike, and prove my title thine.
ALBANY  Stay yet, hear reason. Edmund, I arrest thee
On capital treason, and in thy [attaint],
This gilded serpent [*pointing to Goneril*]. For your claim, fair [sister],
I bar it in the interest of my wife;      85
'Tis she is sub-contracted to this lord,
And I, her husband, contradict your banes.
If you will marry, make your loves to me,
My lady is bespoke.
GONERIL          An enterlude!
ALBANY  Thou art armed, Gloucester, let the trumpet sound.    90
If none appear to prove upon thy person
Thy heinous, manifest, and many treasons,
There is my pledge [*throwing down a glove*]. I'll make it on thy heart,
Ere I taste bread, thou art in nothing less
Than I have here proclaim'd thee.
REGAN          Sick, O, sick!      95
GONERIL  [*Aside.*] If not, I'll ne'er trust medicine.
EDMUND  There's my exchange [*throwing down a
glove*]. What in the world [he is]
That names me traitor, villain-like he lies.
Call by the trumpet; he that dares approach:
On him, on you—who not?—I will maintain      100
My truth and honor firmly.
ALBANY   A herald, ho!
[EDMUND        A herald, ho, a herald!]
[ALBANY] Trust to thy single virtue, for thy soldiers,
All levied in my name, have in my name      104
Took their discharge.
REGAN          My sickness grows upon me.
ALBANY  She is not well, convey her to my tent.

[*Exit Regan, led.*]

---

**79. let-alone:** power of preventing it. **80. Half-blooded fellow:** bastard.
**83. in thy attaint:** as accessory to your treason. **87. banes:** banns of marriage.
**89. enterlude:** interlude, play. **93. make:** prove (which is the Q1 reading).
**94. in nothing less:** in no detail of the charge less guilty. **96. medicine:** i.e. poison.
**97. What:** whoever. **103. single virtue:** unaided valor.

*Enter a* HERALD.

Come hither, herald. Let the trumpet sound,
And read out this.
[CAPTAIN Sound, trumpet!] *A trumpet sounds.*
HERALD (*Reads.*) "If any man of quality or degree          110
within the lists of the army will maintain upon Edmund,
supposed Earl of Gloucester, that he is a manifold
traitor, let him appear by the third sound of the
trumpet. He is bold in his defense."
[EDMUND Sound!]                    *First trumpet.*          115
HERALD Again!                      *Second trumpet.*
HERALD Again!                      *Third trumpet.*
                                   *Trumpet answers within.*

*Enter* EDGAR [*at the third sound,*] *armed,*
[*a Trumpet before him*].

ALBANY Ask him his purposes, why he appears
Upon this call o' th' trumpet.
HERALD                      What are you?
Your name, your quality? and why you answer          120
This present summons?
EDGAR                      Know, my name is lost,
By treason's tooth bare-gnawn and canker-bit,
Yet am I noble as the adversary
I come to cope.
ALBANY                 Which is that adversary?
EDGAR What's he that speaks for Edmund Earl of Gloucester?     125
EDMUND Himself; what say'st thou to him?
EDGAR                            Draw thy sword,
That if my speech offend a noble heart,
Thy arm may do thee justice; here is mine:
Behold, it is my privilege,
The privilege of mine honors,                        130
My oath, and my profession. I protest,
Maugre thy strength, place, youth, and eminence,
[Despite] thy victor-sword and fire-new fortune,
Thy valor, and thy heart, thou art a traitor;
False to thy gods, thy brother, and thy father,     135

---

**122. canker-bit:** worm-eaten.   **124. cope:** encounter.   **130. The privilege . . .
honors:** my privilege as a knight.   **131. profession:** i.e. knighthood.   **protest:** solemnly declare.   **132. Maugre:** in spite of.   **133. fire-new:** brand-new.
**134. heart:** courage.

Conspirant 'gainst this high illustrious prince,
And from th' extremest upward of thy head
To the descent and dust below thy foot,
A most toad-spotted traitor. Say thou "No,"
This sword, this arm, and my best spirits are bent          140
To prove upon thy heart, whereto I speak,
Thou liest.
EDMUND   In wisdom I should ask thy name,
But since thy outside looks so fair and warlike,
And that thy tongue some say of breeding breathes,
What safe and nicely I might well delay          145
By rule of knighthood, I disdain and spurn.
Back do I toss these treasons to thy head,
With the hell-hated lie o'erwhelm thy heart,
Which for they yet glance by, and scarcely bruise,
This sword of mine shall give them instant way          150
Where they shall rest for ever. Trumpets, speak!
   ALARUMS                                    [*They fight. Edmund falls.*]
ALBANY   Save him, save him!
GONERIL                         This is practice, Gloucester.
By th' law of war thou wast not bound to answer
An unknown opposite. Thou art not vanquish'd,
But cozen'd and beguil'd.
ALBANY                         Shut your mouth, dame,          155
Or with this paper shall I [stopple] it. Hold, sir.—
Thou worse than any name, read thine own evil.
No tearing, lady, I perceive you know it.
GONERIL   Say if I do, the laws are mine, not thine;
Who can arraign me for't?
ALBANY                         Most monstrous! O!          160
Know'st thou this paper?
[GONERIL]                         Ask me not what I know.          *Exit.*
ALBANY   Go after her; she's desperate, govern her.
EDMUND   What you have charg'd me with, that have I done,
And more, much more, the time will bring it out.
'Tis past, and so am I. But what art thou          165
That hast this fortune on me? If thou'rt noble,
I do forgive thee.

---

**138. descent:** lowest part.   **139. toad-spotted:** i.e. stained with infamy.   **140. bent:**
prepared, ready for action   **144. that:** since. **say:** trace.   **145. safe and nicely:**
cautiously and with technical correctness.   **147. treasons:** accusations of treason.
**148. hell-hated:** hated as hell is hated.   **149. for:** since.   **152. practice:** trickery.
**156. stopple:** stop up.   **162. govern:** restrain.   **166. fortune on:** victory over.

EDGAR            Let's exchange charity.
I am no less in blood than thou art, Edmund;
If more, the more th' hast wrong'd me.
My name is Edgar, and thy father's son.            170
The gods are just, and of our pleasant vices
Make instruments to plague us:
The dark and vicious place where thee he got
Cost him his eyes.
EDMUND           Th' hast spoken right, 'tis true.
The wheel is come full circle, I am here.         175
ALBANY Methought thy very gait did prophesy
A royal nobleness. I must embrace thee.
Let sorrow split my heart, if ever I
Did hate thee or thy father.
EDGAR            Worthy prince, I know't.
ALBANY Where have you hid yourself?        180
How have you known the miseries of your father?
EDGAR By nursing them, my lord. List a brief tale,
And when 'tis told, O that my heart would burst!
The bloody proclamation to escape,
That follow'd me so near (O, our lives' sweetness!     185
That we the pain of death would hourly die
Rather than die at once!), taught me to shift
Into a madman's rags, t' assume a semblance
That very dogs disdain'd; and in this habit
Met I my father with his bleeding rings,        190
Their precious stones new lost; became his guide,
Led him, begg'd for him, sav'd him from despair;
Never (O fault!) reveal'd myself unto him,
Until some half hour past, when I was arm'd.
Not sure, though hoping, of this good success,      195
I ask'd his blessing, and from first to last
Told him our pilgrimage. But his flaw'd heart
(Alack, too weak the conflict to support!)
'Twixt two extremes of passion, joy and grief,
Burst smilingly.
EDMUND         This speech of yours hath mov'd me,    200
And shall perchance do good: but speak you on,
You look as you had something more to say.
ALBANY If there be more, more woeful, hold it in,

---

**171. pleasant:** pleasurable.    **175. wheel:** wheel of fortune.    **here:** i.e. at the bottom, where I began.    **195. success:** outcome.    **197. flaw'd:** cracked.

For I am almost ready to dissolve,
Hearing of this.
[EDGAR                This would have seem'd a period          205
To such as love not sorrow, but another,
To amplify too much, would make much more,
And top extremity.      Whilst I
Was big in clamor, came there in a man,
Who, having seen me in my worst estate,                          210
Shunn'd my abhorr'd society, but then finding
Who 'twas that so endur'd, with his strong arms
He fastened on my neck and bellowed out
As he'd burst heaven, threw [him] on my father,
Told the most piteous tale of Lear and him                       215
That ever ear received, which in recounting,
His grief grew puissant and the strings of life
Began to crack. Twice then the trumpets sounded,
And there I left him tranc'd.
ALBANY                      But who was this?
EDGAR  Kent, sir, the banish'd Kent, who in disguise             220
Followed his enemy king, and did him service
Improper for a slave.]

                Enter a GENTLEMAN [with a bloody knife].

GENTLEMAN  Help, help! O, help!
EDGAR                          What kind of help?
ALBANY                         Speak, man.
EDGAR  What means this bloody knife?
GENTLEMAN                      'Tis hot, it smokes,
It came even from the heart of— O, she's dead!                   225
ALBANY  Who dead? Speak, man.
GENTEMAN  Your lady, sir, your lady; and her sister
By her is poison'd; she confesses it.
EDMUND  I was contracted to them both; all three
Now marry in an instant.
EDGAR                      Here comes Kent.                      230

                        Enter KENT.

ALBANY  Produce the bodies, be they alive or dead.
                                        [Exit Gentleman.]

206. **love not:** are not in love with.    206–8. **but . . . extremity:** one more such circumstance, amplifying what is already too much, would increase it and pass all limits.
209. **big in clamor:** loud in lamentation.    217. **strings of life:** heart-strings.
219. **tranc'd:** unconscious.    221. **enemy:** hostile.    222. **Improper:** i.e. too menial.

This judgment of the heavens, that makes us tremble,
Touches us not with pity.—O, is this he?
The time will not allow the compliment
Which very manners urges.
KENT          I am come       235
To bid my king and master aye good night.
Is he not here?
ALBANY      Great thing of us forgot!
Speak, Edmund, where's the King? and where's Cordelia?
        *Goneril and Regan's bodies brought out.*
Seest thou this object, Kent?
KENT  Alack, why thus?
EDMUND       Yet Edmund was belov'd!     240
The one the other poison'd for my sake,
And after slew herself.
ALBANY  Even so. Cover their faces.
EDMUND  I pant for life. Some good I mean to do,
Despite of mine own nature. Quickly send    245
(Be brief in it) to th' castle, for my writ
Is on the life of Lear and on Cordelia.
Nay, send in time.
ALBANY      Run, run, O, run!
EDGAR  To who, my lord? Who has the office? Send
Thy token of reprieve.    250
EDMUND  Well thought on. Take my sword. [The captain—]
Give it the captain.
[ALBANY]  Haste thee, for thy life.    *[Exit Edgar.]*
EDMUND  He hath commission from thy wife and me
To hang Cordelia in the prison, and
To lay the blame upon her own despair,    255
That she forbid herself.
ALBANY  The gods defend her! Bear him hence awhile.
        *[Edmund is borne off.]*

    *Enter* LEAR *with Cordelia in his arms,*
    [EDGAR *and a* GENTLEMAN *following*].

LEAR  Howl, howl, howl! O, [you] are men of stones!
Had I your tongues and eyes, I'ld use them so
That heaven's vault should crack. She's gone for ever!  260
I know when one is dead, and when one lives;

234. compliment: ceremony. 239. object: sight. 240. Yet: in spite of all.
256. fordid: destroyed.

She's dead as earth. Lend me a looking-glass,
If that her breath will mist or stain the stone,
Why then she lives.
KENT              Is this the promis'd end?
EDGAR  Or image of that horror?
ALBANY              Fall, and cease!          265
LEAR  This feather stirs, she lives! If it be so,
    It is a chance which does redeem all sorrows
    That ever I have felt.
KENT  [*Kneeling.*]         O my good master!
LEAR  Prithee away.
EDGAR          'Tis noble Kent, your friend.
LEAR  A plague upon you, murderers, traitors all!    270
    I might have sav'd her, now she's gone for ever!
    Cordelia, Cordelia, stay a little. Ha!
    What is't thou say'st? Her voice was ever soft,
    Gentle, and low, an excellent thing in woman.
    I kill'd the slave that was a-hanging thee.    275
GENTLEMAN  'Tis true, my lords, he did.
LEAR               Did I not, fellow?
    I have seen the day, with my good biting falchion
    I would have made [them] skip. I am old now,
    And these same crosses spoil me. Who are you?
    Mine eyes are not o' th' best; I'll tell you straight.    280
KENT  If Fortune brag of two she lov'd and hated,
    One of them we behold.
LEAR  This is a dull sight. Are you not Kent?
KENT                 The same:
    Your servant Kent. Where is your servant Caius?
LEAR  He's a good fellow, I can tell you that;    285
    He'll strike, and quickly too. He's dead and rotten.
KENT  No, my good lord, I am the very man—
LEAR  I'll see that straight.
KENT  That from your first of difference and decay,
    Have follow'd your sad steps—    290

---

**263. stone:** mirror of polished stone. **264. promis'd end:** i.e. end of the world. **265. image:** exact likeness. **Fall, and cease:** i.e. let the earth come to its end. **277. falchion:** light sword. **279. crosses:** adversities. **spoil me:** wear me down. **280. tell you straight:** recognize you in a moment (*straight* = straightway). **281. two . . . hated:** i.e. the two men who best illustrate her fickleness in raising up and then casting down (?) or the man she loved most and the man she hated most (?). **283. This . . . sight:** my eyes really are failing. **288. see:** see to. **289. first . . . decay:** beginning of the deterioration of your fortunes (*difference and decay* = change and decline, i.e. change for the worse).

LEAR                          [You] are welcome hither.
KENT  Nor no man else. All's cheerless, dark, and deadly.
Your eldest daughters have foredone themselves,
And desperately are dead.
LEAR                          Ay, so I think.
ALBANY  He knows not what he says, and vain is it
That we present us to him.
EDGAR                          Very bootless.                          295

*Enter a* MESSENGER.

MESSENGER  Edmund is dead, my lord.
ALBANY                          That's but a trifle here.
You lords and noble friends, know our intent.
What comfort to this great decay may come
Shall be applied. For us, we will resign,
During the life of this old majesty,                          300
To him our absolute power.          [*To Edgar and Kent.*]
                    You, to your rights,
With boot, and such addition as your honors
Have more than merited. All friends shall taste
The wages of their virtue, and all foes
The cup of their deservings. O, see, see!                          305
LEAR  And my poor fool is hang'd! No, no, no life!
Why should a dog, a horse, a rat, have life,
And thou no breath at all? Thou'lt come no more,
Never, never, never, never, never.
Pray you undo this button. Thank you, sir.                          310
Do you see this? Look on her! Look her lips,
Look there, look there!                          *He dies.*
EDGAR                          He faints. My lord, my lord!
KENT  Break, heart, I prithee break!
EDGAR                          Look up, my lord.
KENT  Vex not his ghost. O, let him pass, he hates him
That would upon the rack of this tough world                          315
Stretch him out longer.
EDGAR                          He is gone indeed.
KENT  The wonder is he hath endur'd so long,
He but usurp'd his life.

---

**291. Nor . . . else:** no, neither I nor anyone else.  **293. desperately:** out of despair,
i.e. by their own hands (true only of Goneril's death).  **298. great decay:** great
man fallen into ruin.  **302. boot:** advantage, augmentation. **addition:** additional
marks of distinction.  **306. fool:** Here, as often, a term of endearment; it refers to
Cordelia.  **314. ghost:** departing spirit.

ALBANY  Bear them from hence. Our present business
  Is general woe. [*To Kent and Edgar.*] Friends of my soul, you twain  320
  Rule in this realm, and the gor'd state sustain.
KENT  I have a journey, sir, shortly to go:
  My master calls me, I must not say no.
EDGAR  The weight of this sad time we must obey,
  Speak what we feel, not what we ought to say:  325
  The oldest hath borne most; we that are young
  Shall never see so much, nor live so long.
                       *Exeunt with a dead march.*

**321. gor'd:** wounded.

## NOTE ON THE TEXT

For bibliographical details concerning citations in this note, the reader is asked to consult one or both of the following: the "Key To Works Cited," which precedes the text of *King Lear*, and "the Selected Bibliography in *The Riverside Shakespeare*, 2nd edition, ed. G. Blakemore Evans and John J. M. Tobin. Boston: Houghton Mifflin, 1997, pp. 2021–34, esp. pp. 2022–23 ("The Text: Facsimiles and Studies of Textual History").

   *King Lear* presents a number of extremely complicated and confusing textual problems. There are two primary texts, the First Quarto (Q1) (1608) and the First Folio (F1) (1623). A second quarto (Q2), also dated 1608 but actually printed in 1619, is essentially an occasionally corrected reprint of Q1, with one or two slight additions (see Textual Notes, 3.6.47, 4.6.197); a third quarto (Q3), printed from Q2 and of no textual significance, appeared in 1655.

   The exact provenience of the manuscript underlying Q1 has been variously accounted for: (1) a manuscript resulting from dictation by two boy actors (perhaps those who played Goneril and Regan) one of whom, reading from Shakespeare's "foul papers" (i.e., rough draft), allowed his memory of the play to contaminate his reading, the other, only hearing, not seeing, the text, made aural errors and not infrequently reduced verse to prose (Walker, Duthie [1960]; earlier [1949] Duthie had shown the older stenographic theory [Greg, 1940] to be unworkable); (2) a manuscript taken down in long-hand during one or more performances at the Globe, like (1), allowing for actors' aural and verse / prose errors (Stone); (3) a manuscript sharked up by memorial reconstruction by one or more actors, thus showing (as Q1 appears to do) such typical characteristics of a reported text as anticipations, recollections, transpositions, substitutions, paraphrases, improvisations, and so on, although the resulting text is considerably better in most ways than the memorially reconstructed texts in the "bad" quartos of *Romeo and Juliet* (Q1) and *Hamlet* (Q1) (Kirschbaum, Walton); (4) Shakespeare's holograph "foul papers," the corrupt state of the Q1 text being explained by the occasional difficulty of Shakespeare's handwriting (see the Introduction to *Sir Thomas More*) and an unusually untidy and messy manuscript, plagued with a number of revised "first thoughts" made, *currente calamo*, in the heat of composition, and set by two compositors (one at least inexperienced) in a printing shop (Nicholas Oke's), which, having a comparatively limited supply of type, was faced with printing its first play script (Doran [later withdrawn], Urkowitz, Blayney, Taylor, Halio). Although none of the above explanations can be entirely ruled out, and each presents difficulties of one kind or another, the fourth is at present most widely accepted, in part perhaps because it best fits the new "two-*Lear*" theory (see below), even though, as Greg has said (1955, p. 379), it is difficult to believe that "Shakespeare, and that at the height of his powers, could ever have written the clumsy and fumbling lines we find in Q."

Similar problems of provenience plague the F1 text. It is now generally agreed that, in some way, either directly or through a transcription, the copy underlying the F1 text made use of either Q1 or Q2 (or both), the printed quarto involved having been annotated by collation against some kind of playhouse manuscript, perhaps the official prompt-book. However, several different interpretations within this framework have been advanced: (1) Greg, Duthie, and Walton argue for the direct use of a copy of Q1 that had been annotated, by correction, deletion, and expansion, against a playhouse manuscript; (2) Werstine and Taylor argue for similar copy, but using a copy of Q2 instead of Q1; (3) Doran, Howard-Hill, and Blayney propose that F1 copy was based on a transcript of either (a) Shakespeare's holograph manuscript (? "fair copy") revised and used as the prompt-book (Doran); (b) a transcript of the prompt-book eked out where unclear, substantively or in accidentals, by consultation of a copy of Q2 and, but less immediately, a copy of Q1, particularly by the inexperienced Compositor E, who was responsible for setting the greater part of the F1 text (Howard-Hill); (c) a transcript of a copy of Q1 which had been annotated by a reviser against the official prompt-book (or at least some theater-related manuscript), Compositor E, however, making frequent reference for clarification to a copy of Q2; this manuscript then became the new official prompt-book (Blaney, Halio). It should be noted that, in the case of (b) or (c), the use of manuscript copy for the F1 text (the theory now most widely accepted) opens the way to a fourth source of potential corruption, adding to the other three (collator, compositor, and proof-reader) the scribe responsible for copying out the annotated copy of either Q1 or Q2.

It will, I think, be clear by now that no two edited texts of *Lear*, given the complexity and uncertainty of the whole textual situation, will ever be exactly alike. There are too many points in both the Q1–2 and F1 texts which force an editor to choose between readings on essentially subjective grounds. The present text is based on that of F1, a text that, it is now generally agreed, was significantly influenced whether directly or indirectly by both Q1 and Q2. The F1 text contains about 133 lines and part-lines found in neither Q1 or Q2. In addition, however, roughly 288 lines and part-lines (which include one whole scene, 4.3) unique to Q1 and Q2 have been incorporated, and more than a hundred individual readings from Q1 (and, rarely, from Q2) have been drawn upon to supplement or correct the F1 text. The reasons for this frequent dependence on Q1 (and occasionally its virtual reprint, Q2) are several. First, as noted above, there are numerous textual errors in F1 for which Q1 offers the most authoritative corrections. Second, when the F1 text is influenced by an uncorrected state of Q1 it is occasionally necessary to restore the corrected state of Q1 (as in 3.4.12; 4.1.10, 4.2.28, 29, 60, 79). Third, where F1 follows a reading otherwise unique to Q2, such readings being without textual authority, the Q1 reading has been preferred (e.g., 1.4.22, 31, 137; 2.1.20), except in a few cases where Q2 (1619) reflects a normalized form (e.g., Q1 "a" v. Q2 "he") which would have been altered by the F1 editor(s) (see 4.6.70; also the practice in other F1 plays) regardless of Q2's reading, or where, for metrical, assonantal, or some other special reason, the Q2 / F1 reading seems preferable to that of Q1 (e.g., 4.6.269–70). Fourth, Q1 occasionally offers readings which, it has been generally agreed, are superior to those in F1 (e.g., 2.1.45; 3.7.58, 63), the F1 reading in such cases arising, it is argued, from interference by the book-keeper or actors, who presumably wished to get rid of difficult or esoteric words.

Some few years ago, a group of critics (Warren, Urkowitz, Wells, Taylor, and others, in *The Division of the Kingdoms*, 1983, and elsewhere) proposed that the F1 text represented a version of the play so significantly different from that in Q1–2 in tighter dramatic structure and acting pace, as well as in its treatment of a number of characters (Lear, Albany, the Fool, and Goneril) that it must be considered a separate play in its own right, and that these differences were the result of a careful revision undertaken by Shakespeare himself. No one, of course, would deny that the F1 text differs in several ways from the Q1–2 text; it omits some 288 lines or part-lines, adds some 133 lines or part-lines, differs in a substantial number of substantive readings (single words and phrases; see the Textual Notes), and handles the war theme more diplomatically by getting rid of Q1–2 references to Cordelia's attempt to rescue Lear as a French invasion of England. These are the facts. But the premise on which the proponents of the two-*Lear* theory build their case—that the F1 text represents Shakespeare's own revision of the play as it appears in Q1–2—is, so far as any hard evidence is concerned, grounded on subjective interpretations of the "facts" by critics, who, taking Shakespeare's full involvement as a given, discover exaggerated indications of a planned revision even in the most trifling differences, none of which, except perhaps, but not necessarily, for the lines unique to F1 (a number of which, however, are almost certainly due to omissions by the Q1 compositors), are not beyond the capability of an intelligent, but careless, book-keeper. T. H. Howard-Hill well describes the critical dangers inherent in such an *a priori* approach:

Despite the confidence with which the contributors to *The Division of the Kingdoms* hold that Q/F variations represent literary revision and are not merely the effects of faulty textual transmission, the trivial or indifferent character of many of the variations which are brought forward to illustrate the revision can allow readers reasonably to suspect that (although textual variations do affect the character of the play in which they appear, and variations as numerous as those in Q and F must have considerable effects) the distinctive literary consequences of the variation are more a measure of the critical sensitivity of the scholars who interpret them than an indication of a purposed, consistent revision of an existing play into another distinct form.

(Howard-Hill is quoted from a review of *The Division of the Kingdoms* in *The Library*, 6th ser., 7 (1985), 164; see also similar critiques by Carroll, Edwards, Foakes, Knowles, Muir, Thomas, Trousdale, Honigmann [1990], Kermode, Meyer, and Clare.)

In any case, a reader who wishes to reconstruct the main outlines of the F1 text as it differs from that of Q1–2 may do so by noting those passages found only in Q1–2, which in the present text are enclosed in square brackets; similarly, the main outlines of the Q1–2 text may be reconstructed by marking the following passages omitted from the Q1–2 text (single words or phrases are generally not included): 1.1.40–5 ("while . . . now."), 49–50, 84–5 ("The vines . . . interess'd,"), 86 ("Speak."), 88–9 ("*Lear.* Nothing? *Cor.* Nothing."), 162 ("*Alb., Corn.* Dear sir, forbear."), 245 ("I am firm."); 1.2.18 ("Fine word, 'legitimate'!"), 109–14 ("This . . . graves."), 137 ("*fa, sol, la, mi.*"), 166–71 ("I pray . . . brother?"); 1.4.6 ("So . . . come,"), 261 ("*Alb.* Pray . . . patient."), 274 ("Of . . . you."), 305 ("Ha? . . . so."), 322–33 ("This . . . Oswald?"); 2.2.44 ("Part!"); 2.4.6 ("*Kent.* No, my lord."), 22 ("*Kent.* By . . . ay."), 46–55 ("Winter's . . . year."), 98–9 ("*Glou.* Well, . . . man?"), 103 ("Are . . . blood!"), 140–5 ("*Lear.* Say? . . . blame."); 3.1.22–9; 3.2.79–96; 3.4.17 ("In . . .")–18, 26–7, 37–8 ("*Edg.* Fathom . . . Tom!"), 58–9 ("O do de . . . do de."); 3.6.12–14 ("*Fool.* No . . . him."), 85 ("*Fool.* And . . . noon."); 4.1.6–9 ("Welcome . . . But"), 54 ("And . . . must."); 4.2.26 ("O . . . man."); 4.6.165–70 ("Plate . . . lips."), 185 ("I'll . . . proof,"), 203 ("Sa . . . sa."); 5.1.46 ("And machination ceases."); 5.2.11 ("*Glou.* And . . . too."); 5.3.76, 89 ("*Gon.* An enterlude!"), 90 ("let . . . sound."), 145, 156 ("Hold, sir."), 223 ("O, help!"), 225 ("O, she's dead!"), 256 (omitted Q2 only), 283 ("This . . . sight."), 311–12 ("Do . . . there!").

Since the textual situation is so uncertain, it has seemed worthwhile to include in the Textual Notes all variants between F1 and Q1 (a few elided forms not included).

For further information, see: Madeleine Doran, *The Text of "King Lear"* (Stanford, 1931); W. W. Greg, *The Variants in the First Quarto of "King Lear"* (The Bibliographical Society, London, 1940) [a classic study], and *The Shakespeare First Folio* (Oxford, 1955); Leo Kirschbaum, *The True Text of "King Lear"* (Baltimore, 1940); G. I. Duthie, ed., *Shakespeare's "King Lear"* (Oxford, 1949), *Elizabethan Shorthand and the First Quarto of "King Lear"* (Oxford, 1949), and ed., New Shakespeare *King Lear* (Cambridge, 1960); Philip Williams, "Two Problems in the Folio Text of *King Lear*," *SQ* 4 (1953), 451–60; Alice Walker, *Textual Problems of the First Folio* (Cambridge, 1953); A. S. Cairncross, "The Quartos and the First Folio Text of *King Lear*," *RES*, n.s. 6 (1955), 252–6; Charlton Hinman, "The Prentice Hand in the Tragedies of the Shakespeare First Folio: Compositor E," *SB* 9 (1957), 3–20, and Supplementary Introduction to the Oxford facsimile of Quarto 1 (1964); J. S. G. Bolton, "Wear and Tear as Factors in the Textual History of the Quarto Version of *King Lear*," *SQ* 11 (1960), 427–38; Kenneth Muir, ed., New Arden *King Lear* (London, rev. ed., 1963) and *Shakespeare: Contrasts and Controversies* (Norman, Oklahoma, 1985), 51–66; E. A. J. Honigmann, *The Stability of Shakespeare's Text* (London, 1965) and "Shakespeare's Revised Plays: *King Lear* and *Othello*," *The Library*, 6th ser., 4 (1982), 142–73; J. K. Walton, *The Quarto Copy for the First Folio of Shakespeare* (Dublin, 1971); Michael Warren, "Quarto and Folio *King Lear* and the Interpretation of Albany and Edgar," in *Shakespeare: Pattern of Excelling Nature*, ed. David Bevington and J. L. Halio (Newark, 1976), 95–107, and ed., *The Complete Lear, 1608–1623* (Berkeley, 1989: reviewed by E. A. J. Honigmann, *New York Review of Books* [25 October 1990], pp. 58–60); Steven Urkowitz, *Shakespeare's Revision of "King Lear"* (Princeton, 1980; see reviews by Richard Knowles, *MP* 79 [1981], 197–200; Phillip Edwards, *MLR* 77 [1982], 694–8); P. W. K. Stone, ed. *The Textual History of "King Lear"* (London, 1980); P. W. M. Blayney, *The Texts of "King Lear": Vol. I, Nicholas Okes and the First Quarto* (Cambridge, 1982); T. H. Howard-Hill, "The Problem of Manuscript Copy for Folio *King Lear*," *The Library*, 6th ser. 4 (1982), 1–24 and "Q1 and the Copy for Folio *Lear*," *PBSA* 80 (1986), 419–35; Richard Knowles, "The Printing of the Second Quarto (1619) of *King Lear*," *SB* 35 (1982), 191–206; Gary Taylor, "The Folio Copy for *Hamlet*, *King Lear*, and *Othello*," *SQ* 34 (1983), 44–61; Gary Taylor and Michael Warren, eds., *The Division of the Kingdoms: Shakespeare's Two Versions of "King Lear"* (Oxford, 1983); S. W. Reid, *The Text of "King Lear"* (Stanford, 1983); Sidney Thomas, "Shakespeare's Supposed Revision of *King Lear*," *SQ* 35 (1984), 506–11; Gary Taylor, "Folio Compositors and Folio Copy: *King Lear* and Its Context," *PBSA* 79 (1985), 17–74, and "The Rhetorics of Reaction," in *Crisis in Editing: Texts of the English Renaissance*, ed. Randall McLeod (New York, 1994), 19–59 [a counterattack against what Taylor terms the "reactionary" criticisms levelled at the two-*Lear* hypothesis and the New Oxford Shakespeare]; R. A. Foakes, "Textual Revision and the Fool in *King Lear*," in *Essays in Honour of Peter Davison:*

*Trivium* 20 (Wales, 1985): 33–47; Marion Trousdale, "A Trip Through the Divided Kingdoms," *SQ* 37 (1986): 218–23; Stanley Wells, Gary Taylor, et al., *William Shakespeare: A Textual Companion* (Oxford, 1987); W. C. Carroll, "New Plays vs. Old Readings: *The Division of the Kingdoms* and Folio Deletions in *King Lear,*" *SP* 85 (1988): 225–44; Jay L. Halio, ed., New Cambridge *The Tragedy of King Lear* (Cambridge, 1992) and ed., *The First Quarto of "King Lear"* (Cambridge, 1994); A. R. Meyer, "Shakespeare's Art and the Texts of *King Lear,*" *SB* 47 (1994): 128–46; Sir Frank Kermode, "Disintegration Once More," *Proceedings of the British Academy* 84 (1994): 93–111; Robert Clare, "The Theory of Authorial Revision between Quarto and Folio Texts of *King Lear,*" *The Library*, 6th ser. 17 (1995), 34–59.

## TEXTUAL NOTES

Title: **The . . . Lear**] M. William Shakspeare: His True Chronicle Historie of the life and death of King Lear and his three Daughters. With the vnfortunate life of Edgar, sonne and heire to the Earle of Gloster, and his sullen and assumed humor of Tom of Bedlam: As it was played before the Kings Maiestie at Whitehall vpon S. Stephans night in Christmas Hollidayes. By his Maiesties seruants playing vsually at the Gloabe on the Bancke-side. *Q1 (title-page)*
Dramatis personae: *subs. as first given in Rowe*
Act-scene division: *none in Q1–2; from F1, with the following exceptions: 2.3, 4 (no scene divisions in F1); 4.3 (scene om. F1); 4.4–6 (numbered 4.3–5 in F1); see first note to each of these scenes; present act-scene arrangement as a whole first established by Steevens*

### 1.1
Location: *Theobald (after Rowe)*
o.s.d. **Edmund**] Bastard *Q1–2*
4 **kingdom**] kingdomes *Q1–2*
5 **equalities**] *Q1–2;* qualities *F1*
11 **to't**] to it *Q1–2*
19 **a son, sir**] sir a sonne *Q1–2*
20–1 **this, . . . account.**] *Theobald (subs.);* this; . . . account, *F1;* this, . . . account, *Q1–2*
22 **to**] into *Q1–2*
25 **Edmund**] *Q1–2 (throughout, except Edmond at 5.3.168 in Q1);* Edmond *F1 (through 1.2 and at 5.3.168)*

26 s.p. **Edm.**] Bast. *Q1–2 (subs. throughout)*
27–8 **My . . . friend.**] *as prose, Q1–2; as verse, F1*
33 s.d. **Sound a sennet.**] *Q1–2;* Sennet. *F1 (all after coming. l. 33); placed as in Dyce*
33 s.d. **one . . . then**] *Q1–2; Q1–2 s.d. reads:* Enter one bearing a Coronet, then Lear, then the Dukes of Albany, and Cornwell [Cornwall *Q2*], next Gonorill, Regan, Cordelia, with followers.
33 s.d. **Goneril**] Gonorill *Q1–2 (throughout, except* Gonoril *in* Q1 *at* 3.6.36)
34 **the**] my *Q1–2*
35 **lord**] Leige *Q1–2*
35 s.d. **with Edmund**] *Capell (subs.); s.d. om. Q1–2*
36 **shall**] will *Q1–2*
36 **purpose.**] purposes, *Q1–2*
37 **Give . . . that**] The map there; know *Q1–2*
38 **fast**] first *Q1–2*
39 **from our age**] of our state *Q1–2*
40 **Conferring**] Confirming *Q1–2*
40 **strengths**] yeares *Q1–2*
40–5 **while . . . now.**] *om. Q1–2*
45 **The princes**] The two great Princes *Q1–2*
49–50 **(Since . . . state),**] *om. Q1–2*
53 **nature . . . challenge**] merit doth most challenge it *Q1–2*
55 **I**] I do *Q1–2*
55 **words**] *Q1–2;* word *F1 (line very crowded in F1)*

56 **and**] or *Q1–2*
59 **as . . . lov'd**] a . . . loued *Q1–2*
59 **found**] friend *Q1–2*
62, 76 s.dd. **Aside.**] *Pope*
62 **speak?**] doe, *Q1–2*
64 **shadowy**] shady *Q1–2*
64–5 **and . . . rivers,**] *om. Q1–2*
64 **rich'd,**] *Rowe;* rich'd *F1*
66 **Albany's**] *Rowe;* Albanies *F1, Q2;* Albaines *Q1*
66 **issue**] *Q1–2;* issues *F1*
68 **of Cornwall**] to Cornwell *Q1* (Cornwell *throughout scene*); to Cornwall *Q2* (Cornwall *throughout scene*)
68 **Speak.**] *Q1–2*
69 **I . . . sister**] Sir I am made of the selfe same mettall that my sister is *Q1*, (selfe-same) *Q2*
69 **self metal**] *Capell;* selfe-mettle *F1; see preceding note for Q1–2*
70 **worth.**] worth *Q1–2*
72 **comes too short**] came short *Q1–2*
74 **possesses**] *Q1–2;* professes *F1*
76 **Cordelia**] Cord. *Q1*
77 **love's**] loues *Q1*
78 **ponderous**] richer *Q1–2*
82 **conferr'd**] confirm'd *Q1–2*
82 **Now**] but now *Q1–2*
83 **Although . . . love**] Although the last, not least in our deere loue, *Q1–2*
84–5 **The . . . interess'd,**] *om. Q1–2*
85 **interess'd**] *Malone;* interest *F1*
85 **draw**] win *Q1–2*
86 **opulent**] *Q1–2;* opilent *F1*
86 **sisters'**] *ed.;* Sisters *F1, Q1–2*
86 **Speak.**] *om. Q1–2*
88–9 **Lear. Nothing? Cor. Nothing.**] *om. Q1–2*
90 **Nothing will**] How, nothing can *Q1–2*
93 **no**] nor *Q1–2*
94 **How, how, Cordelia?**] Goe to, goe to, *Q1;* Go too, go too, *Q2*
95 **you**] it *Q1–2*
96 **lov'd**] loued *Q1–2 (the 'd and -ed variants between F1 and Q1–2 are not hereafter recorded, since Q1–2 seem haphazard in making any distinction)*
100 **Happily**] Happely *Q1;* Haply *Q2*
104 **To . . . all.**] *Q1–2*
105 **thy . . . this**] this with thy heart *Q1–2*
105 **Ay, my good**] I good my *Q1–2*
108 **Let**] Well let *Q1–2*
110 **mysteries**] *F2;* miseries *F1;* mistresse *Q1–2*
110 **Hecat**] *F2;* Heccat *F1, Q1–2*

110 **night**] might *Q1–2*
118 **to my bosom**] *om. Q1–2*
124 s.d. **To Cordelia.**] *Rowe*
127 **Burgundy.**] *Rowe (subs.);* Burgundy, *F1, Q1–2*
128 **dow'rs**] dower *Q1–2*
128 **the**] this *Q1–2*
130 **with**] in *Q1–2*
131 **Pre-eminence**] *Jennens;* Preheminence *F1, Q1–2*
135 **turn**] turnes *Q1–2*
135 **we shall**] we still *Q1–2*
136 **th' addition**] the addicions *Q1–2*
139 **between**] betwixt *Q1–2*
146 **mad**] man *Q1*
146 **wouldest**] wilt *Q1–2*
149 **falls**] stoops *Q1–2*
149 **folly. Reserve**] *Rowe (subs.);* folly, reserue *F1;* folly, / Reuerse *Q1–2*
149 **state**] doome *Q1–2*
151 **rashness. . . . judgment,**] *Rowe (subs.);* rashnesse, . . . judgement: *F1;* rashnes, . . . iudgement, *Q1–2*
153–4 **sounds Reverb**] sound / Reverbs *Q1–2*
155 **a**] *Q1–2*
156 **thine enemies, ne'er**] thy enemies, nor *Q1–2*
156 **fear'd**] *Furness conj.;* feare *F1, Q1–2*
157 **motive**] the motiue *Q1–2*
160 s.pp. **Lear. . . . Kent.**] *Q1–2;* Kear. . . . Lent. *F1*
160 **Apollo—**] *Q2;* Apollo, *F1;* Appollo, *Q1*
161 **swear'st**] swearest *Q1*
161 **O**] *om. Q1–2*
161 **miscreant**] recreant *Q1–2*
161 s.d. **Starts . . . sword.**] *Rowe (subs.)*
162 **Alb., Corn. Dear sir, forbear.**] *om. Q1–2; F1 reads s.p. as* Cor.
163 **Kill**] Doe, kill *Q1–2*
163 **the**] *Q1–2;* thy *F1*
164 **gift**] doome *Q1–2*
166–7 **recreant, On thine**] on thy *Q1–2*
168 **That**] Since *Q1–2*
168 **vow**] *Q1–2;* vowes *F1*
169 **strain'd**] straied *Q1–2*
170 **betwixt**] betweene *Q1–2*
170 **sentence**] *F1 (u), Q1–2;* sentences *F1 (c)*
173 **Five**] Foure *Q1–2*
173 **thee, for provision**] *Capell;* thee for prouision, *F1, Q1–2*
174 **disasters**] diseases *Q1–2*
175 **sixt**] fift *Q1–2*
178 **death. Away!**] *Pope (subs.);* death, away. *F1;* death, away, *Q1–2*

180 **Fare**] Why fare *Q1–2*
180 **King; sith**] *Theobald;* King, sith *F1;* king, since *Q1–2*
181 **Freedom**] Friendship *Q1–2*
182 s.d. **To Cordelia.**] *Hanmer*
182 **dear . . . thee**] protection take the *Q1–2*
183 **justly think'st . . . rightly**] rightly thinks . . . iustly *Q1–2*
184 s.d. **To . . . Goneril.**] *Hanmer*
187 s.d. **Flourish.**] *om. Q1–2*
187 s.d. **Enter . . . Attendants.**] Enter France and Burgundie with Gloster. *Q1–2*
188 s.p. **Glou.**] *Q1–2;* Cor. *F1 (possibly correct, if Cor. is an abbreviated form of Cornwall)*
190 **toward**] towards *Q1–2*
190 **this**] a *Q1–2*
193 **Most**] *om. Q1–2*
194 **hath**] *what Q1–2*
195 **less.**] *F4;* lesse? *F1, Q1–2*
197 **price**] prise *Q1*
200 **more**] else *Q1–2*
202 **Will**] Sir will *Q1;* Sir, will *Q2*
204 **Dow'r'd**] Couered *Q1–2*
206 **in**] On *Q1–2*
208 s.d. **To France.**] *Pope*
214 **whom**] that *Q1–2*
214 **best**] *Q1–2*
216 **The best, the**] most best, most *Q1–2*
220 **it,**] *Q1–2;* it: *F1*
220 **your fore-vouch'd affection**] you for voucht affections *Q1–2*
221 **Fall**] Falne *Q1–2*
221 **taint;**] *Steevens;* taint, *F1, Q1–2*
223 **Should**] Could *Q1–2*
225 **well**] *Q1–2;* will *F1*
226 **make known**] may know *Q1–2*
228 **unchaste**] vncleane *Q1–2*
230 **richer**] rich *Q1–2*
231 **still-soliciting**] hyphen, *Warburton*
232 **That**] As *Q1–2*
233 **Better**] Goe to, goe to, better *Q1–2*
235 **but**] no more but *Q1–2*
236 **Which**] That *Q1–2*
238 **Love's**] Loue is *Q1–2*
239 **regards**] respects *Q1–2*
240 **point.**] *Steevens (after Pope);* point, *F1, Q2;* point *Q1*
241 **a dowry**] and dowre *Q1;* and dower *Q2*
241 **King**] Leir *Q1;* Lear *Q2*
245 **Nothing.**] *Rowe (subs.);* Nothing, *F1, Q1–2*
245 **I am firm.**] *om. Q1–2*

248 **respects of fortune**] *Q1–2;* respect and Fortunes *F1*
252 **seize**] ceaze *Q1*
256 **my**] thy *Q1–2*
258 **of**] in *Q1–2*
259 **Can**] Shall *Q1–2*
264 s.d. **To Cordelia.**] *Neilson (after anon. conj. in Cambridge)*
266 s.d. **all . . . Cordelia**] *Globe (after Capell);* Lear and Burgundie *Q1–2*
271 **Love**] vse *Q1–2*
276 s.p. **Reg.**] *Gonorill. Q1–2*
276 **duty**] duties *Q1–2*
276 s.p. **Gon.**] Regan. *Q1–2*
279 **want**] worth *Q1–2*
280 **plighted**] pleated *Q1–2*
281 **with shame**] shame them *Q1–2*
282 **my**] *om. Q1–2*
282 s.d. **Exeunt**] *F3;* Exit *F1, Q1–2*
283–5 **Sister . . . to-night.**] *as prose, Capell; as verse, F1, Q1–2*
283 **little**] a little *Q1–2*
289 **not**] *Q1–2*
292 **grossly**] grosse *Q1–2*
296–7 **from . . . long-ingraff'd**] to receiue from his age not alone the imperfection of long ingrafted *Q1–2*
298 **the unruly**] vnruly *Q1–2*
302 **compliment**] *Johnson;* complement *F1, Q1–2*
303 **Pray you**] pray *Q1–2*
303 **let us**] lets *Q1–2*
303 **hit**] *Q1–2;* sit *F1*
304 **disposition**] dispositions *Q1–2*
307 **of it**] on't *Q1–2*

### I.2

**Location:** *Pope*
o.s.d. **with a letter**] *Theobald*
1 s.p. **Edm.**] *Theobald;* Bast. *F1 (through l. 159),* Q1–2 *(throughout)*
4 **me,**] *Q1–2;* me? *F1*
10 **baseness?**] *Rowe;* basenes *F1;* base, *Q1–2*
10 **bastardy**] *Q1–2;* Barstadie *F1*
10 **base, base?**] *om. Q1–2*
13 **dull, stale, tired**] stale dull lyed *Q1;* stale, dull lied *Q2*
14 **a**] of a *Q1–2*
15 **asleep**] *Capell;* a sleepe *F1, Q1;* sleepe *Q2*
15 **then**] the *Q1–2*
18 **Fine word, "legitimate"!**] *om. Q1–2*
21 **top**] *Edwards conj.;* to' *F1;* too *Q1–2*
24 **Prescrib'd**] subscribed *Q1–2*
27 s.d. **Putting . . . letter.**] *Rowe*
32 **needed**] needes *Q1–2*

32 **terrible**] terribe *Q1*
37 **and**] *om. Q1–2*
39 **o'erlooking**] liking *Q1–2*
41–2 **I . . . blame.**] *as prose, Q1–2; as verse, F1*
46 s.d. **(Reads.)**] *Q1–2 describe ll. 46–54 as A Letter.*
46 **and reverence**] *om. Q1–2*
54 **brother.**] brother *Q1–2*
55 **Sleep . . . wake**] slept . . . wakt *Q1–2*
58 **you to this**] this to you *Q1–2*
64 **his; . . . that,**] his but in respect, of that *Q1;* his, but in respect of that, *Q2*
66 **It is his.**] It is his? *Q1;* Is it his? *Q2*
69 **Has**] Hath *Q1–2*
69 **before**] heretofore *Q1–2*
71 **heard him oft**] often heard him *Q1–2*
72 **perfect**] perfit *Q1–2*
73 **declin'd, the**] declining, his *Q1–2*
74 **his**] the *Q1–2*
77 **sirrah**] sir *Q1–2*
77 **I'll**] I *Q1–2*
78 **Abominable**] *F4;* Abhominable *F1, Q1–2*
82 **his**] this *Q1–2*
86 **that . . . writ**] he hath wrote *Q1–2*
87 **other**] further *Q1–2*
92 **auricular**] aurigular *Q1–2*
95–7 **Edm. Nor . . . earth!**] *Q1–2*
98 **him, . . . the**] him, I pray you frame your *Q1–2*
101 **will**] shall *Q1–2*
102 **find**] see *Q1–2*
105 **it**] *om. Q1–2*
108 **discord**] discords *Q1–2*
108 **in**] *om. Q1–2*
108 **and**] *om. Q1–2*
109 **'twixt**] betweene *Q1–2*
109–14 **This . . . graves.**] *om. Q1–2*
117 **honesty**] honest *Q1–2*
117 **'Tis strange.**] strange strange! *Q1;* strange, strange! *Q2*
117 s.d. **Exit.**] *om. Q1–2*
119 **surfeits**] surfeit *Q1–2*
121 **and**] and the *Q1–2*
122 **on**] by *Q1–2*
123 **treachers**] Trecherers *Q1–2*
123 **spherical**] spirituall *Q1–2*
127 **whoremaster man**] *Q1–2;* Whoremaster-man *F1*
128 **on . . . star**] to the charge of Starres *Q1–2*
131 **Fut**] *Q1–2*
132 **in**] of *Q1–2*
133 **bastardizing.**] bastardy *Q1;* bastardy; *Q2*
133 **Edgar—**] *Q1* (Edgar;); Edgar, *Q2*

133 s.d. **Enter Edgar.**] *in left margin, opposite Edgar— l. 133, Q1*
134 **Pat**] and out *Q1–2*
135 **My cue**] mine *Q1–2*
135 **sigh**] sigh *Q1*
136 **Tom o'**] them of *Q1–2*
137 **fa . . . mi**] *om. Q1–2*
137 s.d. **Humming these notes.**] *Hanmer (subs.)*
142 **with**] about *Q1–2*
143 **writes**] writ *Q1–2*
144–52 **as . . . come,**] *Q1–2*
146 **amities**] armies *Q2*
153 **The**] Why, the *Q1;* Why the *Q2*
155 **Ay**] *Rowe;* I *F1; om. Q1–2*
157 **nor**] or *Q1–2*
161 **until**] till *Q1–2*
163 **scarcely**] scarce *Q1–2*
166 **fear.**] feare brother, *Q1–2*
166–71 **I . . . brother?**] *om. Q1–2 (except for* go arm'd *[l. 170], which follows* I advise you to the best; *[l. 172])*
173 **toward**] towards *Q1–2*
174 **heard;**] heard, *Q1–2*
174 **faintly,**] *Q1–2;* faintly. *F1*
178 s.d. **Exit Edgar.**] *Q1* (Fdgar), *Q2;* Exit. *F1 (after l. 177)*

## 1.3

**Location:** *Rowe*
o.s.d. **Steward Oswald**] *Collier;* Steward *F1;* Gentleman *Q1–2*
2 s.p. **Osw.**] *Collier;* Ste. *F1 (throughout);* Gent. *Q1–2 (throughout scene)*
2 **Ay**] *Rowe;* I *F1;* Yes *Q1–2*
3 **night**] *Q1–2;* night, *F1*
6 **upbraids**] obrayds *Q1*
6–7 **us . . . When**] vs, / On euery trifell when *Q1,* (vs) *Q2*
10 s.d. **Horns within.**] *Capell*
13 **fellows**] fellow seruants *Q1;* fellow-seruants *Q2*
13 **to**] in *Q1–2*
14 **distaste**] dislike *Q1–2*
14 **my**] our *Q1–2*
16–20 **Not . . . abus'd.**] *Q1–2 (as prose; as verse, Theobald)*
21 **have said**] tell you *Q1–2*
21 **Well**] Very well *Q1–2*
22–3 **And . . . so.**] *as verse, Capell (after Hanmer); as prose, F1, Q1–2*
24–5 **I . . . speak.**] *Q1–2 (as prose; as verse, Capell)*
25–6 **I'll . . . dinner.**] *as verse, Hanmer; as prose, F1, Q1–2*
26 **very**] *Q1–2*
26 **Prepare**] goe prepare *Q1–2*

## I.4

Location: ed. (*after* Pelican)
o.s.d. **disguised as Caius**] *Rowe*
1 **well**] *Q1-2*; will *F1*
4 **raz'd**] *Q1*; raiz'd *F1*; raizd *Q2*
6 **So . . . come,**] *om. Q1-2*
6 **lov'st**] louest *Q1-2*
7 **thee**] the *Q1-2*
7 **labors**] labour *Q1-2*
7 s.d. **Knights**] *Rowe; Q1-2 s.d. reads:* Enter Lear.
7 s.d. **from hunting**] *ed.*
9 s.d. **Exit an Attendant.**] *Malone (after Capell)*
21 **be'st**] be *Q1-2*
21 **he's**] he is *Q1-2*
22 **th' art**] *Q1*; thou art *F1, Q2*
31 **canst**] *Q1*; canst thou *F1, Q2*
37 **sir**] *om. Q1-2*
40 **me.**] *Rowe (subs.)*; me, *F1, Q1-2*
42 **Dinner, ho,**] *Theobald*; Dinner ho, *F1, Q2*; dinner, ho *Q1*
43 s.d. **Exit an Attendant.**] *Dyce*
43 s.d. **Enter Steward Oswald.**] *placed as in Capell; after l. 44, F1, Q1-2*
44 **you**] *om. Q1-2*
45 s.d. **Exit**] *om. Q1-2*
46 **clotpole**] clat-pole *Q1-2*
47 s.d. **Exit a Knight.**] *Dyce*
47 **Ho!**] *Rowe;* Ho, *F1, Q2;* ho *Q1*
48 **asleep.**] *Theobald (subs.)*; asleepe, *F1, Q1-2*
48 s.d. **Enter Knight.**] *Dyce*
50 s.p. **Knight.**] Kent. *Q1-2*
50 **daughter**] *Q1-2;* Daughters *F1*
54, 57, 64, 73 s.pp. **Knight.**] seruant. *Q1-2*
56 **He**] A *Q1*
60 **of kindness**] *om. Q1-2*
66 **wrong'd**] is wrong'd *Q2*
70 **purpose**] purport *Q1-2*
71 **my**] this *Q1-2*
75 **well**] *om. Q1-2*
77 s.d. **Exit an Attendant.**] *Dyce*
77 s.d. **Exit another Attendant.**] *Dyce*
77 s.d. **Enter Steward Oswald.**] *placed as in Johnson; after l. 78, F1; om. Q1-2*
78 **you, come**] you sir, come *Q1-2*
78 **hither, sir**] hither *Q1-2*
82-3 **I . . . pardon.**] *as prose, Q1-2; as verse F1*
82 **these**] this *Q1-2*
82-3 **your pardon**] you pardon me *Q1-2*
84 s.d. **Striking him.**] *Rowe*
85 **strucken**] struck *Q1-2*
86 s.d. **Tripping . . . heels.**] *Rowe*
87-8 **I . . . thee.**] *as prose, Q1-2; as verse, F1*
89 **arise, away**] *om. Q1-2*

91-2 **To . . . So.**] you haue wisedome. *Q1-2*
92 **wisdom? So.**] *Theobald (subs.)*; wisedome, so. *F1*; wisedome. *Q1-2*
92 s.d. **Pushes Oswald out.**] *Theobald*
93 **my**] *om. Q1-2*
94 s.d. **Giving Kent money.**] *Johnson*
95 s.d. **Offering . . . cap.**] *Capell*
98 **Kent. Why, Fool?**] *Q1-2; Lear.* Why my Boy? *F1 (anticipating l. 106)*
99 **Why?**] Why *Q1-2*
99 **one's**] on's *Q1*; ones *Q2*
101 **thou'lt**] thou't *Q1-2*
102 **has**] hath *Q1-2*
103 **did**] done *Q1-2*
107 **all my**] any *Q1-2*
111 **Truth's a dog**] Truth is a dog that *Q1*, (is,) *Q2*
112 **the Lady Brach**] Ladie oth'e brach *Q1-2*
114 **gall**] gull *Q1-2*
117 **nuncle**] vncle *Q1-2*
128 s.p. **Kent.**] Lear. *Q1-2*
129 **'tis**] *om. Q1-2*
131 **nuncle**] vncle *Q1-2*
132-3 **Why . . . nothing.**] *as prose, Q1-2; as verse, F1*
134 s.d. **To Kent.**] *Rowe*
137 **Dost**] *Q1* (Doo'st); Do'st thou *F1;* Dost thou *Q2*
138 **one**] foole *Q1-2*
140-55 **That . . . snatching.**] *Q1-2*
153 **an't**] on't *Q2*
154 **ladies**] lodes *Q2*
154 **the**] *om. Q2*
155-6 **Nuncle . . . egg**] giue me an egge Nuncle *Q1-2*
160 **crown**] *Q1-2;* Crownes *F1*
161 **thine**] thy *Q1-2*
161 **on thy**] at'h *Q1*
166, 175 s.dd. **Sings.**] *Rowe (subs.)*
166 **grace**] wit *Q1-2*
167 **wise men**] *Q1-2;* wisemen *F1*
168 **And . . to**] They . . . doe *Q1-2*
172 **e'er**] euer *Q1-2*
173 **mothers**] mother *Q1-2*
178 **fools**] *Q1-2;* Foole *F1*
179 **Prithee**] *F3 (subs.)*; Pry'thy *F1;* prethe *Q1;* prethee *Q2*
181 **sirrah**] *om. Q1-2*
183 **thou'lt**] thou wilt *Q1-2*
184 **sometimes**] sometime *Q1-2*
186 **o'**] of *Q1-2*
187 **o'**] a *Q1-2*
188 **o'**] of *Q1-2*
190 **You**] Me thinks you *Q1;* Me-thinks you *Q2*
190 **Of late**] alate *Q1-2*

192 **frowning**] frowne *Q1–2*
194 s.d. **To Goneril.**] *Pope*
198 **nor crust**] neither crust *Q1–2*
198 **nor**] *Q1–2;* not *F1*
200 s.d. **Pointing to Lear.**] *Johnson*
204 **and . . . riots. Sir,**] *Capell (subs.);*
  and (not to be endur'd) riots Sir.
  *F1;* & (not to be indured riots,)
  Sir *Q1;* and (not to be endured
  riots) Sir, *Q2*
208 **it**] *om. Q1–2*
210 **redresses**] redresse *Q1–2*
213 **Which**] that *Q1–2*
214 **Will**] must *Q1–2*
214 **proceeding**] proceedings *Q1–2*
214 **know**] trow *Q1–2*
215–6 **"The . . . young."**] *as verse, Pope;*
  *as prose, F1, Q1–2*
216 **it had**] *Q1–2;* it's had *F1*
216 **by it**] beit *Q1–2*
219 **I**] Come sir, I *Q1–2*
219 **your**] that *Q1–2*
221 **which . . . transport**] that . . .
  transforme *Q1–2*
225 s.d. **Sings.**] *ed.*
225 **"Whoop . . . thee."**] *quotes,*
  *Furness*
226, 227 **Does**] Doth *Q1–2*
226 **This**] why this *Q1–2*
228 **weakens,**] weakness, or *Q1–2*
229 **lethargied . . . 'Tis**] *(dash, Rowe);*
  lethergie, sleeping, or wakeing; ha!
  sure tis *Q1–2*
231 **Lear's shadow.**] Lears shadow? *Q1–2*
  *(spoken by Lear)*
232–5 **Lear. I . . . father.**] *Q1–2*
  (ll. 232–4 *continued to Lear*).
232–4 **I . . . daughters.**] *as verse, Kittredge*
  *(after Pope); as prose, Q1–2*
237 **This admiration, sir,**] Come sir, this
  admiration *Q1–2*
239 **To**] *om. Q1–2*
239 **aright,**] *Q1–2;* aright: *F1*
240 **should**] you should *Q2*
242 **debosh'd**] deboyst *Q1–2*
245 **Makes it**] make *Q1–2*
245 **a brothel**] brothell *Q1–2*
246 **grac'd**] great *Q1–2*
247 **then**] thou *Q1–2*
250 **remainders**] remainder *Q1–2*
252 **Which**] that *Q1;* and *Q2*
255–6 **You . . . betters.**] *as verse, Rowe; as*
  *prose, F1, Q1–2*
256 s.d. **Albany**] Duke *Q1–2*
257 **Woe . . . repents**] We . . . repent's *Q1;*
  We . . . repent's vs *Q2*
257 **O . . . come?**] *Q1–2*

258 **will? . . . my**] will that wee prepare
  any *Q1–2*
261 **Alb. Pray . . . patient.**] *om. Q1–2*
262 s.d. **To Goneril.**] *Rowe*
262 **liest.**] list *Q1;* lessen *Q2*
263 **are**] and *Q1–2*
268 **Which**] that *Q1–2*
270 **Lear, Lear!**] Lear! *Q1–2*
271 s.d. **Striking his head.**] *Pope*
272 s.d. **Exeunt . . . Kent.**] *Alexander*
274 **Of . . . you.**] *om. Q1–2*
275 **Hear**] harke *Q1–2*
275 **hear!**] *om. Q1–2*
277–8 **fruitful. . . . convey**] fruitful into
  her wombe, conuey *Q1;* fruitefull,
  into her wombe conuey *Q2*
283 **thwart disnatur'd**] thourt
  disuetur'd *Q1–2*
285 **cadent**] accent *Q1–2*
287 **that . . . feel**] *repeated, Q1*
289 **Away, away.**] goe, goe, my people?
  *Q1–2*
289 s.d. **Exit.**] *Lear's exit here and re-entry*
  *at l. 293 om. Q1–2*
291 **more of it**] the cause *Q1–2*
293 **As**] that *Q1–2*
295 **What's**] What is *Q1–2*
296 s.d. **To Goneril.**] *Theobald*
296 **death!**] *Q1–2;* death, *F1*
298 **which**] that *Q1–2*
299 **thee . . . Blasts**] the worst blasts *Q1–2*
299–300 **upon thee! Th'**] vpon the *Q1–2*
301 **thee! Old**] the old *Q1–2*
302 **ye**] you *Q1–2*
303 **cast you**] you cast *Q1–2*
303 **loose**] make *Q1–2*
304 **Yea . . . this?**] *Q1–2*
305 **Ha . . . so:**] *om. Q1–2*
305–6 **I . . . Who**] yet haue I left a
  daughter, whom *Q1–2*
310 **ever.**] euer, thou shalt I warrant thee.
  *Q1–2*
310 **that?**] that my Lord? *Q1–2*
312 **you—**] *Theobald;* you. *F1, Q2;* you, *Q1*
313–4 **Pray . . . more**] Come sir no more,
  you, more *Q1;* Come sir, no more;
  you, more *Q2*
314 s.d. **To the Fool.**] *Johnson*
315–6 **Nuncle . . . thee.**] *as prose, Q1–2;*
  *as verse, F1*
315 **take**] and take *Q1–2*
316–7 **with thee. A**] with a *Q1–2*
322–33 **This . . . unfitness—**] *om. Q1–2*
333 **unfitness—**] *Rowe;* vnfitnesse. *F1*
333 **How now, Oswald?**] Gon. What
  Oswald, ho. Oswald. Here Madam.
  *Q1–2 (Q1–2 om. Oswald's re-entry)*

334 **What,**] Q2 (*Gon.* What,); What *F1;*
Gon. What Q1
334 **that**] this Q1–2
335 **Ay**] *Rowe;* I *F1;* Yes Q1–2
337 **fear**] feares Q1–2
340 s.d. **Exit Oswald.**] *Rowe*
340 **No, no**] now Q1; —now Q2
342 **condemn**] dislike Q1–2
343 **You are**] *F2;* Your are *F1;*
y'are Q1–2
343 **attax'd**] *Greg;* at task *F1;* alapt Q1 (*u*),
Q2; attaskt Q1 (*c*) (*cf. 3.2.16*)
344 **prais'd**] *F2;* prai'sd *F1;* praise Q1–2
346 **better, oft**] better ought, Q1–2
347 **then—**] then. Q1
348 **th' event**] *Rowe;* the'uent *F1;* the
euent Q1–2

### 1.5

**Location:** *Capell (after Theobald)*
o.s.d. **Enter . . . Fool.**] Q2; Enter Lear,
Kent, Gentleman, and Foole. *F1;* Enter
Lear. Q1
5 **afore**] before Q1–2
8 **were**] where Q1
8 **in 's**] in his Q1–2
8 **were't**] *Rowe;* wert *F1,* Q1–2
11 **not**] nere Q1–2
15 **crab's**] crab is Q1–2
16 **can tell**] con, Q1–2
17 **What . . . tell**] Why what canst thou
tell my Q1–2
18 **She will**] Sheel Q1–2
18 **does**] doth Q1–2
19 **Canst**] canst not Q1–2
19–20 **stands . . . on 's**] stande in the
middle of his Q1, (stands) Q2
22 **one's eyes of**] his eyes on Q1–2
23 **he**] a Q1
30 **put 's**] put his Q1–2
31 **daughters**] daughter Q1–2
32 **nature.**] *Pope (subs.);* Nature,
*F1,* Q1–2
34 **'em**] them Q1–2
35 **moe**] more Q1–2
38 **indeed**] *om.* Q1–2
39 **Monster**] Monster, Q1–2
41 **I'ld**] *Globe;* Il'd *F1;* id'e Q1–2
44 **till**] before Q1–2
46–8 **O . . . ready?**] *as verse, Pope; as prose,*
*F1,* Q1–2
46 **not mad,**] *om.* Q1–2
46 **heaven!**] heauen! I would not be
mad, Q1–2
47 s.d. **Enter Gentleman.**] *Theobald*
48 **How now,**] *om.* Q1–2
49 s.p. **Gent.**] Seruant. Q1–2

50 s.d. **Exeunt . . . Gentleman.**] *Capell;*
Exit. Q1–2
51 **that's a**] that is Q1–2
52 **unless**] except Q1–2
52 s.d. **Exit.**] Q1–2; Exeunt. *F1*

### 2.1

**Location:** *Rowe*
o.s.d. **severally**] meeting Q1; meetes
him Q2
1 s.p. **Edm.**] *Theobald;* Bast. *F1,* Q1–2
*(throughout scene)*
2–4 **And . . . night.**] *as prose, Q1–2; as*
*verse, F1*
2 **you**] Q1–2; your *F1*
4 **Regan**] *om.* Q1–2
4 **this night**] to night Q1–2
7 **they**] there Q1–2
8 **ear-bussing**] Q1–2; ear-kissing *F1*
9 **Not I.**] Not, I Q1–2
10–2 **Cur. Have . . . word.**] *om.* Q2
10–1 **Have . . . Albany?**] *as prose, Q1; as*
*verse, F1*
10 **toward**] towards Q1
11 **Dukes**] two Dukes Q1
13 **You . . . sir.**] *as prose, Q1–2; as verse, F1*
13 **do**] *om.* Q1–2
14 **better! best!**] *Pope;* better best, *F1,*
Q1–2
18 **I must act.**] must aske Q1–2
18 **fortune, work**] *Capell;* Fortune worke
*F1;* fortune helpe Q1–2
19 s.d. **Enter Edgar.**] *placed as in Theobald;*
*after l. 18, F1; in left margin opposite l. 15,*
*Q1; after* Which *l. 18, Q2*
20 **sir**] *om.* Q1–2
23 **Cornwall?**] Cornwall ought, Q1–2
26 **'gainst**] against Q1–2
27 **yourself.**] your— Q1–2
28 **coming.**] *Rowe;* comming, *F1,* Q1–2
28–9 **me: In cunning**] me in crauing
Q1–2
30 **Draw**] *om.* Q1–2
31 **Light ho**] light here Q1–2
32 **brother**] brother flie Q1–2
33 s.d. **Wounds his arm.**] *Rowe*
36 s.d. **and . . . torches**] *om.* Q1–2
37 **where's**] where is Q1
39 **Mumbling**] warbling Q1–2
40 **stand 's**] Q1; stand *F1;* stand his Q2
42 **could—**] Q1–2; could. *F1*
43 **ho**] *om.* Q1–2
43 s.d. **Exeunt some Servants.**] *Dyce*
45 **revengive**] Q1–2; reuenging *F1*
46 **the thunder**] their thunders Q1–2
47 **manifold**] many fould Q1–2
48 **in fine**] in a fine Q1–2

49 **loathly**] *Q1*; lothly *F1, Q2*
50 **in**] with *Q1-2*
52 **latch'd**] lancht *Q1*; launcht *Q2*
53 **And**] but *Q1-2*
54 **quarrel's right**] *Pope*; quarrels right
  *F1, Q2*; quarrels, rights *Q1*
56 **Full**] but *Q1-2*
57 **uncaught; . . . dispatch.**] *Steevens*
  *(after Johnson)*; vncaught / And found;
  dispatch, *F1, Q2*; vncaught and found,
  dispatch, *Q1*
62 **coward**] caytife *Q1-2*
68 **would the reposal**] could the
  reposure *Q1-2*
70 **I should**] *Q1-2*; should I *F1*
71 **ay**] *Capell*; I *Q1-2*
72 **I'ld**] id'e *Q1-2*
73 **practice**] pretence *Q1-2*
76 **spirits**] spurres *Q1-2*
77 **O strange**] Strong *Q1-2*
78 **said he**] *om. Q1-2*
78 **I . . . him.**] *Q1-2*
78 s.d. **Tucket within.**] *placed as in*
  *Steevens; after* it." *l. 77, F1; om. Q1-2*
79 **why**] *Q1-2*; wher *F1*
83 **due**] *om. Q1-2*
87 **strange news**] *Q1-2*;
  strangenesse *F1*
90 **O**] *om. Q1-2*
90 **it's**] is *Q1-2*
92 **nam'd,**] named *Q1-2*
93 **O**] I *Q1-2*
95 **tended**] tends *Q1-2*
97 **of that consort**] *om. Q1-2*
100 **th' expense . . . his**] the wast and
  spoyle of his *Q1 (c)*; these—and wast of
  this his *Q1 (u), Q2*
105 **hear**] heard *Q1-2*
106 **It was**] Twas *Q1-2*
107 **bewray**] betray *Q1-2*
115-6 **need; You**] need you, *Q1*; need,
  you *Q2*
116 **sir**] *om. Q1-2*
117 **however**] *Rowe*; how euer *F1, Q1-2*
119 **threading**] threatning *Q1-2*
119 **night:**] *Theobald (subs.)*; night,
  *F1, Q1-2*
120 **poise**] poyse *Q1 (c)*; prise *Q1 (u)*;
  prize *F1, Q2*
121 **advice**] *Q2*; aduise *F1, Q1*
123 **best**] *F1, Q1 (u), Q2*; lest *Q1 (c)*
123 **thought**] *Q1-2*; though *F1*
127 **businesses**] busines *Q1*;
  businesse *Q2*
129 s.d. **Flourish. Exeunt.**] *Cambridge*;
  Exeunt. Flourish. *F1*; Exeunt. *Q1*; Exit.
  *Q2 (both after use. l. 128)*

**2.2**
**Location:** *Capell*
o.s.d. **and**] *Q1-2*; aad *F1*
1 **dawning**] euen *Q1 (c), Q2*;
  deuen *Q1 (u)*
1 **this**] the *Q1-2*
6 **lov'st**] loue *Q1-2*
16-7 **three-suited, hundred-pound**] *F1*
  *(subs.)*; three-suited-hundred pound
  *F1*; three shewted hundred pound
  *Q1 (c), Q2*; three-snyted hundred
  pound *Q1 (u)*
17 **worsted-stocking**] *Theobald*;
  woosted-stocking *F1*; worsted-stocken
  *Q1 (c), Q2*; wosted
  stocken *Q1 (u)*
18 **action-taking**] action taking
  knaue, a *Q1-2*
18-9 **superserviceable, finical**]
  superfinicall *Q1-2*
19 **one-trunk-inheriting**] *F3*; one
  Trunke-inheriting *F1*; one truncke
  inheriting *Q1-2*
23 **one**] *om. Q1-2*
23 **clamorous**] *Q1-2*; clamours *F1*
24 **deni'st**] denie *Q1-2*
24 **thy**] the *Q1-2*
25 **Why**] *om. Q1-2*
26 **that is**] that's *Q1-2*
29 **days**] dayes agoe *Q1-2*
29-30 **tripp'd . . . thee**] beat thee, and
  tript vp thy heeles *Q1-2*
31 **yet**] *om. Q1-2*
32 s.d. **drawing his sword**] *Rowe*
  *(after l. 33); placed as in Craig*
32 **of**] a *Q1-2*
33 **you, you**] you, draw you *Q1-2*
33 **cullionly**] *Q1-2*; Cullyenly *F1*
35 **come with**] bring *Q1-2*
42 s.d. **Beating him.** *Rowe*
43 **murther, murther**] murther,
  helpe *Q1-2*
43 s.d. **Edmund . . . drawn**] *Q1-2*
44 s.p. **Edm.**] *Theobald*; Bast. *F1, Q1-2*
44 **Part!**] *om. Q1-2*
45 **and**] *Q1-2*; if *F1*
45-6 **please! Come,**] *Kittredge*
  *(after Theobald)*; please, come, *F1*; please
  come, *Q1-2*
46 **ye**] you *Q1-2*
46 s.d. **Enter . . . Servants.**] *Staunton*;
  *part of Edmund's entry, F1, Q1-2*
  *(om. Servants)*
48-9 **Keep . . . matter?**] *as verse, Capell*;
  *as prose F1, Q1-2*
49 **What is**] what's *Q1-2*
50 **King.**] *Q1-2*; King? *F1*

51 **What is**] Whats *Q1;* What's *Q2*
51 **difference? speak.**] *Rowe;* difference, speake? *F1, Q1–2*
53 **valor.**] *Theobald (subs.);* valour, *F1, Q1–2*
58 **A**] I, a *Q1–2*
58 **sir;**] *Q1;* Sir, *F1, Q2*
59 **they**] hee *Q1–2*
60 **years o' th'**] houres at the *Q1–2*
61 s.p. **Corn.**] Glost. *Q1–2*
62 **ruffian**] ruffen *Q1 (possibly a Shakespearean form)*
63 **grey beard—**] *F3 (dash, Rowe);* graybeard. *F1, Q1–2*
65 **you'll**] *Q1;* you will *F1, Q2*
66 **wall**] walles *Q1–2*
67 **jakes**] iaques *Q1;* Iaques *Q2*
67 **grey beard**] *Q1;* gray-beard *F1, Q2*
68 **sirrah**] sir *Q1–2*
69 **know you**] you haue *Q1–2*
70 **hath**] has *Q1–2*
73 **Who**] That *Q1–2*
74 **the . . . a-twain**] those cordes in twaine *Q1–2*
75 **t' intrinse t' unloose;**] to intrench, to inloose *Q1–2*
77 **Being**] Bring *Q1–2*
77 **fire**] stir *Q1–2*
77 **the**] their *Q1–2*
77 **colder moods**] colder-moods *Q1*
78 **Renege**] *Q1–2;* Reuenge *F1*
79 **gale**] *Q1–2;* gall *F1*
80 **dogs)**] dayes *Q1–2*
82 **Smile**] *F4;* Smoile *F1, Q2;* smoyle *Q1 (possibly a dialect form)*
83 **and**] *Q1;* if *F1, Q2*
84 **I'ld drive ye**] Id'e send you *Q1–2*
84 **Camelot**] Camulet *Q1–2*
86 **out? say that.**] out, say that? *Q1–2*
89 **What . . . fault?**] what's his offence. *Q1;* what's his offence? *Q2*
91 **nor his, nor**] or his, or *Q1–2*
94 **Than**] *Q2;* Then *F1;* That *Q1*
95 **some**] a *Q1–2*
97 **roughness**] ruffines *Q1–2*
99 **An . . . and**] he must be *Q1–2*
100 **take't,**] *Q1 (comma, Rowe);* take it *F1, Q2*
105 **faith,**] sooth, or *Q1–2*
106 **great**] graund *Q1;* grand *Q2*
108 **On**] In *Q1–2*
108 **flick'ring**] *ed. (after Pope);* flicking *F1;* flitkering *Q1–2*
108 **front—**] *Rowe;* front. *F1, Q1–2*
108 **mean'st**] mean'st thou *Q1–2*
109 **dialect**] dialogue *Q1–2*
114 **What was th'**] What's the *Q1–2*

118 **compact**] coniunct *Q1–2*
121 **That**] that, / That *Q1;* that / That *Q2*
123 **fleshment**] flechuent *Q1–2*
123 **dread**] *Q1–2;* dead *F1*
125 **Ajax**] A'Iax *Q1–2*
125 **their**] *Q1–2;* there *F1*
125 **Fetch . . . stocks.**] Bring . . . stockes ho? *Q1–2*
126 **ancient**] ausrent *Q1 (u);* miscreant *Q1 (c), Q2*
127 **Sir**] *om. Q1–2*
129 **employment**] imployments *Q1–2*
130 **shall**] should *Q1–2*
130 **respects**] respect *Q1–2*
132 **Stocking**] Stopping *Q1 (c), Q2;* Stobing *Q1 (u)*
137 **should**] could *Q1–2*
138 **color**] nature *Q1–2*
139 **speaks**] speake *Q1*
139 s.d. **stocks brought out.**] *placed as in* Dyce; *after l. 37, F1; om. Q1–2*
141–5 **His . . . with**] *Q1–2*
143 **contemned'st**] *Capell;* temnest *Q1 (c), Q2;* contaned *Q1 (u)*
145 **The King must**] *Q1–2;* The King his Master, needs must *F1 (the F1 reading represents metrical padding to compensate for the cutting of ll. 141–5)*
146 **he**] hee's *Q1–2*
149 **gentleman**] Gentlemen *Q1*
150 **For . . . legs.**] *Q1–2*
150 s.d. **Kent . . . stocks.**] *Rowe (after l. 147)*
151 **Come . . . away.**] *continued to Regan, Q1–2; assigned to Cornwall, F1*
151 **good**] *Q1; om. F1, Q2*
151 s.d. **with . . . Kent**] *Globe (subs., after Capell); s.d. om. Q1*
152 **Duke's**] *Q1–2;* Duke *F1*
155 **Pray**] Pray you *Q1–2*
155 **travell'd**] *F3;* trauail'd *F1, Q1–2*
156 **Some time . . . out**] Sometime . . . ont *Q1–2*
159 **Duke's**] Dukes *Q1*
159 **to**] *Q1;* too *F1, Q2*
159 **taken**] tooke *Q1–2*
159 s.d. **Exit.**] *om. Q1*
165 **miracles**] my wracke *Q1 (c), Q2;* my rackles *Q1 (u)*
168 s.d. **reads**] *Jennens (and Jennens' quotes following)*
169 **enormous**] enormious *Q1–2*
170 **o'erwatch'd**] ouerwatch *Q1;* ouerwatcht *Q2*
172 **shameful**] *Q1–2;* shamefnll *F1*
173 **smile once more,**] Smile, once more *Q1–2*
173 s.d. **Sleeps.**] *Q1;* He sleepes. *Q2*

## 2.3

2.3] Steevens
Location: ed. (after Pelican, from A.
Schmidt's ed., 1879)
1 heard] heare Q1
4 unusual] Q1; vnusall F1, Q2
5 Does] Dost Q1–2
5 taking. Whiles . . . scape] taking
while . . . scape, Q1–2
10 elf . . . in] else all my haire with Q1–2
12 winds and persecutions] wind, and
persecution Q1–2
15 arms] bare armes Q1–2
16 wooden pricks] Q2; Wodden-prickes
F1; wodden prickes Q1
17 farms] seruice Q1–2
18 sheep-cotes] Q1–2; Sheeps-Coates F1
19 Sometimes] Sometime Q1–2

## 2.4

2.4] Steevens
Location: ed. (after Pelican)
o.s.d. Enter . . . Gentleman.] Enter King.
Q1; Enter King, and a Knight. Q2
o.s.d. Kent . . . stocks.] Dyce
1 home] hence Q1–2
2 messenger] Q1–2; Messengers F1
2, 61 s.pp. Gent.] Knight. Q1–2
3–4 in . . . this] of his Q1–2
5 Ha?] How, Q1–2
6 thy] Q1–2; ahy F1
6 Kent. No, my lord.] om. Q1–2
7 he] looke he Q1; looke, he Q2
7 cruel] crewell Q1–2
7 garters. Horses.] F2 (subs.); Garters
Horses F1; garters, / Horses Q1–2
8 heads] heeles Q1–2
10 man's] Q2; man F1; mans Q1
10 wooden] Q1–2; wodden F1
19–20 Lear. No . . . have.] Q1–2
22 Kent. By . . . ay.] om. Q1–2
23 could not, would] would not,
could Q1–2
26 mightst . . . impose] may'st . . .
purpose Q1–2
31 panting] Q1–2; painting F1
34 those] whose Q1–2
35 meiny] men Q1–2
40 which] that Q1–2
42 wit about me,] wit, about me Q1
45 The] This Q1–2
46–55 Fool. Winter's . . . year.] om. Q1–2
46 Winter's] F3; Winters F1
46 wild] F2; wil'd F1
57 Hysterica] F4; Historica F1, Q1–2
59 With] Q1–2; Wirh F1
59 here] om. Q1–2

60 here.] there? Q1; there. Q2
61 but] then Q1–2
62 None] No Q1–2
63 number] traine Q1–2
65 thou'dst] thou ha'dst Q1; thou
hadst Q2
70 twenty] a 100. Q1; a hundred Q2
73 following] following it Q1–2
74 upward] vp the hill Q1–2
75, 83 wise man] Q1–2; wiseman F1
76 have] Q1–2; hause F1
78 which] that Q1–2
78 and seeks] om. Q1–2
80 begins] begin Q1
87 fool] om. Q1–2
87 s.d. Enter . . . Gloucester.] placed as
in Q1–2; after l. 85, F1
88 They are . . . they are] th'are . . .
th'are Q1–2
88 sick? . . . weary?] Johnson; sicke, . . .
weary, F1, Q1–2
89 have . . . fetches] traueled hard to
night, meare Iustice Q1–2
89 travell'd] Q1–2; trauail'd F1
90 The] I the Q1–2
95 plague! death!] death, plague, Q1–2
96 Fiery? What quality?] what fierie
quality, Q1; what fiery quality; Q2
97 I'ld] id'e Q1; ide Q2
98–9 Glou. Well . . . man?] om. Q1–2
102 commands, tends] Muir;
commands. tends, F1; come and tends
Q1 (u); commands her Q1 (c), Q2
103 Are . . . blood!] om. Q1–2
104 Fiery . . . Duke?] Fierie Duke, Q1
(c), Q2; The fierie Duke Q1 (u)
104 that—] that Lear, Q1–2
107 Whereto] where to Q1–2
108 commands] Command Q1
112 s.d. Looking on Kent.] Johnson
(after wherefore l. 112); placed as in
Cambridge
115 practice only.] practice, only Q1–2
116 Go tell] Tell Q1–2
116 I'd] F4; Il'd F1; Ile Q1–2
120 s.d. Exit.] om. Q1–2
121 O . . . down!' O my heart, my heart.
Q1; O my heart! my heart. Q2
123 put 'em] put vm Q1; put them vp Q2
123–4 knapp'd 'em o' th'] rapt vm ath
Q1–2
126 s.d. Gloucester, Servants] om. Q1–2
(see l. 120 above)
129 you] Q1–2; your F1
130 so.] Q2 (so;); so, F1, Q1
131 mother's] Q1–2; Mother F1
132 s.d. To Kent.] Rowe

132 **O]** yea *Q1–2*
133 s.d. **Exit Kent.]** *Ringler conj.*
134 **sister's]** *F3;* Sisters *F1;* sister is *Q1–2*
135 **here.]** *Q2;* heere, *F1;* heare, *Q1*
135 s.d. **Points . . . heart.]** *Pope*
136 **thou'lt]** thout *Q1–2*
137 **With]** Of *Q1–2*
137 **deprav'd]** depriued *Q1 (c),* *Q2;* deptoued *Q1 (u)*
137 **quality——]** *Rowe;* quality. *F1;* qualitie, *Q1–2*
138 **you]** *om.* *Q1–2*
140 **scant]** slacke *Q1–2*
140–5 **Lear. Say . . . blame.]** *om.* *Q1–2*
143 **restrain'd]** *F3;* restrained *F1*
143 **followers]** *F2;* Followres *F1*
147 **in]** on *Q1–2*
148 **his]** her *Q1–2*
150 **you]** *om.* *Q1–2*
152 **her.]** her Sir? *Q1;* her sir. *Q2*
153 **but]** *om.* *Q1–2*
154 s.d. **Kneeling.]** *Hanmer (subs.)*
158 s.d. **Rising.]** *Collier MS (subs.)*
158 **Never]** No *Q1–2*
164 **sir, fie]** fie sir *Q1–2*
165 s.p. **Lear.]** *om.* *Q1*
168 **blister!]** blast her pride, *Q1–2*
169 **mood is on.]** mood— *Q1–2*
171 **Thy tender-hefted]** The tender hested *Q1–2*
172 **Thee]** the *Q1*
177 **know'st]** knowest *Q1–2*
182 s.d. **Tucket within.]** *placed as in Collier; after l. 181, F1*
183 **know't,]** know't *Q1–2*
183 **letter]** letters *Q1–2*
184 s.d. **To Oswald.]** *Capell (subs.)*
185 **easy-borrowed]** *hyphen, Theobald*
186 **fickle]** *Q1–2;* fickly *F1*
186 **he]** a *Q1*
188 s.p. **Lear.]** Gon. *Q1–2*
188 **stock'd]** struck *Q1–2*
189 **on't]** ant *Q1–2*
189 **Who]** *Lear.* Who *Q1–2*
190 **your]** you *Q1–2*
191 **you]** *om.* *Q1–2*
193 s.d. **To Goneril.]** *Johnson*
194 **will you]** wilt thou *Q1–2*
210 **owl——]** *Steevens;* Owle, *F1,* *Q1–2*
212 **hot-bloodied]** *F1 (c);* hot-blooded *F1 (u);* hot bloud in *Q1–2*
214 **beg]** bag *Q1*
215 **afoot]** *Q1–2;* a foote *F1*
217 s.d. **Pointing at Oswald.]** *Dyce*
218 **I]** Now I *Q1–2*
222 **that's in]** that lies within *Q1–2*
224 **or]** an *Q1–2*

231 **so]** so sir *Q1–2*
232 **look'd]** looke *Q1–2*
235 **you]** you are *Q1–2*
235 **so——]** *Rowe;* so, *F1,* *Q1–2*
236 **spoken]** spoken now *Q1–2*
237 **What,]** *Rowe;* what *F1,* *Q1–2*
240 **Speak]** Speakes *Q1–2*
240 **one]** a *Q1–2*
245 **ye]** you *Q1–2*
246 **control]** *Q1 (controwle),* *Q2;* comptroll *F1*
250 **all——]** *Rowe;* all. *F1,* *Q1–2*
256 **look]** seem *Q1–2*
258 s.d. **To Goneril.]** *Hanmer*
263 **need]** needes *Q1–2*
264 **need]** deed *Q1–2*
266 **nature . . . needs,]** *Q1–2;* nature, . . . needs: *F1*
267 **life is]** life as *Q1;* life's as *Q2*
267 **beast's]** *Capell;* Beastes *F1,* *Q1–2*
269 **wear'st]** wearest *Q1–2*
270 **warm.]** *Rowe (subs.);* warme, *F1,* *Q1–2*
272 **man]** fellow *Q1–2*
275 **so]** to *Q1;* too *Q2*
276 **tamely]** lamely *Q1–2*
277 **And]** O *Q1–2*
280 **shall——]** shall, *Q1*
280 **things——]** *Hanmer;* things, *F1,* *Q1–2*
281 **are yet]** *Q1;* are yet, *F1;* are, yet *Q2*
285 **into]** in *Q1–2*
285 **flaws]** flowes *Q1–2*
286 s.d. **Lear . . . Fool]** *Ringler conj.;* Lear, Leister, Kent, and Foole *Q1;* Lear, Glocester, Kent, and Foole *Q2*
288 **and 's]** *F2;* an'ds *F1;* and his *Q1–2*
293 s.p. **Gon.]** *Duke.* *Q1–2*
293 **purpos'd]** puspos'd *Q1*
295 s.p. **Corn.]** Reg. *Q1–2*
295 s.d. **Enter Gloucester.]** *placed as in Kittredge; after l. 294, F1,* *Q1–2 (in right margin, Q1)*
296–7 **rage. . . . whither.]** rage, & wil I know not whether. *Q1–2*
298 s.p. **Corn.]** Re. *Q1–2*
298 **best]** good *Q1–2*
300 **bleak]** *Q1–2;* high *F1*
301 **ruffle]** russel *Q1–2*
302 **scarce]** not *Q1–2*
308 **wild]** *Q1–2;* wil'd *F1*
309 **Regan]** Reg *Q1*
309 **o' th']** at'h *Q1;* ath *Q2*

## 3.1

**Location:** *ed. (after Rowe)*
o.s.d. **severally]** at seuerall doores *Q1–2*
1 **Who's there, besides]** Whats here beside *Q1,* (What's) *Q2*

4 **elements**] element *Q1–2*
7–15 **tears . . . all.**] *Q1–2*
11 **to-and-fro-conflicting**] *hyphens,*
 *Theobald*
13 **belly-pinched**] *hyphen, Pope*
18 **note**] Arte *Q1–2*
20 **is**] be *Q1–2*
22–9 **Who . . . furnishings—**] *om. Q1–2*
29 **furnishings—**] *Rowe;* furnishings. *F1*
30–42 **But . . . you.**] *Q1–2*
32 **feet**] fee *Q2;* see *Q3*
43 **further**] farther *Q1–2*
44 **am**] *om. Q1–2*
45 **out-wall,**] *Q1–2;* out-wall; *F1*
48 **that**] your *Q1–2*
53–4 **in . . . this**] Ile this way, you that *Q1–2*
55 **Holla**] hollow *Q1–2*
55 s.d. **severally**] *Theobald*

### 3.2
**Location:** *ed. (after Sisson)*
1 **winds**] wind *Q1–2*
1 **blow!**] *Pope;* blow *F1, Q1–2*
2 **cataracts**] caterickes *Q1;*
 carterickes *Q2*
2 **hurricanoes**] *F2;* Hyrricano's *F1;*
 Hircanios *Q1–2*
3 **drench'd our steeples,**] drencht, /
 The steeples *Q1;* drencht / The
 Steeples, *Q2*
3 **drown'd**] *Q1–2;* drown *F1*
5 **Vaunt-couriers of**] vaunt-currers
 to *Q1–2*
7 **Strike**] smite *Q1–2*
8 **moulds**] Mold *Q1–2*
9 **makes**] make *Q1–2*
11 **o' door**] a doore *Q1–2*
12 **in**] in, and *Q1–2*
13 **neither**] nether *Q1,* neyther *Q2*
13 **wise men**] *Pope.* Wisemen *F1;* wise
 man *Q1–2*
13 **fools**] foole *Q1–2*
14 **bellyful**] *Malone;* belly full *F1, Q1–2*
16 **tax**] taske *Q1–2 (cf. 1.4.343)*
18 **Then**] why then *Q1–2*
22 **will . . . join**] haue . . . join'd *Q1–2*
23 **battles**] battel *Q1–2*
24 **O, ho!**] O *Q1–2*
25 **put 's**] put his *Q1–2*
28–9 **head . . . The**] head, has any the *Q1–2*
33 **of**] haue *Q1–2*
40 **codpiece**] codpis *Q1–2*
41 **wise man**] *Pope;* Wiseman *F1, Q1–2*
42 **are**] sit *Q1–2*
44 **Gallow . . . wanderers**] gallow, . . .
 wanderer *Q1–2*
45 **make**] makes *Q1–2*

47 **never**] ne're *Q1–2*
49 **fear**] force *Q1–2*
50 **pudder**] Powther *Q1;* Thundring *Q2*
54 **of**] man of *Q1–2*
55 **incestuous**] incestious *Q1–2*
55 **to**] in *Q1–2*
57 **Has**] hast *Q1–2*
58 **concealing continents**] concealed
 centers *Q1–2*
60 **than**] their *Q1–2*
63 **while**] whilst *Q1–2*
64 **harder . . . stones**] hard then is the
 stone *Q1–2*
65 **you**] me *Q1–2*
67 **wits begin**] wit begins *Q1–2*
71 **And**] that *Q1–2*
71–2 **your hovel. Poor**] you houell
 poore, *Q1–2*
72 **in**] of *Q1–2*
73 **That's sorry**] That sorrowes *Q1–2*
74 s.d. **Sings.**] *Capell*
74 **has and**] has *Q1–2*
74 **little tine**] *Q1–2;* little-tyne *F1*
77 **Though**] for *Q1–2*
78 **boy**] my good boy *Q1–2*
78 s.d. **with Kent**] *Capell (subs);*
 *s.d. om. Q1–2*
79–96 **Fool. This . . . time.**] *om. Q1–2; ll.*
 *79–80 as prose, Malone; as verse, F1*
85–6 **Then . . . confusion.**] *placed as in*
 *Duthie; after l. 92 in F1*

### 3.3
**Location:** *Rowe (subs.)*
o.s.d. **with lights**] *Q1–2*
1 **this**] this, *Q1*
3 **from me**] me from me *Q1*
3 **perpetual**] their *Q1–2*
5 **or**] nor *Q1–2*
8 **There is**] ther's a *Q1–2*
9 **between**] betwixt *Q1–2*
13 **there is**] Ther's *Q1–2*
13 **footed**] landed *Q1–2*
14 **look**] seeke *Q1–2*
17 **bed. If**] *Rowe (subs.);* bed, if *F1;* bed,
 though *Q1–2*
17 **for't**] *Q1;* for it *F1, Q2*
19 **strange things**] Some strange
 things *Q1–2*
21 **courtesy,**] curtesie *Q1–2*
24 **loses**] *Q2;* looses *F1, Q1*
25 **The**] Then *Q1–2*
25 **doth**] doe *Q1–2*

### 3.4
**Location:** *Rowe (subs.)*
2 **night's**] nights *Q1*

4 **here**] *om. Q1–2*
6 **contentious**] tempestious *Q1 (c)*;
crulentious *Q1 (u), Q2*
7 **skin; so**] ~~Rowe; skinso: F1;~~ skin, so
*Q1–2*
10 **thy**[ *Q1–2*; they *F1*
12 **body's**] *Rowe;* bodies *F1, Q1–2*
12 **this**] *Q1 (c);* the *F1, Q1 (u), Q2*
14 **there—**] *Singer;* there, *F1;* their *Q1–2*
14 **ingratitude!**] *Rowe;* ingratitude, *F1,*
*Q1–2*
16 **home**] sure *Q1–2*
17–8 **In . . . endure.**] *om. Q1–2*
20 **gave**] gaue you *Q1–2*
20 **all—**] *Rowe;* all, *F1, Q1–2*
22 **here**] *om. Q1–2*
23 **thine own**] thy one *Q1;* thy
owne *Q2*
26 s.d. **To the Fool.**] *Johnson*
26–7 **In . . . sleep.**] *om. Q1–2*
26 **poverty—**] *Rowe;* pouertie, *F1*
27 s.d. **Fool**] *Rowe; s.d. follows l. 26 in F1,*
*Rowe; placed as in Hanmer; s.d. om. Q1–2*
29 **storm**] night *Q1–2*
31 **loop'd**] *Q1–2* (loopt); lop'd *F1*
37–8 **Edg. Fathom . . . Tom!**] *om. Q1–2*
37 s.d. **Within.**] *Theobald*
38 s.d. **Enter . . . hovel.**] *from F1* Enter
Edgar, and Foole. *(after l. 36) and*
*Theobald (after l. 40); placed as in Capell;*
*om. Q1–2*
42 **A . . . says**] A spirit, he sayes, *Q1,*
(sayes) *Q2*
45 s.d. **Enter . . . madman.**] *from F1 (see*
*l. 38 s.d.) and Theobald; om. Q1–2*
46–7 **"Through . . . winds."**] *quotes,*
*Staunton*
46 **Through**] thorough *Q1*
47 **blow**] blowes *Q1–2*
47 **cold**] *Q1–2*
47 **winds**] wind *Q1–2*
47 **Humh!**] *om. Q1–2*
48 **bed**] cold bed *Q1–2*
49 **Didst thou give**] Hast thou
giuen *Q1–2*
49 **thy**] thy two *Q1–2*
52 **through fire**] *Q1–2;* though Fire *F1*
52 **through flame**] *om. Q1–2*
53 **ford**] *Q1–2* (foord); Sword *F1*
53 **whirlpool**] whirli-poole *Q1–2*
54 **hath**] has *Q1–2*
55 **porridge**] pottage *Q1–2*
56 **trotting-horse**] *hyphen, Steevens*
57 **four-inch'd**] *hyphen, Capell*
58, 59 **Bless**] *Q1–2,* Blisse *F1*
58 **a-cold**] *Pope;* a cold *F1, Q1–2*
*(throughout)*

58–9 **O . . . de.**] *om. Q1–2*
59 **star-blasting**] starre-blusting *Q1–2*
62 **and there**] *om. Q1–2*
63 **Has**] What, *Q1–2*
64 **Wouldst . . . 'em**] didst . . . them *Q1–2*
68 **light**] fall *Q1–2*
76 **Pillicock-Hill**] *hyphen, Rowe;*
pelicocks hill *Q1–2*
76–7 **alow! alow, loo, loo!**] a lo lo lo.
*Q1–2*
80 **o' th'**] at'h *Q1;* of the *Q2*
81 **word's justice**] *Knight;* words Iustice
*F1;* words iustly *Q1–2*
82 **sweet heart**] *Q1–2;* Sweet-heart *F1*
91 **deeply**] *Q1–2;* deerely *F1*
91 **out-paramour'd**] out paromord *Q1;*
out paramord *Q2*
95 **rustling**] ruslngs *Q1;* ruslings *Q2*
96 **woman**] women *Q1–2*
96 **brothels**] brothell *Q1–2*
97 **plackets**] placket *Q1–2*
97 **books**] booke *Q1–2*
99 **says . . . nonny.**] *after Capell;* Sayes . . .
nonny, *F1;* hay no on ny, *Q1–2*
99 **boy, boy**] boy, my boy *Q1–2*
100 **sessa!**] *Malone;* Sesey: *F1 (in italics)*;
caese *Q1;* cease *Q2*
101 **Thou**] Why thou *Q1–2*
101 **a**] thy *Q1–2*
103 **more than this?**] more, but this *Q1;*
more but this? *Q2*
105 **Ha?**] *om. Q1–2*
108–9 **Come, unbutton here.**] come on
*Q1 (c);* come on bee true. *Q1 (u), Q2*
109 s.d. **Tearing . . . clothes.**] *Rowe*
110 **contented, 'tis**] content, this is *Q1–2*
113 **on 's**] in *Q1–2*
113 s.d. **Enter . . . torch.**] *placed as in*
*Sisson; after l. 109, F1;* Enter Gloster.
*Q1–2 (after l. 114)*
115 **fiend**] *Q1–2*
115 **Flibbertigibbet**] fliberdegibek *Q1 (c)*;
Scriberdegibit *Q1 (u);* Sirberdegibit *Q2*
116 **till the**] *Q1–2;* at *F1*
117 **pin, squinies**] *Greg (after anon. conj.)*;
Pin, squints *F1;* pin-queues *Q1 (u);* pin,
squemes *Q1 (c);* pinqueuer *Q2*
120 **Swithold**] swithald *Q1–2*
120 **'old**] *Cambridge;* old *F1, Q1–2*
122 **alight**] *Rowe;* a-light *F1;* O light *Q1–2*
123 **troth plight**] *Q1–2;* troth-plight *F1*
124 **aroint . . . aroint**] arint thee, witch
arint *Q1 (c);* arint thee, with arint *Q1*
*(u); Q2*
135 **stock-punish'd**] *Q1–2* (-punish);
stockt, punish'd *F1*

135 **had**] Q*1–2*
137 **Horse . . . wear;**] *as part of preceding prose speech in* Q*1–2*
139 **Have**] Hath Q*1–2*
140 **Smulkin**] snulbug Q*1–2*
144 **Mahu.**] ma hu— Q*1–2*
145–6 **Our . . . it.**] *as verse, Pope; as prose,* F*1,* Q*1–2*
145 **my . . . vild**] is growne so vild my Lord Q*1–2*
152 **ventured**] venter'd Q*1–2*
153 **fire and food**] food and fire Q*1–2*
156 **Good my**] My good Q*1–2*
157 **same**] most Q*1–2*
161 **once more**] *om.* Q*1–2*
163 **Ah**] O Q*1–2*
167 **he**] a Q*1*
168 **lately,**] Q*1–2; lately:* F*1*
169 **true**] truth Q*2*
171 **Grace—**] *Capell;* grace. F*1,* Q*1–2*
171–2 **mercy, sir. Noble**] *mercie noble* Q*1–2*
174 **into th'**] in't Q*1*
175–6 **him; . . . still**] him I wil keep stil, Q*1–2*
177 **soothe**] *Collier;* sooth F*1,* Q*1–2*
182 **tower came**] towne come Q*1–2*

### 3.5

**Location:** *Rowe*
1 **his**] the Q*1–2*
2 **How,**] F*4;* How F*1,* Q*1–2*
3 **something**] some thing Q*1;* something Q*2*
10 **which**] *om.* Q*1–2*
12–3 **this . . . not**] his treason were Q*1–2*
20 s.d. **Aside.**] *Theobald*
21 **persever**] perseuere Q*1–2*
25 **dearer**] Q*1–2;* deere F*1*

### 3.6

**Location:** *Capell (subs.)*
o.s.d. **Enter . . . Gloucester.**] Enter Gloster and Lear, Kent, Foole, and Tom. Q*1, (om. first* and*)* Q*2*
5 **his**] *om.* Q*1–2*
5 **reward**] deserue Q*1–2*
5 s.d. **Exit Gloucester.**] *Capell;* Exit. F*1 (after l. 3); s.d. om.* Q*1–2*
6 **Frateretto**] *Capell;* Fraterretto F*1;* Fretereto Q*1–2*
7 **and**] *om.* Q*1–2*
9 **madman**] mad man Q*1–2*
12–4 **Fool. No . . . him.**] *om.* Q*1–2*
16 **'em—**] *Theobald;* 'em. F*1;* them. Q*1–2*
17–56 **Edg. The . . . scape?**] Q*1–2*
21, 36 s.dd. **To Edgar.**] *Capell*
21 **justicer**] *Theobald;* Iustice Q*1–2*

22, 37 s.dd. **To the Fool.**] *Capell*
22 **Now**] Q*2;* no Q*1*
23 **Want'st**] Q*2;* wanst Q*1*
24 **eyes at trial**] Q*2;* eyes, at tral Q*1*
24, 26 s.dd. **Sings.**] *Cambridge conj.*
25 **"Come . . . me"**—] *as verse, Capell; as part of preceding prose speech,* Q*1–2*
25 **bourn**] *Capell (subs.);* broome Q*1–2*
26–7 **"Her . . . speak**] *as two verse lines, Capell; as one verse line,* Q*1–2*
28 **come**] Q*2;* come, Q*1*
33–4 **How . . . cushions?**] *as verse, Theobald; as prose,* Q*1–2*
34 **cushions**] Q*2;* cushings Q*1*
35–9 **I'll . . . too.**] *as verse, Pope (subs.); as prose,* Q*1–2*
36 **robed**] *Pope;* robbed Q*1–2*
38 s.d. **To Kent.**] *Capell*
38 **o' th'**] Q*2;* ot'h Q*1*
40 s.d. **Sings.**] *Cambridge conj.*
41–4 **"Sleepest . . . harm."**] *as verse, Theobald; as prose,* Q*1–2*
47 **she**] Q*2*
52 **join-stool**] ioynt stoole Q*2*
58 **pity!**] *Rowe;* pitty: F*1;* pity Q*1–2*
60 s.d. **Aside.**] *Rowe*
61 **They**] Theile Q*1;* They'l Q*2*
68–9 **mongril grim, Hound**] *Rowe (subs.);* Mongrill, Grim, / Hound F*1;* mungril, grim-hound Q*1;* Mungrel, Grim-hound Q*2*
69 **lym**] *Hanmer;* Hym F*1;* him Q*1;* Him Q*2*
70 **Or**] *om.* Q*1–2*
70 **tike**] Q*1–2;* tight F*1*
70 **trundle-tail**] Q*1 (trundletaile),* Q*2;* Troudle taile F*1*
71 **him**] them Q*1–2*
73 **leapt**] leape Q*1–2*
74–5 **Do . . . dry.**] *as prose, Capell (after* Q*1–2); as verse,* F*1*
74 **Do . . . Sessa**] *Malone;* Do . . . sese F*1;* loudla doodla Q*1–2*
77 **her heart.**] her / Hart Q*1;* her, / Hart Q*2*
78 **make . . . hearts**] F*3;* make these hard-hearts F*1;* makes this hardnes Q*1–2*
78 s.d. **To Edgar.**] *Capell*
79 **for**] you for Q*1–2*
80 **garments . . . say**] garments youle say, Q*1;* garment; you'l say Q*2*
81 **Persian**] Persian attire Q*1–2*
82 **and rest**] *om.* Q*1–2*
84 **So, so**] so, so, so Q*1–2*
84 **morning.**] morning, so, so, so, Q*1, (. . . so.)* Q*2*

85 **Fool. And . . . noon.**] *om. Q1–2*
85 s.d. **Enter Gloucester.**] *Q1–2; after l.*
 *81, F1*
91 **toward**] towards *Q1–2*
95 **Take . . . up**] Take vp the King *Q1 (c);*
 Take vp to keepe *Q1 (u),* Q2
97–101 **Kent. Oppressed . . . behind.**]
 *Q1–2*
98 **balm'd**] *Theobald;* balmed *Q1–2*
99 **allow,**] *Q2;* alow *Q1*
100 s.d. **To the Fool.**] *Theobald*
101 s.p. **Glou.**] *Q1–2*
101 s.d. **all but Edgar**] *Globe*
102–15 **Edg. When . . . lurk.**] *Q1–2*
102–3 **When . . . foes.**] as verse, *Q2;* as
 prose, *Q1*
104 **suffers, suffers**] *Theobald;*
 suffers suffers, *Q1;* suffers, *Q2*
104 **i' th'**] *Q2;* it'h *Q1*
110 **fathered**] fatherd *Q2*
115 s.d. **Exit.**] *Theobald*

### 3.7

**Location:** *Rowe*
1 s.d. **To Goneril.**] *Furness*
2 **him**] hin *F1 (u) (unrecorded)*
3 **traitor**] vilaine *Q1–2*
3 s.d. **Exeunt . . . Servants.**] *Capell*
7 **revenges**] reuenge *Q1–2*
9 **Advise**] *Q1–2;* Advice *F1*
10 **festinate**] *F2;* festiuate *F1;* festuant
 *Q1–2*
11 **posts**] post *Q1–2*
11 **intelligent**] intelligence *Q1–2*
17 **questrists**] questrits *Q1–2*
18 **lord's**] *Rowe;* Lords, *F1;* Lords *Q1–2*
19 **toward**] towards *Q1–2*
22 s.d. **Exeunt . . . Oswald.**] *Capell*
 *(subs., after l. 21; placed as in Dyce);* Exit
 *F1 (after l. 21);* Exit Gon. and Bast.
 *Q1–2 (after l. 21)*
23 s.d. **Exeunt other Servants.**] *Capell*
24 **well**] *om. Q1–2*
26 **court'sy**] *Rowe;* curt'sie *F1;* curtesie
 *Q1–2*
27 **control**] *Q1–2;* comptroll *F1*
27 s.d. **brought . . . three**] *Q1–2;* and *F1*
31 **guests**] *Q2;* Ghests *F1;* gests *Q1*
32 s.d. **Servants bind him.**]
 *Rowe (subs.)*
33 **lady**] *Q1–2;* Lady, *F1*
33 **I'm none**] I am true *Q1–2*
34 **find—**]*Q1–2;* finde. *F1*
34 s.d. **Regan . . . beard.**] *Johnson*
40 **robber's**] *Pope /* Robbers *F1,* *Q1–2*
43 **simple-answer'd**] hyphen, *Hanmer;*
 simple answerer *Q1–2*

44–5 **And . . . kingdom?**] as verse, *Rowe;*
 as prose, *F1,* *Q1–2*
46–7 **King—Speak.**] *ed. (after Duthie);*
 King: Speake. *F1;* King speake? *Q1;*
 king, speak? *Q2*
52 **Wast**] *Q1–2;* Was't *F1*
52 **peril—**] *Q1–2;* perill. *F1*
53 **him**] him first *Q1–2*
55 **Dover**] Douer sir *Q1–2*
58 **rash**] *Q1–2;* sticke *F1*
59 **as his bare**] on his lowd *Q1 (c);* of his
 lou'd *Q1 (u),* Q2
60 **hell-black night**] *Pope;*
 Hell-blacke-night *F1;* hell
 blacke night *Q1–2*
60 **buoy'd**] bod *Q1 (c);* layd *Q1 (u);*
 laid *Q2*
62 **holp**] holpt *Q1–2*
62 **rain**] rage *Q1–2*
63 **howl'd**] heard *Q1–2*
63 **dearn**] *Q1–2;* sterne *F1*
65 **subscribe;**] subscrib'd *Q1;*
 subscrib'd, *Q2*
68 **these**] those *Q1–2*
70 **you**] ye *Q1–2*
71 **th' other too**] tother to *Q1–2*
72 **vengeance—**] *Q1–2;* vengeance. *F1*
72, 76, 79, 81 s.pp. **1. Serv.**] *Capell;* Seru.
 *F1,* *Q1–2*
73 **you**] *om. Q1*
77 **I'ld**] id'e *Q1;* ide *Q2*
78 s.d. **Draw and fight.**] *Q1–2*
79 **Nay**] Why *Q1–2*
79 s.d. **Cornwall is wounded.**] *ed.*
 *(after Rowe)*
80 s.d. **She . . . behind;**] *Q1–2*
80 s.d. **kills him**] *om. Q1–2*
81 **slain!**] slaine *Q1–2*
81 **you have**] yet haue you *Q1–2*
82 s.d. **He dies.**] *Q2*
86 **enkindle**] vnbridle *Q1–2*
87 **treacherous**] *om. Q1–2*
94 s.d. **one**] *Globe*
97 **dunghill. Regan,**] dungell Regan,
 *Q1;* dunghill, Regan *Q2*
98 s.d. **Exit . . . Regan.**] *Theobald;*
 Exeunt, *F1;* Exit. *Q1–2*
99–107 **2. Serv. I'll . . . him!**] *Q1–2*
99 s.p. **2. Serv.**] *Capell;* Seruant. *Q1–2*
100 s.p. **3 Serv.**] *Capell;* 2 Seruant. *Q1–2*
100–2 **If . . .monsters.**] as verse, *Theobald;*
 as prose, *Q1–2*
103 s.p. **2. Serv.**] *Capell;* 1 Ser. *Q1–2*
104 **roguish**] *om. Q1 (c)*
106 s.p. **3. Serv.**] *Capell;* 2 Ser. *Q1–2*
106–7 **Go . . .him!**] as verse, *Warburton;* as
 prose, *Q1–2*

107 s.d. **Exeunt severally.**] *Theobald;* Exit. *Q1–2*

**4.1**

**Location:** *Capell (after Rowe)*
2 **flatter'd. . . . worst,**] *Pope;* flatter'd, to be worst; *F1;* flattered to be worst, *Q1–2*
4 **esperance**] experience *Q1–2*
6–9 **Welcome . . . But**] *om. Q1–2*
9 s.d. **led by**] *Q1–2;* and *F1; Q1–2 s.d. after* age. *l. 12*
9 **who comes**] Who's *Q1–2*
10 **parti-ey'd**] *ed. (after Davenport conj., from* parti, eyd *Q1 (c));* poorlie, leed *Q1 (u);* poorely led *F1, Q2*
14 **These fourscore years.**] this forescore— *Q1–2*
17 **You**] Alack sir, you *Q1–2*
21 **O**] ah *Q1–2*
24 **I'ld**] Id'e *Q1;* Ide *Q2*
25, 27, 37, 52, 54 s.dd. **Aside.**] *Johnson*
26 **e'er**] *Rowe;* ere *F1, Q1–2*
28 **So**] As *Q1–2*
31 **He**] A *Q1*
36 **to**] are toth' *Q1;* are to'th *Q2*
37 **kill**] bitt *Q1;* bit *Q2*
38 **fool**] the foole *Q1–2*
41 **Then prithee**] *Q1–2*
41 **away**] gon *Q1;* gone *Q2*
42 **hence**] here *Q1–2*
45 **Which**] Who *Q1–2*
46 **time's**] *Rowe;* times *F1, Q1–2*
51 **fellow—**] *Capell;* fellow. *F1, Q1–2*
52 **daub it further**] dance it farther *Q1–2*
54 **And . . . must.**] *om. Q1–2*
57 **scar'd**] *Q1–2;* scarr'd *F1*
58 **thee . . . son**] the good man *Q1–2*
58–63 **Five . . . master!**] *Q1–2 (as verse; as prose, Pope)*
61 **Flibbertigibbet**] *Pope;* Stiberdigebit *Q1–2*
61 **mopping**] *Theobald;* Mobing *Q1–2*
62 **mowing**] *Theobald (after Pope);* Mohing *Q1–2 (in italics as proper name)*
64 **plagues**] plagues. *Q1*
66 **heavens,**] *Capell;* Heauens *F1, Q1–2*
68 **slaves**] stands *Q1–2*
70 **undo**] vnder *Q1–2*
74 **fearfully**] firmely *Q1–2*

**4.2**

**Location:** *Capell (after Rowe)*
o.s.d. **Enter . . . Bastard**] *Q1–2;* Enter Gonerill, Bastard, and Steward. *F1*
2 s.d. **Enter . . . Steward.**] *Theobald (subs.);* Enter Steward. *Q1–2 (after l. 2); see above for F1*

10 **most . . . dislike**] hee should most desire *Q1–2*
11 s.d. **To Edmund.**] *Hanmer*
15 **Edmund**] *Q2;* Edmond *F1;* Edgar *Q1*
17 **names**] armes *Q1–2*
24 **fare thee well**] far you well *Q1;* faryewell *Q2*
25 s.d. **Exit.**] *om. Q1–2*
26 **O . . . man!**] *om. Q1–2*
28 **A**] *Q1 (c);* My *F1, Q1 (u), Q2*
28 **fool**] foote *Q1 (u), Q2*
28 **bed**] *Q1 (c);* body *F1, Q1 (u);* head *Q2*
28 s.d. **Exit.**] *Q1–2* (Exit Stew.)
29 **whistling**] *Q1 (c);* whistle *F1, Q1 (u), Q2*
31–50 **I . . . deep.**] *Q1–2*
31 **disposition;**] *Theobald (subs.);* disposition *Q1;* disposition, *Q2*
32 **it**] ith *Q1 (c);* its *Q3*
42 **even**] *om. Q2*
42–3 **lick, . . . madded.**] *Capell;* lick. . . . madded, *Q1;* licke; . . . madded; *Q2*
45 **benefited**] *Q1 (c);* beneflicted, *Q1 (u), Q2*
47 **these**] *Heath conj.;* the *Q1 (u), Q2;* this *Q1 (c)*
49 **Humanity**] Humanly *Q1 (u), Q2*
51 **bear'st**] bearest *Q1–2*
52 **eye discerning**] *Rowe;* eye-discerning *F1;* eye deseruing *Q1–2*
53–9 **that . . . so?**] *Q1–2*
53–4 **know'st Fools**] *Hanmer;* know'st, fools *Q1 (c);* know'st fools, *Q1 (u), Q2*
54 **those**] these *Q2*
56 **noiseless**] noystles *Q1 (u)*
57 **state . . . threat**] *Jennens;* state begins thereat *Q1 (c);* slayer begin threats *Q1 (u);* slaier begins threats *Q2*
58 **Whilst**] Whil's *Q1 (u);* Whiles *Q2*
60 **shows**] *Q1 (c)* (shewes); seemes *F1, Q1 (u), Q2*
62–8 **Alb. Thou . . . mew!**] *Q1–2*
65 **dislocate**] *Q3;* dislecate *Q1–2*
66 **bones. Howe'er**] *Theobald (subs.);* bones, how ere *Q1–2*
68 **mew!**] *Daniel conj.;* mew— *Q1 (c);* now— *Q1 (u), Q2*
68 s.d. **Enter a Messenger.**] *placed as Q2 s.d.; after l. 61, F1;* Enter a Gentleman. *Q1 (after l. 69)*
69 **Alb. What news?**] *Q1–2*
70 s.p. **Mess.**] Gent. *Q1–2 (throughout scene)*
72 **eyes?**] *Q1–2;* eyes. *F1*
73 **thrill'd**] thrald *Q1–2*
75 **thereat enraged**] *Q1–2;* threat-enrag'd *F1*

79 **justicers**] *Q1 (c);* Iustices *F1, Q1 (u), Q2*
83 s.d. **Aside.**] *Johnson*
85 **in**] on *Q1–2*
87 **tart**] tooke *Q1–2*
87 s.d. **Exit.**] *Q1–2*
93 **their**] there *Q1*
96 **thine**] thy *Q1–2*

### 4.3

**4.3**] *Pope*
*Entire scene from Q1–2; om. F1; first included
by Pope*
**Location:** *Capell (subs.)*
2 **no**] the *Q2*
7 **him**] *Pope;* him, *Q1–2*
11 **Ay, sir**] *Johnson;*I say *Q1–2*
13 **seem'd**] *Q2;* seemed *Q1*
14 **Over**] ore *Q2*
15 **mov'd**] *Pope;* moued *Q1–2*
16 **strove**] *Pope;* streme *Q1–2*
17–8 **goodliest. . . . once;**] *Pope
(subs.);* goodliest . . . once, *Q1,*
(goodliest,) *Q2*
18 **Sunshine**] *Q2;* Sun shine *Q1*
19 **way:**] *Globe;* way *Q1;* way, *Q2*
20 **seem'd**] *Pope;* seeme *Q1–2*
21 **eyes,**] *Q2;* eyes *Q1*
22 **dropp'd. In**] *Q2 (subs.);* dropt in *Q1*
28 **Kent!**] *Theobald;* Kent, *Q1;* Kent. *Q2*
28 **storm? i' th'**] *Theobald;* storme ith
*Q1–2*
29 **believ'd!**] *Capell (subs.);* beleeft *Q1;*
beleeu'd, *Q2*
31 **clamor-moistened**] *hyphen first
appears in Theobald's notes (later conj. by
W. S. Walker);* clamour moystened her
*Q1–2 (Theobald first om. her)*
34 **make**] mate *Q2*
35 **since?**] *Q2;* since. *Q1*
39 **sometime**] *Q2;* some time *Q1*
42 **him:**] *Capell;* him *Q1;* him, *Q2*
43–4 **benediction, . . . casualties,**] *Q2;*
benediction turnd her, To forraine
casualties *Q1*
48 **not?**] *Q2;* not. *Q1*
49 **so,**] *Pope;* so *Q1–2*
49 **afoot**] *Q2;* a foote *Q1*
51 **him.**] *Pope;* him *Q1;* him, *Q2*
52 **while**] a while *Q2*
53 **grieve**] *Pope;* greeue, *Q1–2*
55 s.d. **Exeunt.**] *Pope;* Exit. *Q1–2*

### 4.4

**4.4**] *Pope;* Scena Tertia. *F1*
**Location:** *Capell*
o.s.d. **Doctor**] *Q1–2;* Gentlemen *F1*
o.s.d. **Soldiers**] others *Q1–2*

2 **vex'd**] vent *Q1–2*
3 **femiter**] *Q1–2;* Fenitar *F1*
3 **furrow-weeds**] *hyphen, Dyce*
4 **hardocks**] *F3;* Hardokes *F1;* hor-docks
*Q1–2*
4 **cuckoo-flow'rs**] *hyphen, Q2*
6 **sustaining corn.**] sustayning, corne,
*Q1–2*
6 **century**] *Q1–2;* Centery *F1*
6 **send**] is sent *Q1–2*
8 s.d. **Exit an Officer.**] *Malone (after
Capell)*
8 **wisdom**] wisedome do *Q2 (do may
have dropped out of the type line in Q1;
the end of the next line shows evidence of
type dislocation)*
9 **sense?**] *Q2;* Sense; *F1;* sence, *Q1*
10 **helps**] can helpe *Q1–2*
11 s.p. **Doct.**] *Q1–2;* Gent. *F1*
13 **lacks;**] lackes *Q1;* lackes, *Q2*
18 **good man's distress**] *Q1–2;*
Goodmans desires *F1*
26 **importun'd**] important *Q1–2*
27 **incite**] in sight *Q1;* insite *Q2*
28 **right**] *Q1–2;* Rite *F1*

### 4.5

**4.5**] *Pope;* Scena Quarta. *F1*
**Location:** *Capell (subs.)*
2 **there**] *om. Q1–2*
4 **lord**] Lady *Q1–2*
6 **letter**] letters *Q1*
11 **Edmund**] and now *Q1–2*
14 **o' th' enemy**] at'h army *Q1;* of the
Army *Q2*
15 **madam**] *om. Q1–2*
15 **letter**] *letters Q1–2*
16 **troops set**] troope sets *Q1–2*
21 **Some things—**] *Pope (reading
Something);* Some things, *F1;* Some
thing, *Q1;* Some-thing, *Q2*
22 **I had**] I'de *Q1;* Ide *Q2*
25 **eliads**] aliads *Q1–2*
27 **madam?**] Madam. *Q1–2*
28 **y' are;**] for I *Q1–2*
32 **more.**] more *Q1;* more, *Q2*
36 **you**] *om. Q1–2*
39 **him**] *Q1–2*
39 **should**] would *Q1–2*
40 **party**] Lady *Q1–2*

### 4.6

**4.6**] *Pope;* Scena Quinta. *F1*
**Location:** *Theobald (after Rowe)*
o.s.d. **Edgar**] Edmund *Q1–2*
o.s.d. **dressed . . . peasant**] *Theobald (subs.)*
1 **I**] we *Q1–2*

2 **up it now**] it upnow *Q1*; it up
now *Q2*
6 **eyes'**[ *Capell*; eyes *F1, Q1–2*
7 **speak'st**] speakest *Q1*
8 **In**] With *Q1–2*
17 **walk**] *Q1–2*; walk'd *F1*
18 **yond**] yon *Q1–2*
21 **chafes**] chaffes *Q1*; chafe *Q2*
22 **heard so high.**] heard, its so hie *Q1*;
heard: it is so hie *Q2*
30 **further**] farther *Q1–2*
32 **ye**] you *Q1–2*
33 s.d. **Aside.**] *Capell*
34 s.d. **He kneels.**] *Q1–2*
39 **snuff**] snurff *Q1*
40 **him**] *om. Q1–2*
41 s.d. **He falls.**] *Q1–2*
41 **sir;**] *Knight (subs.)*; sir, *F1, Q1–2*
42 **may**] my *Q1*
46 **friend!**] *Rowe*; Friend, *F1; om. Q1–2*
49 **goss'mer**] *Pope*; Gozemore *F1*;
gosmore *Q1–2*
50 **fathom**] fadome *Q1–2*
51 **Thou'dst**] Thou hadst *Q1–2*
52 **speak'st**] speakest *Q1*
56 **no?**] no 1 *Q1*
57 **summit**] *Rowe*; Somnet *F1*; sommons
*Q1–2*
57 **bourn.**] *Pope (subs.)*; Bourne *F1*;
borne, *Q1–2*
58 **a-height**] *hyphen, Warburton*
62 **death?**] death *Q1*
65 **How is't? Feel**] how feele *Q1–2*
67 **cliff,**] *Q2*; cliffe. *F1*; cliffe *Q1*
68 **beggar**] bagger *Q1*; begger *Q2*
69 **methought**] *Q2*; me thought *F1*; me
thoughts *Q1*
70 **he**] a *Q1–2*
71 **welk'd**] *ed.*; wealk'd *F1*; welk't *Q1*;
welkt *Q2*
71 **enridged**] *Q1–2*; enraged *F1*
73 **make them**] made their *Q1–2*
77 **die.**] die *Q1*; dye: *Q2*
78 **'twould**] would it *Q1*; would he *Q2*
79 **fiend!"—**] *Rowe (subs.)*; Fiend, *F1*,
*Q1–2*
80 s.d. **mad . . . flowers**] *ed. (after Duthie-
Wilson)*; mad *Q1–2 (s.d. after l. 82)*
81 **ne'er**] neare *Q1*; nere *Q2*
83 **coining,**] *Q1–2*; crying. *F1*
86 **Nature's**] Nature is *Q1–2*
89 **piece of**] *om. Q1–2*
91–2 **bird . . . hewgh!**] bird in the ayre,
hagh, *Q1*; birde in the ayre. Hagh, *Q2*
93 **marjorum**] Margerum *Q1–2*
96 **Goneril . . . beard?**] Gonorill, ha
Regan, *Q1–2*

97 **the**] *om. Q1–2*
99 **every thing that**] euery thing
*Q1*; all *Q2*
103 **'em . . . 'em**] them . . . them *Q1–2*
105 **ague-proof**] argue-proofe *Q1–2*
107 **Ay**] *Rowe*; I *F1, Q1–2*
107 **every**] euer *Q1*
107 **king!**] King *Q1*; King: *Q2*
111 **die. . . . adultery?**] die for adulterie,
*Q1*; dye for adultery: *Q2*
113 **Does**] doe *Q1–2*
118–31 **Behold . . . thee.**] *as verse, Johnson
(subs.); as prose, F1, Q1–2*
118 **yond**] yon *Q1–2*
119 **presages**] presageth *Q1–2*
120 **does**] do *Q1–2*
121 **To**] *om. Q1–2*
122 **The**] to *Q1–2*
124 **they are**] tha're *Q1 (type-line crowded)*
127 **fiends'**] *Capell*; Fiends *F1, Q1–2*
128 **There . . . sulphurous**] ther's the
sulphury *Q1–2*
129 **consumption**] consumation *Q1–2*
130 **civet;**] Ciuet, *Q1–2*
131 **Sweeten**] to sweeten *Q1–2*
133 **Let me**] Here *Q1–2*
135 **Shall**] should *Q1*; shold *Q2*
135 **Dost thou**] do you *Q1–2*
136 **thine**] thy *Q1–2*
137 **at**] on *Q1–2*
138 **this**] that *Q1–2*
138–9 **but . . . it**] the penning oft *Q1*; the
penning on't *Q2*
140 **thy**] the *Q1–2*
140 **see**] see one *Q1–2*
141 s.d. **Aside.**] *Capell*
144 **What,**] *Q2*; What *F1*; What! *Q1*
145–6 **me? . . . purse?**] me, . . .
purse, *Q1*
150 **this**] the *Q1–2*
151 **thine**] thy *Q1–2*
152 **yond . . . yond**] yon . . . yon *Q1–2*
153 **thine . . . handy-dandy**] thy eare
handy, dandy *Q1*; thy eare, handy
dandy *Q2*
154 **justice . . . thief**] theefe . . .
Iustice *Q1–2*
157 **cur?**] *Q2*; Cur: *F1*; cur, *Q1*
159 **dog's obey'd**] dogge, so bade *Q1*;
dogge, so bad *Q2*
160–3 **Thou . . . cozener.**] *as verse, Pope;
as prose, F1, Q1–2*
161 **thy**] thine *Q1–2*
162 **Thou**] thy bloud *Q1–2*
163–4 **cozener. . . . clothes**] cosioner,
through tottered raggs, *Q1*; cozener,
through tattered ragges *Q2*

164–73 **Thorough . . . so.**] *as verse, Rowe*
 *(subs.)*; *as prose, F1, Q1–2*
164 **small**] *Q1–2*; great *F1 (a reading*
 *defended by J. C. Maxwell in*
 *Duthie-Wilson)*
165 **hide**] hides *Q1–2*
165–70 **Plate . . . lips.**] *om. Q1–2*
165 **Plate sin**] *Theobald (after Pope)*; Place
 sinnes *F1*
170 **glass eyes**] *Q1–2*; glasse-eyes *F1*
172 **Now . . . now.**] no now *Q1*; No,
 now *Q2*
174 s.d. **Aside.**] *Capell*
174 **impertinence mix'd,**] impertinencie
 mixt *Q1*; impertinency, mixt *Q2*
176 **fortunes**] fortune *Q1–2*
179 **know'st**] knowest *Q1*
180 **wawl**] wayl *Q1–2*
180 **Mark**] Marke me *Q1–2*
180 s.d. **Lear . . . flowers.**] *ed. (after*
 *Duthie-Wilson)*
183 **This'**] *Singer;* This *F1*, *Q1–2*
184 **shoe**] shoot *Q1–2*
185 **felt**] fell *Q1–2*
185 **I'll . . . proof,**] *om. Q1–2*
186 **stol'n**] stole *Q1–2*
186 **son-in-laws**] sonnes in law *Q2*
187 s.d. **a Gentleman**] three Gentlemen
 *Q1–2*
187 s.d. **with Attendants**] *Rowe*
188 **hand**] hands *Q1–2*
188 **him.—Sir,**] *Rowe (subs.)*; him, Sir. *F1*;
 him sirs, *Q1*; him sirs. *Q2 (om.* Your . . .
 daughter)
189 **daughter**] *om. Q1 (see preceding note*
 *for Q2)*
190 **even**] eene *Q1–2*
191 **well,**] well *Q1*
192 **surgeons**] a churgion *Q1*; a
 Chirurgeon *Q2*
195 **a man a man**] a man *Q1–2*
197 **Ay . . . sir—**] *Q2 (reading* I; Ay
 *Jennens)*; I and laying
 Autums dust. *Q1*
198 **smug**] *om. Q1–2*
200 **Masters**] my maisters *Q1–2*
202–3 **Then . . . sa.**] *as prose, Q1–2 (om.*
 Sa . . . sa.); *as verse, F1*
202 **Come**] nay *Q1–2*
203 **by**] with *Q1–2*
203 **Sa . . . sa.**] *om. Q1–2*
203 s.d. **running . . . follow**] *Capell;*
 King running. *Q1–2*
205 **one**] *Q1–2*; a *F1*
207 **have**] hath *Q1–2*
209 **sir**] *om. Q1–2*

210 **vulgar; . . . that**] vulgar euery one
 here's that *Q1*; vulgar, euery one
 heares *Q2*
211 **Which . . . sound**] That . . . sence
 *Q1–2*
213 **speedy foot;**] speed fort *Q1*; speed
 for't, *Q2*
213 **descry**] descryes *Q1–2*
214 **Stands**] Standst *Q1*
214 **thought**] thoughts *Q1–2*
216 s.d. **Exit Gentleman.**] *Johnson;* Exit.
 *F1 (after on. l. 216), Q1–2*
217 **ever-gentle**] *hyphen, Capell*
219 **Well**] Well, *Q1*
221 **tame to**] lame by *Q1–2*
226 **To boot, and boot!**] to boot, to
 boot. *Q1 (c), Q2;* to saue thee. *Q1 (u)*
226 **happy!**] *Q2 (happy;)*; happie *F1;*
 happy, *Q1*
228 **old**] most *Q1–2*
231 s.d. **Edgar interposes.**] *Collier*
 *(after Johnson)*
232 **Durst**] *Q1;* Dar'st *F1, Q2*
233 **that th'**] the *Q1–2*
235 **zir**] sir *Q1–2*
235 **vurther**] *om. Q1–2*
235 **cagion**] *Q1–2*; 'casion *F1*
237 **and**] *om. Q1–2*
238 **voke**] *Q1*; volke *F1, Q2*
238 **ha' bin zwagger'd**] haue beene
 swagger'd *Q1*; haue beene zwaggar'd
 *Q2*
239 **'twould . . . 'tis**] it would not haue
 beene so long *Q1*; it wold not haue
 bene zo long *Q2*
241 **Ice**] ile *Q1–2*
241 **ballow**] bat *Q1 (c), Q2;* battero *Q1 (u)*
242 **Chill**] ile *Q1*
243 s.d. **They fight.**] *Q1–2*
244 **zir**] sir *Q1*
245 **vor**] for *Q1–2*
250 **English**] Brittish *Q1 (c)*; British *Q1*
 *(u), Q2 (Q1–2's form is historically correct,*
 *but English must have been in the MS*
 *against which copy for F1 was corrected)*
251 s.d. **He dies.**] *Q1–2*
256 **these**] his *Q1–2*
256 **the**] These *Q1–2*
257 **sorry**] sorrow *Q1*
259 **manners, . . . not:**] *Capell;*
 manners: . . . not *F1;* manners . . . not
 *Q1;* manners . . . not, *Q2*
260 **we**] wee'd *Q1–2*
262 s.d. **Reads the letter.**] A letter. *Q1*
 *(c), Q2; om. Q1 (u)*
262 **our**] your *Q1–2*

265–6 **done, if . . . conqueror;**] *Pope*
(*subs.*); done. If . . . Conqueror, *F1;*
done, If . . . conquerour, *Q1;* done:
If . . . Conqueror, *Q2*
269 **say)**] say) your *Q1;* say) & your *Q2*
269–70 **servant, Goneril.**] seruant and
for you her owne for *Venter, Gonorill.*
*Q1;* seruant, *Gonorill. Q2*
271 **indistinguish'd**] *Q1;* indinguish'd
*F1;* vndistinguisht *Q2*
271 **will**] wit *Q1–2*
273 **brother!**] brother *Q1;* Brother: *Q2*
273 **in the**] *Q1–2;* in rhe *F1*
282 **sever'd**] fenced *Q1–2*
284 s.d. **Drum afar off.**] *placed as in*
*Q1–2* (A drum); *after l. 281, F1*

**4.7**
**Location:** *Capell*
o.s.d. **still . . . Caius**] *ed.*
o.s.d. **Doctor**] *Q1–2;* Gentleman. *F1*
8 **Pardon**] Pardon me *Q1–2*
12 **be't**] beet *Q1;* be it *Q2*
12 **so, . . . lord.**] so, . . . Lord *Q1;* so: my
Lord *Q2*
12 s.d. **To the Doctor.**] *Theobald (subs.)*
13, 16, 42, 50, 77 s.pp. **Doct.**] *Q1–2;* Gent.
*or* Gen. *F1*
15 **jarring**] hurrying *Q1–2*
19 **will.**] *Johnson;* will: *F1, Q2;* will *Q1*
20 s.p. **Gent.**] Doct *Q1–2*
20 **of**] of his *Q1–2*
22 s.p. **Doct.**] *Capell (subs.); speech*
*continued to Gentleman, F1;* Gent. *Q1;*
Kent. *Q2*
22 **Be . . . madam**] Good madam be by
*Q1–2*
23 **not**] *Q1–2*
23 **Cor. Very well.**] *Q1–2*
23 s.d. **Enter . . . Servants.**] *placed as in*
*Duthie-Wilson; after* array'd *l. 19, F1; om.*
*Q1–2*
23 s.d. **Gentleman in attendance.**]
*Neilson*
23 s.d. **Soft music.**] *White*
24 **Doct. Please . . . there!**] *Q1–2*
30 **Did challenge**] Had challengd *Q1–2*
31 **oppos'd**] exposd *Q1–2*
31 **warring**] *Q1–2;* iarring *F1*
32–5 **To . . . helm?**] *Q1–2*
32 **dread-bolted**] *hyphen, Theobald*
34 **lightning?**] *Theobald;* lightning *Q1;*
lightning, *Q2*
34 **watch—poor perdu!—**] *Capell*
(*subs.*); watch poore *Per du, Q1–2*
35 **helm?**] *Q2;* helme *Q1*
35 **enemy's**] iniurious *Q1–2*

37 **wast**] *Q1–2;* was't *F1*
44 **o' th'**] ath *Q1;* a'th *Q2*
47 **scald**] *Q1–2;* scal'd, *F1*
47 **do . . . me?**] know me. *Q1;* know ye
me? *Q2*
48 **You are**] Yar *Q1;* Y' are *Q2*
48 **when**] *Q2;* where *F1, Q1*
51 **I? Fair**] I faire *Q1*
57 **hand**] hands *Q1–2*
58 **No, sir**] *Q1–2*
58 **me**] *om. Q1*
60 **not . . . less**] *om. Q1–2*
69 **I am.**] *om. Q1–2*
78 **kill'd**] cured *Q1–2*
78–9 **and . . . lost.**] *Q1–2* (*as prose; as*
*verse, Theobald*)
82 **Will't**] *Rowe;* Wilt *F1, Q1–2*
83 **you**] *om. Q1–2*
83 s.d. **Manent . . . Gentleman.**] *Q1–2*
(Manet)
84–96 **Gent. Holds . . . fought.**
**Exit.**] *Q1–2*
94 s.d. **Exit.**] *Theobald*
96 **battle's**] *Theobald;* battels *Q1–2*
96 s.d. **Exit.**] *om. Q2*

**5.1**
**Location:** *Capell (after Rowe)*
3 **course. He's**] *Rowe (subs.);* course, he's
*F1, Q1;* course, he is *Q2*
4 s.d. **To . . . out.**] *Globe (after Capell)*
9 **In**] I, *Q1;* I *Q2*
11 **forfended**] *Q1;* fore-fended *F1;*
forefended *Q2*
11–3 **Edm. That . . . hers.**] *Q1–2*
12–3 **I . . . hers.**] *as verse,* Q2; *as prose,* Q1
16 **me**] *Q1–2*
16 **not.**] *Rowe (subs.);* not, *F1, Q1–2*
17 **husband!**] *Delius;* husband. *F1, Q1–2*
18–9 **Gon. I . . . me.**] *Q1–2* (*as prose,* Q1;
*as verse, Theobald, after* Q2)
18 s.d. **Aside.**] *Theobald*
20–1 **bemet. Sir, . . . heard:**] be-met /
For . . . heare *Q1,* (be-met,) *Q2*
23–8 **Where . . . nobly.**] *Q1–2*
25 **touches**] toucheth *Q1–2*
26 **whom,**] *Theobald;* whome *Q1–2*
30 **and particular broils**] dore
particulars *Q1;* doore particulars, *Q2*
31 **the**] to *Q1–2*
31 **Let's**] Let vs *Q1–2*
32 **proceeding**] proceedings *Q1–2*
33 **Edm. I . . . tent.**] *Q1–2*
(*with s.p.* Bast.)
36 **pray**] pray you *Q1–2*
37 s.d. **Aside.**] *Capell*
37 s.d. **As . . . out,**] *Theobald*

37 s.d. **disguised**] *Theobald*
37 s.d. **Albany remains.**] *Pope*
46 **And machination ceases.**]
   *om. Q1–2*
46 **love**] *Q1–2;* loues *F1*
50 **thy**] the *Q1–2*
50 s.d. **Exit Edgar.**] *Dyce;* Exit. *F1, Q1–2*
   (*after l. 49*)
52 **Here**] Hard *Q1–2*
52 **guess**] quesse *Q1*
52 **true**] great *Q1–2*
55 **sisters**] sister *Q1*
56 **stung**] sting *Q1–2*
58 **Both? one?**] both one *Q1–2*
64 **who**] that *Q1–2*
65 **the**] his *Q1–2*
66 **intends**] entends *Q1;* extends *Q2*

## 5.2
**Location:** *Capell (after Rowe)*
o.s.d. **the Powers . . . hand**] *Q1–2;* Lear,
   Cordelia, and Souldiers, ouer the Stage
   *F1*
1 **tree**] bush *Q1–2*
4 s.d. **Edgar**] *Pope*
8 **further**] farther *Q1–2*
11 **all.**] *Rowe (subs.);* all *F1, Q1–2*
11 **Glou. And . . . too.**] *om. Q1–2*

## 5.3
**Location:** *ed. (after Ridley)*
2 **first**] best *Q1–2*
5 **I am**] am I *Q1–2*
8 **No . . . no!**] No, no, *Q1–2*
13 **hear poor rogues**] *Q1–2;* heere
   (poore Rogues) *F1*
24 **good-years**] *hyphen, Globe;*
   good *Q1–2*
24 **them, flesh**] em, fleach *Q1–2*
25 **'em starv'd**] vm starue *Q1;* em starue
   *Q2*
26 **Come.**] *om. Q2*
26 s.d. **with Cordelia, guarded**]
   *Theobald (subs.); s.d. om. Q1*
27 s.d. **giving a paper**] *Malone*
   (*after Capell*)
32 **sword.**] *Rowe (subs.);* Sword, *F1, Q1–2*
33 **thou'lt**] thout *Q1–2*
35 **th' hast**] thou hast *Q1–2*
36 **Mark,**] *Rowe;* Marke *F1, Q1–2*
38–9 **Capt. I . . . do't.**] *Q1–2*
39 s.d. **another Captain**] *Globe; Q1–2 s.d.
   reads:* Enter Duke [the Duke *Q2*], the
   two ladies, and others.
42 **Who**] That *Q1–2*
43 **I . . . them**] We . . . then *Q1–2*
43 **you,**] *Q1;* you *F1, Q2*

47 **and appointed guard**] *Q1 (c), Q2;
   om. Q1 (u)*
48 **had**] has *Q1–2*
49 **on**] of *Q1–2*
51–2 **Queen, My reason**] *Neilson;*
   Queen: / My reason *F1, Q2;* queen /
   My reason, *Q1*
54 **session.**] session *Q1–2 (see next note)*
54–9 **At . . . place.**] *Q1–2 (reading* at)
54 **time**] time, *Q1;* time: *Q2*
55 **We**] *Q1 (c), Q2;* mee *Q1 (u)*
57 **sharpness**] *Q1 (c), Q2;* sharpes *Q1 (u)*
   (*Greg suggests that the uncorrected reading
   may be that of the MS, in the sense of
   "sharp edges or points"*)
62 **might**] should *Q1–2*
65 **immediacy**] imediate *Q1–2*
68 **addition**] aduancement *Q1–2*
68 **rights**] right *Q1–2*
70 s.p. **Gon.**] *Q1–2;* Alb. *F1*
72 **a-squint**] *Rowe;* a squint *F1, Q1–2*
76 **Dispose . . . thine.**] *om. Q1–2*
78 **him**] him then *Q1–2*
79 **let-alone**] *hyphen, Capell*
81 s.p. **Reg.**] Bast. *Q1–2*
81 s.d. **To Edmund.**] *Hanmer (subs.)*
81 **thine**] good *Q1–2*
83 **thy**] thine *Q1–2*
83 **attaint**] *Q1–2;* arrest *F1*
84 s.d. **pointing to Goneril**] *Johnson*
84 **sister**] *Q1–2;* Sisters *F1*
85 **bar**] *Rowe;* bare *F1, Q1–2*
87 **your**] the *Q1–2*
88 **loves**] loue *Q1–2*
89 **Gon. An enterlude!**] *om. Q1–2*
90 **let . . . sound.**] *om. Q1–2*
90 **trumpet**] *F2;* Trmpet *F1*
91 **person**] head *Q1–2*
93, 97 s.dd. **throwing . . . glove**] *Malone
   (after Capell)*
93 **make**] proue *Q1–2*
96 s.d. **Aside.**] *Rowe*
96 **medicine**] poyson *Q1–2*
97 **he is**] *Q1–2;* hes *F1*
99 **the**] thy *Q1–2*
102 **Edm. A . . . herald!**] *Q1–2*
   (*with s.p.* Bast.)
103 s.p. **Alb.**] *Q1–2*
105 **My**] This *Q1–2*
106 s.d. **Exit Regan, led.**] *Theobald*
106 s.d. **Enter a Herald.**] *placed as in
   Hanmer; after l. 101, F1; om. Q1–2*
107 **trumpet**] *Q1–2;* Trumper *F1*
109 **Capt. Sound, trumpet!**] *Q1–2*
109 s.d. **trumpet**] *F2;* Tumpet *F1; s.d. om.
   Q1–2*
111 **within the lists**] in the hoast *Q1–2*

112 **he is**] he's *Q1–2*
113 **by**] at *Q1–2*
115 **Edm. Sound!**] *Q1–2 (with s.p.* Bast.)
115 s.d. **First trumpet.**] *placed as in*
  *Capell; after l. 114, F1* (1. Trumpet.)
116 **Her. Again!**] *Q1–2 assign apparently to*
  Bast. *and om. the repeated* Again! *of*
  *l. 117 and the s.dd. in ll. 115–*  7
  (*including* Trumpet answers within.)
117 s.d. **at . . . sound**] *Q1–2*
117 s.d. **a**] *Q1;* with a *Q2*
118 **purposes,**] purposes *Q1*
120 **your quality**] and qualitie *Q1–2*
121 **Know**] O know *Q1–2*
121–2 **lost, . . . tooth**] *Theobald* (lost;); lost
  . . . tooth: *F1, Q2;* lost . . . tooth. *Q1*
123–4 **Yet . . . cope**] yet are I mou't /
  Where is the aduersarie I come to
  cope with all *Q1* (*Q2 om.* yet . . .
  mou't)
126 **say'st**] saiest *Q1*
129–30 **my . . . honors**] the priuiledge of
  my tongue *Q1–2*
132 **place, youth**] youth, place *Q1–2*
133 **Despite**] *Q1–2;* Despise *F1*
133 **victor-sword . . . fortune**] victor,
  sword and fire new fortun'd *Q1*,
  (sword,) *Q2*
133 **fire-new**] *hyphen, Rowe*
136 **Conspirant**] Conspicuate *Q1–2*
136 **illustrious**] *Q1–2;* illustirous *F1*
138 **below thy foot**] beneath thy feet
  *Q1–2*
139 **traitor. . . . "No,"**] traytor say thou
  no *Q1;* traitor: say thou no, *Q2*
140 **are**] As *Q1;* Is *Q2*
142 **should**] sholud *Q1*
144 **tongue**] being *Q1–2*
144 **some say**] *Q1–2;* (some say) *F1*
145 **What . . . delay**] *om. Q1–2*
146 **rule**] right *Q1–2*
147 **Back . . . these**] Heere . . . those *Q1;*
  *line om.* Q2
148 **hell-hated . . . o'erwhelm**] hell
  hatedly, oreturnd *Q1;* hell hatedly
  ore-turn'd *Q2*
149 **scarcely**] *Q1–2;* scarely *F1*
151 s.d. **Alarums.**] *placed as in Pope;*
  *after l. 152, F1; om. Q1–2*
151 s.d. **They . . . falls.**] *Capell;* Fights. *F1*
  (*after l. 152); om. Q1–2*
152 **practice**] meere practise *Q1–2*
153 **war thou wast**] armes /
  Thou art *Q1–2*
155 **Shut**[ Stop *Q1–2*
156 **stopple**] *Q1;* stop *F1, Q2*
156 **Hold, sir.—**] *om. Q1–2*

157 **name**] thing *Q1–2*
158 **No**] nay no *Q1;* Nay, no *Q2*
158 **know it**] know't *Q1–2*
160 **can**] shal *Q1–2*
160 **Most monstrous! O!**] Most
  monstrous *Q1;* Monster, *Q2*
161 s.p. **Gon.**] *Q1–2;* Bast. *F1*
161 s.d. **Exit.**] *placed as in Q1–2* (Exit.
  Gonorill.); *after* for't *l. 160, F1*
166 **thou'rt**] thou bee'st *Q1–2*
169 **th' hast**] thou hast *Q1–2*
171 **vices**] vertues. *Q1;* vertues *Q2*
172 **plague**] scourge *Q1–2*
174 **Th' hast**] Thou hast *Q1–2*
174 **right, 'tis true.**] *Capell (subs.);* right,
  'tis true, *F1;* truth, *Q1–2*
175 **circle**] circled *Q1;* circkled *Q2*
178–9 **ever I Did**] I did euer *Q1–2*
183 **burst!**] *Theobald;* burst. *F1, Q2;*
  burst *Q1*
186 **we**] with *Q1–2*
191 **Their**] The *Q1–2*
191 **lost;**] lost *Q1*
193 **fault**] Father *Q1–2*
194 **past,**] *Q1;* past *F1, Q2*
197 **our**] my *Q1–2*
205 **Hearing of this.**] *om.* Q2
205–22 **Edg. This . . . slave.**] *Q1–2*
208 **extremity. Whilst**] *Q2;* extreamitie /
  Whil'st *Q1*
212 **endur'd,**] *Q2;* indur'd *Q1*
214 **him**] *Theobald;* me *Q1–2*
215 **Told the most**] And told the *Q2*
218 **crack. Twice**] *Theobald (subs.);* cracke
  twice, *Q1–2*
222 s.d. **a Gentleman**] one *Q1–2*
222 s.d. **with . . . knife**] *Q1–2*
223 **O, help!**] *om. Q1–2*
223–4 **What . . . knife?**] *assigned to* Alb. *in*
  *Q1–2 (reading that for* this *and om.*
  Alb. Speak, man.)
224 **'Tis**] Its *Q1–2*
225 **O, she's dead!**] *om. Q1–2*
226 **Who . . . man.**] Who man, speake?
  *Q1;* Who man? speake. *Q2*
228 **poison'd; she confesses**] poysoned,
  she hath confest *Q1;* poyson'd: she has
  confest *Q2*
231 **the**] their *Q1–2*
231 s.d. **Exit Gentleman.**] *Malone (after*
  *Capell; following l. 233); placed as in*
  *Cambridge*
232 **judgment**] Iustice *Q1–2*
232 **tremble,**] *Q1–2;* tremble. *F1*
233 **pity.**] pity. Edg. Here comes *Kent* sir.
  Enter Kent *Q1–2 (cf. l. 230 and s.d. in F1)*
233 **is this he?**] tis he, *Q1–2*

234 **compliment**] *Pope;* complement *F1,*
    *Q1–2*
235 **Which**] that *Q1–2*
237 s.p. **Alb.**] Duke. *Q1 (throughout rest*
    *of scene);* Q2 *agrees with F1 except for*
    Duke: *at l. 319*
238 s.d. **Goneril . . . out.**] *placed as in*
    *Dyce; after l. 231, F1; after l.*
    *239, Q1–2*
241 **poison'd**] poysoned *Q1*
245 **mine**] my *Q1–2*
246 **brief . . . th'**] briefe, int toth' *Q1;*
    briefe, into the *Q2*
246–7 **castle, . . . Is**] castle for my writ, /
    Is *Q1;* Castle for my / Writ, tis *Q2*
249 **has**] hath *Q1–2*
251 **sword. The captain—**] *ed. (after*
    *Jennens) from Q1* sword the Captaine,
    (the Captaine *om. F1, Q2)*
252 s.p. **Alb.**] *Q2;* Edg. *F1;* Duke. *Q1*
252 s.d. **Exit Edgar.**] *Malone*
256 **That . . . herself.**] *om. Q2*
257 s.d. **Edmund . . . off.**] *Theobald*
257 s.d. **Enter**] *Q1–2;* Entor *F1*
257 s.d. **Edgar . . . following**] *Neilson*
    *(after Capell)*
258 **howl!**] howle, howle, *Q1–2*
258 **you**] *Q1–2;* your *F1*
259 **I'ld**] *F3;* Il'd *F1;* I would *Q1–2*
264 **Why**] *om. Q2*
265 **horror?**] *Q2;* horror. *F1, Q1*
268 s.d. **Kneeling.**] *Theobald*
268 **O**] A *Q1–2*
270 **you, murderers,**] your murderous
    *Q1;* you murdrous *Q2*
274 **woman**] women *Q1–2*
276 s.p. **Gent.**] Cap. *Q1–2*
277 **falchion**] Fauchon *Q1;* Fauchion *Q2*
278 **them**] *Q1–2;* him *F1*
280 **best;**] *Pope (subs.);* best, *F1, Q1–2*
281 **brag**] bragd *Q1–2*
281 **and**] or *Q1–2*
283 **This . . . sight.**] *om. Q1–2*

283 **you not**] not you *Q1–2*
285 **you**] *om. Q1–2*
287 **man—**] *Pope;* man. *F1, Q1–2*
289 **first**] life *Q1–2*
290 **You're**] *Q1* (You'r); Your are *F1;* You
    are *Q2*
292 **foredone**] foredoome *Q1;* fore-
    doom'd *Q2*
293 **Ay . . . think.**] So thinke I to. *Q1;* So
    I thinke too. *Q2*
294 **says**] sees *Q1–2*
294 **is it**] it is *Q1–2*
295 s.d. **Enter a Messenger.**] *placed as*
    *Q1–2 s.d.* Enter Captaine.; *after him. l.*
    *295, F1*
296 s.p. **Mess.**] Capt. *Q1–2*
298 **great**] *om. Q1–2*
301 s.d. **To . . . Kent.**] *Malone*
    *(after Rowe)*
302 **honors**] honor *Q1*
306 **No, no, no**] no, no *Q1–2*
307 **have**] of *Q1*
308 **Thou'lt**] O thou wilt *Q1–2*
309 **Never . . . never!**] neuer, neuer,
    neuer, *Q1;* neuer, neuer, neuer: *Q2*
311–2 **Do . . . there!**] O, o, o, o. *Q1;* O, o,
    o, o, o. *Q2*
312 s.d. **dies**] *F2;* dis *F1; om. Q1–2*
312 **faints.**] *Theobald (subs.);* faints, *F1, Q2;*
    faints *Q1*
313 s.p. **Kent.**] Lear. *Q1–2*
315 **rack**] *F4;* wracke *F1, Q1–2*
316 **He**] O he *Q1–2*
319 s.p. **Alb.**] Duke. *Q1, Q2*
320 **Is**] Is to *Q1–2*
320 s.d. **To . . . Edgar.**] *Johnson*
321 **realm**] kingdome *Q1–2*
323 **calls me,**] cals, and *Q1–2*
324 s.p. **Edg.**] Duke. *Q1–2*
326 **hath**] haue *Q1–2*
327 s.d. **Exeunt . . . march.**] Exeunt . . .
    March. / FINIS. *F1;* FINIS. *Q1–2*

# SOURCES AND CONTEXTS

*Note: Footnotes in the reprinted excerpted material are from the original publication. Footnote numerals, therefore, will correspond to those at the bottom of the page, but expect numerical gaps since sections not excerpted contain the lines and numbers not included here. The location of footnotes in excerpted materials varies. Expect some footnotes at the bottom of the page, others to appear as endnotes. The spelling of Shakespeare's name varies over the centuries, especially prior to the early twentieth century. Some authors in this Evans Shakespeare Edition, for example, may use the spelling "Shakespear" or "Shakspere." The adjectival form of the name is "Shakespearian" in British Commonwealth countries and "Shakespearean" in the United States. Generally an author's particular spelling has been retained. Within square brackets, notes are by Evans Editor, V. F. Petronella.*

## From *The True Chronicle Historie of King Leir and His Three Daughters* (1605)

### Anon.

The Anonymous *King Leir* was entered in the Stationers' Register May 14, 1594 and again May 8, 1605 before it was printed in 1605. The play was produced at Philip Henslowe's Rose Theatre on Bankside April 6, and April 9, 1594 by the Queen's Men together with Sussex's Men. A production of *King Leir* in 1605 may be the one that influenced Shakespeare to write his *King Lear* with its Gloucester sub-plot and unhappy ending. Debate continues as to the authorship of the anonymous play. Playwrights who have been put forth as candidates are Thomas Lodge, George Peele, Robert Greene, and Thomas Kyd, all of them University Wits.

### ACTUS I [SCENE I]

*Enter* KING LEIR *and* NOBLES.

THUS TO our griefe the obsequies performd
Of our (too late) deceast and dearest Queen,
Whose soule I hope, possest of heavenly joyes,
Doth ride in triumph 'mongst the Cherubins;
Let us request your grave advice, my Lords,
For the disposing of our princely daughters,
For whom our care is specially imployd,
As nature bindeth to advaunce their states,          10
In royall marriage with some princely mates:
For wanting now their mothers good advice,

Under whose government they have receyved
A perfit patterne of a vertuous life:
Lest as it were a ship without a sterne,
Or silly sheepe without a Pastors care;
Although our selves doe dearely tender them,
Yet are we ignorant of their affayres:
For fathers best do know to governe sonnes;
But daughters steps the mothers counsell turnes.　　　20
A sonne we want for to succeed our Crowne,
And course of time hath cancelled the date
Of further issue from our withered loynes:
One foote already hangeth in the grave,
And age hath made deepe furrowes in my face:
The world of me, I of the world am weary,
And I would fayne resigne these earthly cares,
And thinke upon the welfare of my soule:
Which by no better meanes may be effected,
Then by resigning up the Crowne from me,　　　30
In equall dowry to my daughters three.
SKALLIGER A worthy care, my Liege, which well declares,
　　The zeale you bare unto our *quondam* Queene:
　　And since your Grace hath licens'd me to speake,
　　I censure thus; Your Majesty knowing well,
　　What severall Suters your princely daughters have,
　　To make them eche a Joynter more or lesse,
　　As is their worth, to them that love professe.
LEIR No more, nor lesse, but even all alike,
　　My zeale is fixt, all fashiond in one mould:　　　40
　　Wherefore unpartiall shall my censure be,
　　Both old and young shall have alike for me.
　　　　　　　　　　　　　　　　　　　　[*Exeunt.*


# [SCENE 2]
### Enter GONORILL and RAGAN.

GONORILL I marvell, *Ragan*, how you can indure
　　To see that proud pert Peat, our youngest sister,
　　So slightly to account of us, her elders,
　　As if we were no better then her selfe!　　　100
　　We cannot have a quaynt device so soone,
　　Or new made fashion, of our choyce invention;
　　But if she like it, she will have the same,
　　Or study newer to exceed us both.

Besides, she is so nice and so demure;
So sober, courteous, modest, and precise,
That all the Court hath worke ynough to do,
To talke how she exceedeth me and you.
RAGAN What should I do? would it were in my power,
  To find a cure for this contagious ill:          110
  Some desperate medicine must be soone applyed,
  To dimme the glory of her mounting fame;
  Els ere't be long, sheele have both prick and praise,
  And we must be set by for working dayes.
  Doe you not see what severall choyce of Suters
  She daily hath, and of the best degree?
  Say, amongst all, she hap to fancy one,
  And have a husband when as we have none:
  Why then, by right, to her we must give place,
  Though it be ne're so much to our disgrace.
GONORILL By my virginity, rather then she shall have
  A husband before me,
  Ile marry one or other in his shirt:
  And yet I have made halfe a graunt already
  Of my good will unto the King of Cornwall.
RAGAN Sweare not so deeply (sister) here commeth my L. *Skalliger:*
  Something his hasty comming doth import.

          [*Enter* SKALLIGER.

SKALLIGER Sweet Princesses, I am glad I met you heere so luckily,
  Having good newes which doth concerne you both,
  And craveth speedy expedition.          130
RAGAN For Gods sake tell us what it is, my Lord,
  I am with child untill you utter it.
SKALLIGER Madam, to save your longing, this it is:
  Your father in great secrecy to day,
  Told me, he meanes to marry you out of hand,
  Unto the noble Prince of Cambria;
  You, Madam, to the King of Cornwalls Grace:
  Your yonger sister he would fayne bestow
  Upon the rich King of Hibernia:
  But that he doubts, she hardly will consent;      140
  For hitherto she ne're could fancy him.
  If she do yeeld, why then, betweene you three,
  He will devide his kingdome for your dowries.
  But yet there is a further mystery,
  Which, so you will conceale, I will disclose.

GONORILL Thanks, gentle *Skalliger*, thy kindnes undeserved,
　　　Shall not be unrequited, if we live.

　　　　　　　　　　　　　　　　　　　　　[*Exit Skalliger.*

RAGAN Now have we fit occasion offred us,
　　　To be reveng'd upon her unperceyv'd.　　　　　　　　170

GONORILL Nay, our revenge we will inflict on her,
　　　Shall be accounted piety in us:
　　　I will so flatter with my doting father,
　　　As he was ne're so flattred in his life.
　　　Nay, I will say, that if it be his pleasure,
　　　To match me to a begger, I will yeeld:
　　　For why, I know what ever I do say,
　　　He meanes to match me with the Cornwall King.

RAGAN Ile say the like: for I am well assured,　　　　　　180
　　　What e're I say to please the old mans mind,
　　　Who dotes, as if he were a child agayne,
　　　I shall injoy the noble Cambrian Prince:
　　　Only, to feed his humour, will suffice,
　　　To say, I am content with any one
　　　Whom heele appoynt me; this will please him more,
　　　Then e're *Apolloes* musike pleased Jove.

GONORILL I smile to think, in what a wofull plight
　　　Cordella will be, when we answere thus:
　　　For she will rather dye, then give consent
　　　To joyne in marriage with the Irish King:　　　　　　190
　　　So will our father think, she loveth him not

　　　　　　　[*Enter* PERILLUS, *with the three daughters.*

LEIR Well, here my daughters come: I have found out
　　　A present meanes to rid me of this doubt.　　　　　220

GONORILL Our royall Lord and father, in all duty,
　　　We come to know the tenour of your will,
　　　Why you so hastily have sent for us?

LEIR Deare *Gonorill*, kind *Ragan*, sweet *Cordella*,
　　　Ye florishing branches of a Kingly stocke,
　　　Sprung from a tree that once did flourish greene,
　　　Whose blossomes now are nipt with Winters frost,
　　　And pale grym death doth wayt upon my steps,
　　　And summons me unto his next Assizes.
　　　Therefore, deare daughters, as ye tender the safety　　230
　　　Of him that was the cause of your first being,
　　　Resolve a doubt which much molests my mind,
　　　Which of you three to me would prove most kind;

Which loves me most, and which at my request
Will soonest yeeld unto their fathers hest.
GONORILL  I hope, my gracious father makes no doubt
Of any of his daughters love to him:
Yet for my part, to shew my zeale to you,
Which cannot be in windy words rehearst,                    240
I prize my love to you at such a rate,
I thinke my life inferiour to my love.
Should you injoyne me for to tye a milstone
About my neck, and leape into the Sea,
At your commaund I willingly would doe it:
Yea, for to doe you good, I would ascend
The highest Turret in all Brittany,
And from the top leape headlong to the ground:
Nay, more, should you appoynt me for to marry
The meanest vassayle in the spacious world,                 250
Without reply I would accomplish it:
In briefe, commaund what ever you desire,
And if I fayle, no favour I require.
LEIR  O, how thy words revive my dying soule!
CORDELLA  O, how I doe abhorre this flattery!
LEIR  But what sayth *Ragan* to her fathers will?
RAGAN  O, that my simple utterance could suffice,
To tell the true intention of my heart,
Which burnes in zeale of duty to your grace,
And never can be quench'd, but by desire
To shew the same in outward forwardnesse.                   260

[SCENE 12]

*Enter* CORNWALL, GONORILL, *and* ATTENDANTS.

CORNWALL  Ah, *Gonorill*, what dire unhappy chaunce
Hath sequestred thy father from our presence,
That no report can yet be heard of him?
Some great unkindnesse hath bin offred him,
Exceeding far the bounds of patience:
Else all the world shall never me perswade,                 950
He would forsake us without notice made.
GONORILL  Alas, my Lord, whom doth it touch so neere,
Or who hath interest in this griefe, but I,
Whom sorrow had brought to her longest home,

But that I know his qualities so well?
I know, he is but stolne upon my sister
At unawares, to see her how she fares,
And spend a little time with her, to note
How all things goe, and how she likes her choyce:
And when occasion serves, heele steale from her,                    960
And unawares returne to us agayne.
Therefore, my Lord, be frolick, and resolve
To see my father here agayne e're long.

CORNWALL  I hope so too; but yet to be more sure,
Ile send a Poste immediately to know
Whether he be arrived there or no.                    [*Exit.*

GONORILL  But I will intercept the Messenger,
And temper him before he doth depart,
With sweet perswasions, and with sound rewards,
That his report shall ratify my speech,
And make my Lord cease further to inquire.
If he be not gone to my sisters Court,
As sure my mind presageth that he is,
He happely may, by travelling unknowne wayes,
Fall sicke, and as a common passenger,
Be dead and buried: would God it were so well;
For then there were no more to do, but this,
He went away, and none knowes where he is.
But say he be in Cambria with the King,
And there exclayme against me, as he will:                    980
I know he is as welcome to my sister,
As water is into a broken ship.
Well, after him Ile send such thunderclaps
Of slaunder, scandall, and invented tales,
That all the blame shall be remov'd from me,
And unperceiv'd rebound upon himselfe.
Thus with one nayle another Ile expell,
And make the world judge, that I usde him well.


.     .     .


LEIR  Camst thou from France, of purpose to do this?

MESSENGER  From France? zoones, do I looke like a Frenchman?
Sure I have not mine owne face on; some body hath chang'd
faces with me, and I know not of it: But I am sure, my apparell
is all English. Sirra, what meanest thou to ask that question?
I could spoyle the fashion of this face for anger. A French face!

LEIR  Because my daughter, whom I have offended,
And at whose hands I have deserv'd as ill,
As ever any father did of child,
Is Queene of Fraunce, no thanks at all to me,          1580
But unto God, who my injustice see.
If it be so, that shee doth seeke revenge,
As with good reason she may justly do,
I will most willingly resigne my life,
A sacrifice to mittigate her ire:
I never will intreat thee to forgive,
Because I am unworthy for to live.
Therefore speake soone, & I will soone make speed:
Whether *Cordella* will'd thee do this deed?
MESSENGER  As I am a perfit gentleman, thou speakst French to me:
I never heard *Cordellaes* name before,
Nor never was in Fraunce in all my life:
I never knew thou hadst a daughter there,
To whom thou didst prove so unkind a churle:
But thy owne toung declares that thou hast bin
Avyle old wretch, and full of heynous sin.
LEIR  Ah no, my friend, thou art deceyved much:
For her except, whom I confesse I wrongd,
Through doting frenzy, and o're-jelous love.
There lives not any under heavens bright eye,          1600
That can convict me of impiety.
And therfore sure thou dost mistake the marke:
For I am in true peace with all the world.
MESSENGER  You are the fitter for the King of heaven:
And therefore, for to rid thee of suspence,
Know thou, the Queenes of Cambria and Cornwall,
Thy owne two daughters, *Gonorill* and *Ragan*,
Appoynted me to massacre thee here.
Why wouldst thou then perswade me, that thou art
In charity with all the world? but now
When thy owne issue hold thee in such hate,          1610
That they have hyred me t'abbridge thy fate,
Oh, fy upon such vyle dissembling breath,
That would deceyve, even at the poynt of death.
PERILLUS  Am I awake, or is it but a dreame?
MESSENGER  Feare nothing, man, thou art but in a dreame,
And thou shalt never wake untill doomes day,
By then, I hope, thou wilt have slept ynough.
LEIR  Yet, gentle friend, graunt one thing ere I die.

MESSENGER Ile graunt you any thing, except your lives.     1620
LEIR Oh, but assure me by some certayne token,
    That my two daughters hyred thee to this deed:
    If I were once resolv'd of that, then I
    Would wish no longer life, but crave to dye,
MESSENGER That to be true, in sight of heaven I sweare.
LEIR Sweare not by heaven, for feare of punishment:
    The heavens are guiltlesse of such haynous acts.
MESSENGER I sweare by earth, the mother of us all.
LEIRE Sweare not by earth; for she abhors to beare
    Such bastards, as are murtherers of her sonnes.     1630
MESSENGER Why then, by hell, and all the devils I sweare.
LEIR Sweare not by hell; for that stands gaping wide,
    To swallow thee, and if thou do this deed.
                    [*Thunder and lightning.*
MESSENGER I would that word were in his belly agayne,
    It hath frighted me even to the very heart:
    This old man is some strong Magician:
    His words have turned my mind from this exployt.
    Then neyther heaven, earth, nor hell be witnesse;
    But let this paper witnesse for them all.
                    [*Shewes Gonorils letter.*
    Shall I relent, or shall I prosecute ?
    Shall I resolve, or were I best recant?
    I will not crack my credit with two Queenes,
    To whom I have already past my word.
    Oh, but my conscience for this act doth tell,
    I get heavens hate, earths scorne, and paynes of hell.
                    [*They blesse themselves.*
PERILLUS Oh just Jehova, whose almighty power
    Doth governe all things in this spacious world,
    How canst thou suffer such outragious acts
    To be committed without just revenge?'...


[SCENE 24]

*Enter the* GALLIAN KING *and* QUEENE, *and*
MUMFORD, *with a basket, disguised like Countrey folke.*


*Enter* LEIR & PERILLUS *very faintly.*     2109

.     .     .

LEIR Ah, *Gonorill*, was halfe my Kingdomes gift     2143
    The cause that thou dist seeke to have my life?

Ah, cruell *Ragan*, did I give thee all,
And all could not suffice without my bloud?
Ah, *poore Cordella*, did I give thee nought,
Nor never shall be able for to give?
O, let me warne all ages that insueth,
How they trust flattery, and reject the trueth.
Well, unkind Girles, I here forgive you both,      2150
Yet the just heavens will hardly do the like;
    [Cf. *King Lear*, 4.2.46–49 ~ *Evans Editor*]
And only crave forgivenesse at the end
Of good *Cordella*, and of thee, my friend;
Of God, whose Majesty I have offended,
By my transgression many thousand wayes:
Of her, deare heart, whom I for no occasion
Turn'd out of all, through flatterers perswasion:
Of thee, kind friend, who but for me, I know,
Hadst never come unto this place of wo.

CORDELLA  Alack, that ever I should live to see
My noble father in this misery.

KING  Sweet Love, reveale not what thou art as yet,
Untill we know the ground of all this ill.

CORDELLA  O, but some meat, some meat: do you not see,
How neere they are to death for want of food?

PERILLUS  Lord, which didst help thy servants at their need,
Or now or never send us helpe with speed.
Oh comfort, comfort! yonder is a banquet,
And men and women, my Lord: be of good cheare:
For I see comfort comming very neere.
O my Lord, a banquet, and men and women!

LEIR  O, let kind pity mollify their hearts,
That they may helpe us in our great extreames.

PERILLUS  God save your, friends; & if this blessed banquet
Affordeth any food or sustenance,
Even for his sake that saved us all from death,
Vouchsafe to save us from the gripe of famine.
                    *[She bringeth him to the table.*

CORDELLA  Here father, sit and eat, here, sit & drink:
And would it were far better for your sakes.
              *[Perillus takes Leir by the hand to the table.*

PERILLUS  Ile give you thanks anon: my friend doth faynt,
And heedeth present comfort.         *[Leir drinks.*

LEIR And now I am constraind to seeke reliefe
    Of her, to whom I have bin so unkind;
    Whose censure, if it do award me death,
    I must confesse she payes me but my due:
    But if she shew a loving daughters part,
    It comes of God and her, not my desert.
CORDELLA No doubt she will, I dare be sworne she will.
LEIR How know you that, not knowing what she is? 2290
CORDELLA My selfe a father have a great way hence,
    Usde me as ill as ever you did her;
    Yet, that his reverend age I once might see,
    Ide creepe along, to meet him on my knee.
LEIR O, no mens children are unkind but mine.
CORDELLA Condemne not all, because of others crime:
    But looke, deare father, looke behold and see
    Thy loving daughter speaketh unto thee. [*She kneeles.*
LEIR O, stand thou up, it is my part to kneele,
    And aske forgivenesse for my former faults. [*he kneeles.* 2300
CORDELLA O, if you wish I should injoy my breath,
    Deare father rise, or I receive my death. [*he riseth.*
LEIR Then I will rise to satisfy your mind,
    But kneele againe, til pardon be resignd. [*he kneeles.*
CORDELLA I pardon you: the word beseemes not me:
    But I do say so, for to ease your knee.
    You gave me life, you were the cause that I
    Am what I am, who else had never bin.
LEIR But you gave life to me and to my friend,
    Whose dayes had else had an untimely end. 2310
CORDELLA You brought me up, when as I was but young,
    And far unable for to helpe my selfe.
LEIR I cast thee forth, when as thou wast but young,
    And far unable for to helpe thy selfe.
CORDELLA God, world and nature say I do you wrong,
    That can indure to see you kneele so long.
PERILLUS Let me breake off this loving controversy,
    Which doth rejoyce my very soule to see.
    Good father, rise, she is your loving daughter, [*He riseth.*
    And honours you with as respective duty,
    As if you were the Monarch of the world. 2320
CORDELLA But I will never rise from off my knee, [*She kneeles.*
    Untill I have your blessing, and your pardon
    Of all my faults committed any way,
    From my first birth unto this present day.

LEIR The blessing, which the God of *Abraham* gave
Unto the trybe *juda*, light on thee,
And multiply thy dayes, that thou mayst see
Thy childrens children prosper after thee.
Thy faults, which are just none that I do know,
God pardon on high, and I forgive below.     *[She riseth.*
CORDELLA Now is my heart at quiet, and doth leape
Within my brest, for joy of this good hap:
And now (deare father) welcome to our Court,
And welcome (kind *Perillus*) unto me,
Myrrour of vertue and true honesty.
LEIR O, he hath bin the kindest friend to me,
That ever man had in adversity.
PERILLUS My toung doth faile, to say what heart doth think,
I am so ravisht with exceeding joy.
KING All you have spoke: now let me speak my mind,
And in few words much matter here conclude:     *[he kneeles.*
If ere my heart do harbour any joy,
Or true content repose within my brest,
Till I have rooted out this viperous sect,
And repossest my father of his Crowne,
Let me be counted for the perjurdst man,
That ever spake word since the world began.     *[rise.*
MUMFORD Let me pray to, that never pray'd before; 
    *[Mumford kneeles.*
If ere I resalute the Brittish earth,
(As (ere't be long) I do presume I shall)
And do returne from thence without my wench,
Let me be gelded for my recompence.     *[rise.*
KING Come, let's to armes for to redresse this wrong:
Till I am there, me thinks, the time seemes long.     *[Exeunt.*

.   .   .

### [SCENE 32]

*Alarums and excursions, then sound victory.*
*Enter* LEIR, PERILLUS, KING, CORDELLA, *and* MUMFORD.

KING Thanks be to God, your foes are overcome,
And you againe possessed of your right.
LEIR First to the heavens, next, thanks to you, my sonne,
By whose good meanes I repossesse the same:
Which if it please you to accept your selfe,

With all my heart I will resigne to you:
For it is yours by right, and none of mine.
First, have you raisd, at your owne charge, a power
Of valiant Souldiers; (this comes all from you)
Next have you ventured your owne persons scathe.
And lastly, (worthy *Gallia* never staynd)
My kingly title I by thee have gaynd.
KING Thank heavens, not me, my zeale to you is such,
Commaund my utmost, I will never grutch.
CORDELLA He that with all kind love intreats his Queene,
Will not be to her father unkind seene.
LEIR Ah, my *Cordella*, now I call to mind,
The modest answere, which I tooke unkind:
But now I see, I am no whit beguild,
Thou lovedst me dearely, and as ought a child.
And thou (*Perillus*) partner once in woe,
Thee to requite, the best I can, Ile doe:
Yet all I can, I, were it ne're so much,
Were not sufficient, thy true love is such.
Thanks (worthy, *Mumford*) to thee last of all,
Not greeted last, 'cause thy desert was small;
No, thou hast Lion-like layd on to day,
Chasing the Cornwall King and Cambria;
Who with my daughters, daughters did I say?
To save their lives, the fugitives did play.
Come, sonne and daughter, who did me advaunce,
Repose with me awhile, and then for Fraunce.
                    *Sound Drummes and Trumpets.*                    [*Exeunt:*

[From the anonymous *True Chronicle Historie of King Leir* (1605). In *Narrative and Dramatic Sources of Shakespeare*, 7, ed. Geoffrey Bullough. New York: Columbia UP, 1975, pp. 337–38; 339–40; 341; 342–43; 360–61; 376–77; 389–90; 393–94; and 401–2.]

# From THE COUNTESSE OF PEMBROKES ARCADIA (1590)

## Sir Philip Sidney

Sir Philip Sidney (1554–1586), the eldest son of Sir Henry Sidney, Lord Deputy of Ireland, was born at Penshurst Place, Tonbridge, in the county of Kent. He was the nephew of Robert Dudley, Earl of Leicester and brother of Mary, Countess of Pembroke, who was among the first English women to achieve a major literary reputation. Sir Philip was named after his godfather, staunch Catholic King Philip II of Spain, who married Catholic Queen ("Bloody") Mary Tudor—the political and religious rivals of Elizabeth I. King Philip took pride in his almost invincible Armada until the English navy destroyed the fleet in 1588. Despite his godfather's Catholicism, Sir Philip Sidney was very much interested in establishing a Protestant League.

During Shakespeare's lifetime Sidney composed and then published in 1595 a monumental critical work: *An Apology for Poetry* (also known as *The Defence of Poesy*). In the treatise, Sidney's classicism demands adherence to the "unities" of action, place, and time: dramatic events should be limited to a single plot, encompassed in a single space, and occur within a 24-hour period. According to Sidney there should be no mixture of tragedy and comedy—that is, no mingling of kings and clowns.

In *King Lear*, by contrast, Shakespeare widens, deepens, and heightens the tragedy with a brilliant double-plot structure, expands the geography with an epic, far-reaching sweep, creates a tension-filled brew when he mixes the seriousness of tragedy with the levity of comedy; and ultimately achieves timelessness by refusing to be limited to a 24-hour stage-clock.

[In Bk. II Ch. 10 Pyrocles and Musidorus have an adventure 'worthy to be remembered for the un-used examples therin, as well of true natural goodnes, as of wretched ungratefulnesse'.]

IT WAS in the kingdome of *Galacia*, the season being (as in the depth of winter) very cold, and as then sodainely growne to so extreame and foule a storme, that never any winter (I thinke) brought foorth a fouler child: so that the Princes were even compelled by the haile, that the pride of the winde blew into their faces, to seeke some shrowding place within a certaine hollow rocke offering it unto them, they made it their shield against the tempests furie.[1] And so stay-ing there, till the violence thereof was passed, they heard the speach of a couple, who not perceiving them (being hidde within that rude canapy) helde a straunge and pitifull disputation which made them steppe out; yet in such sort, as they might see unseene. There they perceaved an aged man, and a young, scarcely come to the age of a man, both poorely arayed, extreamely weather-beaten;[2] the olde man blinde, the young man leading him: and yet through all those miser-ies, in both these seemed to appeare a kind of noblenesse, not sutable to that affliction. But the first words they heard, were these of the old man. Well *Leonatus* (said he) since I cannot perswade thee to lead me to that which should end my griefe, & thy trouble, let me now entreat thee to leave me: feare not, my miserie cannot be greater then it is, & nothing doth become me but miserie; feare not the danger of my blind steps, I cannot fall worse then I am. And doo not I pray thee, doo not obstinately continue to infect thee with my wretchednes. But flie, flie from this region; onely worthy of me. Deare father (answered he) doo not take away from me the onely remnant of my happinesse: while I have power to doo your service, I am not wholly miserable. Ah my sonne (said he, and with that he groned, as if sorrow strave to breake his harte,) how evill fits it me to have such a sonne, and how much doth thy kindnesse upbraide my wickednesse? These dolefull speeches, and some others to like purpose (well shewing they had not bene borne to the fortune they were in,) moved the Princes to goe out unto them, and aske the younger what they were? Sirs (answered he, with a good grace, and made the more agreable by a certaine noble kinde of pitiousnes) I see well you are straungers, that know not our miserie so well here knowne, that no man dare know, but that we must be miserable. In deede our state is such, as though nothing is so need-full unto us as pittie, yet nothing is more daungerous unto us, then to make our selves so knowne as may stirre pittie. But your presence promiseth, that cruelty shall not over-runne hate. And if it did, in truth our state is soncke below the degree of feare.

This old man (whom I leade) was lately rightfull Prince of this countrie of *Paphlagonia*, by the hard-harted ungratefulnes of a sonne of his, deprived, not onely of his kingdome (whereof no forraine forces were ever able to spoyle him) but of his sight, the riches which Nature graunts to the poorest creatures. Whereby, and by other his unnaturall

---

**1.** This no doubt suggested the hovel in Lear's storm 3.2 and 4.   **2.** Edgar has to disguise his nobleness, 4.1, etc.

dealings, he hath bin driven to such griefe, as even now he would have had me to have led him to the toppe of this rocke, thence to cast him-selfe headlong to death: and so would have made me (Who received my life of him) to be the worker of his destruction. But noble Gentle-men (said he) if either of you have a father, and feele what duetifull affection is engraffed in a sonnes hart, let me intreate you to convey this afflicted Prince to some place of rest and securitie. Amongst your worthie actes it shall be none of the least, that a King, of such might and fame, and so unjustly oppressed, is in any sort by you relieved.

But before they could make him answere, his father began to speake, Ah my sonne (said he) how evill an Historian are you, that leave out the chiefe knotte of all the discourse! my wickednes, my wickednes. And if thou doest it to spare my eares, (the onely sense nowe left me proper for knowledge) assure thy selfe thou dost mistake me. And I take witnesse of that Sunne which you see (with that he cast up his blinde eyes, as if he would hunt for light,) and wish my selfe in worse case then I do wish my selfe, which is as evill as may be, if I speake untruely; that nothing is so welcome to my thoughts, as the publish-ing of my shame. Therefore know you Gentlemen (to whom from my harte I wish that it may not prove ominous foretoken of misfortune to have mette with such a miser as I am) that whatsoever my sonne (O God, that trueth binds me to reproch him with the name of my sonne) hath said, is true. But besides those truthes, this also is true, that having had in lawful mariage, of a mother fitte to beare royall children, this sonne (such one as partly you see, and better shall knowe by my shorte declaration) and so enjoyed the expectations in the world of him, till he was growen to justifie their expectations (so as I needed envie no father for the chiefe comfort of mortalitie, to leave an other ones-selfe after me) I was caried by a bastarde sonne of mine (if at least I be bounde to beleeve the words of that base woman my concubine, his mother) first to mislike, then to hate, lastly to destroy, to doo my best to destroy, this sonne (I thinke you thinke) undeserving destruc-tion. What waies he used to bring me to it, if I should tell you, I should tediously trouble you with as much poysonous hypocrisie, desperate fraude, smoothe malice, hidden ambition, and smiling envie, as in any living person could be harbored. But I list it not, no remembrance, (no, of naughtines) delights me, but mine own; and me thinks, the accusing his traines might in some manner excuse my fault, which certainly I loth to doo. But the conclusion is, that I gave order to some servants of mine, whom I thought as apte for such charities as my selfe, to leade him out into a forrest, and there to kill him.

But those theeves (better natured to my sonne then my selfe) spared his life, letting him goe, to learne to live poorely: which he did, giving himselfe to be a private souldier, in a countrie here by. But as he was redy to be greatly advaunced for some noble peeces of service which he did, he hearde newes of me: who (dronke in my affection to that unlawfull and unnaturall sonne of mine) suffered my self so to be governed by him, that all favors and punishments passed by him, all offices, and places of importance distributed to his favourites; so that ere I was aware, I had left my self nothing but the name of a King: which he shortly wearie of too, with many indignities (if any thing may be called an indignity, which was laid upon me) threw me out of my seat, and put out my eies; and then (proud in his tyrannie) let me goe, nether imprisoning, nor killing me: but rather delighting to make me feele my miserie;[1] miserie indeed, if ever there were any; full of wretchednes, fuller of disgrace, and fullest of guiltines. And as he came to the crowne by so unjust meanes, as unjustlie he kept it, by force of stranger souldiers in *Cittadels*, the nestes of tyranny, & murderers of libertie; disarming all his own countrimen, that no man durst shew himself a welwisher of mine: to say the trueth (I think) few of them being so (considering my cruell follie to my good sonne, and foolish kindnes to my unkinde bastard:) but if there were any who fell to pitie of so great a fall, and had yet any sparkes of unstained duety lefte in them towardes me, yet durst they not shewe it, scarcely with giving me almes at their doores;[2] which yet was the onelie sustenaunce of my distressed life, no bodie daring to shewe so much charitie, as to lende me a hande to guide my darke steppes:[3] Till this sonne of mine (God knowes, woorthie of a more vertuous, and more fortunate father) forgetting my abhominable wrongs, not recking danger, and neglecting the present good way he was in doing himselfe good, came hether to doo this kind office you see him performe towards me, to my unspeakable griefe; not onely because his kindnes is a glasse even to my blind eyes, of my naughtines, but that above all griefes, it greeves me he should desperatly adventure the losse of his soul-deserving life for mine, that yet owe more to fortune for my deserts, as if he would cary mudde in a chest of christall. For well I know, he that now raigneth, how much soever (and with good reason) he despiseth me, of all men despised; yet he will not let slippe any advantage to make away him, whose just title (ennobled by courage and goodnes) may one day shake the seate of a never secure tyrannie. And for this cause I craved of him to leade me to the toppe of this rocke, indeede I must confesse, with meaning to free him from

---

**1.** Cf. Regan, 3.7.93–94: 'Let him smell his way to Dover!' Edmund is not present but knows that his father is to be punished' horribly.   **2.** So Gloucester is ordered not to help Lear, 3.3.1–6. But he does so.   **3.** One of Gloucester's servants dies trying to save him; others 'get the Bedlam to lead him' (3.7.73–82ff.).

so Serpentine a companion as I am. But he finding what I purposed, onely therein since he was borne, shewed himselfe disobedient unto me.[1] And now Gentlemen, you have the true storie, which I pray you publish to the world, that my mischievous proceedinges may be the glorie of his filiall pietie, the onely reward now left for so great a merite. And if it may be, let me obtaine that of you, which my sonne denies me: for never was there more pity in saving any, then in ending me; both because therein my agonies shall ende, and so shall you preserve this excellent young man, who els wilfully folowes his owne ruine.

The matter in it self lamentable, lamentably expressed by the old Prince (which needed not take to himselfe the gestures of pitie, since his face could not put of the markes thereof) greatly moved the two Princes to compassion, which could not stay in such harts as theirs without seeking remedie. But by and by the occasion was presented: for *Plexirtus* (so was the bastard called) came thether with fortie horse, onely of purpose to murder this brother; of whose comming he had soone advertisement, and thought no eyes of sufficient credite in such a matter, but his owne; and therefore came him selfe to be actor, and spectator. And as soone as he came, not regarding the weake (as he thought) garde of but two men, commaunded some of his followers to set their handes to his, in the killing of *Leonatus*. But the young Prince (though not otherwise armed but with a sworde) how falsely soever he was dealt with by others, would not betray him selfe: but bravely drawing it out, made the death of the first that assaulted him, warne his fellowes to come more warily after him.[2] But then *Pyrocles* and *Musidorus* were quickly become parties (so just a defence deserving as much as old friendship) and so did behave them among that companie (more injurious then valiant) that many of them lost their lives for their wicked maister.

Yet perhaps had the number of them at last prevailed, if the King of Pontus (lately by them made so) had not come unlooked for to their succour. Who (having had a dreame, which had fixt his imagination vehemently upon some great daunger presently to follow those two Princes whom he most deerely loved) was come in all hast, following as well as he could their tracke with a hundreth horses in that countrie, which he thought (considering who then raigned) a fit place inough to make the stage of any Tragedie.

But then the match had ben so ill made for *Plexirtus*, that his ill-led life, and worse gotten honour should have tumbled together to destruction; had there not come in *Tydeus* and *Telenor*, with fortie or fiftie in their suit, to the defence of *Plexirtus*. . . . And briefly so they did, that if they overcame not yet were they not overcome, but caried away that ungratefull maister of theirs to a place of securitie; howsoever the Princes laboured to the contrary.[1] But this matter being thus far begun, it became not the constancie of the Princes so to leave it; but in all hast making forces both in *Pontus* and *Phrygia*, they had in fewe dayes lefte him but only that one strong place where he was. For feare having bene the onely knot that had fastned his people unto him, that once untied by a greater force, they all scattered from him; like so many birdes, whose cage had bene broken.

In which season the blind King (having in the chief cittie of his Realme, set the crowne upon his sonne *Leonatus* head) with many teares (both of joy and sorrow) setting forth to the whole people, his owne fault and his sonnes vertue, after he had kist him, and forst his sonne to accept honour of him (as of his newe-become subject) even in a moment died, as it should seeme: his hart broken with unkindnes and affliction, stretched so farre beyond his limits with this excesse of comfort, as it was able no longer to keep safe his roial spirits.[2] But the new King (having no lesse lovingly performed all duties to him dead, then alive) pursued on the siege of his unnatural brother, asmuch for the revenge of his father, as for the establishing of his owne quiet. In which siege truly I cannot but acknowledge the prowesse of those two brothers, then whom the Princes never found in all their travell two men of greater habilitie to performe, nor of habler skill for conduct.

---

1. Cf. Edmund's apparent victory (5.3) turned to defeat by Albany.  2. Cf. Gloucester's death: 'Twixt two extremes of passion, joy and grief' (5.3.199).

[From Sir Philip Sidney's *The Countesse of Pembrokes Arcadia* (1590). In *Narrative and Dramatic Sources of Shakespeare*, 7, ed. Geoffrey Bullough. New York: Columbia UP, 1975, pp. 402-7.]

# From *The Second Booke of the Historie of England* (1587 edn.)

## R. Holinshed

Raphael Holinshed (1529?-c. 1589), the great chronicler, was assigned the task of assembling a world history starting with the Flood and ending with the era of Queen Elizabeth. He never brought to fruition the scope of his original idea, but more importantly he did produce in 1577 a history of England, Scotland, and Ireland. The volume was reprinted and enlarged in 1587. This edition was the one that Shakespeare used as one of the principle sources for his English history plays and for sections of *Cymbeline* and *King Lear*. See Fig. 6 from Holinshed's 1577 edition.

### [XII.2.59]

**LEIR** THE SONNE of Baldud was admitted ruler over the Britaines, in the yeare of the world 3105, at what time Joas reigned in Juda. This Leir was a prince of right noble demeanor, governing his land and subjects in great wealth. He made the towne of Caerleir now called Leicester, which standeth upon the river of Sore. It is written that he had by his wife three daughters without other issue, whose names were Gonorilla, Regan, and Cordeilla, which daughters he greatly loved, but specially Cordeilla the yoongest farre above the two elder. When this Leir therefore was come to great yeres, & began to waxe unweldie through age, he thought to understand the affections of his daughters towards him, and preferre hir whome he best loved, to the succession over the kingdome, Wherupon he first asked Gonorilla the eldest, how well she loved him: who calling hir gods to record, protested that she 'loved him more than hir owne life, which by right and reason should be most deere unto hir'. With which answer the father being well pleased, turned to the second, and demanded of hir how well she loved him: who answered (confirming hir saiengs with great othes) that she loved him 'more than toong could expresse, and farre above all other creatures of the world.'

Then called he his yoongest daughter Cordeilla before him, and asked of hir what account she made of him, unto whome she made this answer as followeth: 'Knowing the great love and fatherlie zeale that you have alwaies borne towards me (for the which I maie not answere you otherwise than I thinke and as my conscience leadeth me)

I protest unto you, that I have loved you ever, and will continuallie (while I live) love you as my naturall father. And if you would more understand of the love that I beare you, assertaine your selfe, that so much as you have, so much you are woorth, and so much I love you, and no more'. The father being nothing content with this answer, married his two eldest daughters, the one unto Henninus the duke of Cornewall, and the other unto Maglanus the duke of Albania, betwixt whome he willed and ordeined that his land should be divided after his death, and the one halfe thereof immediatlie should be assigned to them in hand: but for the third daughter Cordeilla he reserved nothing.'

Nevertheles it fortuned that one of the princes of Gallia (which now is called France) whose name was Aganippus, hearing of the beautie, womanhood, and good conditions of the said Cordeilla, desired to have hir in mariage, and sent over to hir father, requiring that he might have hir to wife: to whome answer was made, that he might have his daughter, but as for anie dower he could have none, for all was promised and assured to hir other sisters alreadie. Aganippus notwithstanding this answer of deniall to receive anie thing by way of dower with Cordeilla, tooke hir to wife, onlie moved thereo (I saie) for respect of hir person and amiable vertues. This Aganippis was one of the twelve kings that ruled Gallia in those daies, as in the British historie it is recorded,[1] But to proceed.

After that Leir was fallen into age, the two dukes that had married his two eldest daughters, thinking it long yer the government of the land did come to their hands, arose against him in armour, and reft from him the governance of the land, upon conditions to be continued for terme of life:[2] by the which he was put to his portion, that is, to live after a rate assigned to him for the maintenance of his estate, which in processe of time was diminished as well by Maglanus as by Henninus. But the greatest griefe that Leir tooke, was to see the unkindnesse of his daughters, which seemed to thinke that all was too much which their father had, the same being never so little: in so much that going from the one to the other, he was brought to that miserie, that scarslie they would allow him one servant[3] to wait upon him.

In the end, such was the unkindnesse, or (as I maie saie) the urnaturalnesse which he found in his two daughters, notwithstanding their faire and pleasant words uttered in time past, that being constreined of necessitie, he fled the land, & sailed into Gallia, then to seeke some comfort of his yongest daughter Cordeilla, whom before time he hated. The

---

**1.** *In margin*: 'He governed the third part of Gallia as *Gal. Min.* saith.' **2.** Cf. 1.1.130–8. Lear makes his own conditions. **3.** Cf. Goneril and then Regan at 2.4.260–64. In *Leir* he has Perillus, in *King Lear* the Fool, but also numerous knights. (3.7.14–20.)

ladie Cordeilla hearing that he was arrived in poore estate, she first sent to him privilie a certeine summe of monie to apparell himselfe withall,[1] and to reteine a certeine number of servants that might attend upon him in honorable wise, as apperteined to the estate which he had borne; and then so accompanied she appointed him to come to the court, which he did, and was so joifullie, honorablie, and lovinglie received, both by his sonne in law Aganippus, and also by his daughter Cordeilla, that his hart was greatlie comforted: for he was no lesse honored, than if he had been king of the whole countrie himselfe.

Now when he had informed his sonne in law and his daughter in what sort he had been used by his other daughters, Aganippus caused a mightie armie to be put in a readinesse, and likewise a great navie of ships to be rigged, to passe over into Britaine with Leir his father in law, to see him againe restored to his kingdome. It was accorded, that Cordeilla should also go with him to take possession of the land, the which he promised to leave unto hir, as the rightfull inheritour after his decesse, notwithstanding any former grant made to hir sisters or to their husbands in anie maner of wise.

Hereupon, when this armie and navie of ships were readie, Leir and his daughter Cordeilla with hir husband[2] tooke the sea, and arriving in Britaine, fought with their enimies, and discomfited them in battell, in the which Maglanus and Henninus were slaine: and then was Leir restored to his kingdome, which he ruled after this by the space of two yeeres, and then died, fortie yeeres after he first began to reigne. His bodie was buried at Leicester in a vaut under the chanell of the river of Sore beneath the towne.

## THE SIXT CHAPTER

The gunarchie[3] of queene Cordeilla, how she was vanquished, of hir imprisonment and selfe-murther: the contention betweene Cunedag and Margan nephewes for governement, and the evill end thereof.

CORDEILLA the yoongest daughter of Leir was admitted Q. and supreme governesse of Britaine, in the yeere of the world 3155, before the bylding of Rome 54, Uzia then reigning in Juda, and Jeroboam over Israell. This Cordeilla after hir fathers deceasse ruled the land of Britaine right worthilie during the space of five yeeres, in which meane time hir husband died, and then about the end of those five yeeres, hir two nephewes Margan and Cunedag, sonnes to hir aforesaid

---

1. In *Leir*, 216–80, she gives him food; Cf. 4.7.20–1, where he is clothed while asleep. 2. In *Leir* he defeats the enemy. 3. gynarchy, governement by a woman.

sisters, disdaining to be under the government of a woman, levied warre against hir, and destroied a great part of the land, and finallie tooke hir prisoner, and laid hir fast in ward, wherewith she tooke such griefe, being a woman of a manlie courage, and despairing to recover libertie, there she slue hirselfe, when she had reigned (as before is mentioned) the tearme of five yeeres.

[From *The Second Booke of the Historie of England* (1587). In *Narrative and Dramatic Sources of Shakespeare*, 7, ed. Geoffrey Bullough. New York: Columbia UP, 1975, pp. 316–19.]

# From THE MIRROR FOR MAGISTRATES
## (1574)
### John Higgins

John Higgins (c.1545–1602), poet, historian, and antiquarian, was associated with Christ Church, Oxford. He is linked closely to *The Mirror for Magistrates*, first published in 1559, with its metaphorical title referring to the looking glass into which humankind gazes to be mindful of the fickle ways of Fortune in this imperfect terrestrial world. The 1559 *Mirror* relates nineteen "tragedies" in verse dealing with legendary, historical, political, and religious luminaries whose lives are subject to the random rotations of Fortune's wheel—a theme at the center of pre-Shakespearean literary works, from which in part *King Lear* descends, concerning the falls (*de casibus*) of illustrious men and women. In the 1574 *Mirror*, Higgins presents his Cordelia (spelled variously as "Cordila," "Cordilla," "Cordell," and "Cordile") in a first-person narrative that Shakespeare no doubt consulted in composing *King Lear*.

THE FIRST parte of the Mirour for Magistrates, containing the falles of the first infortunate Princes of this lande: From the comming of Brute to the incarnation of our saviour and redemer Jesu Christe. Ad. Romanos. 13.2. Quisquis se opponit potestati, Dei ordina resistit. Imprinted at London by Thomas Marshe. Anno. 1574. Cum Privilegio.

*Cordila shewes how by despaire when she was in prison she slue herselfe, the yeare before Christe. 800.*

Yf any wofull wight have cause, to waile her woe:
Or griefes are past do pricke us Princes tel our fal;
My selfe likewise must needes constrained eke do so,
And shew my like misfortunes and mishaps withal.
Should I keepe close my heavy haps and thral?
Then did I wronge: I wrongde my selfe and thee,
Which of my facts, a witnes true maist bee.

A woman yet must blushe when bashfull is the case,
Though truth bid tell the tale and story as it fell:
But sith that I mislike not audience time nor place      10
Therefore, I cannot still keep in my counsaile well:
No greater ease of hart then griefes to tell,

It daunteth all the dolours of our minde,
Our carefull harts thereby great comfort finde.

        .     .     .

Therefore if I more willing be to tell my fall,
And shew mishaps to ease my burdened brest and minde:
That others haply may avoide and shunne like thrall,
And thereby in distresse more ayde and comfort finde.      25
They maye keepe measure where as I declinde,
And willing be to flye like bruite and blame:
As I to tell, or thou to write the same.

For sith I see the[e] prest to heare that wilt recorde,
What I *Cordilla* tell to ease my inward smart:      30
I will resite my storye tragicall ech worde,
To the that givst an eare to heare and ready art,
And lest I set the horse behinde the cart,
I minde to tell ech thinge in order so,
As thou maiste see and shewe whence sprang my wo.

My grandsyre *Bladud* hight that found the Bathes by skill,
A fethered king that practisde for to flye and soare:
Whereby he felt the fall God wot against his will,
And never went, roode, raignde nor spake, nor flew no more.
Who dead his sonne my father *Leire* therefore,      40
Was chosen kinge, by right apparent heyre,
Which after built the towne of *Leircestere*.

He had three daughters, first and eldest hight *Gonerell*:
Next after hir, my sister *Ragan* was begote:
The thirde and last was, I the yongest namde *Cordell*,
And of us all, our father *Leire* in age did dote.
So minding hir that lovde him best to note,
Because he had no sonne t'enjoye his lande:
He thought to give, where favoure most he fande.[1]

What though I yongest were, yet men me judgde more wise      50
Then either *Gonorell*, or *Ragan* had more age,
And fayrer farre: wherefore my sisters did despise
My grace, and giftes, and sought my praise t'swage:[2]
But yet though vice gainst vertue die with rage,
It cannot keepe her underneth to drowne,[1]
But still she flittes above, and reapes renowne.

---

1. Skalliger in *Leir* (37–8) suggests an unequal division; *Lear* is ambiguous at 1.1.
52–3. 2. 'and sought my wrecke to wage', 1587; hence their plot in *Leir*, Sc. 2.
1. Shakespeare goes into this more deeply in his tragedy.

Yet nathelesse, my father did me not mislike:
But age so simple is, and easye to subdue:
As childhode weake, thats voide of wit and reason quite:
They thincke thers nought you flater fainde, but all is true:     60
Once olde and twice a childe, tis said with you,
Which I affirme by proofe, that was definde:
In age my father had a childishe minde.

He thought to wed us unto nobles three, or Peres:
And unto them and theirs, devide and part the lande:
For both my sisters first he sent as first their yeares
Requirde their mindes, and love, and favour t'understand.
(Quod he) all doubtes of duty to abande,
I must assaye and eke your frendships prove:
Now tell me eche how much you do me love.     70

Which when they aunswered, they lovde him wel and more
Then they themselves did love, or any worldly wight:
He praised them and said he would againe therefore,
The loving kindnes they deservde in fine requite:
So found my sisters favour in his sight,
By flatery fayre they won their fathers hart:
Which after turned him and mee to smart.

But not content with this he minded me to prove,
For why he wonted was to love me wonders[2] well:
How much dost thou (quoth he) *Cordile* thy father love?     80
I will (said I) at once my love declare and tell;
I lovde you ever as my father well,
No otherwise, if more to know you crave:
We love you chiefly for the goodes[3] you have.

Thus much I said, the more their flattery to detect,
But he me answered therunto again with Ire,
Because thou dost thy fathers aged yeares neglect,
That lovde the more of late then thy desertes require,
Thou never shalt, to any part aspire
Of this my realme, among thy sisters twayne,     90
But ever shalt undoted ay remayne.

---

**2.** wondrous.   **3.** Word-play. He is all goodness to them so they should love him
accordingly; but the sisters may love him for his wealth.

[From *The Mirror for Magistrates* (1574). In *Narrative and Dramatic Sources of
Shakespeare*, 7, ed. Geoffrey Bullough. New York: Columbia UP, 1975, pp. 323–25.]

# From *The Faerie Queene* (1590)

## Book 2, Canto 10
### Verses 27–32
### Edmund Spenser

Jonathan Bate and Eric Rasmussen, in their edition of *William Shakespeare: Complete Works* (New York: Modern Library, 2007), explain that one of the sixteenth- and seventeenth-century works familiar to Shakespeare and a source for *King Lear* was Edmund Spenser's epic poem, *The Faerie Queene* of 1590. In this lengthy poem made up of six complete books and a portion of a seventh, Spenser (1552–1599) uses a mixture of Arthurian legend and sustained allegory to narrate the adventures of various medieval knights in quest of the courtly favor of the beautiful, virtuous Fairy Queen or Gloriana, an idealized portrait of the literal, historical personage, Queen Elizabeth I of England. Spenser draws many of his details from medieval romance, which affects how he tells his version of the Lear story in Book 2, canto 10 of *The Faerie Queene*. Bate and Rasmussen do well to point out that "in all versions of the story [of King Lear] before Shakespeare's, there is a 'romance' ending whereby the old king is restored to his daughter Cordelia and to the throne" (p. 2007). Understandably, then, Shakespeare, who is much less given to idealizing than is Spenser, will proceed in a very different direction in his drama of Lear and Cordelia.

Battles in Spenser's poem have about them an element of romance combined with the theological tradition of the *psychomachia* ('soul-combat')—the age-old battle between forces of vice and those of virtue on the figurative battlefield of the human soul. As discussed in the "Introduction," *King Lear* may be read, heard, or viewed as a complex *psychomachia*.

See the section titled "Psychomachia" in the Evans Editor's "Introduction."

27
Next him[1] king *Leyr* in happie peace long raynd,
But had no issue male him to succeed,
But three faire daughters, which were well uptraind,
In all that seemed fitt for kingly seed:
Mongst whom his realme he equally decreed

To have divided. Tho when feeble age
Nigh to his vtmost date he saw proceed,
He cald his daughters; and with speeches sage
Inquyrd, which of them most did love her parentage.

28

The eldest *Ganerill* gan to protest,
  That she much more then her owne life him lou'd:
  And *Regan* greater love to him profest.
Then all the world, when euer it were proou'd;
But *Cardeill* said she lou'd him, as behoou'd:
  Whose simple answere, wanting colours fayre
  To paint it forth, him to displeasaunce moon'd,
  That in his crown he counted her no hayre,
But twist the other twain his kingdom whole did shayre.

29

So wedded th'one to *Maglan* king of Scottes,
  And thother to the king of *Cambrin*,
  And twixt them shayrd his rcalme by equall lottes:
But without dowre the wise *Cordelia*,
Was sent to *Aggannip* of *Celtica*.
  Their aged Syre, thus eased of his crowne,
  A private life ledd in *Albania*,
  With *Gonorill*, long had in great renowne,
That nought him grieu'd to beene from rule deposed downe.

30

But true it is that when the oyle is spent,
  The light goes out, and weeke is throwne away;
  So when he had resignd his regiment,
His daughter gan despise his drouping day,
And wearie wax of his continuall stay.
  Tho to his daughter *Regan* he repayrd,
  Who him at first well used every way;
  But when of his departure she despayrd,
Her bountie she abated, and his cheare empayrd.

[1. In verse 27, line 1, the pronoun "him" refers to Baldud, a figure in
Britain's legendary history. Baldud was the father of King Leir, the pre-
cursor of Shakespeare's *King Lear*. See chapter 5 of Raphael Holinshed's
*Chronicles: The Historie of England* (1587). ~ *Evans Editor*] **Stanza 27 1.** him:
Bladud **9.** parentage: parents; here, parent. **Stanza 28 4.** proou'd: put to the test.
**5.** as behoon'd: as was fitting (to a father). **7.** displeasaunce: displeasure.
**Stanza 29 2.** Cambria: Wales. **5.** Celtica: France. **7.** Albania: Scotland.
**Stanza 30 1–2.** weeke wick; with a pun on 'weak', alluding to Lear's 'feeble age'
(27.6). **3.** regiment: office. **9.** cheare: kindly reception.

31

The wretched man gan then auise to late,
  That loue is not, where most it is profest,
  Too truely tryde in his extremest state;
  At last resolu'd likewise to prove the rest,
  He to *Cordelia* him selfe addrest,
  Who with entyre affection him receau'd
  As for her Syre and king her seemed best;
  And after all an army strong she leau'd,
To war on those, which him had of his realme bereau'd.

32

So to his crowne she him restord againe,
  In which he dyde, made ripe for death by eld,
  And after wild, it should to her remaine:
  Who peaceably the same long time did weld:
  And all mens harts in dew obedience held:
  Till that her sisters children, woxen strong,
  Through proud ambition against her rebeld,
  And overcommen kept in prison long,
Till weary of that wretched life, her selfe she hong.

**Stanza 31   1.** auise: reflect.   **3.** tryde: proven.   **6–7.** entyre: sincere; perfect.
**8.** after all: afterwards, lean'd: levied.   **Stanza 32 3.** after wild: willed that afterwards.   **4.** weld: wield.

[From *The Faerie Queene*, ed. A. C. Hamilton, Hiroshi Yamashita, and Toshiyuki
Suzuki London, U.K.: Longman, 2001, pp. 251–2.]

# From *A Declaration of Egregious Popish Impostures* (1603)

## Samuel Harsnett[1]

Samul Harsnett (1561–1631) was educated at Pembroke Hall, Cambridge and later became Master and Vice-Chancellor of the University. In 1629 he was appointed Bishop of Chichester and in 1629 the Archbishop of York. His *Declaration of Popish Impostures* (published 1603) developed out of the investigation of exorcisms conducted by Jesuits. Harsnett argued in this tract that English Catholic priests were responsible for fraudulent exorcisms that were used to convert Anglicans to the Roman Catholic faith. These attempts at conversion led to staged exorcisms during which supposedly possessed individuals would not only enact the physical gestures of those in the grips of demons but also utter the language of the possessed and shout out demonic names. Harsnett wisely recorded several of the words used in these performances, providing readers like Shakespeare with "actual" names of devils: Frateretto, Fliberdigibbet, Purre, Maho, and Modu, to use some of Harsnett's spellings. Edgar in the role of Poor Tom of Bedlam invokes such demonic creatures in 3.4 and 3.6 of *King Lear*. One of the priests whom Harsnett cites as a performer of exorcisms is referred to, at different times, as Edmund Campion or Father Edmunds or Father William Weston. This is a curious coincidence in view of Shakespeare's villainous Edmund.

### CHAP. 10

*The strange names of their devils*

NOW THAT I have acquainted you with the names of the Maister, and his twelve disciples, the names of the places wherein, and the names of the persons upon whom these wonders were shewed: it seemes not incongruent that I relate unto you the names of the devils, whom in this glorious pageant they did dispossesse. Wherein, we may call unto *Porphyrins, Proclus, Iamblicus,* and *Trismegistus,* the old Platonicall sect, that conversed familiarly, and kept company with devils, and desire their help to expound us these new devils names: and

---

1. At London Printed by James Roberts, dwelling in Barbican. 1603.

to tell us at what solemne feast, and meeting in hell, these devils were dubbed, and halowed with these new strange names. It cannot be but our holy devill-crue had surely met with *Menippus,* proclaiming him-selfe new come out of hell: *ad sum profoundo Tartari emissus specu:* Else they could never have beene so deeply sighted, and acquainted with the Muster-booke of hell. Or else it may seeme that our vagrant devils heere did take theyr fashion of new names from our wandring Jesuits, who to dissemble themselves, have alwaies three, or foure odde con-ceited names in their budget: or els they did so plague the poore devils with theyr holy charmes, and enchaunted geare, and did so intoxicate them with their dreadful fumigations, as they made some so giddy-headed, that they gave themselves giddy names, they wist not what. Or else there is a confederation between our wandring Exorcists, and these walking devils, and they are agreed of certaine uncouth non-significant names, which goe currant amongst themselves, as the Gipsies are of gi-bridge,[1] which none but themselves can spell without a paire of specta-cles. Howsoever it is, it is not amisse that you be acquainted with these extravagant names of devils, least meeting them otherwise by chance, you mistaken them for the names of Tapsters, or Juglers.

First then, to marshall them in as good order, as such disorderly cattell will be brought into, you are to understand, that there were in our possessed 5. Captaines, or Commaunders above the rest: Captaine *Pippin, Marwoods* devill, Captaine *Philpot, Trayfords* devil, Captaine *Maho, Saras* devil, Captaine *Modu, Maynies* devill, and Captaine *Soforce, Anne Smiths* devil. These were not all of equal authoritie, & place, but some had more, some fewer under theyr commaund. *Pippin, Marwoods* devill was a Captaine, (marry either cassierd for some part of bad ser-vice hee had done, or else a male-content standing upon his worth) like some of our high Puntilios, scorned to sort himselfe with any of his ranke, and therefore like a melancholick *Privado,* he affects *Mar-wood* to lie in the fields, and to gape at the Moone, and so of a *Caesars* humor, he raignes in *Marwood* alone.

Captaine *Philpot, Trayfords* devill, was a Centurion, (as himselfe tels you) and had an hundred under his charge. Mary he was (as seemes) but a white-livered devill, for he was so hastie to be gone out of *Tray-ford,* for feare of the Exorcist, that hee would scarce give him leave, beeing a bed, to put on his breeches. The names of ther punie spirits cast out of *Trayford* were *these, Hilco, Smolkin,*[2] *Hillio, Hiaclito,* and *Lustie huffe-cap:* this last seemes some swaggering punie devill, dropt out of a Tinkers budget. But *Hiaclito* may not be slipped over without your ob-servation: for he scorning a great while (as the Author saith) to tell his

1. gibberish, unintelligible language.   2. 3.4.140.

name, at last he aunswered most proudly, *my name is* Hiaclito, *a Prince, & Monarch of the world.* And beeing asked by the Exorcist, what fellowes he had with him: hee said that *hee had no fellowes, but two men, and an urchin boy.* It was little beseeming his state (I wis) beeing so mighty a Monarch, to come into our coasts so skurvily attended, except hee came to see fashions in England, and so made himselfe private till the Exorcist reveald him: or els that he was of the new Court cut, affecting no other traine then two crasie fellowes, and an urchin butter-flie boy.

*Soforce, Anne Smiths* possedent, was but a musty devill; there was neither mirth, nor good fellowship with him, affecting so much sullennesse, as he would hardlie speake. Yet as all melancholike creatures use to have, he had a restie tricke with him. For whether *Alexander* the Apothecarie had put too much *Assa Foetida* in the fumigation for the devill, or had done the devill some other shrewd turne with his drugges, sure it is that *Alexander* the Apothecarie, riding one day towards London, to fetch more Priests to *Denham*, his horse fell a plunging, and *Alexander* came downe: and returning to *Denham*, hee constantly affirmed, that it was *Anne Smiths* devill, that playd the Jade with him.

*Modu*, Ma: *Maynies* devill, was a graund Commaunder, Mustermaister over the Captaines of the seaven deadly sinnes:[1] *Cliton, Bernon, Hilo, Motubizanto,* & the rest, himselfe a Generall of a kind and curteous disposi[ti]on: so saith *Sara Williams,* touching this devils acquaintance with Mistres *Plater,* and her sister *Fid.*

*Sara Williams* had in her at a bare word, *all the devils in hell. The* Exorcist askes *Maho, Saras* devil,[2] what company he had with him, and the devil makes no bones, but tels him in flat termes, *all the devils in hell.* Heere was a goodly fat *otium* this meane while in hell: the poore soules there had good leave to play: such a day was never seene since hell was hell: not a doore-keeper left, but all must goe a maying to poore *Saras* house. It was not kindly done of the devils, to leave the poore soules behind, especially going to make merry amongst theyr friends. But what if the soules had fallen a madding, or maying as fast, as the devils, and had gone a roming abroade amongst their good friends, had not this (trow we,) made a prettie peece of worke in hell?

And if I misse not my markes, this *Dictator Modu* saith, hee had beene in *Sara* by the space of two yeeres, then so long hell was cleere,

---

**1.** 3. 4. 143; [Cf. The Seven Deadly Sins are Pride, Anger (or Wrath), Lust (or Lechery), Covetousness, Gluttony, Envy, and Sloth. They appear prominently in two important Elizabethan works: Spenser's *Faerie Queene* (1590), Book 1, canto 4 and Christopher Marlowe's *Doctor Faustus* (1592), Act 2, scene 2. See also John Jewell's "Homilie" (including note 20) later in "Sources and Contexts." ~ *Evans Editor*] 4.1.61. **2.** Cf. 3.4.144; 4.1.60.

and had not a devill to cast at a mad dogge. And sooth, I cannot much blame the devils for staying so long abroade, they had taken up an Inne, much sweeter then hell: & an hostesse that wanted neither wit, nor mirth, to give them kinde welcome.

Heere, if you please, you may take a survey of the whole regiment of hell: at least the chiefe Leaders, and officers, as we finde them enrolled by theyr names.

First *Killico*, *Hob*, and a third *anonymos*, are booked downe for three graund Commaunders, every one having under him 300 attendants.

. . .

But the devill is like some other good fellowes in the world, that will not sweare, except he allow theyr Commission[1] that tenders him his oath: and Commissioners for the devill, are onely holy Exorcists, and then it must be the sacrament of the Masse to, else I wis it is not all worth a beane.

*Frateretto*,[2] *Fliberdigibbet*,[3] *Hoberdidance*,[4] *Tocobatto* were foure devils of the round, or Morrice, whom *Sara* in her fits, tuned together, in measure and sweet cadence.[5] And least you should conceive, that the devils had no musicke in hell, especially that they would goe a maying without theyr musicke, the Fidler comes in with his Taber, & Pipe, and a whole Morice after him, with motly visards for theyr better grace. These foure had forty assistants under them, as themselves doe confesse.

---

1. Lear has a 'commission' of justice in 3.6.39–58. 2. 3.6.6; 4.1.60–61. 3. 3.4.115; 4.1.60–61. 4. 3.6.30. 5. Cf. Edgar, 4.1.58–59: 'Five fiends have been in Poor Tom at once.'

[For a highly informative study of Harsnett's work, see Frank Brownlow's *Shakespeare, Harsnett, and the Devils of Denham*. Associated University Presses: London. 1993. ~ *Evans Editor*]

[From *A Declaration of Egregious Popish Impostures* (1603). In *Narrative and Dramatic Sources of Shakespeare*, 7, ed. Geoffrey Bullough. New York: Columbia UP, 1975, pp. 414–18.]

# THE GENEVA BIBLE (1560)

## EVANS EDITOR'S MODERNIZED VERSION

The two Bibles associated with Shakespeare are The Geneva Bible (1560), an extensively annotated text intended for Calvinists, and The Bishops' Bible (1568), which was the official Bible of the Anglican Church during the reign of Elizabeth I. The King James Bible appeared in 1611. (See Color Plate 1.) Excerpted below are passages from The Geneva Bible in modern spelling prepared by the Evans Editor for this volume. The facsimile of the 1560 edition is usually a challenge for modern readers in the light of old spelling forms and typography. Removed here are all but two of the hundreds of marginal sixteenth-century explanatory commentaries (i.e., glosses) on the scriptural verses. Also removed are all of the alphabetical cues that were keyed to those glosses.

## JOB 9

1    THEN JOB answered, and said, . . .

17   For he destroys me with a tempest, & wounds me without cause.

18   He will not suffer me to take my breath, but fills me with bitterness.

19   If *we speak* of strength, behold, he is strong: if *we speak* of judgement, who shall bring me in to plead?

20   If I would justify my self, mine own mouth shall condemn me: if I would be perfect, he shall judge me wicked.

21   *Though* I were perfect, *yet* I know not my soul: *therefore* abhor I my life.

22   This is one point: therefore I said, He destroys the perfect and the wicked.

23   If the scourge should suddenly slay, should *God* laugh at the punishment of the innocent?

24   The earth is given into the hand of the wicked: he covers the faces of the judges thereof: if not, where is he? or who is he?

25   My days have been more swift than a post: they have fled, & have seen no good thing.

## JOB 10

1 My soul is cut off though I live: I will leave my complaint upon myself, & will speak in the bitterness of my soul. . . .

11 Thou hast clothed me with skin and flesh, and joined me together with bones and sinews.

12 Thou hast given me life, and grace: & thy visitation has preserved my spirit.

13 Though thou hast hid these things in thine heart, *yet* I know that it is so with thee.

14 If I have sinned, then you will straightly look unto me, and will not hold me guiltless of mine iniquity.

15 If I have done wickedly, woe unto me: if I have done righteously, I will not lift up my head, being full of confusion, because I see my affliction.

16 But let it increase: hunt thou me as a lion: return and show thy self marvelous upon me.

17 You renew your plagues against me, and you increase your wrath against me: changes and armies of sorrows are against me.

18 Wherefore then hast thou brought me out of the womb? Oh that I had perished, and that no eye had seen me!

19 *And* that I were as I had not been, but brought from the womb to the grave.

20 Are not my days few? let him cease, *and* leave off from me, that I may take a little comfort,

21 Before I go and shall not return, even to the land of darkness and shadow of death:

22 Into a land, I say, dark as darkness it self, & into the shadow of death, where is no order, but the light *is there* as darkness.

## JOB 30

1 But now they that are younger than I, mock me: *yea*, they whose fathers I have refused to set with the dogs of my flocks.

2 For where to should the strength of their hands have served me, *seeing* age perished in them?

3 For poverty and famine *they were* solitary, fleeing into the wilderness, which is dark, desolate and waste.

4 They cut up nettles by the bushes, and the juniper roots *was* their meat.

5 They were chased forth from among *men*: they shouted at them, as at a thief.

6 Therefore they dwelt in the clefts of rivers, in the holes of the earth and rocks.

7 They roared among the bushes, and under the thistles they gathered them selves.

8 *They were* the children of fools and the children of villains, which were more vile than the earth.

9 And now am I their song, and I am their talk. [Geneva Bible explanatory sidenote gloss: *They make songs of me, & mock at my misery.*]

10 They abhor me, *and* flee far from me, and spare not to spit in my face. . . .

21 You [God] turn yourself cruelly against me, and are enemy unto me with the strength of your hand.

22 You [God] take me up *and* cause me to ride upon the wind, and make my strength to fail.

23 Surely I know that you [God] will bring me to death, and to the house appointed for all the living. [Geneva Bible explanatory sidenote gloss: *He compares his afflictions to a tempest or a whirlwind.*]

24 Doubtless none can stretch his hand unto the grave, though they cry in his destruction.

25 Did not I weep with him that was in trouble? was not my soul in heaviness for the poor?

26 Yet when I looked for good, evil came unto me: and when I waited for light, there came darkness.

27 My bowels did boil without rest: *for* the days of affliction are come upon me.

28 I went mourning without sun: I stood up in the congregation and cried.

29 I am a brother to the dragons, and a companion to the ostriches.

30 My skin is black upon me, and my bones are burnt with heat.

31 Therefore mine harp is turned to mourning, and mine organs into the voice of them that weep.

## JOB 31

1 I made a covenant with mine eyes: why then should I think on a maid?

2 For what portion *should I have* of God from above? and *what* inheritance of the Almighty from on high? . . .

14 What then shall I do when God stands up? and when he shall visit me, what shall I answer?

15 He that hath made me in the womb, hath he not made him? hath not he alone fashioned us in the womb?

16 If I restrained the poor of *their* desire, or have caused the eyes of the widow to fail,

17 Or have eaten my morsels alone, & the fatherless hath not eaten thereof...

34 Though I could have made afraid a great multitude, yet the most contemptible of the families did fear me: so I kept silence, and went not out of the door.

35 Oh that I had some to hear me! behold my sign that the Almighty will witness for me: though my adversary should write a book *against me,*

36 Would not I take it upon my shoulder, & bind it as a crown unto me?

37 I will tell him the number of my goings, and go unto him as to a prince.

38 If my land cry against me, or the furrows thereof complain together,

39 If I have eaten the fruits thereof without silver: or if I have grieved the souls of the masters thereof,

40 Let thistles grow instead of wheat, & cockle instead of barley. The words of Job are ended.

## LUKE 2

1 And it came to pass in those days, that there came a commandment from Augustus Caesar, that all the world should be taxed....

41 Now his parents went to Jerusalem every year, at the feast of the Passover.

42 And when he was twelve years old, and they were come up to Jerusalem, after the custom of the feast,

43 And had finished the days *thereof,* as they returned, the child Jesus remained in Jerusalem, and Joseph knew not, nor his mother,

44 But they supposing, that he had been in the company, went a day's journey, and sought him among *their* kinsfolk, and acquaintances.

45 And when they found him not, they turned back to Jerusalem, and sought him.

46 And it came to pass three days after, that they found him in the Temple, sitting in the midst of the doctors, both hearing them, and asking them questions.

47 And all that heard him, were astonished at his understanding and answers.

48 So when they saw him, they were amazed, and his mother said unto him, Son, why hast thou thus dealt with us? Behold, thy father and I have sought thee with very heavy hearts.

49 Then said he unto them, How is it that ye sought me? knew ye not that I must go about my Father's business?

50 But they understood not the word that he spoke to them.

## ACTS 6

7  And the word of God increased, & the number of the disciples was multiplied in Jerusalem greatly, and a great company of the Priests were obedient to the faith.

8  Now Steven full of faith and power, did great wonders and miracles among the people.

9  Then there arose certain of the Synagogue, which are called Libertines, and Cyrenians, and of Alexandria, and of them of Cilicia, and of Asia, and disputed with Stephen.

10  But they were not able to resist the wisdom, & the Spirit by the which he spoke.

11  Then they suborned men, which said, We have heard him speak blasphemous words against Moses, and God.

12  Thus they moved the people & the Elders, and the Scribes, and running upon him, caught him, and brought him to the Council,

13  And set forth false witnesses, which said, This man ceases not to speak blasphemous words against this holy place, and the Law.

14  For we have heard him say, that this Jesus of Nazareth shall destroy this place, and shall change the ordinances, which Moses gave us.

15  And as all that sat in the Council looked steadfastly on him, they saw his face as *it had been* the face of an Angel.

## ACTS 7

55  But he being full of the holy Ghost, looked steadfastly into heaven, and saw the glory of God, and Jesus standing at the right hand of God,

56  And said, Behold, I see the heavens open, and the Son of man standing at the right hand of God.

57  Then they gave a shout with a loud voice, and stopped their ears, and ran upon him all at once,

58  And cast him out of the city, and stoned him: and the witnesses laid down their clothes at a young man's feet, named Saul.

59  And they stoned Stephen, who called on *God*, & said, Lord Jesus, receive my spirit.

60  And he kneeled down, and cried with a loud voice, Lord, lay not this sin to their charge. And when he had thus spoken, he slept.

[From *The Geneva Bible: A Facsimile of the 1560 Edition.* Introduction by Lloyd E. Berry. Madison: U of Wisconsin P, 1969.]

# From AN ACT AGAINST FOND AND FANTASTICAL PROPHECIES (1563)

This statement was prompted by the great uneasiness that false prophecies caused in the political arena. Henry VIII, who reigned from 1509 to 1547, deemed it necessary to prohibit political prophecies in the light of the way they provided rhetorical weight to propaganda during the fifteenth and early sixteenth centuries. His son Edward VI continued the policy. Eventually Parliament addressed the issue and enacted a law whereby those involved with false prophecy would be convicted and imprisoned for one year and fined ten pounds.

The Fool in *King Lear* utters an apparently garbled prophecy (3.2. 80–96) that represents no political threat but does make an implicit comment on the absurdity of expending excessive faith on prophecy.

FORASMUCH as since the expiration and ending of the statute made in the time of King Edward the Sixth, entitled "An Act against fond and fantastic prophecies," diverse evil disposed persons, inclined to the stirring and moving of factions, seditions and rebellions within this realm, have been the more bold to attempt the like practice in feigning, imagining, inventing and publishing of such fond and fantastical prophecies, as well concerning the Queen's Majesty as diverse honorable personages, gentlemen and others of this realm, as was used and practised before the making of the said statute, to the great disquiet, trouble and peril of the Queen's Majesty, and of this her realm. For remedy whereof: Be it ordained and enacted by the authority of this present Parliament, That if any person or persons, after the first day of May next coming, do advisedly and directly advance, publish and set forth by writing, printing, singing or any other open speech or deed to any person or persons, any fond, fantastical or false prophecy, upon or by the occasion of any arms, fields, beasts, badges or such other like things accustomed in arms, cognizances or signets, or upon or by reason of any time, year or day, name, bloodshed or war to the intent thereby to make any rebellion, insurrection, dissension, loss of life or other disturbance within this realm or [of] other the Queen's dominions—that then every such person being thereof lawfully convicted according to the due course of the laws of this realm, for every such offense shall suffer imprisonment of his body by the space of one year, without bail or mainprise,[1] and shall forfeit for every such offense the sum of ten pounds. And if any such offender do after such conviction eftsoons[2] offend in any of the premises, and be thereof lawfully convicted, as is aforesaid, that then every such offender shall for his second offence and conviction as is aforesaid, suffer imprisonment of his body without bail or mainprise during his life, and shall forfeit all his goods and chattels, reals and personals.[3]

1. mainprise: suretyship; responsibility or obligation of one person undertaken on behalf of another.   2. eftsoons: again, soon after.   3. chattels . . . personals: property, real (i.e., land) and personal belongings

[From *At the Parliament holden at Westminster the xii of January, in the fifth year of the reign of our Sovereign Lady Elizabeth . . . were enacted as followeth. London,* 1563. Reprinted in *William Shakespeare, Macbeth: Texts and Contexts,* ed. William C. Carroll. Boston: Bedford / St. Martin's, 1999, pp. 335-36.]

From The Earl of Northampton's

# A DEFENSIVE STATEMENT AGAINST THE POISON OF COUNTERFEIT PROPHECIES (1563)

## EVANS EDITOR'S MODERNIZED VERSION

### HENRY HOWARD

Henry Howard, 1st Earl of Northampton (1540–1614), a prominent English aristocrat and courtier, was looked upon with suspicion throughout his life as a shadow Catholic. He was man of artistic / architectural tastes, overseeing the building of Northumberland House in London and had definite philanthropic interests, supporting, for example, the founding of several hospitals. His reputation as a man of learning is reflected in his *Defensive Statement against the Poison of Counterfeit Prophecies* (1563), which Shakespeare might have read before composing *King Lear*.

Northampton was also thought of as being a treacherous religious intriguer, a view based on strong opposition to his Roman Catholic tendencies. He was the second son of the poet Henry Howard, Earl of Surrey, and the younger brother of Thomas Howard, 4th Duke of Norfolk, who appears as a character in Shakespeare's *Henry 6-Part 3*. Northampton's mother was the former Lady Frances de Vere, daughter of the 15th Earl of Oxford—the grandfather of the 17th Earl of Oxford—the Shakespeare claimant thought by Oxfordians to be the author of the plays usually attributed to Shakespeare.

Northampton's statement about planetary predictions and prophecy in general should be seen in connection with Gloucester's and Edmund's contrasting views of astrology in *King Lear* (1.2.103–33) and with the Fool as prophet (3.2.80–96).

The complete digitized old-spelling Elizabethan English text of the Earl of Northampton's treatise (1563) is available on the digital database Early English Books Online. The Evans Editor's modern-spelling adaptation below is an excerpt from Image 41, columns 1 and 2. Howard, Henry, Earl of Northampton. *A Defensative against the Poyson of Supposed Prophecies* (1563). EEBO. Web. 5 July 2010.

.   .   .

R EASON HAS her limits, and prophecy is not attained by active endeavor but inspired by the receiving of free grace and
mercy. Farmers, ship-pilots, and physicians may not be called
prophets or reputed as such even though sometimes they light upon
truth. Common persons cannot discern truth because they proceed
no further than the most conveniently acceptable explanation. Nor
do they take it upon themselves to think any more than others might
think with similar regard and diligence. With these persons we may
compare and match the wise men of this world and military gener-
als in the field, who assume the title of *Prudentes a Providendo* ('those
who under the aegis of Providence are prudent or sagacious'). These
persons are capable of linking speculation to practice [i.e., thought to
action] and the precedents of the past to the overall ideas of the present. This is done with due regard for every circumstance that pertains
to the matter in hand at the present time and to the figuring out of
grave events to come. This procedure is carried out by way of sober
skill rather than by a leap of arrogant recklessness; by the navigator's
accurate compass rather than by the plodding wheel of a cart. Serious
scenarios do not only represent the onset of lamentable tragedies—as
when dumb shows or pantomimes anticipate tragedies that will in
time unfold—but also provide direction as to how those same scenarios may be prevented and thwarted by political means.

. . . Wise men do not predict the likelihood or unlikelihood of
war or peace by drawing up a figure-chart on a sheet of paper, but by
actively reasoning about the political conditions and human dispositions of surrounding neighbors; and not by observing the planets but
by the act of preparing. Again, after the war begins, we proceed to the
continuance thereof not by dreams but by rational judgment; not by
the good or bad aspect of Mars and Saturn, but by the good or bad
ideas of mighty princes that gather and band together. This is the ideal
purview of wisdom; other approaches are but shells of error without
any kernel of effectiveness or benefit.

Stories are filled with examples of these sensible and respectable
kinds of prophets, who only by the navigational compass of deep wisdom and a long period of experience have found such ready means
to prevent the mishaps that light divining [i.e., light-headed proph-
esying] fools were never able to think of or understand, much less to
foresee or prognosticate.

[Evans Editor's modern-spelling version of A *Defensative against the Poyson of
Supposed Prophesies* (1583) based on digitized old-spelling version / Early English
Books Online: Henry Howard, Earl of Northampton from A *Defensative against
the Poyson of Supposed Prophesies* (1583). John Charlewood, Printer.]

# From *The Discovery of Witchcraft*
## (1584)
### Reginald Scot

Reginald Scot was born about 1538 and died in 1599. His forebears were Scottish, but he became an Englishman. He, in fact, was a Member of the English Parliament. His *Discoverie of Witchcraft* (1584) was written against the belief in witches in order to show that witchcraft did not exist. He argued that both reason and religion reject belief in witchcraft and magic and that spiritual manifestations were either contrived impostures or illusory experiences brought on by mental unbalance. Actually, Scot was attempting to defend the innocent against persecution regarding accusations of witchcraft, but his book was misread so that it appeared as if he were advocating the practice of sorcery. King James I, who believed that witches did indeed exist and who fiercely opposed witchcraft, considered Scot as one who was trying to deny the existence of witches. Not only did James order the burning of all copies of Scot's book, he also wrote his own treatise, *Demonology* (Edinburgh, 1597), to denounce *The Discoverie* and to underscore the view that witches are slaves of the Devil.

### CHAPTER 3

*That certeine observations are indifferent, certeine ridiculous, and certeine impious, whence that cunning is derived of Apollo, and of Aruspices.*

The ridiculous art of nativitiecasting.

I KNOW NOT whether to disallow or discommend the curious observation used by our elders, who conjectured upon nativities: so as, *if Saturne* and *Mercurie* were opposite in anic brute signe, a man then borne should be dumbe or stammer much; whereas it is dailie scene, that children naturallie imitate their parents conditions in that behalfe. Also they have noted, that one borne in the spring of the moone, shalbe healthie; in that time of the wane, when the moone is utterlie decaied, the child then borne cannot live; and in the conjunction, it cannot long continue.

But I am sure the opinion of *Julius Maternus* is most impious, who writeth, that he which is borne when *Saturne* in *Leone*, shall live long, and after his death shall go to heaven presentlie. And so is this of *Albumazar*, who saith, that whosoever praieth to God, when the moone is in *Capita draconis*, shalbe heard, and obteine his praier. Furthermore, to plaie the cold prophet, as to recount it good or bad lucke, when salt or wine falleth on the table, or is shed, &c: or to prognosticate that ghests approch to your house, upon the chattering of pies or haggisters, wherof there can be yeelded no probable reason, is altogether vanitie and superstition: as hereafter shalbe more largelie shewed. But to make simple people beleeve, that a man or woman can foretell good or evill fortune, is *mere* witchcraft or cousenage. For God is the onlie searcher of the heart, and delivereth not his counsell to so lewd reprobates. I know diverse writers affirme, that witches foretell things, as prompted by a reall divell; and that he againe learneth it out of the prophesies written in the scriptures, and by other nimble sleights, wherein he passeth anie other creature earthlie; and that the same divell, or some of his fellowes runnes or flies as farre as *Rochester,* to mother *Bungie;* or to *Canturburie* to M. *T;* or to Delphos, to *Apollo;* or to *Aesculapius,* in *Pargamo*; or to some other idoll or witch, and mere by waie of oracle answers all questions, through, his understanding of the prophesies conteined in the old testament, especiallie in *Daniel* and *Esaie;* whereby the divell knew of the translation of the monarchic from *Babylon to Gracie, &* c. But either they have learned this of some oracle or witch; or else I know not where the divell they find it. Marrie certeine it is, that herein they shew themselves to be witches and fond divinors; for they find no such thing written in Gods word.

Of the idoll called *Apollo,* I have somewhat already spoken in the former title of *Ob* or *Pytho;* and some occasion I shall have to speake thereof hereafter; and therfore at this time it shall suffice to tell you, that the credit gained thereunto, was by the craft and cunning of the priests, which tended thereupon; who with their counterfeit miracles so bewitched the people, as they thought such vertue to have beene conteined in the bodies of those idols, as God hath not promised to anie of his angels, or elect people. For it is said, that if *Apollo* were in a chafe [i.e., chase, hunt], he would sweat: if he had remorse to the afflicted, and could not help them, he would shed teares, which I beleeve might have beene wiped awaie with that handkerchiefe, that wiped and dried the Rood of graces face, being in like perplexities. Even as another sort of

*Apollos passions.*

witching priests called *Aruspices*, prophesied victorie to *Alexander*, bicause an eagle lighted on his head: which eagle might (I beleeve) be cooped or caged with *Mahomets* dove, that picked peason [peas, grain] out of his ear.

## CHAPTER 4

*The predictions of sootksaiers and lewd priests, the prognostications of astronomers and physicians allowable, divine prophesies holie and good.*

The cousening tricks of oracling priests and monkes, are and have beene speciallie most abhominable. The superstitious observations of sensles augurors and soothsaiers (contrarie to philosophie, and without authoritie of scripture) are very ungodlie and ridiculous. Howbeit, I reject not the prognostications of astronomers, nor the conjectures or forewarnings of physicians, nor yet the interpretations of philosophers; although in respect of the divine prophesies conteined in holie scriptures, they are not to be weighed or regarded. For the end of these and the other is not onlie farre differing; but whereas these conteine onlie the word and will of God, with the other are mingled most horrible lies and cousenages. For though there may be many of them learned and godlie, yet lurke there in corners of the same profession, a great number of counterfets and couseners. *J. Bodin*[1] putteth this difference betweene divine prophets and inchantors; to wit, the one saith alwaies true, the others words (proceeding from the divell) are alwaies false; or for one truth they tell a hundred lies. And then why maie not everie witch be thought as cunning as *Apollo?* And why not everie counterfeit cousener as good a witch as mother *Bungie?* For it is ods, but they will hit the truth once in a hundred divinations as well as the best.

*What prophesies allowable.*

[1. Scot refers to the learned French Renaissance political philosopher, natural philosopher, humanist, historian, lawyer, and economist Jean Bodin (c.1529–1596), who was concerned about the contagious rise of sorcery—the topic of his treatise, *De la démonomanie des sorciers* (1581). ~ *Evans Editor*]

[From *The Discoverie of Witchcraft* by *Reginald Scot* (1584). Introduction by Montague Summers. 1930. Rpt. New York: Dover, 1972.]

# From 'AN HOMILIE AGAINST DISOBEDIENCE AND WILFULL REBELLION'

## PART I, IN CERTAINE SERMONS OR HOMILIES APPOINTED TO BE READ IN CHURCHES

### (1623)

### John Jewel

John Jewel (1522–1571) was Bishop of Salisbury from 1559 to 1571. He is the primary author of "An Homily against disobedience and wilful rebellion" (1571). In Shakespeare's day, parsons, vicars and curates were not fully informed about the Reform movement, nor were they sufficiently educated to compose sermons. Bishops were qualified in these areas and hence wrote the sermons or homilies that were to be read on Sundays and holy days. Even today, under Article 35 of the Thirty-Nine Articles of the Anglican Church, the reading of homilies is still called for. "An Homily against disobedience and wilful rebellion" is particularly well known for its stylistic lucidity and for its important Elizabethan-Jacobean theme of the need for social and political order to be maintained lest chaos come again.

A s GOD the Creator and Lord of all things appointed his angels and heavenly creatures in all obedience to serve and to honour his majesty, so was it his will that man, his chief creature upon the earth, should live under the obedience of his Creator and Lord; and for that cause, GOD, as soon as He had          5
created man, gave unto him a certain precept and law, which he (being yet in the state of innocency, and remaining in Paradise) should observe as a pledge and token of his due and bounden obedience, with denunciation of death if he did transgress and break the said law and commandment. And as GOD would have man to be his obedient subject, so did He make all earthly creatures sub-          10
ject unto man, who kept their due obedience unto man so long as man remained in his obedience unto GOD; in the which obedience if man had continued still, there had been no poverty, no diseases, no sickness, no death, nor other miseries wherewith mankind is now infinitely and most miserably afflicted and oppressed . . . . For          15

as long as in this first kingdom the subjects continued in due obedience to GOD their king, so long did GOD embrace all his subjects with his love, favour, and grace, which to enjoy is perfect felicity, whereby it is evident that obedience is the principal virtue of all virtues, and indeed the very root of all virtues and the cause    20
of all felicity. But as all felicity and blessedness should have continued with the continuance of obedience, so with the breach of obedience, and breaking in of rebellion, all vices and miseries did withal break in and overwhelm the world. The first author of which rebellion, the root of all vices and mother of all mis-    25
chiefs, was Lucifer, first GOD's most excellent creature and most bounden subject, who, by rebelling against the majesty of GOD, of the brightest and most glorious angel, is become the blackest and most foulest fiend and devil; and from the height of Heaven is fallen into the pit and bottom of Hell.    30

Here you may see the first author and founder of rebellion and the reward thereof; here you may see the grand captain and father of rebels; who, persuading the following of his rebellion against GOD their Creator and Lord unto our first parents Adam and Eve, brought them in high displeasure with GOD, wrought    35
their exile and banishment out of Paradise, a place of all pleasure and goodness, into this wretched earth and vale of misery. . . .

Thus do you see that neither Heaven nor Paradise could suffer any rebellion in them, neither be places for any rebels to remain in. Thus became rebellion, as you see, both the first and the    40
greatest and the very foot of all other sins, and the first and principal cause both of all worldly and bodily miseries, sorrows, diseases, sicknesses, and deaths, and, which is infinitely worse than all these, . . . . the very cause of death and damnation eternal also. After this breach of obedience to GOD, . . . . GOD forthwith,    45
by laws given unto mankind, repaired again the rule and order of obedience thus by rebellion overthrown, and besides the obedience due unto his majesty, He not only ordained that, in families and households, the wife should be obedient unto her husband, the children unto their parents, the servants unto their masters, but    50
also, when mankind increased and spread itself more largely over the world, He by his holy word did constitute and ordain in cities and countries several and special governors and rulers, unto whom the residue of his people should be obedient. . . .

By these two places of the Holy Scriptures [Romans 13:1–7;    55
I Peter 2:13–18], it is most evident that kings, queens, and other princes (for he speaketh of authority and power be it in men or women) are ordained of GOD, are to be obeyed and honoured of

their subjects; that such subjects, as are disobedient or rebellious against their princes, disobey GOD and procure their own 60 damnation; that the government of princes is a great blessing of GOD, given for the commonwealth, specially of the good and godly; for the comfort and cherishing of whom GOD giveth and setteth up princes, and, on the contrary part, to the fear and for the punishment of the evil and wicked. Finally, that if servants 65 ought to obey their masters, not only being gentle, but such as be froward, as well and much more ought subjects to be obedient, not only to their good and courteous but also to their sharp and rigorous princes. It cometh therefore neither of chance and fortune (as they term it), nor of the ambition of mortal men and 70 women climbing up of their own accord to dominion, that there be kings, queens, princes, and other governors over men being their subjects, but all kings, queens, and other governors are specially appointed by the ordinance of GOD.... Unto the which similitude of heavenly government, the nearer and nearer that 75 an earthly prince doth come in his regiment the greater blessing of GOD's mercy is he unto that country and people over whom he reigneth, and the further and further that an earthly prince doth swerve from the example of the heavenly government the greater plague is he of GOD's wrath, and punishment by GOD's 80 justice, unto that country and people over whom GOD for their sins hath placed such a prince and governor....

What shall subjects do then? Shall they obey valiant, stout, wise, and good princes and contemn, disobey, and rebel against children being their princes, or against undiscreet and evil 85 governors? God forbid: for first, what a perilous thing were it to commit unto the subjects the judgment which prince is wise and godly and his government good, and which is otherwise, as though the foot must judge of the head: an enterprise very heinous, and must needs breed rebellion.... And who are most 90 ready to the greatest mischiefs but the worst men? ... What an unworthy matter were it then to make the naughtiest subjects, and most inclined to rebellion and all evil, judges over their princes, over their government, and over their councillors to determine which of them be good or tolerable and which be 95 evil and so intolerable....

Here you can see that GOD placeth as well evil princes as good, and for what cause he doth both.... If we will have an evil prince (when GOD shall send such a one) taken away and a good in 100 his place, let us take away our wickedness which provoketh GOD to place such a one over us, and GOD will either displace him, or of an

evil prince make him a good prince, so that we first will change
our evil into good. . . .                                                           105
   What shall we say of those subjects? May we call them by the
name of subjects, who neither be thankful nor make any prayer to
GOD for so gracious a sovereign, but also themselves take armour
wickedly, assemble companies and bands of rebels, to break the
public peace so long continued and to make, not war, but rebellion    110
to endanger the person of such a gracious sovereign, to hazard
the estate of their country (for whose defence they should be
ready to spend their lives), and, being Englishmen, to rob, spoil,
destroy, and burn in England Englishmen, to kill and murder
their own neighbours and kinsfolk, their own countrymen, to          115
do all evil and mischief, yea, and more too than foreign enemies
would or could do?. . .


## NOTES

   6. *precept and law* Genesis 2:17.
  17. *first kingdom* i.e. God's rule over the angels and man and man's rule
      over the 'creatures' in the Garden of Eden.
  20. *obedience . . . virtue* Note the continual stress laid on obedience as the
      cardinal virtue. In the third part of this homily, its opposite, disobe-
      dience or rebellion, is described as the source of the Seven Deadly
      Sins: pride, envy, wrath, covetousness, sloth, gluttony, and lechery.
  26. *mother* i.e. rebellion.
  27. *Lucifer* The name means 'light bearer' '(Latin), another name for
      Satan.
  30. *most foulest* The double superlative was not uncommon in
      Elizabethan usage.
  38. *vale* valley.
  42. *foot* basis.
  56–62. *By these . . . damnation* The real point to which the whole hom-
      ily has been leading: the sanctity and divinely appointed status of the
      sovereign . . . against whom rebellion must be considered as a crime
      against God.
  58. *women* inserted with special reference to Queen Elizabeth.
  63. *commonwealth* public welfare.
  68. *froward* evilly disposed.
  68–70. *ought subjects . . . princes* an important part of Tudor doctrine: no
      rebellion against a bad sovereign . . . A bad sovereign was sent as a
      punishment by God to a wicked people and would be removed by
      God in His own good time.

76. *similitude . . . government* i.e. kings are sometimes referred to as 'gods' in the Bible.

77. *regiment* rule.

85. *contemn* despise.

85–6. *rebel . . . children* Child monarchs were thought of as dangerous to a kingdom because of the power struggles that tended to prevail among different factions during their minority. Shakespeare illustrates the danger in *I Henry VI,* and compare *Richard III,* 2.3.2: 'Woe to that land that's govern'd by a child!' (proverbial, Tilley W600).

90. *foot . . . head* i.e. the lowest judge of the highest (proverbial, Tilley F562).

93. *naughtiest* most wicked.

105. *those subjects* reference to the unsuccessful rebellion of the Duke of Norfolk and the Northern Earls in favour of Mary Queen of Scots in 1569, an event that led to the publication of this homily in 1571.

107. *take armour* i.e. arm themselves.

112–16. *being Englishmen . . . do* Sounds the dreaded theme of civil war, further developed in the third part of this homily, where war is described as 'the greatest of these worldly mischiefs; but of all wars, civil war is the worst.' [*King Lear* is an excellent illustration of the massive political and social disruption that can come from disobedience and willful rebellion. ~ *Evans Editor*]

[From *Elizabethan-Jacobean Drama: A New Mermaid Background Book,* ed. G. Blakemore Evans, London: A & C Black, 1987.]

# From *Christ's Tears over Jerusalem*
## (1593)
### Thomas Nashe

Pamphleteer and dramatist Thomas Nashe (1567-1601), was educated at St, John's Cambridge, in the 1580s. He became one of the University Wits (representing both Cambridge and Oxford) along with Robert Greene, Christopher Marlowe, Thomas Lodge, Thomas Kyd, and George Peele. Critical targets of the Wits included non-university playwrights like Shakespeare.

*Christ's Tears Over Jerusalem* suggests a devotional work, but Nashe, ever a University Wit, could not completely restrain his satirical bent. When material in *Christ's Tears* offended the London civic authorities, Nashe was briefly imprisoned in Newgate, but later released, thanks to the intervention of supporters among the nobility. Shakespeare must have been intrigued by the angular features of Nashe's literary style and his unconventional social conduct, for both the style and the conduct at times correspond to the tone and unsettling quality of *King Lear*.

SINCE THESE be the dayes of dolor and heauinesse, wherein (as holy *David* saith) *The Lord is knowne by executing judgment*, and the axe of his anger is put to the roote of the Tree, and his Fan is in his hande to purge his Floore; I suppose it shal not be amisse to write something of mourning, for *London* to harken counsaile of her great Grand-mother, *Jerusalem*.

Omnipotent Sauiour, it is thy Teares I intende to write of, those affectionate Teares, which in the 23. and 24. of *Mathew* thou wepst ouer *Jerusalem* and her Temple; Be present with me (I beseech thee) personating the passion of thy loue. O dew thy Spyrit plentifully into my incke, and let some part of thy divine dreariment liue againe in myne eyes. Teach mee how to weepe as thou wepst, & rent my hart in twaine with the extremity of ruth. I hate in thy name to speake coldly to a quick-witted generation. Rather let my braines melt all to incke, and the floods of affliction driue out mine eyes before them, then I should be dull and leaden in describing the dollour of thy loue. Farre be from me any ambitious hope of the vaine merite of Arte; may that liuing vehemence I vse in lament onely proceed from a heauen-bred hatred of vncleannesse and corruption. Mine owne wit I cleane disinherite: thy fiery Clouen-tongued inspiration be my Muse. Lende my wordes the forcible wings of the Lightnings, that they may peirce vnawares into the marrow and reynes of my Readers.

Could the least and sencelessest of our sences into the quietest corner of hel be transported in a vision but three minutes, it woulde breede in vs such an agasting terror, and shyuering mislike of it, that to make vs more wary of sinne-meriting it, we would have it painted in our Gardens, our banquetting-houses, on our gates, in our Gallaries, our Closets, our bed-chambers.

Againe, were there no hell but the accusing of a mans owne conscience, it were hell and the profundity of hel to any sharpe transpercing soule that had never so lyttle inckling of the joys of heaven, to be seperate from them to heare and see tryumphing and melody, and, *Tantalus* like, not bee suffered to come neere them or partake them; to thinke when all els were entred, hee should be excluded. Our best methode to preuent this excluding, or seperating from Gods presence, is heere on earth (what soeuer we goe about) to thinke we see him present. Let vs fancy the firmament as his face, the all-seeing Sun to be his right eye, and the Moone hys left, (although hys eyes are farre more fiery pointed and subtile,) that the Starres are but the congemmed twincklings of those his cleare eyes, that the winds are the breath of his nostrils, and the lightning & tempests the troubled action of hys ire: that his frownes bring forth  frost & snowe, and hys smiles faire weather, that the Winter is the image of the first world, wherein *Adam* was unparadized, & the fruit-fostering Summer the representation of the seede of womans satisfying, for the unfortunate fruite of lyfe which he pluckt. Who is there entertayning these diuise allusiue cogitations, that hath not God vnremoueable in his memory? Hee that hath God in his memorie, and aduaunceth him before his eyes ever-more, will be bridled and pluckt backe from much abusion and bestialnesse. Many sinnes be there, which if none but man should over-eye vs offending in, wee woulde never exceede or offend in. In the presence of his Prince, the dissolutest misliuer that lyues wil not offend or misgouerne himselfe: how much more ought we (abyding alwaies in Gods presence) precisely to straighten our pathes? Harde is it when we shall have our Iudge an eye-witnes against vs. There is no demurring or exceptioning against his testimony.

Purblind *London*, neyther canst thou see that GOD sees thee, nor see into thy selfe. Howe long wilt thou clowde his earthly prospect with the misty night of thy mounting iniquities? Therefore hath hee smytten thee and strooke thee, because thou wouldest not believe he was present with thee. He thought, if nothing els might move thee to looke backe, at least thou wouldest looke back to thy striker. Had it not beene so to cause thee to looke back & repent, with no crosse or plague would he haue visited, or sought to call thee. He could have beene reuenged on thee superaboüdantly at the day of thy dissolution & soules general Law-day, though none of thy chyldren or allies by his hand had been sepulchred. Hys hande I may well terme it, for on many that are arrested with the Plague is the print of a hand seene, and in the very moment it first takes the, they feele a sencible blow gyuen them, as it were with the hande of some stander by. As Gods hand wee will not take it, but the hande of fortune, the hande of hote weather, the hande of close smouldry ayre. The Astronomers, they assigne it to the regiment and operation of Planets. They say, *Venus, Mars,* or *Saturne,* are motiues therof, and never mention our sinnes, which are his chiefe procreatours. The vulgar menialty conclude, therefore it is like to encrease, because a Hearneshaw [heronshaw / heron; cf. "hand-saw" in *Hamlet,* 2.2.379. ~ *Evans Editor*] (a whole afternoone together) sate on the top of S. *Peters* Church in Cornehill. They talke of an Oxe that tolde the bell at *Wolwitch,* & howe from an Oxe hee trans-formed himselfe to an olde man, and from an old man to an infant, & from an infant to a young man. Strange propheticall reports (as touching the sicknes) the mutter he gaue out, when in trueth they are nought els but cleanly coyned lyes, which some pleasant sportiue wittes have deuised, to gull them most groselie. Vnder Maister *Dees* name, the lyke fabulous diuinations have they bruted, [i.e., "bruited" / 'announced abroad' ~ *Evans Editor*] when (good reuerend old man) hee is as farre from any such arrogant prescience, as the superstitious spreaders of it are from peace of conscience.

If we would hunt after signes and tokens, we should ominate [i.e., 'utter omens' ~ *Evans Editor*] from our hardnes of hart and want of charitie amongst bretheren, that Gods iustice is harde entring. No certainer conjecture is there of the ruine of any kingdom then theyr reuolting from God. Certaine conjectures have we had that we are reuolted from God and that our ruine is not far of. In diuers places of our Land it hath raigned blood, the ground hath been removed, and horrible, deformed byrthes conceiued. Did the Romans take it for an ill signe, when their Capitol was strooken with lightning, how much more ought *London* to take it for an ill signe, when her chiefe steeple is strooken with lightning? They with thunder from any enterprise were disanimated, we nothing are amated [i.e., 'dismayed' ~ *Evans Editor*]. The blazing starre, the Earthquake, the dearth and famine some fewe yeeres since, may nothing afright vs. Let vs looke for the sworde next to remembrance and warne vs. As there is a tyme of peace, so is there

a time of warre. No prosperity lasteth alwaies. The Lord by a      5
solemne oath bound himselfe to the Iewes; yet when they were
obliuious of him, he was obliuious of the couenant he made
with their forefathers, and left theyr Citty desolate unto them.
Shall he not then (we starting from him, to whom by no bonde      10
he is tyde) leaue our house desolate unto vs? Shall we receiue
of God (a long time) al good, and shall we not looke in the end
to receiue of hym some ill? O ye disobedient chyldren, returne,
and the Lorde shall heale your infirmities. Lye downe in your
confusion, & cover your faces with shame. From my youth to      15
thys day, haue you sinned, and not obeyed the voyce of the Lord
your God. Now, in the age of your obstinacie and vngrateful
abandonments, repent and be conuerted. With one united inter-
cessionment, thus reconcile your selues unto hym.

O Lord, our refuge from one generation to another, whether      20
from thy sight shall we goe, or whether, but to thee, shall we flye
from thee? Iust [i.e., Just] is thy wrath; it sendeth no man to hell
vniustly. Rebuke vs not in thine anger, neyther chastise vs in thy
displeasure. We have sinned, we confesse, & for our sinnes thou
hast plagued vs, with the sorrowes of death thou hast compast      25
vs, & thy snares haue over-tooke vs: out of Natures hande hast
thou wrested the sword of Fate, and now slayest euery one in
thy way. Ah, thou presenter of men, why hast thou sette vs vp
as a marke against thee? Why wilt thou breake a leafe driuen to      30
and fro with the wind, & pursue the dry stubble? Returne &
shew thy selfe meruailous vpon vs. None haue we like *Moyses*,
to stand betwixt life & death for vs. None to offer himselfe to
die for the people, that the Plague may cease. O deere Lord, for
*Jerusalem* didst thou die, yet could'st not drive backe the plagues
destinate to *Jerusalem*. No image or likenes of thy *Jerusalem on
earth* is there left, but *London*. Spare *London*, for *London* is like
the Citty that thou louedst. Rage not so farre against *Jerusalem*,
as not onely to desolate her, but to wreake thy selfe on her      5
likenes also. All the honor, of thy miracles thou loosest, which
thou hast shewed so many and sundry, times, in rescuing vs with
a strong hand from our enemies, if now thou becommest our
enemie. Let not worldlings iudge thee inconstant, or vndeliber-      10
ate in thy choyse, in so soone reiecting the Nation thou hast
chosen. In thee we hope beyond hope. Wee have no reason to
pray to thee to spare vs, and yet have wee no reason to spare
from prayer, since thou hast [willed] vs. Thy will be done, which
willeth not the death of any sinner. Death let it kill sinne in vs,      15
and reserue vs to prayse thee. Though thou kilst vs, wee will

prayse thee: but more prayse shalt thou reape by preseruing then killing, since it is the onely prayse to preserue where thou maist kill. With the Leaper [i.e., Leper] we cry out, *O Lorde, if thou wilt, thou canst make vs cleane.* We clayme thy promise, *That those which*     20 *mourne shall be comforted.*

Comfort vs, Lord; we mourne, our bread is mingled with ashes, and our drinke with teares. With so manie Funerals are wee oppressed, that wee have no leysure to weepe for our sinnes for howling     25 for our Sonnes and Daughters. O heare the voyce of our howling, withdraw thy hand from vs, & we will draw neere vnto thee.

[From *The Works of Thomas Nashe*, ed. Ronald B. McKerrow. 1958. Rpt. New York: Barnes & Noble, 1966.]

# From *BASILICON DORON*

## (EDINBURGH 1598; LONDON 1603)

### King James I

Born two years after Shakespeare, King James VI of Scotland became King James I of England in 1603. He died in 1625 and was succeeded by his son Charles I. James was the first monarch of the House of Stuart (or Stewart) and succeeded Queen Elizabeth I, the last monarch of the House of Tudor. He was the staunchly Protestant son of Roman Catholic Mary, Queen of Scots. His father was Henry Stewart, Duke of Albany (known as Lord Darnley). James became the king of Scotland at age one (1567) when his mother was forced to abdicate the throne, and later upon the death of Elizabeth I, he became King James I of England. His *Basilicon Doron* (also known as *Basilikon Doron*—Greek for 'The King's Gift') was addressed to his eldest son, Henry, Duke of Rothesay, who was born 1594 and died in 1612. Thereupon James gave the work to his second son, the future King Charles I.

In the manner of Renaissance political manuals such as Machiavelli's *The Prince* (c. 1513), Erasmus's *Education of a Christian Prince* (1516), and Thomas More's *Utopia* (1516) or courtesy books like Castiglione's *The Courtier* (1528), James provides guidelines for an exemplary monarch and does so in terms of Christian duty to God, the responsibilities of the regal office, and the need for proper personal behavior. James emphasizes the dangers of division in the kingdom—the implicit idea at the heart of *King Lear*.

BUT TO returne to the purpose of garments, they ought to be used according to their first institution by God, which was for three causes: first to hide our nakednesse and shame; next and consequently, to make vs more comely; and thirdly, to preserve vs from the injuries of heate and colde. If to hide our nakednesse and shamefull parts, then these naturall parts ordained to be hid, should not be represented by any vndecent formes in the cloathes: and if they should helpe our comelinesse, they should not then by their painted preened fashion, serue for baites to filthie lecherie, as false haire and fairding ['face-coloring cosmetics' ~ *Evans Editor*] does amongst vnchast women: and if they should preserue vs from the iniuries of heat and colde, men should not, like senselesse stones, contemne God, in lightlying ['making light of' ~ *Evans Editor*] the seasons, glorying to conquere honour on heate and colde. And although it be praiseworthy and necessarie in a Prince, to be *pattens algoris & æstus*,[393] when he shall have adoe with warres upon the fields; yet I thinke it meeter that ye goe both cloathed and armed, then naked to the battell, except you would make you light for away-running: and yet for cowards, *metus addit alas*.[394] And shortly, in your cloathes keepe a proportion, aswell with the seasons of the yeere, as of your aage: in the fashions of them being carelesse, vsing them according to the common forme of the time, some-times richlier, some-times meanlier cloathed, as occasion serueth, without keeping any precise rule therein: For if your mind be found occupied vpon them, it wil be thought idle otherwaies, and ye shall bee accounted in the number of one of these *compti iuuenes;*[397] which wil make your spirit and iudgment to be lesse thought of. But specially eschew to be effeminate in your cloathes, in perfuming, preening, or such like: and faile never in time of warres to bee galliardest ['spruced-up' ~ *Evans Editor*] and brauest, both in cloathes and countenance. And make not a foole of yourselfe in disguising or wearing long haire or nailes, which are but excrements ['dregs' ~ *Evans Editor*] of nature, and bewray such misusers of them, to bee either of a vindictiue, or a vaine light naturall. Especially, make no vowes in such vaine and outward things, as concerne either meate or cloathes.

Let your selfe and all your Court weare no ordinarie armour with your cloathes, but such as is knightly and honourable; I meane rapier-swordes, and daggers: For tuilyesome ['burdensome' ~ *Evans Editor*] weapons in the Court, betokens confusion in the countrey. And therefore banish not onely from your Court, all traiterous offensiue weapons, forbidden by the Lawes, as guns and such like (whereof I spake alreadie) but also all traiterous defensiue armes, as secrets, plate-sleeves ['concealed weapons, armorial sleeves' ~ *Evans Editor*], and such like vnseene armour: For, besides mat the wearers thereof, may be presupposed to have a secret euill intention, they want both the vses that defensiue armour is ordained for; which is, to be able to holde out violence, and by their outward glancing in their enemies eyes, to strike a terrour in their hearts: Where by the contrary, they can serve for neither, being not onely vnable to resist, but dangerous for shots, and giving no outward showe against the enemie; beeing onely ordained, for betraying vnder trust, whereof honest men should be ashamed to beare the outward badge, not resembling the thing they are not. And for answere against these arguments, I know none but the olde Scots fashion; which if it be wrong, is no more to be allowed for ancient-nesse, then the olde Masse is, which also our forefathers used.

The next thing that yee haue to take heed to, is your speaking and language; whereunto I ioyne your gesture, since action is one of the chiefest qualities, that is required in an oratour: for as the tongue speaketh to the eares, so doeth the gesture speake to the eyes of the auditour. In both your speaking and your gesture, use a naturall and plaine forme, not fairded ['highly decorated' ~ Evans Editor] with artifice: for (as the French-men say) *Rien contre-faict fin*:[403] but eschew all affectate formes in both.

In your language be plaine, honest, naturall, comely, cleane, short, and sententious, eschewing both the extremities, aswell in not using any rusticall corrupt leide, ['base lead in writing implements' ~ *Evans Editor*] as booke-language, and pen and inke-horne termes: and least of all mignard and effoeminate tearmes. But let the greatest part of your eloquence consist in a naturall, cleare, and sensible forme of the deliuerie of your minde, builded euer vpon certaine and good grounds; tempering it with grauitie, quickenesse, or merinesse, according to the subject, and occasion of the time; not taunting in Theologie, nor alleadging and prophaning the Scripture in drinking purposes, as over many doe.

Vse also the like forme in your gesture; neither looking sillily, like a stupide pedant; nor vnsetledly, with an vncouth morgue, like a new-come-ouer Cavalier: but let your behauiour be naturall, graue, and according to the fashion of the countrey. Be not ouersparing in your courtesies, for that will be imputed to inciuilitie and arrogancie: nor yet ouer prodigall in iowking or nodding at every step: for that forme of being popular, becommeth better aspiring *Absalom* ['son of David; see 2 Samuel' ~ *Evans Editor*], then lawfull Kings: framing ever your gesture according to your present actions: looking grauely and with a maiestie when yee sit in iudgement, or giue audience to Embassadours, homely, when ye are in private with your owne seruants: merily, when ye are at any pastime or merrie discourse; and let your countenance smell of courage and magnanimitie when ye are at the warres. And remember (I say ouer againe) to be plaine and sensible in your language: for besides that it is the tongues office, to be the messenger of the mind, it may be thought a point of imbecillitie of spirit in a King, to speake obscurely, much more vntrewly; as if he stood in awe of any in vttering his thoughts.

Remember also, to put a difference betwixt your forme of language in reasoning, and your pronouncing of sentences, or declaratour of your wil in iudgement, or any other waies in the points of your office: For in the former case, yee must reason pleasantly and patiently, not like a king, but like a priuate man and a scholer; otherwaies, your impatience of contradiction will be interpreted to be for lacke of reason on your part. Where in the points of your office, ye should ripely aduise indeede, before yee giue foorth your sentence: but fra it be giuen foorth, the suffering of any contradiction diminisheth the maiestie of your authoritie, and maketh the processes endlesse. The like forme would also bee obserued by all your inferiour Iudges and Magistrates. Now as to your writing, which is nothing else, but a forme of enregistrate speech;[416] vse a plaine, short, but stately stile, both in your Proclamations and missiues, especially to forraine Princes. And if your engine spur you to write any workes, either in verse or in prose, I cannot but allow you to practise it: but take no longsome workes in hand, for distracting you from your calling.

## NOTES

393. able to bear cold and heat
394. fear supplies wings
397. adorned youths
403. Nothing counterfeit is estimable
[416. 'enregistrate' is a nonce-word, an invented word for the occasion, here pertaining to writing and style worthy of a Prince. ~ Evans Editor]

[See James I's treatise on *Demonology* in the introductory remarks to Reginald Scot's *The Discovery of Witchcraft*. ~ Evans Editor]

[From *King James VI and I: Political Writings*, ed. Johann P. Sommerville. Cambridge, U.K.: Cambridge UP, 1994.]

# From *A Brief Discourse of a Disease Called the Suffocation of the Mother* (1603)

Edward Jorden

Jorden (1569–1633) was an English physician and chemist. His gynecological treatise, *A Disease Called the Suffocation of the Mother*, appeared in London, 1603. Very importantly, his thesis centers on female hysteria not as a sign of demonic possession but as a medically treatable physiological condition. Jorden traveled extensively in Italy, where he received his medical education; attended classes at the universities of Bologna, Ferrara, and Venice; and in 1591 earned the equivalent of an MD from the university in Padua, one year before Galileo joined the university as a mathematics professor.

Shakespeare found in Harsnett's *Declaration of Egregioius Popish Impostures* (1603) and in Jorden's treatise, two terms (the "mother" and "[Hysterica passio]") denoting the hysteria related to a disorder of the womb, to which King Lear refers in 2.4.56–57. When Jorden speaks of "corruption," he does not refer to moral corruption but to natural processes such as menstruation or pregnancy that find a woman's body producing an excess of fluids, blood included—normal physiological realities that become associated with illnesses of various kinds.

T HAT THIS *disease doth oftentimes give occasion unto simple and unlearned people, to suspect possession, withcraft, or some such like supernatural cause.*
The passive condition of womankind is subject unto more diseases and of other sorts and natures than men are, and especially in regard of that part from whence this disease which we speak of doth arise. For as it hath more variety of offices belonging unto it than other parts of the body have, and accordingly is supplied from other parts with whatsoever it hath need of for those uses: so it must needs thereby be subject unto more infirmities than other parts are, both by reason of such as are bred in the part itself, and also by reason of such as are communicated unto it from other parts, with which it hath correspondence. And as those offices in their proper kinds are more excellent than other; so the diseases whereby they are hurt or

depraved, are more grievous. But amongst all the diseases whereunto that sex is obnoxious,[1] there is none comparable unto this which is called *The Suffocation of the Mother,* either for variety, or for strangeness of accidents.[2] For whatsoever strange accident may appear in any of the principal functions of man's body, either animal, vital, or natural, the same is to be seen in this disease, by reason of the community and consent which this part hath with the brain, heart, and liver, the principal seats of these three functions; and the easy passage which it hath unto them by the veins, arteries, and nerves. And whatsoever humor in other parts may cause extraordinary effects, by reason of the abundance or corruption of it, this part will afford the like in as plentiful a manner, and in as high a degree of corruption: and with this advantage, that whereas in the other, some one or two of the faculties only one are hurt (as in apoplexies, epilepsies, syncopies,[3] subversions of the stomach, etc.) and not all (unless as in syncopies by consent, where the vital function ceasing, all the rest must needs cease), in this case all the faculties of the body do suffer; not as one may do from another, but all directly from this one fountain, in such sort as you shall oftentimes perceive in one and the same person diverse accidents of contrary natures to concur at once.

And hereupon the symptoms of this disease are said to be monstrous and terrible to behold, and of such a variety as they can hardly be comprehended within any method or bounds. Insomuch as they which are ignorant of the strange affects which natural causes may produce, and of the manifold examples which our profession of physic doth minister in this kind, have sought above the moon for supernatural causes: ascribing these accidents either to diabolical possession, to witchcraft, or to the immediate finger of the Almighty.

*What this disease is, and by what means it*
*causeth such variety of symptoms*

This disease is called by diverse names amongst our authors. *Passio Hysterica, Suffocatio, Praefocatio,* and *Strangulatus uteri, Caducus matricis, etc.* In English "the Mother," or "the Suffocation of the Mother," because most commonly it takes them with choking in the throat: and it is an effect of the Mother or womb wherein the principal parts of the body by consent do suffer diversely according to the diversity of the causes and diseases wherewith the matrix[4] is offended.

---

1. **sex . . . obnoxious:** i.e., which are harmful to the female sex.   2. **accidents:** i.e., the symptoms.   3. **syncopies:** failures of the heart's action, resulting in unconsciousness.   4. **matrix:** uterus.

## Of the causes of this disease

And as the want and scarcity of blood may procure this grief, so the abundance and excess thereof doth more commonly cause it, where the patients do want those monthly evacuations which should discharge their bodies of this superfluity: as we see in strong and lusty maidens, who having ease and good fare enough, have their veins filled with plenty of blood, which wanting⁵ sufficient vent distendeth them in bulk and thickness, and so contracteth them in their length, whereby the matrix is drawn upwards or sidewards, according as the repletion is, whereupon followeth a compression of the neighbor parts, as of the midriff which causeth shortness of breath, by straightening the instruments of respiration of their due scope.

But if this blood wanting his proper use do degenerate into the nature of an excrement [i.e., 'something excreted' ~ Evans Editor], then it offendeth in quality as well as in excess, and being detained in the body, causeth diverse kinds of symptoms, according to the quality and degree of the distemperature thereof. . . .

Lastly, the perturbations of the mind are oftentimes to blame both for this and many other diseases. For seeing we are not masters of our own affections, we are like battered cities without walls, or ships tossed in the sea, exposed to all manner of assaults and dangers, even to the overthrow of our own bodies.

5. **wanting:** lacking.

[From *A Disease Called the Suffocation of the Mother* (London 1603). Rpt. New York: Da Capo Press, 1971.]

# From *The Bel-Man of London* (1608)

*A Discoverie of all the idle Vagabonds in England*

Thomas Dekker

Born in London, perhaps of Dutch ancestry, Thomas Dekker (*c.* 1570–1632) was a highly prolific playwright. He was involved in the War of the Theaters to which Rosencrantz, Hamlet, and Guildenstern allude (2.2.341–59). In his *Bel-Man of London* (1608), Dekker offers a verbal sketch of the world of rogues and notorious villainies. What Shakespeare found of interest in Dekker for *King Lear* was the language of an underworld of vagabonds, beggars, cheats, and hoodwinkers—the ingredients for the speeches as well as the antics of the Fool and of Edgar as Poor Tom.

## THE BEL-MAN OF LONDON

Discovering the most notable villanies now in *the Kingdoms*.

ENTRING INTO a contemplation of the *Changes of Time*; how all things that are under the Moone are as variable as her lookes are: how *Goodness* grows crooked, and hath almost lost her shape: how *Vertue* goes poorely, and is not regarded: how *Villany* jets [i.e., 'struts or walks pompously' ~ *Evans Editor*] in silkes, and, (like a God) adored: And when I consider, how all the pleasures of this life are but as childrens dreames, how all the glories of the world are but artificiall fire workes that keepe a blazing for a time, and yet die in stinking smoakes: and how al the labours of man are like the toiling of the winds, which strive to cast up heapes of dust, that in the ende are not worth the gathering: Then, even, then, doe I grow wearie of myselfe: then am I neither in love with the beautie of the Sunne, neither stand I gazing at the dancing of the starres: I neither wonder at the stately measures of the cloudes, the nimble galliards of the water, nor, the wanton trippings of the wind, nor am I delighted when the earth dresses up her head with flowers; I wish my selfe a *Beast*, because men are so bad that *Beasts* excell them in goodness, and abhorre all company, because the best is but tedious, the worser loathsome, both are the destroyers of *Time,* and both must be maintained with cost.

Since then that in the *Noblest Streames* there are such *Whirlepooles* to swallow us up, such *Rocks* that threaten danger, (if not shipwracke,) and such *Quick-sands* to make us sinke, who would not willingly take downe all the sayles of his ambition, and cast anchore on a safe and retired shore, which is to be found in no place, if not in the Countrie. O blessed life! patterne / of that which our first Parents lead, the state of Kinges (now) being but a slavery to that of theirs. O schoole of contemplation! O thou picture of the whole world drawne in a little compasse! O thou *Perspective* glasse, in whom we may behold upon earth, all the *Frame* and *Wonders* of heaven. . . .

Dost thou call for *Music?* No Prince in the worlde keepes more skilfull musitions: the birds are thy consort, and the winde instruments they play upon, yeeld ten thousand tunes. Art, thou addicted to studie; Heaven is thy Library; the *Sunne; Moone,* and starres are thy bookes and teach thee *Astronomies:* By observing them, thou makest Almanacks; to thy selfe, that serve for all seasons. That great *Volume* is thine *Ephemerides* [i.e., 'almanac / record book' ~ *Evans Editor*], out of which thou maist calculate the predictions of times to follow; yea in the very cloudes are written lessons of *Divinity* for thee, to instruct thee in wisdome: the turning over their leaves, teach thee the variations of seasons, and how to dispose, thy businesse for all weathers. If the practise of *Phisicke* delight thee, what *Aphorismes* can all the Doctours in the worlde set downe more certaine? what rules for good diet can they hushed [i.e., 'send us' ~ *Evans Editor*]; whilst *Hee* that played the maisterdivels [i.e., 'master-devils' ~ *Evans Editor*] part amongst these *Hell-hounds,* after a shrug or two given, thus began to speake to him that was new-entered into the damned *Fraternitie.* Brother *Begger* (quoth he) because thou art yet but a méere fresh-man in our *Colledge,* I charge thee to hang thine eares to my lippes, and to learne the *Orders* of our house which thou must observe, upon paine either to be beaten with our cudgels the next time thou art met, or else to bee stript out of any garments that are worth the taking from thee.

There are *Rogues,* (the livery thou thy self now wearest: Next are *Wilde Rogues* [and then] *Tom of Bedlam's* band of madcaps, otherwise called *Poor Tom's Flocke of Wilde-geese* whome here thou seest by his blacke and blew naked armes to be a man beaten to the world. . . .

My noble hearts, my old weather-beaten fellowes, and brave English Spirits, I am to give you that which all the land knowes you justly deserve (a *Roaguish* commendation,) and you shall have it. I am to give *Beggers* their due praise, yet / what neede I doe that, sithence no man, I thinke, will take any thing from them that is their due. To be a *Begger* is to be a *Braveman,* because tis now in fashion for very brave men to *Beg.*

[From Thomas Dekker. *The Guls Handbook* and *The Bel-Man of London* [no editor given] London: J. M. Dent, 1928.]

# THAT MAN IS (AS IT WERE)
# A LITTLE WORLD

From *THE HISTORY OF THE WORLD* (1614)
BK. I, CHAP. 2, SECTION 5

Sir Walter Raleigh

"Ralegh" is the preferred way that Sir Walter Raleigh (c.1552–1618) spelled his name. As a first-rate poet, he practiced the art of peace, but as a prominent courtier he was caught up in the warfare of court life, for although many friends were at his side, he had enemies on all sides of him. Eventually he ended up a political prisoner and was sentenced to be beheaded but escaped the block, if not continued imprisonment, thanks to a reprieve. He spent thirteen years in the Tower of London, wrote there his *History of the World* (London, 1614), and was finally liberated in 1615. Raleigh knew very well the world, including the New World, and the environment of the court with its political ups and downs and questions pertaining to "Who loses and who wins; who's in, who's out," as Lear expresses it (5.3.15). Raleigh's *History* speaks eloquently of the role of man, the microcosm, within the greater system of the macrocosm, a theme that also resounds in the description of Lear in the storm where he "Strives in his little world of man" (3.1.10), which epitomizes the microcosm-macrocosm relationship. See Benjamin West's painting, Plate 3.

$M$AN, THUS compounded and formed by God, was an abstract or model, or brief story of the universal. . . . And whereas God created three sorts of living natures, to wit, angelical, rational, and brutal; giving to angels an intellectual, and to beasts a sensual nature, he vouchsafed unto man both the intellectual of angels, the sensitive of beasts, and the proper rational belonging unto man . . . and because in the little frame of man's body there is a representation of the universal, and (by allusion) a kind of participation of all the parts thereof, therefore was man called *microcosmos*, or the little world . . . for out of earth and dust was

formed the flesh of man, and therefore heavy and lumpish; the bones
of his body we may compare to the hard rocks and stones, and there-  15
fore strong and durable. . . . His blood, which disperseth itself by the
branches of veins through all the body, may be resembled to those
waters which are carried by brooks and rivers over all the earth; his
breath to the air; his natural heat to the enclosed warmth which the
earth hath in itself, which, stirred up by the heat of the sun, assisteth  20
nature in the speedier procreation of those varieties which the earth
bringeth forth; our radical moisture, oil, or balsamum (whereon the
natural heat feedeth and is maintained) is resembled to the fat and
fertility of the earth; the hairs of man's body, which adorns or over-
shadows it, to the grass, which covereth the upper face or skin of the  25
earth; our generative power, to nature, which produceth all things; our
determinations, to the light, wandering, and unstable clouds, carried
every where with uncertain winds; our eyes, to the light of the sun
and moon; and the beauty of our youth, to the flowers of the spring,
which, either in a very short time, or with the sun's heat, dry up and  30
wither away, or the fierce puffs of wind blow them from the stalks;
the thoughts of our mind, to the motion of angels; and our pure
understanding (formerly called *mens*, and that which always looketh
upwards), to those intellectual natures which are always present with
God; and, lastly, our immortal souls (while they are righteous) are by  35
God himself beautified with the title of his own image and similitude.
. . . In this also is the little world of man compared, and made more
like the universal (man being the measure of all things) . . . that the
four complexions resemble the four elements, and the seven ages of
man the seven planets; whereof our infancy is compared to the Moon,  40
in which we seem only to live and grow, as plants; the second age to
Mercury, wherein we are taught and instructed; our third age to Venus,
the days of love, desire, and vanity; the fourth to the Sun, the strong,
flourishing, and beautiful age of man's life; the fifth to Mars, in which
we seek honour and victory, and in which our thoughts travel to am-  45
bitious ends; the sixth age is ascribed to Jupiter, in which we begin to
take account of our times, judge of ourselves, and grow to the perfection of our understanding; the last and seventh to Saturn, wherein our
days are sad and overcast, and in which we find by dear and lamentable
experience, and by the loss which can never be repaired, that of all  50
our vain passions and affections past, the sorrow only abideth: our attendants are sicknesses and variable infirmities; and by how much the
more we are accompanied with plenty, by so much the more greedily
is our end desired, whom when time hath made unsociable to others,
we become a burden to ourselves: being of no other use than to hold  55
the riches we have from our successors.

## NOTES

1–2. *abstract or model* Raleigh's whole discussion turns on the Greek idea of man as being in himself a 'little world,' a microcosm of the great world or 'macrocosm' (see ll. 9–10), which included not only the earth but the whole planetary system as described in the Ptolemaic (geo-centric) system.

[3. *three. . .natures* In this section Raleigh refers to hierarchal elements in the Great Chain of Being. ~ *Evans Editor*]

4–5. *an intellectual. . .nature* Angels, by intellection, could 'know' intuitively without the necessity (as in man) of going through the process of logical reasoning.

5–7. *vouchsafed. . .man* Raleigh here differs from the usual account, which gave man a 'tripartite soul': rational, sensitive and vegetal (the last two of which he shared with the beasts and plant life).

10. *earth and dust* Compare Genesis 2:7.

16. *natural heat* body temperature.

20. *radical moisture* the humour or moisture naturally inherent in all plants and animals; 'oil' (essential oils, necessary to life in man and plants) and 'balsamum' (preservative essence, conceived by Paracelsus to exist in all organic bodies) are here used as equal to 'radical moisture.'

25. *determinations* decisions, conclusions.

30. *motion* apprehension. Compare *Hamlet* 2.2.306: 'how like an angel in apprehension, how like a god!' (see below, ll. 31–3). The whole speech is relevant to a number of Raleigh's comments.

31. *pure understanding* the faculty of comprehending and reasoning, our right reason (as it was before being clouded by the Fall). *mens* intellectual faculty.

32. *looketh upwards* i.e. with the 'eyes of the mind.'

34–5. *title. . .image* Thus man is a microcosm of God.

37. *four complexions* the four humours.

38. *four elements* earth, water, air, fire.

*seven ages of man* There are many treatments of the several periods of man's life (the number of ages may differ); the most famous statement is that of Jaques in *As You Like It* (2.7.139–66).

38–9. *seven planets* as arranged in the Ptolemaic system: (above the spheres of the four elements, Earth as the centre) Moon, Mercury, Venus, Sun, Mars, Jupiter and Saturn (followed, in ascending order, by the Circle of the Fixed Stars, the Crystalline Sphere, the Primum Mobile or First Mover, and the Empyrean, or Highest Heaven).

45. *travel* probably here with the sense of 'travail' (= labour, work).

52. *variable* diverse, various; changeable, fluctuating.

[From Sir Walter Raleigh. *The History of the World* (1614), Book I, chapter 2, section 5. Rpt. In *Elizabethan-Jacobean Drama: A New Mermaid Background Book*, ed. G. Blakemore Evans. London: A & C Black, 1987.]

# From *The Ballad of King Lear and His Three Daughters* (Pre-1620)

## Anonymous

As Stanley Wells writes in his Oxford edition of *King Lear* (2000), an important reason for his reprinting *The Ballad of King Lear and His Three Daughters* (pre-1620) is that it may be based on a recollection of a play in performance. The ballad first appeared, as far as is known, in *Golden Garland of Princely Pleasures and Delicate Delights* by Richard Johnson (1573–1659?). Charlotte Lennox reprinted the ballad in her 3-volume *Shakespear Illustrated* of 1753–54 and argues that the ballad was written before Shakespeare's *King Lear* and that the presentation of Lear's death is an exact copy of Shakespeare's version (3: 301–2). The ballad, like Shakespeare, speaks not only of the cruelty of the older daughters but also of of Lear's madness. (See Charlotte Lennox's *Shakespeare's Misuse of His Sources* in the "Classic Essays" section of this volume. Also see the "Earliest Productions" section of the Evans Editor's "Performance History.")

*A Lamentable Song of the Death of King Lear and his Three Daughters*

### TO THE TUNE OF 'WHEN PLYING FAME'

KING LEAR once rulèd in this land
   With princely power and peace,
   And had all things with heart's content
That might his joys increase.
Amongst those gifts that nature gave      5
   Three daughters fair had he,
So princely-seeming beautiful
   As fairer could not be.

So on a time it pleased the king
   A question thus to move:      10
Which of his daughters to his grace
   Could show the dearest love;
'For to my age you bring content,'
   Quoth he, 'then let me hear
Which of you three in plighted troth      15
   The kindest will appear.'

To whom the eldest thus began:
 'Dear father mine,' quoth she,
'Before your face to do you good
 My blood shall tendered be.      20
And for your sake my bleeding heart
 Shall here be cut in twain
Ere that I see your reverend age
 The smallest grief sustain.'

'And so will I,' the second said,     25
 'Dear father, for your sake
The worst of all extremities
 I'll gently undertake,
And serve your highness night and day
 With diligence and love,      30
That sweet content and quietness
 Discomforts may remove.'

'In doing so you glad my soul,'
 The agèd king replied;
'But what sayst thou, my youngest girl,   35
 How is thy love allied?'
'My love,' quoth young Cordela then,
 'Which to your grace I owe,
Shall be the duty of a child,
 And that is all I'll show.'      40

'And wilt thou show no more,' quoth he,
 'Than doth thy duty bind?
I well perceive thy love is small
 Whenas no more I find.
Henceforth I banish thee my court,    45
 Thou art no child of mine,
Nor any part of this my realm
 By favour shall be thine.

'Thy elder sisters' loves are more
 Than well I can demand,     50
To whom I equally bestow
 My kingdom and my land,
My pompal state and all my goods,
 That lovingly I may
With these thy sisters be maintained   55
 Until my dying day.'

**44. Whenas** seeing that  **53. pompal** splendid, showy; first rec. 1650; rare

Thus flattering speeches won renown
   By these two sisters here;
The third had causeless banishment,
   Yet was her love more dear.             60
For poor Cordela patiently
   Went wand'ring up and down,
Unhelped, unpitied, gentle maid,
   Through many an English town,

Until at last in famous France             65
   She gentler fortunes found,
Though poor and bare, yet was she deemed
   The fairest on the ground.
Where when the king her virtues heard,
   And his fair lady seen,             70
With full consent of all his court
   He made his wife and queen.

Her father, old King Lear, this while,
   With his two daughters stayed.
Forgetful of their promised loves,          75
   Full soon the same denayed,
And living in Queen Ragan's court,
   The elder of the twain,
She took from him his chiefest means,
   And most of all, his train.          80

.     .     .

Even thus possessed with discontents      145
   He passèd o'er to France,
In hope from fair Cordela there
   To find some gentler chance.
Most virtuous dame, where when she heard
   Of this her father's grief,         150
As duty bound, she quickly sent
   Him comfort and relief.

And by a train of noble peers
   In brave and gallant sort,
She gave in charge he should be brought     155
   To Aganippus' court,

---

**67. bare** destitute; defenceless

Her royal king, whose noble mind
   So freely gave consent
To muster up his knights at arms,
   To fame and courage bent.             160

And so to England came with speed
   To repossess King Lear,
And drive his daughters from their thrones
   By his Cordela dear.
Where she, true-hearted noble queen,      165
   Was in the battle slain,
Yet he, good king, In his old days
   Possessed his crown again.

But when he heard Cordela dead,
   Who died indeed for love          170
Of her dear father, in whose cause
   She did this battle move,
He swooning fell upon her breast,
   From whence he never parted,
But on her bosom left his life,         175
   That was so truly-hearted.

The lords and nobles when they saw
   The end of these events,
The other sisters unto death

They doomèd by consents,         180
And being dead, their crowns were left
   Unto the next of kin.
Thus have you heard the fall of pride
   And disobedient sin.

     FINIS

---

172. **move** instigate   **176. That** i.e. Cordela   **180. doomèd** . . . consents condemned by general agreement

[From the ballad as reprinted in *King Lear*, ed. Stanley Wells (Oxford: Oxford UP, 2000), pp. 280–82; 284–85.] Used by permission of Oxford University Press.

Fig. 14. *Cordelia Departing from the Court* (Act 1. Scene 1, *King Lear*), an engraving (1792), by William Sharp after a painting by Robert Smirke for the Boydell Shakespeare Gallery.

In "Shakespeare's Misuse of His Sources" (1753-54), the next "Classic Critical Essay" in this Evans Edition, Charlotte Lennox writes that in *King Lear*, the King of France "lavishes the warmest Praises on [Cordelia's] Virtues" and offers her "Refuge in France," where she will be Queen. Similarly, the anonymous ballad (pre-1620), a source for *King Lear* that Lennox quotes and discusses in her essay, sings of how "in famous France / [Cordelia] gentler fortunes found" (ll. 65-66).

Sharp's engraving of Smirke's romantic painting portrays a couple almost resembling Romeo and Juliet —Cordelia and a youthful King of France, in an ermine-trimmed robe, depart Lear's court—made grand by its architectural, theatrical setting. Unlike her father, Cordelia, is fully aware of the nature of her sisters. At the moment of her departure she says: "I know you what you are" (1.1. 268-69). Regan, whose hand is extended as if ushering Cordelia out, and Goneril, her left arm magisterially akimbo, now rule a divided Britain. Behind them are Cornwall and Albany.

The artist, Robert Smirke (1752-1845), whose painting inspired Sharp's engraving, was the son of the architect-designer of the British Museum, Sir Robert Smirke (1780 –1867). Robert Smirke, the younger, was a major contributor to the Boydell Shakespeare Gallery, for which he produced twenty-six works. A master engraver, William Sharp (1749-1824), also made a much-admired engraving (1793) of Benjamin West's *King Lear in the Storm* (1788; see Color Plate 3).

*Footnotes in the reprinted excerpted material are from the original publication. Footnote numerals, therefore, will correspond to those at the bottom of the essay, but expect numerical gaps since sections not excerpted contain the lines and numbers not included here. The spelling of Shakespeare's name varies over the centuries, especially prior to the early twentieth century. Some authors in this Evans Shakespeare Edition, for example, may use the spelling "Shakespear" or "Shakspere." The adjectival form of the name is "Shakespearian" in British Commonwealth countries and "Shakespearean" in the United States. Generally an author's particular spelling has been retained. Within square brackets, notes are by Evans Editor, V. F. Petronella.*

# From *SHAKESPEARE'S MISUSE*
# *OF HIS SOURCES* (1753-4)

## Charlotte Lennox

As a novelist and playwright, Charlotte Ramsay Lennox (1730–1804) won acclaim as the author of *The Female Quixote* (1752), an adaptation and critique of the Cervantes masterpiece. One of her plays, *Old City Manners* (1775), is based on a comedy by Ben Jonson, George Chapman, and John Marston. It is called *Eastward Ho* (1605) and was performed in 1775 at Theatre Royal, Drury Lane. Some biographical accounts say that Shakespearean actor David Garrick (a famous Lear), who knew of Lennox's writings, was involved in the performance. Her interest in the theater led to a study of Shakespeare's work and in particular the sources for the plays. Despite her having adapted the works of others, Lennox disliked adaptations of Shakespeare—a sophisticated view in an age that appropriated his work freely. Intellectual strengths and her ability as a critic of Shakespearean drama were no doubt bolstered by her friendship with Samuel Johnson.

## [ON *KING LEAR*]

T HIS FABLE, although drawn from the foregoing History of King *Leir*, is so altered by *Shakespeare* in several Circumstances, as to render it much, more improbable than the Original. There we are sufficiently disgusted with the Folly of a Man who gives away one Half of his Kingdom to two of his Daughters because they flatter him with Professions of the most extravagant Love, and deprives his youngest Child of her Portion for no other Crime but confining her Expressions of Tenderness within the Bounds of plain and simple Truth. But *Shakespeare* has carried this Extravagance much farther. He shews us a King resigning his Kingdom, his Crown and Dignity to his two Daughters, reserving nothing to himself, not even a decent Maintenance, but submitting to a mean Dependance on the Bounty of his Children, whom, by promising Rewards proportionable to the Degree of Flattery they lavish on him, he has stimulated to outvie each other in artful Flourishes on their Duty and Affection toward him.

LEAR Tell me, Daughters,
    (Since now we will divest us, both of Rule,
    Int'rest of Territory, Cares of State)
    Which of you, shall we say, doth love us most?
    That we our largest Bounty may extend
    Where Nature doth with Merit challenge. *Goneril*,
    Our eldest born, speak first.        [1.1.47ff.]

What Wonder, when thus bribed *Goneril* should answer

I love you, Sir,
Dearer than Eye-sight, Space and Liberty.    [1.1.54f.]

*Lear* does not run mad till the third Act. Yet his Behaviour towards *Cordelia* in this first Scene has all the Appearance of a Judgment totally depraved: He asks *Cordelia* what she has to say to draw a Dowry more opulent than her Sisters. Thus he suggested to her a Motive for exceeding them in Expressions of Love. The noble Disinterestedness of her Answer afforded the strongest Conviction of her Sincerity, and that she possessed the highest Degree of filial Affection for him, who hazarded the Loss of all her Fortune to confine herself to simple Truth in her Professions of it. Yet for this *Lear* banishes her his Sight, consigns her over to Want, and loads her with the deepest Imprecations. What less than Phrenzy can inspire a Rage so groundless and a Conduct so absurd! *Lear*, while in his Senses, acts like a mad Man, and from his first Appearance to his last seems to be wholly deprived of his Reason.

In the History *Lear* Disinherits *Cordelia*, but we read of no other kind of Severity exerted towards her. The King of *France*, as well in the History as the Play, charm'd with the Virtue and Beauty of the injured *Cordelia*, marries her without a Portion. *Shakespeare* does not introduce this Prince till after the absurd Trial *Lear* made of his Daughters' Affection is over. The Lover who is made to Marry the disinherited *Cordelia* on account of her Virtue is very injudiciously contrived to be Absent when she gave so glorious a Testimony of it, and is touch'd by a cold Justification of her Fame, and that from herself, when he might have been charm'd with a shining Instance of her Greatness of Soul and inviolable Regard to Truth.

So unartfully has the Poet managed this Incident that *Cordelia's*
noble Disinterestedness is apparent to all but him who was to, be
the most influenced by it. In the Eyes of her Lover she is debased,
not exalted; reduced to the abject Necessity of defending her own
Character, and seeking rather to free herself from the Suspicion
of Guilt than modestly enjoying the conscious Sense of superior
Virtue.

*Lear's* Invective against her to the King of *France* is conceived in the
most shocking Terms:

> I would not from your Love make such a stray,
> To Match you where I Hate; therefore beseech you,
> T'avert your Liking a more worthy Way,
> Than on a Wretch, whom Nature is asham'd
> Almost t' acknowledge her's. [1.1.209ff.]

Well might the King of *France* be startled at such Expressions as these
from a Parent of his Child. Had he been present to have heard the
Offence she gave him to occasion them, how must her exalted Merit
have been endeared to him by the extream Injustice she suffered! But
as it is, a bare Acquittal of any monsterous Crime is all the Satisfaction
she can procure for herself, and all the Foundation her Lover has for
the Eulogium he afterwards makes on her.

CORDELIA I yet beseech your Majesty,
(If, for I want that glib and oily Art,
To speak and purpose not; since what I well intend,
I'll do't before I Speak) that you make known
It is no vicious Blot, Murther, or Foulness,
No unchast Action, or dishonour'd Step,
That hath depriv'd me of your Grace and Favour.
But ev'n for want of that, for which I'm richer,
A still soliciting Eye, and such a Tongue,
That I am glad I've not; though not to have it
Hath lost me in your Liking.
LEAR Better thou
Hadst not been Born, than not to have pleased me better. [1.1.223ff.]

From this Speech of *Cordelia's*, and *Lear's* Answer, *France* collects
Matter for extenuating a supposed Error in his Mistress, not for Admiration of her Worth.

FRANCE Is it but this? a Tardiness in Nature,
Which often leaves the History unspoke,
That it intends to do. [1.1.235ff.]

Yet a Moment after, without knowing any more of the Matter, he lavishes the warmest Praises on her Virtues and offers to make her (loaded as she is with her Father's Curses, and deprived of the Dower he expected with her) Queen of *France*. This Conduct would be just and natural had he been a Witness of her noble Behaviour, but doubtful as it must have appeared to him in such perplexing Circumstances 'tis extravagant and absurd.

*Shakespeare* has deviated widely from History in the Catastrophe of his Play. The Chronicle tells us that King *Lear*, having been dispossessed by his rebellious Sons-in-Law of that Half of the Kingdom which he had reserved for himself, and forced by repeated Indignities from his Daughters to take Refuge in *France*, was received with great Tenderness by *Cordelia*, who prevailed upon her Husband to attempt his Restoration. Accordingly an Army of *Frenchmen* pass'd over into *Britain*, by which, the Dukes of *Cornwal* and *Albany* being defeated, King *Lear* was restored to his Crown, died in Peace two Years after, and left his Kingdom to *Cordelia*. In *Shakespeare* the Forces of the two wicked Sisters are victorious, *Lear* and the pious *Cordelia* are taken Prisoners, she is hanged in Prison and the old King dies with Grief. Had *Shakespeare* followed the Historian he would not have violated the Rules of poetical Justice: he represents Vice punished, and Virtue rewarded. In the Play one Fate overwhelms alike the Innocent and the Guilty, and the Facts in the History are wholly changed to produce Events neither probable, necessary, nor just.

Several Incidents in this Play are borrowed from the History of the old Prince of *Paphlagonia* in *Sidney's Arcadia*, which I shall here Transcribe. . . . (III, 286–91)

The under Plot of *Gloster* and his two Sons in the Tragedy of King *Lear* is borrowed from this foregoing short History of *Leonatus;* several of the Circumstances closely copied, and the Characters of the Brothers nearly the same. The Adventure of the Rock is heightened by *Shakespeare*, perhaps with too little Attention to Probability. *Gloster*, though deprived of Sight, might easily be sensible of the Difference between walking on a level Plain and ascending a steep and craggy Rock; nor could he possibly suppose, when he fell gently on that Plain, that he had precipitated himself from an immense Height to the Margin of the Sea.

*Shakespeare*, in the pathetic Description he makes *Edgar* give of his Father's Death, had certainly the following Passage of the *Arcadia* in his Eye:

The blind King, having in the chief City of his Realm set the Crown upon his Son *Leonatus's* Head, with many Tears, both of Joy and Sorrow, setting forth to the People his own Fault, and his Son's

Virtue; after he had kissed him, and forced his Son to accept Honour of him, as of his new become Subject, even in a Moment died, as it should seem, his Heart broken with Unkindness and Affliction, stretched so far beyond his Limits with his Excess of Comfort, as it was able no longer to keep safe his vital Spirits.

EDGAR  I met my Father with his bleeding Rings,
　　　　Their precious Gems new lost; became his Guide;
　　　　Led him, begg'd for him, sav'd him from Despair;
　　　　Never (O Fault!) reveal'd myself unto him,
　　　　Until some half Hour past, when I was arm'd,
　　　　Not sure, though hoping, of this good Success,
　　　　I asked his Blessing, and from first to last
　　　　Told him my Pilgrimage: but his flaw'd Heart,
　　　　Alack, too weak the Conflict to support,
　　　　'Twixt two Extremes of Passion, Joy and Grief,
　　　　Burst smilingly.　　　　　　　　　　　[5.3.189ff.]

The Chronicle of *Holinshed*, and *Sidney's Arcadia* are not the only Resources *Shakespeare* had for his Tragedy of *Lear*, if we may believe the Editor of a Collection of old Ballads published in the Year 1726. In his Introduction to an old Ballad called, *A Lamentable Song of the Death of King Lear and his three Daughters*, he has these Words:

> I cannot be certain directly as to the Time when this Ballad was written; but that it was some Years before the Play of *Shakespeare* appears from several Circumstances, which to mention would swell my Introduction too far beyond its usual Length.

It is to be wished that this Writer, since he was resolved not to exceed a certain Length in his Introduction, had omitted some Part of it in order to introduce those Circumstances that were of infinitely more Consequence than any thing else he has said on the Subject of that old Ballad: if it was really written before *Shakespeare's* Play that great Poet did not disdain to consult it, but has copied it more closely than either the Chronicle or *Sidney*. [See *The Ballad of King Lear and His Three Daughters*—the previous selection in this Evans Edition], From thence (for 'tis mentioned no where else) he took the Hint of *Lear's Madness*, and the extravagant and wanton Cruelty his Daughters exercised on him; the Death of King *Lear* is also exactly copied.

*Spenser* seems to have furnished *Shakespeare* with the Hint of *Cordelia's* Manner of Death. In the tenth Canto of the second Book of his *Faerie Queene* he relates the Story of King *Lear* and his three Daughters. *Cordelia*, he tells us, after having restored her Father to his Crown and succeeded to it after his Death, was by her Sister's Children dethroned and confined a long Time in Prison, so that, overcome by Despair, she hanged herself. In *Shakespeare Cordelia* does not hang herself but is hanged by a Soldier, a very improper Catastrophe for a Person of such exemplary Virtue. (III, 300–2)

[From *Shakespear Illustrated*, Vol. 3 (1753-54). Rpt. in *Shakespeare: The Critical Heritage*, Vol. 4 (1753-1765), ed. Brian Vickers. London: Routledge & Kegan Paul, 1981.]

# From the "PREFACE" and "END-NOTE TO KING LEAR" (1765)

## Samuel Johnson

Samuel Johnson (1709–1784), poet, journalist / essayist, lexicographer, and the author of a novella, *Rasselas, Prince of Abyssinia* (1759), has the distinction of being Shakespeare's sixth major editor after Nicholas Rowe (1674–1718), who was the first. Since boyhood Johnson was fascinated by the plays of Shakespeare. His response to the death of Cordelia was one of shock. So jolted was he that he rejected the idea of ever again reading the closing scenes of *Lear*. When editing Shakespeare later, however, he could not ignore the painful scene that stunned him in earlier years. His great wealth of knowledge, revealed in conversation and writing, made Johnson so great an authoritative leader—a "cham" like Kubla Kahn or Tamerlane—that he was known as "The Great Cham." Reflecting well the Age of Reason his skeptical and critical bent of mind explored conflicts of thought, believing that any issue should be judged from two or more sides. Possessing mental gifts that made him a formidable organizer and communicator of ideas, he was highly qualified to produce his famous *Dictionary* (1755). Here Shakespeare is the most quoted author. In 1765, Trinity College, Dublin awarded him a Doctor of Laws degree for his scholarly work, and a year later Oxford followed suit with a Doctor of Civil Law degree. Deservedly he was now "Dr. Johnson."

1765 was also the year of his eight-volume dictionary and edition of Shakespeare with its famous "Preface." Johnson's interest in poetic justice in literature, which calls for the good to be rewarded and the evil punished, is particularly relevant to a study of *King Lear*. His distrust of puns, however, flies in the face of Shakespeare as a leading exponent of the pun. James Boswell (1740–1795), in the biographical masterpiece devoted to his wise and learned friend, wrote that in "candidly admitting the faults" of Shakespeare, Johnson had bestowed on him "deserved and indisputable praise." Not a strict classicist, Johnson defended Shakespeare's mixing of comedy with tragedy and forgoing the classical unities of time, place, and action, the last having to do with sub-plots, a hallmark of *King Lear*.

# FROM THE "PREFACE"

A NTIQUITY, LIKE every other quality that attracts the notice of mankind, has undoubtedly votaries that reverence it, not from reason, but from prejudice. Some seem to admire indiscriminately whatever has been long preserved, without considering that time has sometimes co-operated with chance; all perhaps are more willing to honour past than present excellence; and the mind contemplated genius through the shades of age, as the eye surveys the sun through artificial opacity. The great contention of criticism is to find the faults of the moderns, and the beauties of the ancients.

## [END-NOTE TO KING LEAR]

The Tragedy of Lear is deservedly celebrated among the dramas of Shakespeare. There is perhaps no play which keeps the attention so strongly fixed; which so much agitates our passions and interests our curiosity. The artful involutions of distinct interests, the striking opposition of contrary characters, the sudden changes of fortune, and the quick succession of events fill the mind with a perpetual tumult of indignation, pity, and hope. There is no scene which does not contribute to the aggravation of the distress or conduct of the action, and scarce a line which does not conduce to the progress of the scene. So powerful is the current of the poet's imagination that the mind which once ventures within it is hurried irresistibly along.

On the seeming improbability of Lear's conduct it may be observed that he is represented according to histories at that time vulgarly received as true. And perhaps, if we turn our thoughts upon the barbarity and ignorance of the age to which this story is referred, it will appear not so unlikely as while we estimate Lear's manners by our own. Such preference of one daughter to another, or resignation of dominion on such conditions, would be yet credible if told of a petty prince of Guinea or Madagascar. Shakespeare, indeed, by the mention of his Earls and Dukes has given us the idea of times more civilised, and of life regulated by softer manners; and the truth is that though he so nicely discriminates, and so minutely describes the characters of men he commonly neglects and confounds the characters of ages, by mingling customs ancient and modern, English and foreign.

My learned friend Mr. Warton [ Joseph Warton (1722-1800) ~ Evans Editor], who has in the Adventurer very minutely criticised this play, remarks that the instances of cruelty are too savage and shocking, and that the intervention of Edmund destroys the simplicity of the story. These objections may, I think, be answered by repeating that the cruelty of the daughters is an historical fact, to which the poet has added little, having only drawn it into a series by dialogue and action. But I am not able to apologise with equal plausibility for the extrusion of *Gloucester's* eyes, which seems an act too horrid to be endured in dramatic exhibition, and such as must always compel the mind to relieve its distress by incredulity. Yet let it be remembered that our author well knew what would please the audience for which he wrote.

The injury done by *Edmund* to the simplicity of the action is abundantly recompensed by the addition of variety, by the art with, which he is made to co-operate with the chief design, and the opportunity which he gives the poet of combining perfidy with perfidy and connecting the wicked son with the wicked daughters, to impress this important moral, that villany is never at a stop, that crimes lead to crimes, and at last terminate in ruin.

But though this moral be incidentally enforced, *Shakespeare* has suffered the virtue of *Cordelia* to perish in a just cause, contrary to the natural ideas of justice, to the hope of the reader, and, what is yet more strange, to the faith of chronicles. Yet this conduct is justified by the *Spectator*, who blames *Tate* for giving *Cordelia* success and happiness in his alteration, and declares that in his opinion *the tragedy has lost half its beauty*. [Poet and dramatist John Dennis (1657-1734) ~ *Evans Editor*] has remarked, whether justly or not, that to secure the favourable reception of *Cato* [Dr. Johnson's tragic stage-play of 1713 ~ *Evans Editor*], *the town was poisoned with much false and abominable criticism*, and that endeavours had been used to discredit and decry poetical justice. A play in which the wicked prosper, and the virtuous miscarry, may doubtless be good because it is a just representation of the common events of human life: but since all reasonable beings naturally love justice, I cannot easily be persuaded that the observation of justice makes a play worse; or that if other excellencies are equal the audience will not always rise better pleased from the final triumph of persecuted virtue.

In the present case the publick has decided. *Cordelia*, from the time of *Tate*, has always retired with victory and felicity. And, if my sensations could add any thing to the general suffrage, I might relate that I was many years ago so shocked by *Cordelia's* death that I know not whether I ever endured to read again the last scenes of the play till I undertook to revise them as an editor.

There is another controversy among the criticks concerning this play. It is disputed whether the predominant image in *Lear's* disordered mind be the loss of his kingdom or the cruelty of his daughters. Mr. *Murphy*, a very judicious critick has evinced by induction of particular passages, that the cruelty of his daughters is the primary source of his distress, and that the loss of royalty affects him only as a secondary and subordinate evil. He observes with great justness that *Lear* would move our compassion but little did we not rather consider the injured father than the degraded king.

The story of this play, except the episode of *Edmund*, which is derived, I think, from *Sidney*, is taken originally from *Geoffry* of *Monmouth*, whom *Holinshed* generally copied. ... [Johnson now prints excerpts from 'an old historical ballad', 'A lamentable SONG of the Death of King Leir and his Three Daughters', as a possible source, and argues that it was written before the play, since 'the ballad has nothing of *Shakespeare's* nocturnal tempest, which is too striking to have been omitted', and that 'it has the rudiments of the play, but none of its amplifications: it first hinted *Lear's* madness, but did not array it in circumstances.' ~ *Evans Editor*] (6, 158–60).

[From Johnson's *The Plays of Shakespeare in Eight Volumes . . . by Sam. Johnson* (1765). Rpt. in *Shakespeare: The Critical Heritage*, Vol. 4 (1753-1765), ed. Brian Vickers. London: Routledge & Kegan Paul, 1981.]

# From ON KING LEAR (c. 1813)

## Samuel Taylor Coleridge

Samuel Taylor Coleridge (1772–1834), the great Romantic poet who gave us the haunted Ancient Mariner, a haunting Christabel, and an opium-inspired portrait of Kubla Khan's pleasure dome and its environs, did not compose his Shakespearean criticism in a single manuscript or set of manuscripts. Instead, his writings on Shakespeare are available to us today thanks to editors who painstakingly organized Coleridge's jottings, lecture notes, letters, and other scattered texts into a relatively methodical discourse on what Coleridge thought about Shakespeare. In keeping with the Romantic tradition, Coleridge's approach is subjective since he saw himself in many of the characters of the plays, especially Hamlet. Coleridge's view represents the reverse of the objectivity that Keats valued in Shakespeare—the ability of a writer to remove or negate oneself in what is being written, especially in dramatic writing. (See the section on Keats and "Negative Capability" in the Evans General Editor's "Shakespeare's Life." Also see the Evans Editor's "History of Performance" and the "Headnote / Introduction" to Keats's "Sonnet on *King Lear*"). Nevertheless, the comments and insights of Coleridge, as we now have them in carefully edited form, are both readable and central to the history of classic Shakespearean criticism.

Material in square brackets within Coleridge's text *below* is that of Coleridge's editor, Thomas Raysor.

[Coleridge's note on the opening lines of the play (1.1.1–6) is illustrative of the way in which the Romantic conception of tragic unity allowed the critic to pay attention to minor characters (such as Cornwall and Albany) and to spin almost infinite webs of meaning out of individual words and phrases. Coleridge's painstaking 'practical criticism' of the text (it was he who invented the term) allows him, for instance, to note the apparent contradiction at the very opening of *King Lear,* where the division of the kingdoms is referred to as a *fait accompli* even though it has not yet actually happened. And Romantic emphasis on motivation rather than on action enables Coleridge to treat the figure of Edmund with extraordinary perception and sympathy. . . .]

IT WAS [not] without forethought, and it is not without its due significance, that the triple division is stated here as already determined and in all its particulars, previously to the trial of professions, as the relative rewards of which the daughters were to be made to consider their several portions. The strange, yet by no means unnatural, mixture of selfishness, sensibility, and habit of feeling derived from and fostered by the particular rank and usages of the individual; the intense desire to be intensely beloved, selfish, and yet characteristic of the selfishness of a loving and kindly nature—a feeble selfishness, self-supportless and leaning for all pleasure on another's breast; the selfish craving after a sympathy with a prodigal disinterestedness, contradicted by its own ostentation and the mode and nature of its claims; the anxiety, the distrust, the jealousy, which more or less accompany all selfish affections, and are among the surest contradistinctions of mere fondness from love, and which originate ['give origin to' ~ *Evans Editor*] Lear's eager wish to enjoy his daughter's violent professions, while the inveterate habits of sovereignty convert the wish into claim and positive right, and the incompliance with it into crime and treason;—these facts, these passions, these moral verities, on which the whole tragedy is founded, are all prepared for, and will to the retrospect be found implied in, these first four or five lines of the play. They let us know that the trial is but a trick; and that the grossness of the old king's rage is in part the natural result of a silly trick suddenly and most unexpectedly baffled and disappointed. This having been provided in the fewest words, in a natural reply to as natural [a] question, which yet answers a secondary purpose of attracting our attention to the difference or diversity between the characters of Cornwall and Albany; the premises and data, as it were, having been thus afforded for our after-insight into the mind and mood of the person whose character, passions, and sufferings are the main *subject-matter* of the play;—from Lear, the *persona patiens* of his drama, Shakespeare passes without delay to the second in importance, to the main *agent* and prime mover—introduces Edmund to our acquaintance, and with the same felicity of judgement . . . prepares us for his character in the seemingly casual communication of its origin and occasion. From the first drawing up of the curtain he has stood before us in the united strength and beauty of earliest manhood. Our eyes have been questioning him. Gifted thus with high advantages of *person,* and further endowed by nature with a powerful intellect and a strong energetic will, even without any concurrence of circumstances and accident, pride will be the sin that most easily besets him. But he is the known and acknowledged son of the princely Gloster. Edmund, therefore, has *both* the germ of pride and the conditions best fitted to evolve and ripen it into a predominant feeling. Yet hitherto no reason appears why it should be other than the not unusual pride of person, talent, and birth, a pride auxiliary if not akin to many virtues, and the natural ally of honorable [impulses?]. But alas! in his own presence his own father takes shame to himself for the frank avowal that he is his father—has 'blushed so often to acknowledge him that he is now braz'd to it'. He hears his mother and the circumstances of his birth spoken of with a most degrading and licentious levity—described as a wanton by her own paramour, and the remembrance of the animal sting, the low criminal gratifications connected with her wantonness and prostituted beauty assigned as the reason why 'the whoreson must be acknowledged'. This, and the consciousness of its notoriety—the gnawing conviction that every show of respect is an effort of courtesy which recalls while it represses a contrary feeling—this is the evertrickling flow of wormwood and gall into the wounds of pride, the corrosive virus which inoculates pride with a venom not its own, with envy, hatred, a lust of that power which in its blaze of radiance would hide the dark spots on his disk, [with] pangs of shame personally undeserved and therefore felt as wrongs, and a blind ferment of vindictive workings towards the occasions and causes, especially towards a brother whose stainless birth and lawful honors were the constant remembrancers of *his* debasement, and were ever in the way to prevent all chance of its being unknown or overlooked and forgotten. Add to this that with excellent judgement, and provident for the claims of the moral sense, for that which relatively to the drama is called poetic justice; and as the fittest means for reconciling the feelings of the spectators to the horrors of Gloster's after sufferings—at least, of rendering them somewhat less unendurable (for I will not disguise my conviction that in this one point the tragic has been urged beyond the outermost mark and *ne plus ultra* of the dramatic)—Shakespeare has precluded all excuse and palliation of the guilt incurred by both the parents of the base-born Edmund by Gloster's confession that he was at the time a married man and already blest with a lawful heir of his fortunes. The mournful alienation of brotherly love occasioned by primogeniture in noble families, or rather by the unnecessary distinctions engrafted thereon, and this in children of the same stock, is still almost proverbial on the continent —especially, as I know from my own observation, in the south of Europe—and appears to have been scarcely less common in our own island before the Revolution of 1688, if we may judge from the characters and sentiments so frequent in our elder comedies. . . . Need it be said how heavy an aggravation the stain of bastardy must have been, were it only that the younger brother was liable to hear his own dishonor and his mother's infamy related by his father with an excusing shrug of the shoulders, and in a tone betwixt waggery and shame.

By the circumstances here enumerated as so many predisposing causes, Edmund's character might well be deem'd already sufficiently explained and prepared for. But in this tragedy the story or fable constrained Shakespeare to introduce wickedness in an outrageous form, in Regan and Goneril. He had read nature too heedfully not to know that courage, intellect, and strength of character were the most impressive forms of power, and that to power in itself, without reference to any moral end, an inevitable admiration and complacency appertains. . . . But in the display of such a character it was of the highest importance to prevent the guilt from passing into utter *monstrosity*—which again depends on the presence or absence of causes and temptations sufficient to account for the wickedness, without the necessity of recurring to a thorough fiendishness of nature for its origination. For such are the appointed relations of intellectual power to truth, and of truth to goodness, that it becomes both morally and poetic[ally] unsafe to present what is admirable—what our nature compels us to admire—in the mind, and what is most detestable in the heart, as coexisting in the same individual without any apparent connection, or any modification of the one by the other. . . . [I]n the present tragedy, in which he [was] compelled to present a Goneril and Regan, it was most carefully to be avoided; and, therefore, the one only conceivable addition to the inauspicious influences on the preformation of Edmund's character is given in the information that all the kindly counteractions to the mischievous feelings of shame that might have been derived from co-domestication with Edgar and their common father, had been cut off by an absence from home and a foreign education from boyhood to the present time, and the prospect of its continuance, as if to preclude all risk of his interference with the father's views for the elder and legitimate son:

He hath been out nine years, and away he shall again [1.1.32-33].

[From *Coleridge's Shakespearean Criticism*, ed. Thomas Raysor, in 2 vols., New York: Dutton, 1960.]

# "To See Lear Acted"

## From "On the Tragedies of Shakespeare" (1838)

### Charles Lamb

Charles Lamb (1775–1834) has been for the last two hundred years associated with *Tales from Shakespeare* (1807), which he wrote in collaboration with his sister Mary (1764–1847), who may have been the better writer of the two. *Tales from Shakespeare* is often reprinted for young readers and presents the "gentle Shakespeare," to use the descriptive phrase of Shakespeare's fellow playwright and friendly rival, Ben Jonson (1572-1637), who was no doubt referring to his Stratford friend as one not given to dramatizing overly sensational events and incorporating gratuitous violence. Ironically if Charles Lamb did not want to dwell on the pain and suffering in Shakespeare's plays, he faced in actual life grim realities that would have destroyed a lesser person. Mary Lamb, who had serious mental problems, had been for years caring meticulously for her mother until one day Mary suddenly became so distraught that she stabbed the old woman to death. Charles Lamb's own mental instability, of course, was not helped by the matricide, which seemed to have come straight from the pages of a lurid Elizabethan-Jacobean melodrama, the kind of drama he did not wish to witness. It is no surprise, then, that Charles Lamb, more so than Samuel Taylor Coleridge, his close friend since schooldays, questioned whether a play like *King Lear* can or should be performed on the stage.

S O  T O  see Lear acted . . . to see an old man tottering about the stage with a walking-stick, turned out of doors by his daughters in a rainy night—has nothing in it but what is painful and disgusting. We want to take him into shelter and relieve him. That is all the feeling which the acting of Lear ever produced in me. But the Lear of Shakspeare cannot be acted. The contemptible machinery by which they mimic the storm which he goes out in, is not more inadequate to represent the horrors of the real elements than any actor can be to represent Lear; they might more easily propose to personate the Satan of Milton upon a stage, or one of Michael Angelo's terrible figures. The greatness of Lear is not in corporal dimension, but in intellectual: the explosions of his passion are terrible as a volcano: they are storms turning up and disclosing to the bottom that sea, his mind, with all its vast riches. It is his mind which is laid bare. This case of flesh, and blood seems too insignificant to be thought on; even as he himself neglects it. On the stage we see nothing but corporal infirmities and weakness, the impotence of rage; while we read it, we see not Lear, but we are Lear,—we are in his mind, we are sustained by a grandeur which baffles the malice of daughters and storms; in the aberrations of his reason, we discover a mighty irregular power of reasoning, immethodised from the ordinary purposes of life, but exerting, its powers, as the wind blows where it [wishes], at will upon the corruptions and abuses of mankind. What have looks, or tones, to do with that sublime identification of his age with that of the *heavens themselves,* when, in his reproaches to them for conniving at the injustice of his children, he reminds them that 'they themselves are old'? What gesture shall we appropriate to this? What has the voice or the eye to do with such things? But the play is beyond all art, as the temperings with it show; it is too hard and stony; it must have love-scenes and a happy ending. It is not enough that Cordelia is a daughter, she must shine as a lover too. [Nathan Tate, author of the happy-ending adaptation of *King Lear* (1681)], has put his hook into the nostrils of this Leviathan, for Garrick and his followers, the showmen of the scene, to draw the mighty beast about more easily. A happy ending!—as if the living martyrdom that Lear had gone through,—the flaying of his feelings, alive, did not make a fair dismissal from the stage of life the only decorous thing for him. If he is to live and be happy after, if he could sustain this world's burden after, why all this pudder and preparation,—why torment us with all this unnecessary sympathy? As if the childish pleasure of getting his gilt robes and sceptre again could tempt him to act over again his misused station,—as if at his years, and with his experience, anything was left but to die.

Lear is essentially impossible to be represented on a stage.

[From Charles Lamb. "On the Tragedies of Shakespeare," in *Prose Works,* in 3 vols. London: Edward Moxon, 1838, pp. 121. Rpt. in King Lear: *A New Variorum Edition of Shakespeare,* 1880. Rpt. New York: Dover, 1963.]

# From "*The Character of King Lear*"

## (1817)

### William Hazlitt

William Hazlitt (1778–1830) was John Keats's favorite Shakespearean critic. Among his critical works are *Characters of Shakespeare* (1817), *A View of the English Stage* (1818), *English Poets* (1818), and *English Comic Writers* (1819). As a prolific writer with an engaging prose style, whether discussing literature or politics, he attracted the attention of poets Samuel Taylor Coleridge (1772–1834) and William Wordsworth (1770–1850), who were steeped in the pro-republican liberal politics of the Romantic era. In the late 1790s, Hazlitt, along with Coleridge, lived as a guest for a time at the country house called Alfoxden, which William and his sister Dorothy rented in the Quantock Hills of Somerset. Hazlitt's literary criticism often stressed the social and political responsibilities of the artist.

W E WISH that we could pass this play over, and say nothing about it. All that we can say must fall far short of the subject; or even of what we ourselves conceive of it. To attempt to give a description of the play itself or of its effect upon the mind, is mere impertinence: yet we must say something.—It is then the best of all Shakespear's plays, for it is the one in which he was the most in earnest. He was here fairly caught in the web of his own imagination. The passion which he has taken as his subject is that which strikes its root deepest into the human heart; of which the bond is the hardest to be unloosed; and the cancelling and tearing to pieces of which gives the greatest revulsion to the frame. This depth of nature, this force of passion, this tug and war of the elements of our being, this firm faith in filial piety, and the giddy anarchy and whirling tumult of the thoughts at finding this prop failing it, the contrast between the fixed, immoveable basis of natural affection, and the rapid, irregular starts of imagination, suddenly wrenched from all its accustomed holds and resting-places in the soul, this is what Shakespear has given, and what nobody else but he could give. So we believe.—The mind of Lear, staggering between the weight of attachment and the hurried movements of passion, is like a tall ship driven about by the winds, buffeted by the furious waves, but that still rides above its anchor fixed in the bottom of the sea; or it is like the sharp rock circled by the eddying whirlpool that foams and beats against it, or like, the solid promontory pushed from its basis by the force of an earthquake.

The character of Lear itself is very finely conceived for the purpose. It is the only ground on which such a story could be built with the greatest truth and effect. It is his rash haste, his violent impetuosity, his blindness to every thing but the dictates of his passions or affections, that produces all his misfortunes, that aggravates his impatience of them, that enforces our pity for him. The part which Cordelia bears in the scene is extremely beautiful: the story is almost told in the first words she utters. We see at once the precipice on which the poor old king stands from his own extravagant and credulous importunity, the indiscreet simplicity of her love (which, to be sure, has a little of her father's obstinacy in it) and the hollowness of her sisters' pretensions. Almost the first burst of that noble tide of passion, which runs through the play, is in the remonstrance of Kent to his royal master on the injustice of his sentence against his youngest daughter—"Be Kent unmannerly, when Lear is mad!" This manly plainness, which draws down on him the displeasure of the unadvised king, is worthy of the fidelity with which he adheres to his fallen fortunes. The true character of the two eldest daughters, Regan and Gonerill (they are so thoroughly hateful that we do not even like to repeat their names) breaks out in their answer to Cordelia who desires them to treat their father well—"Prescribe not us our duties"—their hatred of advice being in proportion to their determination to do wrong, and to their hypocritical pretension to do right. Their deliberate hypocrisy adds the last finishing to the odiousness of their characters. It is the absence of this detestable quality that is the only relief in the character of Edmund the Bastard, and that at times reconciles us to him. We are not tempted to exaggerate the guilt of his conduct, when he himself gives it up as a bad business, and writes himself down "plain villain". Nothing more can be said about it. His religious honesty in this respect is admirable. One speech of his is worth a million. . . .—The whole character, its careless, lighthearted villainy, contrasted with the sullen, rancorous malignity of Regan and Gonerill, its connection with the conduct of the underplot, in which Gloster's persecution of one of his sons and the Ingratitude of another, form a counterpart to the mistakes and misfortunes of Lear,—his double amour with the two sisters, and the share which he has in bringing about the fatal catastrophe, are all managed with an uncommon degree of skill and power.

It has been said, and we think justly, that the third act of *Othello* and the three first acts of LEAR, are Shakespear's great master-pieces in the logic of passion: that they contain the highest examples not only of the force of individual passion, but of its dramatic vicissitudes and striking effects arising from the different circumstances and characters of the persons speaking. We see the ebb and flow of the feeling, its pauses and feverish starts, its impatience of opposition, its accumulating force when it has time to recollect itself, the manner in which it avails itself of every passing word or gesture, its haste to repel insinuation, the alternate contraction and dilatation of the soul, and all 'the dazzling fence of controversy' in this mortal combat with poisoned weapons, aimed at the heart, where each wound is fatal. . . . In . . . [*King Lear*] that which aggravates the sense of sympathy in the reader, and of uncontroulable anguish in the swoln heart of Lear, is the petrifying indifference, the cold, calculating, obdurate selfishness of his daughters. His keen passions seem whetted on their stony hearts. The contrast would be too painful, the shock too great, but for the intervention of the Fool, whose well-timed levity comes in to break the continuity of feeling when it can no longer be borne, and to bring into play again the fibres of the heart just as they are growing rigid from over-strained excitement. The imagination is glad to take refuge in the half-comic, half-serious comments of the Fool, just as the mind under the extreme anguish of a surgical operation vents itself in sallies of wit. The character was also a grotesque ornament of the barbarous times, in which alone the tragic groundwork of the story could be laid. In another point of view it is indispensable, inasmuch as while it is a diversion to the too great intensity of our disgust, it carries the pathos to the highest pitch of which it is capable, by showing the pitiable weakness of the old king's conduct and its irretrievable consequences in the most familiar point of view. Lear may well 'beat at the gate which let his folly in,' after, as the Fool says, 'he has made his daughters his mothers'. The character is dropped in the third act to make room for the entrance of Edgar as Mad Tom, which well accords with the increasing bustle and wildness of the incidents; and nothing can be more complete than the distinction between Lear's real and Edgar's assumed madness, while the resemblance in the cause of their distresses, from the severing of the nearest ties of natural affection, keeps up a unity of Interest. Shakespear's mastery over his subject, if it was not art, was owing to a knowledge of the connecting links of the passions, and their effect upon the mind, still more wonderful than any systematic adherence to rules, and that anticipated and outdid all the efforts of the most refined art, not inspired and rendered instinctive by genius. . . .

Four things have struck us in reading LEAR:

1. That poetry is an interesting study, for this reason, that it relates to whatever is most interesting in human life. Whoever therefore has a contempt for poetry, has a contempt for himself and humanity.

2. That the language of poetry is superior to the language of painting; because the strongest of our recollections relate to feelings, not to faces.

3. That the greatest strength of genius is shewn in describing the strongest passions: for the power of the imagination, in works of invention, must be in proportion to the force of the natural impressions, which are the subject of them.

4. That the circumstance which balances the pleasure against the pain in tragedy is, that in proportion to the greatness of the evil, is our sense and desire of the opposite good excited; and that our sympathy with actual suffering is lost in the strong impulse given to our natural affections, and carried away with the swelling tide of passion, that gushes from and relieves the heart.

[From *Characters of Shakespeare's Plays*. 1817; rpt. London: J. M. Dent, 1906.]

# "On Sitting Down to Read King Lear Once Again" (1818)

John Keats

John Keats (1795-1821), the foremost English Romantic poet, struggled from an early age with a tubercular condition that eventually caused his death at the age of twenty-five. He died in Rome after being cared for by his friend, artist Joseph Severn (1793-1879), in a house overlooking the Spanish Steps in the Piazza di Spagna. Keats is buried in what is officially known as Il Cimitero Acatollico, the cemetery for non-Catholics that is generally known as the "Protestant" Cemetery.

Keats left a rich literary legacy of various kinds of brilliant poems, among them odes, narrative verse, and sonnets. Two of his sonnets—one of them, "On Sitting Down to Read *King Lear* Once Again," reprinted here—are associated with Shakespeare's great tragic drama and offer lyrical yet perceptive insights. "On the Sea" (April 1817) was written while Keats was staying in Carisbrooke on the Isle of Wight. Writing to John Hamilton Reynolds (*The Letters*, ed. Rollins, 1: 132-33), Keats included a copy of his poem. He comments on it in the light of his having been "haunted . . . intensely" by one particular passage in *King Lear* (4.6.3-4) that sparked his imagination. In the play, Edgar, dressed as a beggar, is trying to create the illusion of Dover Cliff's brink, picturing how "Horrible steep" the area is. Edgar then asks the blinded, despairing Gloucester, who seeks death by falling from the cliffs, "Hark, do you hear the sea?" Keats, by compiling sibilants throughout his poem, presents the sea as a living, haunting presence:

It keeps eternal whisperings around
Desolate shores, and with its mighty swell
Gluts twice ten thousand caverns . . .

Keats, inspired by lines from *King Lear*, invokes the power of water in this sonnet, whereas in "On Sitting Down to Read *King Lear* Once Again," with the totality of the tragedy in mind, he concentrates on the element of fire with its suggestion of purgation. For a photographic image of the holograph of the sonnet, see Fig. 8, which shows not only Keats's personally handwritten poem following the play of *Hamlet* but also—on the very next page—the opening of *King Lear* with Keats's own marginal markings. Keats's absorbing letters are required reading when studying his works.

A great admirer of Shakespeare's works, Keats during his last years was intent, as poet and aspiring playwright, on developing the kind of aesthetic distancing or objectivity that Shakespeare achieved in his plays. It is in his letters that Keats discusses Shakespeare as the master of "Negative Capability." J. J. M. Tobin, the General Editor of this Evans Edition, deals with the Keatsian concept, as does the *King Lear* Evans Editor in "Performance History" (See, for example, the comments on the *Psychomachia* and those devoted to *Lear* and Shakespeare's "Negative Capability."

O golden-tongued Romance with serene lute!
　　Fair plumèd Syren, Queen of far-away!
　　Leave melodizing on this wintry day,
Shut up thine olden pages, and be mute:
Adieu! for, once again, the fierce dispute
　　Betwixt damnation and impassioned clay
　　Must I burn through, once more humbly assay
The bitter-sweet of this Shakespearian fruit:
Chief Poet! and ye clouds of Albion,
　　Begetters of our deep eternal theme!
When through the old oak forest I am gone,
　　Let me not wander in a barren dream,
But, when I am consumèd in the fire,
Give me new Phoenix wings to fly at my desire.

[From *John Keats: The Complete Works*, ed. John Barnard (Harmondsworth, U.K.: Penguin, 1973), p. 220. Penguin English Poets, gen. ed. Christopher Ricks.]

# From "CORDELIA" (1832)

## Anna Brownell Murphy Jameson

Anna Brownell Murphy Jameson (1794–1860) was born in Dublin, Ireland, where her father was a miniaturist painter who adorned enamels. He served as court artist in residence at Windsor Castle, and his artistic abilities stimulated Jameson to become an art historian. She studied the Italian Renaissance and specialized in Christian iconography. Her most important publication was *Sacred and Legendary Art* (1848–1860) in two volumes. Novelist Nathaniel Hawthorne said of Jameson that she was able to read a painting as if she were reading a book. Art, books, and drama were her central interests.

During a journey to Germany, Jameson met A. W. Schlegel (1767–1845) and Ludwig Tieck (1773–1853), the translators of Shakespeare in an edition that was completed by Tieck's daughter Dorothea (1799–1841) and Wolf Heinrich Friedrich Karl, Count Von Baudissin (1789–1878). This translation of Shakespeare was so exemplary that the great English playwright was sometimes considered a German author. Some also thought that Shakespeare wrote his plays in German as well as in English. No wonder that Jameson's attachment to Shakespeare was intense. Her *Shakespeare's Heroines: Characteristics of Women, Moral, Poetical and Historical* was published by Ticknor and Fields of Boston in 1832, two years before the Schlegel-Tieck translation appeared.

It is in *Shakespeare's Heroines* that Jameson's essay on Cordelia appears. In her beautiful, often Wordsworthian prose, she analyzes Cordelia in a manner that anticipates the criticism of A. C. Bradley, whose work is represented in the last Classic Critical Essay in this volume. Furthermore, in the course of her comments, she likens Cordelia to Sophocles' Antigone, evokes the values of classical Greece, and speaks of Cordelia in the light of Italian religious art. All of these comparisons remain fruitful topics of discussion for young and seasoned critics alike.

.    .    .

THERE IS in the beauty of Cordelia's character an effect too sacred for words, and almost too deep for tears[1]; within her heart is a fathomless well of purest affection, but its waters sleep in silence and obscurity,—never failing in their depth and never overflowing in their fulness. Every thing in her seems to lie beyond our view, and affects us in a manner which we feel rather than perceive. The character appears to have no surface, no salient points upon which the fancy can readily seize: there is little, external development of intellect, less of passion, and still less of imagination. It is completely made out in the course of a few scenes, and we are surprised to find that in those few scenes there is matter for a life of reflection, and materials enough for twenty heroines. If Lear be the grandest of Shakspeare's tragedies, Cordelia in herself, as a human being, governed by the purest and holiest impulses and motives, the most refined from all dross of selfishness and passion, approaches near to perfection; and in her adaptation, as a dramatic, personage, to a determinate plan of action, may be pronounced altogether perfect. The character, to speak of it critically as a poetical conception, is not, however, to be comprehended at once; or easily; and in the same manner Cordelia, as a woman, is one whom we must have loved before we could have known her, and known her long before we could have known her truly. . . .

Amid the awful, the overpowering interest of the story, amid the terrible convulsions of passion and suffering, and pictures of moral and physical wretchedness which harrow up the soul, the tender influence of Cordelia, like that of a celestial visitant, is felt and acknowledged without being quite understood. Like a soft star that shines for a moment from behind a stormy cloud and the next is swallowed up in tempest and darkness, the impression it leaves is beautiful and deep,— but vague. Speak of Cordelia to a critic or to a general reader, all agree in the beauty of the portrait, for all must feel it; but when we come to details, I have heard more various and opposite opinions relative to her than any other of Shakspeare's characters—a proof of what I have advanced in the first instance, that from the simplicity with which the character is dramatically treated, and the small space it occupies, few are aware of its internal power, or its wonderful depth of purpose.

It appears to me that the whole character rests upon the two sublimest principles of human action, the love of truth and the sense of duty; but these, when they stand alone, (as in the Antigone,) are apt to strike us as severe and cold. Shakspeare has, therefore, wreathed them round with the dearest attributes of our feminine nature, the power of feeling and inspiring affection. The first part of the play shows us how Cordelia is loved, the second part how she can love.

. . . We lose sight of Cordelia during the whole of the second and third, and great part of the fourth act; but towards the conclusion she reappears. Just as our sense of human misery and wickedness, being carried to its extreme height, becomes nearly intolerable ["Jameson at this point quotes powerful lines from *King Lear* (1.4.268-69) and with additional quotation marks her own resonating, Shakespeare-like phrase", "like an engine wrenching our frame of nature from its fixed place,"[2] then, like a redeeming angel, she descends to mingle in the scene, "loosening the springs of pity in our eyes,"[3] ~ *Evans Editor*] and relieving the impressions of pain and terror by those of admiration and a tender pleasure. For the catastrophe, it is indeed terrible! wondrous terrible! When Lear enters with Cordelia dead in his arms, compassion and awe so seize on all our faculties, that we are left only to silence and to tears.

. . . In Cordelia it is not the external coloring or form, it is not what she says or does, but what she is in herself, what she feels, thinks, and suffers, which continually awaken our sympathy and interest. The heroism of Cordelia is more passive and tender—it melts into our heart; and in the veiled loveliness and unostentatious delicacy of her character, there is an effect more profound and artless, if it be less striking and less elaborate than in the Grecian heroine. To Antigone we give our admiration, to Cordelia our tears. Antigone stands before us in her austere and statue-like beauty, like one of the marbles of the Parthenon. If Cordelia reminds us of any thing on earth, it is of one of the Madonnas in the old Italian pictures, "with downcast eyes beneath th' almighty dove?"[4] and as that heavenly form is connected with our human sympathies only by the expression of maternal tenderness or maternal sorrow, even so Cordelia would be almost too angelic, were she not linked to our earthly feelings, bound to our very hearts, by her filial love, her wrongs, her sufferings, and her tears.

[1. The phrase, "too deep for tears" is from the last line of Wordsworth's great ode, *Intimation of Immortality from Recollections of Early Childhood* (completed 1804; published 1807). ~ *Evans Editor*] [2. Jameson is here quoting two powerful lines from *King Lear* (1.4.268-69). ~ *Evans Editor*] [3. The quotation here is Jameson's own resonating, Shakespeare-like phrase. ~ *Evans Editor*] 4. The line is from Lord Byron's *Don Juan* (1819-20), Canto 3, stanza 103, line 6.

[From Jameson's *Shakespeare's Heroines* (1832); rpt. in Jameson, *Characteristics of Women, Moral, Political, and Historical* (Ticknor and Fields: Boston, 1863).]

# From *"KING LEAR," STUDIES IN SHAKESPEARE: A BOOK OF ESSAYS* (1869)

Mary Preston

The preface to Mary Preston's *Studies in Shakespeare: Book of Essays* (1869) voices a Victorian practicality: "I have not endeavored, in this book, to say anything *very new* to the reader. My aim has been to direct attention to very old truths [apparent in Shakespeare's works] which amid the multifarious [stage] productions of our day are often overlooked. And though the plays of 'Avon's bard' have been the favorite theme of the learned, on which they have lavished the riches of their fancies and of their thoughts,—still these plays remain an inexhaustible mine of wealth. I hope I may offer—without incurring the charge of presumption — some portion of these treasures as an offset to the quantity of worthless currency which is debasing modern taste and morals in literature." (Dated *August* 18, 1868, Garlands, Hartford County, Maryland).[1] Aside from being listed in Steven Austin Allibone's *Dictionary of English Literature and British and American Authors* (1877) very little is known about Mary Preston, as Ann Thompson and Sasha Roberts point out in *Women Reading Shakespeare*.[2]

## *KING LEAR*

WE HEAR a *great deal of* the *ingratitude* of children; *very little* of the *injustice* of parents. 'Honor thy father and mother,' is of frequent quotation. 'Parents, provoke not your child to wrath,' is seldom mentioned . . . The world embraces and fondles in its false bosom many a father, upon whose unfilial treatment rests the faults of his miserable offspring. I am persuaded that many of the errors, nay, of the crimes of humanity, spring from neglect of paternal duties—from unjustifiable harshness at a father's hand . . .

---

1. The quotation is from "Preface," *Studies in Shakespeare: A Book of Essays*. Philadelphia: Claxton, Remsen, and Haffelfinger, 1869, n.pag. Preston's commentary on King Lear (also from *Studies in Shakespeare: A Book of Essays*) is reprinted in *Women Reading Shakespeare: 1660–1900*, eds. Ann Thompson and Sasha Roberts. Manchester, U.K.: Manchester UP, 1997, pp. 127–28. 2. Thompson and Roberts, p. 126.

It is then a proof of Shakspeare's correct reading of human nature, when he makes the play of King Lear teach a lesson to the unjust parent, as striking as to the ungrateful child . . . This play, then, has a twofold meaning, upon which parents might reflect with equal benefit with the children their Creator has given them, to shield, not to expose them to the storms of adversity. From many a homeless man, from many a heart-broken woman, from many a cheerless home, a mute appeal goeth up to Heaven, against parental injustice, parental cruelty. And if at the bar of the Just Judge there stands an accuser against his children, a white-haired old man, a King Lear, near him is seen the saintly angel of the meek, the lovely, the injured daughter, the Cordelia of domestic history. . . .

There have been tears over the white, discrowned Lear, driven from those homes his injustice had showered upon ungrateful daughters. But few seem to reflect upon the *greater wrong*, inflicted by a king, by a father, whose judgment experience might have ripened, whose passions time and reason should have cooled, turning from his door his youngest daughter, *friendless*, as far as he could deprive her of friends; exiling an old and faithful counsellor, also, because he remonstrated against such injustice to Cordelia. And what was her offence? She is punished because she 'most rightly said,' [1.1.183] as her courageous defender puts it. But King Lear's outrages on his youngest daughter do not even stop here. His ill-will seems to be nourished by his power to do Cordelia harm. His wounded vanity is doubly hurt, by reflecting that he cannot alter the judgment of his daughter, either by appeals to her self-interest, or threats of his anger. And this is all true to real life. Let a parent once take offence at his child's conduct,—without Charity drives out the vexing thoughts,—the consequences are the same as those traced in King Lear. Everything that malice or envy can invent to keep the flame of rage burning, is hearkened to by the father. He desires to justify his unkind feelings to his child, *to himself*, for he has a lurking suspicion that such feelings are not right. Therefore, he regards all those who befriend his child as attacking him; all those who let him see they do not approve of harsh measures to the offender, as being offenders themselves. All 'extenuating circumstances' are never to be mentioned in the unjust father's presence. They are an offence unto him. And there are people *base* enough to pander to such a parental state of mind.

[From *King Lear, Studies in Shakespeare: A Book of Essays*. Philadelphia: Claxton, Remsen, and Haffelfinger, 1869. Rpt. in *Women Reading Shakespeare: 1660-1900*, ed. Ann Thompson and Sasha Roberts. Manchester, U.K.: Manchester UP, 1997.]

# From "SALVINI'S KING LEAR" (1883)

## Emma Lazarus

A plaque adorning the Statue of Liberty in New York Harbor features Lazarus's sonnet, "The New Colossus" (1883), with its famous lines: "Give me your tired, your poor, / Your huddled masses yearning to breathe free . . . " The poet is Emma Lazarus (1849–1887), who lived in the Union Square neighborhood of New York City and was very proud of her Sephardic heritage and her immigrant family's descent from the first Jewish settlers in the United States. As a poet and essayist Lazarus became acquainted with Ralph Waldo Emerson, with whom she carried on a correspondence. She also corresponded with Russian novelist-playwright Ivan Turgenev and Emily Dickinson's first co-editor: author, clergyman, and Civil War officer Thomas Wentworth Higginson.

As one very much interested in father-daughter relationships, Lazarus was attracted to the characters of fathers and daughters in Shakespeare and to the portrayal of Lear by Italian actor Tommaso Salvini (1829–1915), whom Anglo-Saxon critics, she complains, unfairly assailed as being too Italian. Lazarus steps in to support Salvini and to argue for Shakespeare's comprehensive or universal soul and how enacting his great text should not be viewed myopically and hence evaluated on the basis of the particular national or ethnic origin of the actor or actress involved. Lazarus also defends Lear's paternal anger in the light of Cordelia's behavior early and late in the play.

SALVINI [a leading Italian tragedian] understands the *motif* of *Lear* to be, not the local peculiarities of a king of ancient Britain, but the passion of fatherhood. 'Is not a father in Italy the same as a father in Britain?' are his own words upon the subject, and they clearly illustrate his conception. For him the whole tragedy rests upon the fact that the royal martyrdom is *undeserved;* the moment a thought is entertained that it was occasioned by the king's own lack of foresight or justice, its sublime quality disappears. . . .

What wiser and more appropriate act than, while retaining the title and honors of royalty, to renounce its duties and cares, rendered irksome by the inevitable weariness of a ripe old age? His own nature is exuberantly and demonstratively affectionate, and in presence of his whole court he asks his daughters who among them loves him best, simply for the delight of hearing their filial, graceful replies. From *Regan* and *Goneril* he receives dutiful response; then, overflowing with paternal pride and love, he turns to his darling youngest child, the gentlest and meekest of the three, and receives a rebuff discourteous and irreverent enough to affront even a modern and non-royal father: 'I love you according to my bond, neither more nor less. I am not yet married, but the first stranger who appears and claims me as his wife will obtain from me a greater meed of affection than you can possibly expect' [a paraphrase of 1.1.91-93 ~ Evans Editor.] Whoever transports himself mentally into the period, place, and circumstances of this scene will not consider the wrath of *Lear* exaggerated. Only because of our own difficulty in laying aside the knowledge of Cordelia's true character, which the later portions of the play reveal, do we here sympathize with her, and condemn the perfectly justifiable indignation of the aggrieved parent and monarch.

*Lear*, as conceived by Salvini, is a man of noble generosity, of exquisite tenderness and sensitiveness, of powerful intellect and imagination. His robust physical force is beginning to wane, though still as a man of eighty he delights in the pleasures of the chase. But there is no trace of senility in the vigorous richly endowed mind. This conception is amply borne out by the text; for, if the insanity of *Lear* were occasioned by dotage and decrepitude, instead of by the stunning blows of unparalleled misfortunes, there could be no return of reason before his death. Yet, in the last two scenes, Shakspere represents him to be as lucid and sane as though his brain had never been clouded. By accumulating the black and subtle crimes of *Regan* and *Goneril*, the poet emphasizes for us the fact that *Lear* was not imbecile in misjudging them, but that he was dealing here with unnatural monsters such as no human foresight, much less the loving heart of a parent could have divined. . . .

After every new Shaksperean interpretation offered by Salvini, a chorus of critics promptly exclaim against its non-Shaksperean inspiration, its essentially *Italian* quality. If it could be urged as a fault against Salvini's *Othello* that it was 'not Anglican,' all the more emphatic is the dissatisfaction expressed with a so-called 'Italian *Lear*.' It is but a repetition of truisms to say that Shakspere's personages are human, universal, that they move in a world of passion, of dramatic and psychological complications over and above all distinctions of race, country, creed, and even sex. . . . Any actor, therefore, who brings out for us the profound human significance of his great characters, is the true interpreter of Shakspere, and such a one is Salvini. It has always seemed to us a curious fact that any who speak the tongue of Shakspere should wish to rob him of his chief claim to immortality. There are those who insist upon his being insular and local, rather than comprehensive and universal; who resent as an impertinence the very suggestion that his genius may speak as clearly and, as intimately to an Italian or a Frenchman as to an Anglo-Saxon. If it were not so—'the less Shakspere he,' as Browning puts it.[1] They might as well attempt to confine him to the limits of Stratford, and assert that outside of Warwickshire he could not be properly understood, as to restrict him to the English-speaking or Teutonic races.

[1. Emma Lazarus quotes from the last stanza of Robert Browning's "House" (1876), a poetic statement opposing autobiographical readings of Shakespeare's works. Like John Keats, Browning admired Shakespeare for his objective, distanced approach to literary composition, especially for his ability to negate his own selfhood in his plays. See the comments on Keats's concept of "Negative Capability" in the "History of Performance" and the General Editor's "Shakespeare's Life" for the Evans Shakespeare Edition as well as in the introductory remarks devoted to Keats's sonnet, "On Sitting Down to Read *King Lear* Once Again" (1818) in Critical Essays: Classic Essays in this Evans Edition.]

[From *Century Magazine*, 26: 10 (May 1883): 89-91. Rpt. in *Women Reading Shakespeare: 1660–1900*, ed. Ann Thompson and Sasha Roberts. Manchester, U.K.: Manchester UP, 1997.]

# NOTE-BOOK—AND THE PLAY
# [KING LEAR]

FROM *THE PHILOSOPHY OF THE PLAYS OF*
*SHAKSPEARE UNFOLDED. WITH A PREFACE BY*
*NATHANIEL HAWTHORNE* (1857)

Delia Bacon

Ill-fated in love, Delia Bacon (1811–1859) first experienced notoriety
not in matters pertaining to Shakespeare but of an unwanted kind when
she found herself at the center of a bitter ecclesiastical trial involving
a marital breach of promise. Her supporters were two luminaries of
Hartford, Connecticut: novelist Harriet Beecher Stowe (1811–1896)
and Harriet's sister, educator Catharine Beecher (1800–1878). After
enduring this fiasco, Delia went to Boston to seek New England
authors who might champion a cause with which she had become
obsessed—a controversial theory as to who wrote Shakespeare's plays.
Although she preferred to think so, she was not herself a descendant
of Sir Francis Bacon, who, according to Delia, was the author of the
plays usually linked with Shakespeare's name. Determined to continue
her quest to contest the Stratford man's authorship of the plays, Delia
Bacon managed to go to England to seek the aid of luminaries there.
She visited novelist Nathaniel Hawthorne, then the U.S. Consul to
Liverpool. Although he was sympathetic, he did not anticipate at all
that he would be called upon to provide direct financial and editorial
assistance as well as rational support of her theory. In fact, there is no
evidence that Hawthorne ever read in its entirety her tortuous *Philo-*
*sophy of the Plays of Shakspere Unfolded* with its many sections of turgid
prose, as exemplified by the reading that follows.

THE FACT that the design of this play [*King Lear*], whatever it
may be, is one deep enough to go down to that place in the
social system which Tom o'Bedlam was then peacefully oc-
cupying,—thinking of anything else in the world but a social revolution on his behalf—to bring him up for observation; and that

313

it is high enough to go up to that apex of the social structure on which the crown was then fastened, to fetch down the impersonated state itself, for an examination not less curious and critical; the fact too, that it was subtle enough to penetrate the retirement of the domestic life, and bring out its innermost passages for scientific criticism;—the fact that the relation of the Parent to the Child, and that of the Child to the Parent, the relation of Husband and Wife, and Sister and Brother, and Master and Servant, of Peasant and Lord, nay, the transient relation of Guest and Host, have each their place and part here, and the question of their duty marked not less clearly, than that prominent relation of the King and his Subjects;—the fact that these relations come in from the first, along with the political, and demand a hearing, and divide throughout the stage with them; the fact of the mere range of this social criticism, as it appears on the surface of the play, in these so prominent points,—is enough to show already, that it is a *Radical* of no ordinary kind, who is at work behind this drop-scene. . . .

But notwithstanding that the subject of this piece appears to be so general . . . it is not very difficult to perceive that it does, in fact, involve a local exhibition of a different kind; and that, under the cover of that great revolution in the human estate . . . another revolution,—that revolution which was then so near at hand, was clearly outlined, . . . one towards which this Poet appears to '*incline*' in a manner which would not have seemed, perhaps, altogether consistent with his position and assumptions elsewhere, if these could have been produced against him. . . . This Play was evidently written at a time when the conviction that the state of things which it represents could not endure much longer, had taken deep hold of the Poet's mind; at a time when those evils had attained a height so unendurable,—when that evil which lay at the heart of the commonweal, so fearful, that it might well seem, even to the scientific mind, to require the fierce '*drug*' of the political revolution,—so fearful as to make, even to such a mind, the rude surgery of the civil wars at last welcome.

For, indeed, it cannot be denied that the state of things which this Play represents, is that with which the author's own experience was conversant; and that all the terrible tragic satire of it, points—not to that age in the history of Britain in which the Druids were still responsible for the national culture. . . . Down to its most revolting, most atrocious detail, it is still the Elizabethan civility that is painted here . . . we all know what a king's favourite felt himself competent to undertake then; and, if the clearest intimations of such men as Bacon . . . and Raleigh, on such a question, are of any worth, the household of James the First was not without a parallel even for that performance, if not when this play was written, when it was published.

It is all one picture of social ignorance, and misery, and *frantic* misrule. It is a faithful exhibition of the degree of personal security which a man of honourable sentiments, and humane and noble intentions, could promise himself in such a time. It shows what chance there was of any man being permitted to sustain an honourable and intelligent part in the world, in an age in which all the radical social arts were yet wanting, in which the rude institutions of an ignorant past spontaneously built up, without any science of the natural laws, were vainly seeking to curb and quench the Incarnate soul of new ages,—the spirit of a scientific human advancement; and, when all the common welfare was still openly intrusted to the unchecked caprice and passion of one selfish, pitiful, narrow, low-minded man.

[From *The Philosophy of the Plays of Shakespeare Unfolded*. With a Preface by Nathaniel Hawthorne. London: Groombridge and Sons, 1857. Rpt. in *Women Reading Shakespeare: 1660–1900*, ed. Ann Thompson and Sasha Roberts. Manchester, U.K.: Manchester UP, 1997.]

# From *Shakespearean Tragedy*

## LECTURE VIII: *King Lear* (1904)

### A. C. Bradley

Educated at Balliol College, Oxford, A. C. [Andrew Cecil] Bradley (1851–1935) earned two doctorates, an LL.D. and a Litt.D. In time he became Professor of Poetry at Oxford University. A. C. Bradley's published works, *Shakespearean Tragedy* (1904) and *Oxford Lectures on Poetry* (1909), were based on his university lectures. He has been thought of as a paternal figure among students of Shakespeare, young and old alike, for his careful guidance through literary works. For many years, he represented a learned, authoritative, and forthright approach, but in recent decades, poststructuralist criticism has relegated Bradley to the old-fashioned school of nineteenth-century character-criticism. He is now thought of as one who too much looked upon Shakespeare's characters as real people.

Katharine Cooke, in *A. C. Bradley and His Influence in Twentieth-Century Shakespeare Criticism* (191–2) quotes (as others have done over the years) a set of witty rhymed couplets that sum up the place of Bradley among Shakespeareans, young and old.

> I dreamt last night that Shakespeare's Ghost
> Sat for a civil service post.
> The English paper for that year
> Had several questions on *King Lear*
> Which Shakespeare answered very badly
> Because he hadn't read his Bradley.

I

WHEN THE conclusion arrives, the old King has for a long while been passive. We have long regarded him not only as 'a man more sinned against than sinning', [3.2.59-60] but almost wholly as a sufferer, hardly at all as an agent. His sufferings too have been so cruel, and our indignation against those who inflicted them has been so intense, that recollection of the wrong he did to Cordelia, to Kent, and to his realm, has been well-nigh effaced. Lastly, for nearly four Acts he has inspired in us, together with this pity, much admiration and affection. The force of his passion has made us feel that his nature was great; and his frankness and generosity, his heroic effects to be patient, the depth of his shame and repentance, and the ecstasy of his re-union with Cordelia, have melted our very hearts. Naturally, therefore, at the close we are in some danger of forgetting that the storm which has overwhelmed him was liberated by his own deed.

Yet it is essential that Lear's contribution to the action of the drama should be remembered; not at all in order that we may feel that he 'deserved' what he suffered, but because otherwise his fate would appear to us at best pathetic, at worst shocking, but certainly not tragic. And when we were reading the earlier scenes of the play we recognized this contribution clearly enough. At the very beginning, it is true, we are inclined to feel merely pity and misgivings. The first lines tell us that Lear's mind is beginning to fail with age. Formerly he had perceived how different were the characters of Albany and Cornwall, but now he seems either to have lost this perception or to be unwisely ignoring it. The rashness of his division of the kingdom troubles us, and we cannot but see with concern that its motive is mainly selfish. The absurdity of the pretence of making the division depend on protestations of love from his daughters, his complete blindness to the hypocrisy which is patent to us at a glance, his piteous delight in these protestations, the openness of his expressions of preference for his youngest daughter—all make us smile, but all pain us. But pity begins to give way to another feeling when we witness the precipitance, the despotism, the uncontrolled anger of his injustice to Cordelia and Kent, and the 'hideous rashness' of his persistence in dividing the kingdom after the rejection of his one dutiful child. . . .

The old King who in pleading with his daughters feels so intensely his own humiliation and their horrible ingratitude, and who yet, at fourscore and upward, constrains himself to practise a self-control and patience so many years disused; who out of old affection for his Fool, and in repentance for his injustice to the Fool's beloved mistress, tolerates incessant and cutting reminders of his own folly and wrong; in whom the rage of the storm awakes a power and a poetic grandeur surpassing even that of Othello's anguish; who comes in his affliction to think of others first, and to seek, in tender solicitude for his poor boy, the shelter he scorns for his own bare head; who learns to feel and to pray for the miserable and houseless poor, to discern the falseness of flattery and the brutality of authority, and to pierce below the differences of rank and raiment to the common humanity beneath; whose sight is so purged by scalding tears that it sees at last how power and place and all things in the world are vanity except love; who tastes in his last hours the extremes both of love's rapture and of its agony, but could never, if he lived on or lived again, care a jot for aught beside— there is no figure, surely, in the world of poetry at once so grand, so pathetic, and so beautiful as his. Well, but Lear owes the whole of this to those sufferings which made us doubt whether life were not simply evil, and men like the flies which wanton boys torture for their sport. Should we not be at least as near the truth if we called this poem *The Redemption of King Lear*, and declared that the business of 'the gods' with him was neither to torment him, nor to teach him a 'noble anger', but to lead him to attain through apparently hopeless failure the very end and aim of life?

. . .Why does Cordelia die? I suppose no reader ever failed to ask that question, and to ask it with something more than pain,—to ask it, if only for a moment, in bewilderment or dismay, and even perhaps in tones of protest. These feelings are probably evoked more strongly here than at the death of any other notable character in Shakespeare; and it may sound a wilful paradox to assert that the slightest element of reconciliation is mingled with them or succeeds them. Yet it seems to me indubitable that such an element is present, though difficult to make out with certainty what it is or whence it proceeds. And I will try to make this out, and to state it methodically.

(*a*) It is not due in any perceptible degree to the fact, which we have just been examining, that Cordelia through her tragic imper- fection contributes something to the conflict and catastrophe; and I drew attention to that imperfection without any view to our present problem. The critics who emphasize it at this point in the drama are surely untrue to Shakespeare's mind; and still more completely astray are those who lay stress on the idea that Cordelia in bringing a foreign army to help her father was guilty of treason to her country. When she dies we regard her, practically speaking, simply as we regard Ophelia or Desdemona, as an innocent victim swept away in the convulsion caused by the error or guilt of others.

(*b*) Now this destruction of the good through the evil of others is one of the tragic facts of life, and no one can object to the use of it, within certain limits, in tragic art. And, further, those who because of it declaim against the nature of things, declaim without thinking. It is obviously the other side of the fact that the effects of good spread far and wide beyond the doer of good; and we should ask ourselves whether we really could wish (supposing it conceivable) to see this doubled-sided fact abolished. Nevertheless the touch of reconciliation that we feel in contemplating the death of Cordelia is not due, or is due only in some slight degree, to a perception that the event is true to life, admissible in tragedy, and a case of a law which we cannot seriously desire to see abrogated.

(c) What then is this feeling, and whence does it come? I believe that we shall find that it is a feeling not confined to *King Lear*, but present at the close of other tragedies; and that the reason why it has an exceptional tone or force at the close of *King Lear*, lies in that very peculiarity of the close which also—at least for the moment—excites bewilderment, dismay, or protest. The feeling I mean is the impression that the heroic being, though in one sense and outwardly he has failed, is yet in another sense superior to the world in which he appears; is, in some way which we do not seek to define, untouched by the doom that overtakes him; and is rather set free from life than deprived of it. Some such feeling as this—some feeling which, from this description of it, may be recognized as their own even by those who would dissent from the description—we surely have in various degrees at the deaths of Hamlet and Othello and Lear, and of Antony and Cleopatra and Coriolanus. It accompanies the more prominent tragic impressions, and, regarded alone, could hardly be called tragic. For it seems to imply (though we are probably quite unconscious of the implication) an idea which, if developed, would transform the tragic view of things. It implies that the tragic world, if taken as it is presented, with all its error, guilt, failure, woe and waste, is no final reality, but only a part of reality taken for the whole, and, when so taken, illusive; and that if we could see the whole, and the tragic facts in their true place in it, we should find them, not abolished, of course, but so transmuted that they had ceased to be strictly tragic,—find, perhaps, the suffering and death counting for little or nothing, the greatness of the soul for much or all, and the heroic spirit, in spite of failure, nearer to the heart of things than the smaller, more circumspect, and perhaps even 'better' beings who survived the catastrophe. The feeling which I have tried to describe, as accompanying the more obvious tragic emotions at the deaths of heroes, corresponds with some such idea as this.

Now this feeling is evoked with a quite exceptional strength by the death of Cordelia. It is not due to the perception that she, like Lear, has attained through suffering; we know that she had suffered and attained in his days of prosperity. It is simply the feeling that what happens to such a being does not matter: all that matters is what she is.

[From Lecture VIII of A. C. Bradley's *Shakespearean Tragedy*. 1904. Third Edition, ed. John Russell Brown. New York: St. Martin's Press, 1992.]

"Cordelia, Cordelia," *King Lear*, Act 5 Scene 3, illustration from Tales from Shakespeare by Charles and Mary Lamb, 1905 (color litho), Private Collection / The Stapleton Collection / The Bridgeman Art Library International Image ID: STC 30858

Fig. 13. "Cordelia, Cordelia," by Norman Mills Price. Although never having been linked to Bradley's commentary, Price's painting is an excellent visual evocation of A. C. Bradley's question, "Why does Cordelia die?" Every reader of *King Lear* is likely to voice a similar, if not identical, question. A year after the publication in 1904 of Bradley's *Lear* lecture, Price's painting appeared as an illustration in a 1905 edition of *Lamb's Tales*, a work that had been addressed to children ever since its original publication in 1807. Charles and Mary Lamb present neither the specific details of Cordelia's death nor the scene of intense mourning depicted in Price's painting. They wished rather to stress for their youthful audience the moral of Cordelia's plight—namely that innocence and piety are not always successful in this world. See the section on Charles Lamb earlier in the "Classic Critical Essays" in this Evans Edition.

*Footnotes in the reprinted excerpted material are from the original publication. Footnote numerals, therefore, will correspond to those at the bottom of the essay, but expect numerical gaps since sections not excerpted contain the lines and numbers not included here. Notes within square brackets are by Evans Editor, V. F. Petronella*

# From "KING LEAR AND THE COMEDY OF THE GROTESQUE" (1930)

## G. Wilson Knight

THE HEART of a Shakespearian tragedy is centred in the imaginative, in the unknown; and in *King Lear,* where we touch the unknown, we touch the fantastic. The peculiar dualism at the root of this play which wrenches and splits the mind by a sight of incongruities displays in turn realities absurd, hideous, pitiful. This incongruity is Lear's madness; it is also the demonic laughter that echoes in the *Lear* universe. In pure tragedy the dualism of experience is continually being dissolved in the masterful beauty of passion, merged in the sunset of emotion. But in comedy it is not so softly resolved—incompatibilities stand out till the sudden relief of laughter or its equivalent of humour: therefore incongruity is the especial mark of comedy. Now in *King Lear* there is a dualism continually crying in vain to be resolved either by tragedy or comedy. Thence arises its peculiar tension of pain: and the course of the action often comes as near to the resolution of comedy as to that of tragedy. So I shall notice here the imaginative core of the play, and, excluding much of the logic of the plot from immediate attention, analyse the fantastic comedy of *King Lear.*

From the start, the situation has a comic aspect. It has been observed that Lear has, so to speak, staged an interlude, with himself as chief actor, in which he grasps expressions of love to his heart, and resigns his sceptre to a chorus of acclamations. It is childish, foolish—but very human. So, too, is the result. Sincerity forbids play-acting, and Cordelia cannot subdue her instinct to any judgement advising tact rather than truth. The incident is profoundly comic and profoundly pathetic. It is, indeed, curious that so storm-furious a play as *King Lear* should have so trivial a domestic basis: it is the first of our many incongruities to be noticed. The absurdity of the old King's anger is clearly indicated by Kent:

Kill thy physician, and the fee bestow
Upon the foul disease.

(1.1.161–162)

[The quoted Shakespearean lines in Knight's essay are not from *The Riverside Shakespeare* but from an edition Knight chose for his discussion. ~ *Evans Editor*]

The result is absurd. Lear's loving daughter Cordelia is struck from his heart's register, and he is shortly, old and grey-haired and a king, cutting a cruelly ridiculous figure before the cold sanity of his unloving elder daughters. Lear is selfish, self-centred. The images he creates of his three daughters' love are quite false, sentimentalized: he understands the nature of none of his children, and demanding an unreal and impossible love from all three, is disillusioned by each in turn. But, though sentimental, this love is not Weak. It is powerful and firm-planted in his mind as a mountain rock embedded in earth. The tearing out of it is hideous, cataclysmic. A tremendous soul is, as it were, incongruously geared to a puerile intellect. Lear's senses prove his idealized love-figments false, his intellect snaps, and, as the loosened drive flings limp, the disconnected engine of madness spins free, and the ungeared revolutions of it are terrible, fantastic. This, then, is the basis of the play: greatness linked to puerility. Lear's instincts are themselves grand, heroic—noble even. His judgement is nothing. He understands neither himself nor his daughters:

REGAN 'Tis the infirmity of his age: yet he hath ever but slenderly known himself.

GONERIL The best and soundest of his time hath been but rash . . .

(1.1.288–290)

Lear starts his own tragedy by a foolish misjudgement. Lear's fault is a fault of the mind, a mind unwarrantably, because selfishly, foolish. And he knows it:

O Lear, Lear, Lear!
Beat at this gate that let thy folly in,
And thy dear judgement out!

(1.4.254–256)

His purgatory is to be a purgatory of the mind, of madness. Lear has trained himself to think he cannot be wrong: he finds he is wrong. He has fed his heart on sentimental knowledge of his children's love: he finds their love is not sentimental. There is now a gaping dualism in his mind, thus drawn asunder by incongruities, and he endures madness. Thus the theme of the play is bodied continually into a fantastic incongruity, which is implicit in the beginning—in the very act of Lear's renunciation, retaining the 'title and addition' of King, yet giving over a king's authority to his children. As he becomes torturingly aware of the truth, incongruity masters his mind, and fantastic madness ensues; and this peculiar fact of the Lear-theme is reflected in the *Lear* universe:

> GLOUCESTER These late eclipses in the sun and the moon portend
> no good to us: though the wisdom of nature can reason it
> thus and thus, yet nature finds itself scourged by the sequent
> effects: love cools, friendship falls off, brothers divide: in
> cities, mutinies; in countries, disorder; in palaces, treason;
> and the bond cracked 'twixt son and father. This villain of
> mine comes under the prediction; there's son against father:
> the King falls from bias of nature; there's father against
> child. We have seen the best of our time: machinations,
> hollowness, treachery, and all ruinous disorders, follow us
> disquietly to our graves.
>
> (1.2.98–108)

Gloucester's words hint a universal incongruity here: the fantastic incongruity of parent and child opposed. And it will be most helpful later to notice the Gloucester-theme in relation to that of Lear.

From the first signs of Goneril's cruelty, the Fool is used as a chorus, pointing us to the absurdity of the situation. He is indeed an admirable chorus, increasing our pain by his emphasis on a humour which yet will not serve to merge the incompatible in a unity of laughter. He is not all wrong when he treats the situation as matter for a joke. Much here that is always regarded as essentially pathetic is not far from comedy. For instance, consider Lear's words:

> I will have such revenges on you both
> That all the world shall—I will do such things—
> What they are, yet I know not; but they shall be
> The terrors of the earth.
>
> (2.4.275–278)

What could be more painfully incongruous, spoken, as it is, by an old man, a king, to his daughter? It is not far from the ridiculous. The very thought seems a sacrilegious cruelty, I know: but ridicule is generally cruel. The speeches of Lear often come near comedy. Again, notice the abrupt contrast in his words:

> But yet thou art my flesh, my blood, my daughter;
> Or rather a disease that's in my flesh,
> Which I must needs call mine: thou art a boil,

A plague-sore, an embossed carbuncle,
In my corrupted blood. But I'll not chide thee. . .
(2.4.217–221)

This is not comedy, nor humour. But it is exactly the stuff of which
humour is made. Lear is mentally a child; in passion a titan. The
absurdity of his every act at the beginning of his tragedy is contrasted
with the dynamic fury which intermittently bursts out, flickers—then
flames and finally gives us those grand apostrophes lifted from man's
stage of earth to heaven's rain and fire and thunder:

Blow, winds, and crack your cheeks! rage! blow!
You cataracts and hurricanoes, spout
Till you have drench'd our steeples, drown'd the cocks!
(3.2.1–3)

Two speeches of this passionate and unrestrained volume of Promethean curses are followed by:

No, I will be the pattern of all patience;
I will say nothing.
(3.2.36–37)

Again we are in touch with potential comedy: a slight shift of
perspective, and the incident is rich with humour. A sense of self-
directed humour would, indeed, have saved Lear. It is a quality he
absolutely lacks.

Herein lies the profound insight of the Fool: he sees the potentiali-
ties of comedy in Lear's behaviour. This old man, recently a king, and,
if his speeches are fair samples, more than a little of a tyrant, now goes
from daughter to daughter, furious because Goneril dares criticize his
pet knights, kneeling down before Regan, performing, as she says, 'unsightly tricks' (2.4.152)—the situation is excruciatingly painful, and its
painfulness is exactly of that quality which embarrasses in some forms
of comedy. In the theatre, one is terrified lest some one laugh: yet,
if Lear could laugh—if the Lears of the world could laugh at themselves—there would be no such tragedy. In the early scenes old age and
dignity suffer, and seem to deserve, the punishments of childhood:

Now, by my life,
Old fools are babes again; and must be used
With checks as flatteries.
(1.3.18–20)

The situation is summed up by the Fool:

LEAR When were you wont to be so full of songs, sirrah?

FOOL I have used it, nuncle, ever since thou madest thy daughters
thy mother: for when thou gavest them the rod, and put'st down
thine own breeches ....

(1.4.155–158)

The height of indecency in suggestion, the height of incongruity. Lear
is spiritually put to the ludicrous shame endured bodily by Kent in the
stocks: and the absurd rant of Kent, and the unreasonable childish temper
of Lear, both merit in some measure what they receive. Painful as it may
sound, that is, provisionally, a truth we should realize. The Fool realizes it.
He is, too, necessary. Here, where the plot turns on the diverging tugs of
two assurances in the mind, it is natural that the action be accompanied
by some symbol of humour, that mode which is built of unresolved
incompatibilities. Lear's torment is a torment of this dualistic kind, since
he scarcely believes his senses when his daughters resist him. ...

The tragedy is most poignant in that it is purposeless, unreasonable.
It is the most fearless artistic facing of the ultimate cruelty of things in
our literature. That cruelty would be less were there not this element
of comedy which I have emphasized, the insistent incongruities, which
create and accompany the madness of Lear, which leap to vivid shape in
the mockery of Gloucester's suicide, which are intrinsic in the texture
of the whole play. Mankind is, as it were, deliberately and comically
tormented by 'the gods'. He is not even allowed to die tragically. Lear is
'bound upon a wheel of fire' and only death will end the victim's agony:

Vex not his ghost: O, let him pass! he hates him
That would upon the rack of this tough world
Stretch him out longer.

(5.3.313–315)

*King Lear* is supreme in that, in this main theme, it faces the very
absence of tragic purpose; wherein it is profoundly different from
*Timon of Athens*. Yet, as we close the sheets of this play, there is no
horror, nor resentment. The tragic purification of the essentially
untragic is yet complete.

Now in this essay it will, perhaps, appear that I have unduly
emphasized one single element of the play, magnifying it, and leaving
the whole distorted. It has been my purpose to emphasize. I have not
exaggerated. The pathos has not been minimized: it is redoubled. Nor
does the use of the words 'comic' and 'humour' here imply disrespect
to the poet's purpose: rather I have used these words, crudely no doubt,
to cut out for analysis the very heart of the play—the thing that man
dares scarcely face: the demonic grin of the incongruous and absurd
in the most pitiful of human struggles with an iron fate. It is this that
wrenches, splits, gashes the mind till it utters the whirling vapourings of

lunacy. And, though love and music—twin sisters of salvation—temporarily may heal the racked consciousness of Lear, yet, so deeply planted in the facts of our life is this unknowing ridicule of destiny, that the uttermost tragedy of the incongruous ensues, and there is no hope save in the broken heart and limp body of death. This is of all the most agonizing of tragedies to endure: and if we are to feel more than a fraction of this agony, we must have sense of this quality of grimmest humour. We must beware of sentimentalizing the cosmic mockery of the play.

And is there, perhaps, even a deeper, and less heart-searing, significance in its humour? Smiles and tears are indeed most curiously interwoven here. Gloucester was saved from his violent and tragic suicide that he might recover his wronged son's love, and that his heart might

'Twixt two extremes of passion, joy and grief,
Burst smilingly.

(5.3.198–199)

Lear dies with the words

Do you see this? Look on her, look, her lips,
Look there, look there!

(5.3.310–311)

What smiling destiny is this he sees at the last instant of racked mortality? Why have we that strangely beautiful account of Cordelia's first hearing of her father's pain:

. . . patience and sorrow strove
Who should express her goodliest. You have seen
Sunshine and rain at once: her smiles and tears
Were like a better way: those happy smilets,
That play'd on her ripe lip, seem'd not to know
What guests were in her eyes; which parted thence,
As pearls from diamonds dropp'd. In brief,
Sorrow would be a rarity most beloved,
If all could so become it.

(4.3.15–23)

What do we touch in these passages? Sometimes we know that all human pain holds beauty, that no tear falls but it dews some flower we cannot see. Perhaps humour, too, is inwoven in the universal pain, and the enigmatic silence holds not only an unutterable sympathy, but also the ripples of an impossible laughter whose flight is not for the wing of human understanding; and perhaps it is this that casts its darting shadow of the grotesque across the furrowed pages of *King Lear*.

[From Knight's *The Wheel of Fire*. London: Methuen, 1930.] Used by permission of Taylor & Francis Group.

# From *KING LEAR IN OUR TIME* (1965)

Maynard Mack

OUBTLESS ONE cause of the play's strong appeal today is that its "tragic-heroic" content, like that of most contemporary plays, is ambiguous and impure. This is not simply to refer to its well-known vein of grotesqueries, or those events and speeches which have the character of poignant farce and even of inspired music-hall fooling, like the Fool's mouthings, Edgar's gyrations, Gloucester's leap. The play does blur the ordinary tragic-heroic norms. Consider the death of the protagonist, for instance. This is usually in Shakespeare climactic and distinctive, has sacrificial implications, dresses itself in ritual, springs from what we know to be a Renaissance mystique of stoical self-dominion. How differently death comes to Lear! Not in a moment of self-scrutiny that stirs us to awe or exaltation or regret at waste, but as a blessing at which we must rejoice with Kent, hardly more than a needful afterthought to the death that counts dramatically, Cordelia's. To die with no salute to death, with the whole consciousness launched toward another; to die following a life-experience in which what we have been shown to admire is far more the capacity to endure than to perform: this is unique in Shakespeare, and sits more easily with our present sensibility (which is pathologically mistrustful of heroism) than the heroic resonances of the usual Shakespearean close.

The miscellaneousness and very casualness of death in *King Lear* is perhaps also something to which the generations that have known Hiroshima are attuned. In the other tragedies, as a student of mine has noticed in an interesting unpublished paper, there is always a hovering suggestion that death is noble, that the great or good, having done the deed or followed the destiny that was in them to do or follow, go out in a blaze of light. So Romeo and Juliet seem to go. So Cleopatra goes, turning to air and fire to meet Mark Antony. Hamlet goes in a glimpse of some felicity, Othello in a recollection of a deed of derring-do and justice, even Macbeth in a kind of negative glory like the transcendent criminal he has become. But *King Lear* repudiates this.

> The dramatic emphasis is on the generality of death; death is not noble or distinctive; nearly every character dies and for nearly every sort of reason. The reiterated fact of the multiple deaths is processional

in quality. It is like an enormous summarial obituary. The Fool disappears of causes mysterious; Oswald, tailor-made servant, is killed by Edgar; Goneril and Regan are poisoned and dagger-slain; Gloucester dies offstage of weariness, conflicting emotion, and a broken heart; Kent is about to die of grief and service; Edmund is killed by his brother in a duel; Cordelia dies (by a kind of mistake— "Great thing of us forgot!") at a hangman's hands; and King Lear dies of grief and deluded joy and fierce exhaustion. . . . Death is neither punishment nor reward: it is simply in the nature of things.[1]

To this we may add, I think, a third factor that brings *King Lear* close to our business and bosoms today. As we saw in the preceding chapter, intimations of World's End run through it like a yeast. In the scenes on the heath, the elements are at war as if it were indeed Armageddon. When Lear awakes with Cordelia at his side, he imagines that already apocalypse is past, she is a soul in bliss, he bound upon a wheel of fire. Appearing in the last act with Cordelia dead in his arms, he wonders that those around him do not crack "heaven's vault" with their grief, and they wonder in turn if the *pietà* they behold is "the promis'd end" or "image of that horror." These are but some of the overt allusions. Under them everywhere run tides of doomsday passion that seem to use up and wear away people, codes, expectations, all stable points of reference, till only a profound sense remains that an epoch, in fact a whole dispensation, has forever closed.

> The oldest hath borne most: we that are young
> Shall never see so much, nor live so long.

To this kind of situation, we of the mid-twentieth century are likewise sensitively attuned. I shall quote from another student, partly because the comment is eloquent, but chiefly because I think it is significant that everywhere in the fifties and sixties the young are responding to *King Lear* as never before in my experience. "Every great critic," this student writes,

> from Johnson on . . . at some time or other begins to think of the sea. The most moving example of this common image, perhaps, is Hazlitt's: he speaks of the passion of King Lear as resembling an ocean, "swelling, chafing, raging, without bound, without hope, without beacon, or anchor," and of how on that sea Lear "floats, a mighty wreck in the wide world of sorrows." . . . The sea plays no direct part in the action. But the smell of it and the sound of it are omnipresent. The sea licks up at Dover relentlessly, its "murmuring surge" is endless and inescapable and everywhere — an archetype not of an individual drowning, but of the flooding of the world. *King*

*Lear* is alive again: it is our myth, our dream, as we stand naked and unaccommodated, listening to the water rise up against our foothold on the cliff of chalk.[2]

This statement is incomplete. It leaves out of account the strong undertow of victory in the play which carves on those same chalk walls Lear's "new acquist" of self-knowledge and devotion o Cordelia, the majesty of his integrity and endurance, the invincibleness of his hope. These give to an audiences's applause at the close of a great performance a quality of exaltation. The statement is incomplete; but what it includes and what it leaves out both make clear why *King Lear* above all others is the Shakespearean tragedy for our time.

·        ·        ·

I turn now to a closer scrutiny of the play. In the remarks that follow I shall address myself primarily to three topics, which I believe to be both interesting in themselves and well suited to bring before us other qualities of this tragedy which stir the twentieth-century imagination. The first topic is the externality of Shakespeare's treatment of action in *King Lear*; the second is the profoundly social orientation of the world in which he has placed this action; and the third is what I take to be the play's dominant tragic theme, summed up best in Lear's words to Gloucester in Dover fields: "We came crying hither."

As we watch it in the theatre, the action of *King Lear* comes to us first of all as an experience of violence and pain. No other Shakespearean tragedy, not even *Titus*, contains more levels of raw ferocity, physical as well as moral. In the action, the exquisite cruelties of Goneril and Regan to their father are capped by Gloucester's blinding onstage, and this in turn by the wanton indignity of Cordelia's murder. In the language, as Miss Caroline Spurgeon has pointed out, allusions to violence multiply and accumulate into a pervasive image as of "a human body in anguished movement—tugged, wrenched, beaten, pierced, stung, scourged, dislocated, flayed, gashed, scalded, tortured, and finally broken on the rack." [*Shakespeare's Imagery and What It Tells Us* (Cambridge, UK: Cambridge UP, 1935, p. 342)]

. . . It goes without saying that in a world of such contentiousness most of the *dramatis personae* will be outrageously self-assured. The contrast with the situation in *Hamlet*, in this respect, is striking and instructive. There . . . the prevailing mood tends to be interrogative. Doubt is real in *Hamlet*, and omnipresent. Minds, even villainous minds, are inquiet and uncertain. Action does not come readily to anyone except Laertes and Fortinbras, who are themselves easily deflected by the stratagems of the king, and there is accordingly much emphasis on the fragility of the human will. All this is changed in *King Lear*. Its mood, I would suggest (if it may be caught in a single word at all), is imperative. The play asks questions, to be sure, as *Hamlet* does, and far more painful questions because they are so like a child's, so simple and unmediated by the compromises to which much experience usually impels us: "Is man no more than this?" "Is there any cause in nature that makes these hard hearts?" "Why should a dog, a horse, a rat have life And thou no breath at all?" Such questionings in *King Lear* stick deep, like Macbeth's fears in Banquo.

Yet it is not, I think, the play's questions that establish its distinctive coloring onstage. (Some of its questions we shall return to later.) It is rather its commands, its invocations and appeals that have the quality of commands, its flat-footed defiances and refusals: "Come not between the dragon and his wrath." "You nimble lightnings, dart your blinding flames into her scornful eyes!" "Blow, winds, and crack your cheeks! rage! blow!" "Thou shalt not die; die for adultery, no!" "A plague upon you, murderers, traitors, all! I might have sav'd her . . ." In the psychological climate that forms round a protagonist like this, there is little room for doubt, as we may see from both Lear's and Goneril's scorn of Albany. No villain's mind is inquiet. Action comes as naturally as breathing and twice as quick. And, what is particularly unlike the situation in the earlier tragedies, the hero's destiny is self-made. Lear does not inherit his predicament like Hamlet; he is not duped by an antagonist like Othello. He walks into disaster head on. . . .

. . . Movements of the will, then, have a featured place in *King Lear*. But what is more characteristic of the play than their number is the fact that no one of them is ever exhibited to us in its inward origins or evolution. Instead of scenes recording the genesis or gestation of an action—scenes of introspection or persuasion or temptation like those which occupy the heart of the drama in *Hamlet*, *Othello*, and *Macbeth*—*King Lear* offers us the moment at which will converts into its outward expressions of action and consequence; and this fact, I suspect, helps account for the special kind of painfulness that the play always communicates to its audiences. In *King Lear* we are not permitted to experience violence as an externalization of a psychological drama which has priority in both time and significance, and which therefore partly palliates the violence when it comes.

. . . The violences in *King Lear* are thrust upon us quite otherwise — with the shock that comes from evil which has nowhere been inwardly accounted for, and which, from what looks like a studiedly uninward point of view on the playwright's part, must remain unaccountable, to characters and audience alike: "Is there any cause in nature that makes these hard hearts?"

. . . *King Lear,* as I see it, confronts the perplexity and mystery of human action at a later point. Choice remains in the forefront of the argument, but its psychic antecedents have been so effectively shrunk down in this primitivized world that action seems to spring directly out of the bedrock of personality. We feel sure no imaginable psychological process could make Kent other than loyal, Goneril other than cruel, Edgar other than "a brother noble." Such characters, as we saw earlier, are qualities as well as persons: their acts have consequences but little history. The meaning of action here, therefore, appears to lie rather in effects than in antecedents, and particularly in its capacity, as with Lear's in the opening scene, to generate energies that will hurl themselves in unforeseen and unforeseeable reverberations of disorder from end to end of the world.

1. From a paper by Evelyn G. Hooven of the Yale Graduate School in English.
2. From a paper by Leslie Epstein, formerly of the Yale School of Drama.

[From Mack, Maynard. *King Lear in Our Time.* Berkeley: U of California P, 1965]
Used by permission of the author

# From "The Patriarchal Bard: Feminist Criticism and Shakespeare" (1994)

### Kathleen McLuskie

I N ORDER to assert the moral connection between the mimetic world of Shakespeare's plays and the real world of the audience, the characters have to be seen as representative men and women and the categories male and female are essential, unchanging, definable in modern, commonsense terms.

The essentialism of this form of feminism is further developed in Marilyn French's *Shakespeare's Division of Experience*. Like [Linda Bamber, whose essay, "The Woman Reader in *King Lear*," follows the present one in this Evans Edition] she constructs a godlike author who 'breathed life into his female characters and gave body to the principles they are supposed to represent'.[15] Although shored up by references to feminist philosophy and anthropology, this feminine principle amounts to little more than the power to nurture and give birth and is opposed to a masculine principle embodied in the ability to kill. These principles are not, however, located in specific men or women. When men are approved of they are seen as embracing feminine principles whereas women are denied access to the male and are denigrated when they aspire to male qualities. French suggests that Shakespeare divides experience into male (evil) and female (good) principles and his comedies and tragedies are interpreted as 'either a synthesis of the principles or an examination of the kinds of worlds that result when one or other principle is abused, neglected, devalued or exiled'.[16]

The essentialism which lies behind Marilyn French's and Linda Bamber's account of the men and women in Shakespeare is part of a trend in liberal feminism which sees the feminist struggle as concerned with reordering the values ascribed to men and women without fundamentally changing the material circumstances in which their relationships function. It presents feminism as a set of social attitudes, rather than as a project for fundamental social change. As such it can equally easily be applied to an analysis of Shakespeare's plays which situates them in the ideological currents of his own time. In *Shakespeare and the*

*Nature of Women*, for example, Juliet Dusinberre admires 'Shakespeare's concern . . . to dissolve artificial distinctions between the sexes'[17] and can claim that concern as feminist in both twentieth-century and seventeenth-century terms. She examines Shakespeare's women characters—and those of some of his contemporaries—in the light of Renaissance debates over women conducted in puritan handbooks and advice literature. Building on the Hallers' essay on 'The puritan art of love',[18] she notes the shift from misogyny associated with Catholic asceticism to puritan assertions of the importance of women in the godly household as partners in holy and companionate marriage. The main portion of the book is an elaboration of themes—Chastity, Equality, Gods and Devils—in both polemic and dramatic literature. The strength of her argument lies in its description of the literary shift from the discourses of love poetry and satire to those of drama. However her assertions about the feminism of Shakespeare and his contemporaries depend once again upon a mimetic model of the relationship between ideas and drama. Contemporary controversy about women is seen as a static body of ideas which can be used or rejected by dramatists whose primary concern is not with parallel fictions but simply to 'explore the real nature of women'. By focusing on the presentation of women in puritan advice literature, Dusinberre privileges one side of a contemporary debate, relegating expressions of misogyny to the fictional world of 'literary simplification' and arbitrarily asserting more progressive notions as the dramatists' true point of view.[19]

A more complex discussion of the case would acknowledge that the issues of sex, sexuality, sexual relations and sexual division were areas of conflict of which the contradictions of writing about women were only one manifestation alongside the complexity of legislation and other forms of social control of sex and the family. The debates in modern historiography on these questions indicate the difficulty of assigning monolithic economic or ideological models to the early modern family, while the work of regional historians has shown the importance of specific material conditions on both the ideology and practice of sexual relations.[20] Far from being an unproblematic concept, 'the nature of women' was under severe pressure from both ideological discourses and the real concomitants of inflation and demographic change.

The problem with the mimetic, essentialist model of feminist criticism is that it would require a more multi-faceted mirror than Shakespearean drama to reflect the full complexity of the nature of women in Shakespeare's time or our own. Moreover this model obscures the particular relationship between Shakespearean drama and its readers which feminist criticism implies. The demands of the academy insist that feminist critics reject 'a literary version of placard carrying',[21] but they cannot but reveal the extent to which their critical practice expresses new demands and a new focus of attention on the plays. Coppelia Kahn concedes that 'Today we are questioning the cultural definitions of sexual identity we have inherited. I believe Shakespeare questioned them too . . .'[22] and, rather more frankly, Linda Bamber explains: 'As a heterosexual feminist . . . I have found in Shakespeare what I want to imagine as a possibility in my own life'.[23] However, the alternative to this simple co-option of Shakespeare is not to assert some spurious notion of objectivity. Such a procedure usually implies a denigration of feminism[24] in favour of more conventional positions and draws the criticism back into the institutionalised competition over 'readings.'

A different procedure would involve theorising the relationship between feminism and the plays more explicitly, accepting that feminist criticism, like all criticism, is a reconstruction of the play's meaning and asserting the specificity of a feminist response. This procedure differs from claiming Shakespeare's views as feminist in refusing to construct an author behind the plays and paying attention instead to the narrative, poetic and theatrical strategies which construct the plays' meanings and position the audience to understand their event? from a particular point of view. For Shakespeare's plays are not primarily explorations of 'the real nature of women' or even 'the hidden feelings in the human heart.' They were the products of an entertainment industry which, as far as we know, had no women shareholders, actors, writers, or stage hands. His women characters were played by boys and, far from his plays being an expression of his idiosyncratic views, they all built on and adapted earlier stories.

The witty comic heroines, the powerful tragic figures, the opposition between realism and romance were the commonplaces of the literary tradition from which these tests emerged. Sex and sexual relations within them are, in the first analysis, sources of comedy, narrative resolution and *coups de théâtre*. These textual strategies limit the range of meaning which the text allows and circumscribe the position which a feminist reader may adopt *vis-à-vis* the treatment of gender relations and sexual politics within the plays. The feminist reader may resist the position which the text offers but resistance involves more than simple attitudinising.

.        .        .

In traditional criticism Shakespeare's plays are seldom regarded as the sum of their dramatic devices. The social location of the action, their visual dimension and the frequent claims they make for their own authenticity, invite an audience's engagement at a level beyond the plot. The audience is invited to make some connection between the events of the action and the form and pressure of their own world. In the case of sex and gender, the concern of feminists, a potential connection is presented between sexual relations as an aspect of narrative—who will marry whom and how?—and sexual relations as an aspect of social relations—how is power distributed between men and women and how are their sexual relations conducted? The process of interpretative criticism is to construct a social meaning for the play out of its narrative and dramatic realisation. However this is no straightforward procedure: the positions offered by the texts are often contradictory and meaning can be produced by adopting one of the positions offered, using theatrical production or critical procedures to close off others. The critic can use historical knowledge to speculate about the possible creation of meaning in the light of past institutions and ideologies but the gap between textual meaning and social meaning can never be completely filled for meaning is constructed every time the text is reproduced in the changing ideological dynamic between text and audience.

...[Any] dispassionate analysis of the mystification of real socio-sexual relations in *King Lear* is the antithesis of our response to the tragedy in the theatre where the tragic power of the play endorses its ideological position at every stage. One of the most important and effective shifts in the action is the transfer of our sympathy back to Lear in the middle of the action. The long sequence of Act 2, scene 4 dramatises the process of Lear's decline from the angry autocrat of Act 1 to the appealing figure of pathetic insanity. The psychological realism of the dramatic writing and the manipulation of the point of view, forges the bonds between Lear as a complex character and the sympathies of the audience.

The audience's sympathies are engaged by Lear's fury at the insult offered by Kent's imprisonment and by the pathos of Lear's belated attempt at self-control (2.4.101–4). His view of the action is further emotionally secured by his sarcastic enactment of the humility which his daughters recommend:

> Do you but mark how this becomes the house:
> Dear daughter, I confess that I am old.
> Age is unnecessary. On my knees I beg
> That you'll vouchsafe me raiment, bed and food.
>    (2.4. [153–56])

As Regan says, these are unsightly tricks. Their effect is to close off the dramatic scene by offering the only alternative to Lear's behaviour as we see it. The dramatic fact becomes the only fact and the audience is thus positioned to accept the tragic as inevitable, endorsing the terms of Lear's great poetic appeal:

O reason not the need! Our basest beggars
Are in the poorest things superfluous.
Allow not nature more than nature needs,
Man's life is cheap as beasts.
(2.4.[264-7]) [The Evans Shakespeare Edition uses the Folio reading:"beast's"]

The ideological power of Lear's speech lies in his invocation of nature to support his demands on his daughters; its dramatic power lies in its movement from argument to desperate assertion of his crumbling humanity as the abyss of madness approaches. However, once again, that humanity is seen in gendered terms as Lear appeals to the gods to

. . . touch me with noble anger,
And let not women's weapons, water drops
Stain my man's cheeks.                    (2.4.275–7)

The theatrical devices which secure Lear at the centre of the audience's emotional attention operate even more powerfully in the play's denouement.The figure of Cordelia is used as a channel for the response to her suffering father. Her part in establishing the terms of the conflict is over by Act 1; when she reappears it is as an emblem of dutiful pity. Before she appears on stage, she is described by a 'gentleman' whose speech reconstructs her as a static, almost inanimate daughter of sorrows. The poetic paradoxes of his speech construct Cordelia as one who resolves contradiction,which is her potential role in the narrative and her crucial function in the ideological coherence of the text:

. . . patience and sorrow strove
Who should express her goodliest.You have seen
Sunshine and rain at once: her smiles and tears
Were like a better way: those happy smilets
That played on her ripe lip seemed not to know
What guests were in her eyes, which parted thence
As pearls from diamonds dropped.          (4.3.15–23)

With Cordelia's reaction pre-empted by the gentleman, the scene where Lear and Cordelia meet substitutes the pleasure of pathos for suspense. The imagery gives Cordelia's forgiveness divine sanction, and the realism of Lear's struggle for sanity closes off any responses other than complete engagement with the characters' emotions.Yet in this encounter Cordelia denies the dynamic of the whole play. Lear fears that she cannot love him:

> ... for your sisters
> Have, as I do remember, done me wrong.
> You have some cause, they have not.      (4.7.73–5)

But Cordelia demurs with 'No cause, no cause'.

Shakespeare's treatment of this moment contrasts with that of the earlier chronicle play from which he took a number of details, including Lear kneeling and being raised. In the old play the scene is almost comic as Leir and Cordella kneel and rise in counterpoint to their arguments about who most deserves blame. The encounter is used to sum up the issues and the old play allows Cordella a much more active role in weighing her debt to Leir. In Shakespeare's text, however, the spectacle of suffering obliterates the past action so that audience with Cordelia will murmur 'No cause, no cause'. Rather than a resolution of the action, their reunion becomes an emblem of possible harmony, briefly glimpsed before the tragic debacle.

The deaths of Lear and Cordelia seem the more shocking for this moment of harmony but: their tragic impact is also a function of thwarting the narrative expectation of harmony restored which is established by the text's folk-tale structure.

... An important part of the feminist project is to insist that the alternative to the patriarchal family and heterosexual love is not chaos but the possibility of new forms of social organisation and affective relationships. However, feminists also recognise that our socialisation within the family and, perhaps more importantly, our psychological development as gendered subjects make these changes no simple matter. They involve deconstructing the sustaining comforts of love and the family as the only haven in a heartless world. Similarly a feminist critique of the dominant traditions in literature must recognise the sources of its power, not only in the institutions which reproduce them but also in the pleasures which they afford. But feminist criticism must also assert the power of resistance, subverting rather than co-opting the domination of the patriarchal Bard.

### NOTES

15. Marilyn French, *Shakespeare's Division of Experience* (London: Cape, 1982). [It is on p. 31 that French speaks of Shakespeare's breathing life into his female characters and giving body to the principles they represent. ~ *Evans Editor*]
16. *Ibid.*, p. 25.

17. Juliet Dusinberre, *Shakespeare and the Nature of Women* (London: Macmillan, 1975) P.153. Dusinberre's understanding of feminism has been challenged by Martha Anderson-Thom, 'Thinking about Women and their Prosperous Art: a Reply to Juliet Dusinberre's *Shakespeare and the Nature of Women*', *Shakespeare Studies*, II (1978), 259–76.

18. William Haller and Malleville Haller, 'The Puritan Art of 'Love', *Huntington Library Quarterly*, 5, (1942) 235–72. Cf. K. Davies, '"The sacred condition of equality": how original were Puritan doctrines of marriage?' *Social History*, 5 (1977), 566–7.

19. Juliet Dusinberre, *op. cit.*, p. 183.

20. Chapter 4, 'Husbands and Wives, Parents and Children' of Keith Wrightson, *English Society 1580–1680* (London: Hutchinson, 1982) provides a comprehensively informed discussion of the controversy. See also Lawrence Stone, *The Family, Sex and Marriage in England, 1500–1800* (London: Weidenfeld and Nicolson, 1977); G. R. Quaife, *Wanton Wenches and Wayward Wives: Peasants and Illicit Sex in Early Seventeenth Century England* (London: Croom Helm, 1969); Margaret Spufford, *Contrasting Communities: English Villagers in the Sixteenth and Seventeenth Centuries* (Cambridge University Press, 1974).

21. Lenz, Greene and Neely, *op. cit.* preface, p. ix.

22. Coppelia Kahn, *op. cit.*, p. 20.

23. Linda Bamber, *op. cit.*, p.43. [Citation refers to Bamber's *Comic Women, Tragic Men: Gender and Genre in Shakespeare*. Palo Alto, CA: Stanford University Press, 1982. ~ *Evans Editor*]

24. See for example Lisa Jardine's summary dismissal of feminist criticism in favour of historical criticism in *Still Harping on Daughters: Women and Drama in the Age of Shakespeare* (Brighton: Harvester, 1983), introduction, or Inga-Stina Ewbank reminding her audience at the bicentennial congress of the Shakespeare Association of America of Ibsen's distinction between 'feminism' and the truth about men and women: 'Shakespeare's Portrayal of Women: a 1970s View' in Bevington and Halio, eds. [*Shakespeare's Pattern of Excelling Nature* (Associated University Presses: Newark, 1978)], pp. 222–9.

[From *Political Shakespeare: Essays in Cultural Materialism*. 2nd edition, eds. Jonathan Dollimer and Alan Sinfield. Ithaca, New York: Cornell UP.] Reprinted by permission of Cornell University Press.

# From "The Woman Reader
in *King Lear*" (1986)

Linda Bamber

F OR WOMEN the problem of locating ourselves in literature is complicated by the fact that so much of the literature of the past is written by men. Who is "like me" when the character offered as a version of the self is a man? When I began to read the great literature of the past I never thought to ask this question. My (excellent) teachers were almost all men, and I read stories and poems and plays by men without noticing the difference. In the end you could say I imprinted to a different species. I thought I was a man, just as Tarzan thought he was an ape. Of course, I also knew I wasn't. But my responses to literature were confused by an identity problem generated for me by literature itself.

In *King Lear*, the character who is "like me" is of course King Lear. Lear is passionate, articulate, capable of growth, capable of catastrophic error, important to himself and to everyone else in the play. He claims he is "more sinned against than sinning," and that's how I feel, too. But King Lear is a man while I am a woman. When I identify with him, an important part of my identity, my femininity, is homeless. If the *King Lear* world is organized around a man, what is the status of women in it? Are women important in this world, or are they (fictionally) second-class citizens? If I can find satisfactory answers to these questions I am free to identify with Lear as much as I can; otherwise, identifying with Lear means denigrating a part of myself.

The best solution would be finding an alternative, female home in the play. Is there a woman character who represents us as well as Lear himself? If so, we could breathe a sigh of relief and simply graph the play as an ellipse (which has two focal points) instead of a circle. But authors—women as well as men—tend to represent "us" much more fully in characters of their own sex than in characters of the opposite sex, and Shakespeare is no exception. In *King Lear* the women are either more or less than human. Goneril and Regan are too bad to live, much less to represent us, and Cordelia is perfect. The evil sisters present no temptations to the woman reader, but it is worth dealing in some detail with the problems of identifying with perfection.

Cordelia is never selfish or aggressive; when she hurts her father it is only because she is separate from him, not because of a failure of love:

> Good my lord,
> You have begot me, bred me, loved me. I
> Return those duties back as are right fit,
> Obey you, love you and most honor you.
> Why have my sisters husbands, if they say
> They love you all? Haply, when I shall wed,
> That lord whose hand must take my plight shall carry
> Half my love with him, half my care and duty.
> Sure I shall never marry like my sisters,
> To love my father all.                    (1.1.97–106)

This is the only moment in the play in which Cordelia asserts herself, and even here she is not so much asserting herself as mediating between the claims of her father and the claims of her future husband. Her characteristic gestures are of selfless love. No matter how well I think of myself, I would never go so far as to say that she is "like me."

Cordelia's perfection is maintained in this play by her silence. First she refuses to speak the self-serving language of flattery; next she listens in silence when her father disinherits her. "The barbarous Scythian," he tells her,

> Or he that makes his generation messes
> To gorge his appetite, shall to my bosom
> Be as well neighbored, pitied, and relieved,
> As thou my sometime daughter.       (1.1.118–122)

...There is no single woman character, then, who represents me in the play. But if we group the three sisters together and call them something like "the feminine" or "the Other" (as opposed to Lear, who represents "the Self"), we can find a kind of rough sexual justice in *King Lear*. Women are important here not as I am important to myself but as the outside world is important to me. They are like the rock on which the hero is broken and remade; they are the thing outside the Self that cannot be controlled and cannot be renounced. "The Other" is equal to the tragic hero as the second term in a dialectic is equal to the first. Women play the role of "the Other" not only in *King Lear* but in all Shakespeare's plays. In all four genres—comedy, history, tragedy, and romance—the nature of the feminine reflects the nature of the world outside the Self. Before returning to *King Lear* it is worth pausing to consider how this works.

In the comedies, the world outside us is manifestly reliable and orderly, a source of pleasure rather than a threat—and so is the nature of the feminine. In *As They Liked It*, Alfred Harbage has made a statistical survey of Shakespeare's characters, dividing them by groups into good and bad. The highest percentage of good characters in any group is the percentage of good women in the comedies: 96 percent good, 4 percent bad. The possibility of betrayal in this world is very slight. The women will not betray the men, the comic world will not betray its central characters, the playwright will not betray our expectations of a happy ending. The world of Shakespearean comedy is fundamentally safe and its women are fundamentally good. We are free in this world to play, to court danger in sport.

...In Shakespearean tragedy, the world outside the Self seems to thicken. It becomes hard to make out. It is not necessarily evil, although it *may* be evil; in any case, it causes so much suffering that it will at certain moments at least *appear* evil. It is a world that is separate from us who inhabit it; it will not yield to our desires and fantasies no matter how desperately we need it to do so. This means that in tragedy, recognition—*anagnorisis*, the banishing of ignorance—is a major goal. We question the tragic universe to discover its laws, since they are what we must live by. The worlds of comedy and romance, by contrast, are shaped by our hearts' desires; and in history, we are busily remaking the world to suit ourselves.

The feminine in the tragedies can be similarly defined in terms of evil, obduracy, and the problem of *anagnorisis*. First of all, women in the tragedies constitute the *single* group in which Harbage finds more bad than good: 58 percent bad and only 42 percent good. Like the world outside the Self, the feminine causes suffering, appears evil, and may actually *be* evil. And like the world outside the Self, women in the tragedies are notably separate from us, governed by their own laws whether their natures are good or evil. The hero can only recognize them for what they are or fail to do so. The effort to control them is useless; neither the feminine Other nor the world outside the Self is within our power in Shakespeare's tragedy. . . .

It is time to return to my original question. Am I content with the role played in *King Lear* by the wandering portion of my identity, the part I cannot invest in King Lear? On the whole, I think I should be. For one thing, I am flattered to think that I may be capable of such thrilling modulations between good and evil as exist in the world of *King Lear*. It makes me interesting to myself. Identifying with the intensely problematic world outside the hero gives me another way of participating in the major questions of the play, questions about the violent extremes we find within ourselves and in our experience. More importantly, I am content to identify with the world outside the hero because the dialectic between King Lear and the outside world is what creates the satisfactions of tragedy. It is when Lear cannot get what he wants from the outside world that *he* becomes interesting. We do not really want the tragic world to yield to the hero's desires; we want to see what happens to him when his suffering cracks him open, and he goes out on the heath to become something new. There, thanks to the resistance offered by the tragic world, we are in the presence of exciting possibilities. The hero may triumph over his losses; naked, he may be more splendid than he appeared when he was clothed. Or, like Coriolanus, the hero of one of the Roman plays, he may collapse. Both the risk and the possibility of Shakespearean tragedy depend on the Otherness of the tragic universe to the masculine Self. In identifying with the world outside the hero, I am identifying with something as powerful in creating the drama as the hero himself.

What is the nature of the resistance offered by the feminine Other in *King Lear* On the one hand, it is a matter of malice: Goneril and Regan are selfish beasts who wish their father ill. On the other hand, it is a matter of pure separateness. Cordelia, as we have seen, is guilty of nothing but being a separate person from her father, of having her own social role to play. In many ways the resistance Cordelia offers is more interesting. Cordelia simply resists Lear's claim to be the sun around which everything revolves. The mere presence of another inviolable person is enough to shatter Lear's identity. The tragic hero wants to be the only star in the sky.

The feminine Other creates drama by resisting the hero, but also by being endlessly desirable to him. The desire of the hero for women and the world keeps him both alive and vulnerable; it keeps open the possibility of both suffering and fulfillment. A comparison between Lear and Gloucester will illustrate the point. Gloucester, who has sons instead of daughters, loses his capacity for desire and with it both his vulnerability to his experience and his chance of happiness. He tries to kill himself, is rescued by Edgar, feels suicidal again when he witnesses Lear's madness, urges Oswald to kill him, and finally is parked by Edgar in "the shadow of this tree." "A man may rot even here" (5.2.8), he tells Edgar when Edgar returns. Since Edgar and Gloucester are in the middle of a battle there is no time for an elaborate response. "Men must endure / Their going hence, even as their coming hither," Edgar tells his father briefly. "Ripeness is all. Come on." Gloucester gets up and plods on. "And that's true, too," he says. Nothing makes much difference to him anymore. Lear, by contrast, dies upon a wish. "Do you see this?" he asks urgently, bent over the dead Cordelia's head. "Look on her," he cries, tortured by hope. "Look, her lips, / Look there, look there." Lear's feelings stay alive to the end of the play. . . .

[From Bamber, Linda. "The Woman Reader in *King Lear*." In *King Lear*, ed. Russell Fraser, Signet Classic Shakespeare. New York: New American Library, 1986, pp. 291-300.] Used by permission of the author.

# From "*KING LEAR:* THE AVOIDANCE OF LOVE" (2003)

## Stanley Cavell

I N *KING Lear* shame comes first, and brings rage and folly in its train. Lear is not maddened because he had been wrathful, but because his shame brought his wrath upon the wrong object. It is not the fact of his anger but the irony of it, specifically and above all the *injustice* of it, which devours him.

That Lear is ashamed, or afraid of being shamed by a revelation, seems to be the Fool's understanding of his behavior. It is agreed that the Fool keeps the truth present to Lear's mind, but it should be stressed that the characteristic mode of the Fool's presentation is *ridicule*—the circumstance most specifically feared by shame (as accusation and discovery are most feared by guilt). Part of the exquisite pain of this Fool's comedy is that in riddling Lear with the truth of his condition he increases the very cause of that condition, as though shame should finally grow ashamed of itself, and stop. The other part of this pain is that it is the therapy prescribed by love itself. We know that since Cordelia's absence "the fool hath much pin'd away" (1. 4. 78), and it is generally assumed that this is due to his love for Cordelia. That need not be denied, but it should be obvious that it is directly due to his love for Lear; to his having to see the condition in Lear which his love is impotent to prevent, the condition moreover which his love has helped to cause, the precise condition therefore which his love is unable to comfort, since its touch wounds. This is why the Fool dies or disappears; from the terrible relevance, and the horrible irrelevance, of his only passion. This is the point of his connection with Cordelia, as will emerge.

I call Lear's shame a hypothesis, and what I have to say here will perhaps be hard to make convincing. But primarily it depends upon not imposing the traditional interpretations upon the opening events. Lear is puerile? Lear, senile? But the man who speaks Lear's words is in possession, if not fully in command, of a powerful, ranging mind; and its eclipse into madness only confirms its intelligence, not just because what he says in his madness is the work of a marked intelligence, but because the nature of his madness, his melancholy and antic disposition, its incessant invention, is the sign, in fact and in Renaissance thought, of genius; an option of escape open only to minds of the highest reach. How then can we understand such a mind seriously to believe that what Goneril and Regan are offering in that opening scene is love, proof of his value to them; and to believe that Cordelia is withholding love? We cannot so understand it, and so all the critics are right to regard Lear in this scene as psychologically incomprehensible, or as requiring from them some special psychological makeup—if, that is, we assume that Lear believes in Goneril and Regan and not in Cordelia. But we needn't assume that he believes anything of the kind.

We imagine that Lear *must* be wildly abused (blind, puerile, and the rest) because the thing works out so badly. But it doesn't *begin* badly, and it is far from incomprehensible conduct. It is, in fact, quite ordinary. A parent is bribing love out of his children; two of them accept the bribe, and despise him for it; the third shrinks from the attempt, as though from violation. Only this is a king, this bribe is the last he will be able to offer; everything in his life, and in the life of his state, depends upon its success. We need not assume that he does not know his two older daughters, and that they are giving him false coin in return for his real bribes, though perhaps like most parents he is willing not to notice it. But more than this: There is reason to assume that the open possibility—or the open fact—that they are *not* offering true love is exactly what he wants. Trouble breaks out only with Cordelia's "Nothing," and her broken resolution to be silent.—What does he want, and what is the meaning of the trouble which then breaks out?

Go back to the confrontation scene with Gloucester:

If thou wilt weep my fortunes, take my eyes. [4.6.76 ~ *Evans Editor*]

The obvious rhetoric of those words is that of an appeal, or a bargain. But it is also warning, and a command: If you weep for me, the same thing will happen to me that happened to you; do not let me see what you are weeping for. Given the whole scene, with its concentrated efforts at warding off Gloucester, that line says explicitly what it is Lear is warding off: Gloucester's sympathy, his love. And earlier:

GLOUCESTER O! Let me kiss that hand.
LEAR Let me wipe it first, it smells of mortality.
(4.6.134–5)

Mortality, the hand without rings of power on it, cannot be lovable. He feels unworthy of love when the reality of lost power comes over him. That is what his plan was to have avoided by exchanging his fortune for his love at one swap. He cannot bear love when he has no reason to be loved, perhaps because of the helplessness, the passiveness which that implies, which some take for impotence. And he wards it off for the reason for which people do ward off being loved, because it presents itself to them as a demand:

LEAR No. Do thy worst, blind Cupid; I'll not love.

(4.6.139)

Gloucester's presence strikes Lear as the demand for love; he knows he is being offered love, he tries to deny the offer by imagining that he has been solicited (this is the relevance of "blind Cupid" as the sign of a brothel); and he does not want to pay for it, for he may get it, and may not, and either is intolerable. Besides, he has recently done just that, paid his all for love. The long fantasy of his which precedes this line ("Let copulation thrive. . . . There is the sulphurous pit—burning, scalding, stench, consumption . . .") contains his most sustained expression of disgust with sexuality (11. 116ff.)—as though furiously telling himself that what was wrong with his plan was not the debasement of love his bargain entailed, but the fact that love itself is inherently debased and so unworthy from the beginning of the bargain he had made for it. That is a maddening thought; but still more comforting than the truth. For some spirits, to be loved knowing you cannot return that love is the most radical of psychic tortures.

This is the way I understand that opening scene with the three daughters. Lear knows it is a bribe he offers, and—part of him anyway—wants exactly what a bribe can buy: (1) false love and (2) a public expression of love. That is, he wants something he does not have to return *in kind*, something which a division of his property fully pays for. And he wants to *look* like a loved man—for the sake of the subjects, as it were. He is perfectly happy with his little plan, until Cordelia speaks. Happy not because he is blind, but because he is getting what he wants, his plan is working. Cordelia is alarming precisely because he *knows* she is offering the real thing, offering something a more opulent third of his kingdom cannot, must not, repay; putting a claim upon him he cannot face. She threatens to expose both his plan for returning false love with no love, and expose the necessity for that plan—his terror of being loved, of needing love.

Reacting to oversentimental or over-Christian interpretations of her character, interpreters have made efforts to implicate her in the tregedy's source, convincing her of a willfulness and hardness kin to that later shown by her sisters. But her complicity is both less and more than such an interpretation envisages. That interpretation depends, first of all, upon taking her later speeches in the scene (after the appearance of France and Burgundy) as simply uncovering what was in her mind and heart from the beginning. But why? Her first utterance is the aside:

What shall Cordelia speak? Love, and be silent.

This, presumably, has been understood as indicating her decision to refuse her father's demand. But it needn't be. She asks herself what she can say; there is no necessity for taking the question to be rhetorical. She wants to obey her father's wishes (anyway, there is no reason to think otherwise at this stage, or at any other); but how? She sees from Goneril's speech and Lear's acceptance of it what it is he wants, and she would provide it if she could. But to pretend publicly to love, where you do not love, is easy; to pretend to love, where you really do love, is not obviously possible. She hits on the first solution to her dilemma: Love, and be silent. That is, love *by being* silent. That will do what he seems to want, it will avoid the expression of love, keep it secret. She is his joy; she knows it and he knows it. Surely that is enough? Then Regan speaks, and following that Cordelia's second utterance, again aside:

> Then poor Cordelia!
> And yet not so; since I am sure my love's
> More ponderous than my tongue.
>
> (1.1.76–8)

Presumably, in line with the idea of a defiant Cordelia, this is to be interpreted as a reaffirmation of her decision not to speak. But again, it needn't be. After Lear's acceptance of Regan's characteristic outstripping (she has no ideas of her own; her special vileness is always to increase the measure of pain others are prepared to inflict; her mind is itself a lynch mob). Cordelia may realize that she will *have* to say something. "More ponderous than my tongue" suggests that she is going to move it, not that it is immovable—which would make it more ponderous than her love. And this produces her second groping for an exit from the dilemma: to speak, but making her love seem less than it is, out of love. Her tongue will move, and obediently, but against her condition—then poor Cordelia, making light of her love. And yet *she* knows the truth. Surely that is enough?

But when the moment comes, she is speechless:"Nothing, my lord." I do not deny that this can be read defiantly, as can the following "You have begot me, bred me, lov'd me" speech. She is outraged, violated, confused, so young; Lear is torturing her, claiming her devotion, which she wants to give, but forcing her to help him betray (or not to betray) it, to falsify it publicly. (Lear's ambiguity here, wanting at once to open and to close her mouth, further shows the ordinariness of the scene, its verisimilitude to common parental love, swinging between absorption and rejection of its offspring, between encouragement to a rebellion they failed to make and punishment for it.) It may be that with Lear's active violation, she snaps; her resentment provides her with words, and she levels her abdication of love at her traitorous, shameless father:

> Happily, when I shall wed,
> That lord whose hand must take my plight shall carry
> Half my love with him.

(1.1.100–2)

The trouble is, the words are too calm, too cold for the kind of sharp rage and hatred real love can produce. She is never in possession of her situation, "her voice was ever soft, gentle and low" (5.3.272–3); she is young, and "least" (1.1.83). (This notation of her stature and of the quality of her voice is unique in the play. The idea of a defiant *small* girl seems grotesque, as an idea of Cordelia.) All her words are words of love; to love is all she knows how to do. That is her problem, and at the cause of the tragedy of King Lear.

The final scene opens with Lear and Cordelia repeating or completing their actions in their opening scene; again Lear abdicates, and again Cordelia loves and is silent. Its readers have for centuries wanted to find consolation in this end: Heavy opinion sanctioned Tate's Hollywood ending throughout the eighteenth century, which resurrects Cordelia; and in our time, scorning such vulgarity, the same impulse fastidiously digs itself deeper and produces redemption for Lear in Cordelia's figuring of transcendent love. But Dr. Johnson is surely right, more honest and more responsive: Cordelia's death is so shocking that we would avoid it if we could—if we have responded to it. And so the question, since her death is restored to us, is forced upon us: Why does she die? And this is not answered by asking, What does her death mean? (cp. Christ died to save sinners); but by answering, What killed her? (cp. Christ was killed by us, because his news was unendurable).

Lear's opening speech of this final scene is not the correction but the repetition of his strategy in the first scene, or a new tactic designed to win the old game; and it is equally disastrous.

> CORDELIA Shall we not see these daughters and these sisters?
> LEAR No, no, no, no!

(5.3. 7–8)

He cannot finally face the thing he has done; and this means what it always does, that he cannot bear being seen. He is anxious to go off to prison, with Cordelia; his love now is in the open—that much circumstance has done for him; but it remains imperative that it be

348

confined, out of sight. (Neither Lear nor Cordelia, presumably, knows that the soldier in command is Gloucester's son; they feel unknown.) He is still ashamed, and the fantasy expressed in this speech ("We two alone will sing like birds i' the cage") is the same fantasy he brings on the stage with him in the first scene, the thwarting of which causes his maddened destructiveness. There Cordelia had offered him the marriage pledge ("Obey you, love you, and most honor you"), and she has shared his fantasy fully enough to wish to heal political strife with a kiss (or perhaps it is just the commonest fantasy of women):

> CORDELIA Restoration hang
>      Thy medicine on my lips.
>
> (4.7.26–7)

(But after such abdication, what restoration? The next time we hear the words "hang" and "medicine," they announce death.) This gesture is as fabulous as anything in the opening scene. Now, at the end, Lear returns her pledge with his lover's song, his invitation to voyage (". . . so we'll live, and pray, and sing, and tell old tales, and laugh"). The fantasy of this speech is as full of detail as a day-dream, and it is clearly a happy dream for Lear. He has found at the end a way to have what he has wanted from the beginning. His tone is not: We shall love *even though* we are in prison; but: Because we are hidden together we can love. He has come to accept his love, not by making room in the world for it, but by denying its relevance to the world. He does not renounce the world in going to prison, but flees from it, to earthly pleasure. The astonishing image of "God's spies" (5.3.17) stays beyond me, but in part it contains the final emphasis upon looking without being seen; and it cites an intimacy which requires no reciprocity with real men. Like Gloucester toward Dover, Lear anticipates God's call. He is hot experiencing reconciliation with a daughter, but partnership in a mystic marriage.

If so, it cannot be, as is often suggested, that when he says,

> Upon such sacrifices, my Cordelia,
> The Gods themselves throw incense.
>
> (5.3.20–1)

he is thinking simply of going to prison with Cordelia as a sacrifice.

[From Cavell, Stanley. *Disowning Knowledge in Seven Plays of Shakespeare.* Updated Edition. Cambridge, UK: Cambridge UP, 2003. Originally published 1987.]
Reprinted with the permission of Cambridge University.

# From "SHAKESPEARE AND THE EXORCISTS" (1988)

## Stanley Greenblatt

I N  THE *Declaration [of Egregious Popish Impostures,]* Harsnett specifically attacks exorcism as practiced by Jesuits, but he had earlier leveled the same charges at a Puritan exorcist. And he does so not, as we might expect, to claim a monopoly on the practice for the Anglican church but to expose exorcism itself as a fraud. On behalf of established religious and secular authority, Harsnett wishes to cap permanently the great rushing geysers of charisma released in rituals of exorcism. Spiritual *potentia* will henceforth be distributed with greater moderation and control through the whole of the Anglican hierarchy, at whose pinnacle sits the sole legitimate possessor of absolute charismatic authority, the monarch, Supreme Head of the Church in England.

The arguments that Harsnett marshals against exorcism have a rationalistic cast that may mislead us, for despite appearances we are not dealing with the proto-Enlightenment attempt to construct a rational faith. Harsnett denies the presence of the demonic in those whom Father Edmunds claimed to exorcise but finds it in the exorcists themselves: "And who was the devil, the broacher, herald, and persuader of these unutterable treasons, but *Weston* [alias Edmunds] the Jesuit, the chief plotter; and . . . all the holy Covey of the twelve devilish comedians in their several turns: for there was neither devil, nor urchin, nor Elf, but themselves" (154–55). Hence, writes Harsnett, the "Dialogue between *Edmunds, &* the devil" was in reality a dialogue between "the devil *Edmunds,* and *Edmunds* the devil, for he played both parts himself" (86). [The Harsnett citations are drawn from the 1603 J. Roberts printing of *A Declaration of Egregious Popish Impostures* ~ *Evans Editor*]

This strategy—the reinscription of evil onto the professed enemies of evil—is one of the characteristic operations of religious authority in the early modern period and has its secular analogues in more recent history when famous revolutionaries are paraded forth to be tried as counter-revolutionaries. The paradigmatic Renaissance instance is the case of the *benandanti,* analyzed brilliantly by the historian Carlo

Ginzburg.[8] The *benandanti* were members of a northern Italian folk cult who believed that they went forth seasonally to battle with fennel stalks against their enemies, the witches. If the *benandanti* triumphed, their victory assured the peasants of good harvests; if they lost, the witches would be free to work their mischief. The Inquisition first became interested in the practice in the late sixteenth century; after conducting a series of lengthy inquiries, the Holy Office determined that the cult was demonic and in subsequent interrogations attempted, with some success, to persuade the witch-fighting *benandanti* that they were themselves witches.

Harsnett does not hope to persuade exorcists that they are devils; he wishes to expose their fraudulence and relies on the state to punish them. But he is not willing to abandon the demonic altogether, and it hovers in his work, half accusation, half metaphor, whenever he refers to Father Edmunds or the pope. Satan's function was too important for him to be cast off lightly by the early seventeenth-century clerical establishment. The same state church that sponsored the attacks on superstition in *A Declaration of Egregious Popish Impostures* continued to cooperate, if less enthusiastically than before, in the ferocious prosecutions of witches. These prosecutions, significantly, were handled by the secular judicial apparatus—witchcraft was a criminal offense like aggravated assault or murder—and hence reinforced rather than rivaled the bureaucratic control of authority. The eruption of the demonic into the human world was not denied altogether, but the problem would be processed through the proper secular channels. In cases of witchcraft, the devil was defeated in the courts through the simple expedient of hanging his human agents, not, as in cases of possession, compelled by a spectacular spiritual counterforce to speak out and depart.

Witchcraft then was distinct from possession, and though Harsnett himself is skeptical about accusations of witchcraft, his principal purpose is to expose a nexus of chicanery and delusion in the practice of exorcism.[9] By doing so he hopes to drive the practice out of society's central zone, to deprive it of its prestige, and to discredit its apparent efficacy.[10] In late antiquity, as Peter Brown has demonstrated, exorcism was based on the model of the Roman judicial system: the exorcist conducted a formal *quaestio* in which the demon, under torture, was forced to confess the truth.[11] Now, after more than a millennium, this power would once again be vested solely in the state.

Harsnett's efforts, backed by his powerful superiors, did seriously restrict the practice of exorcism. Canon 72 of the new Church Canons of 1604 ruled that henceforth no minister, unless he had the special permission of his bishop, was to attempt "upon any pretense whatsoever, whether of possession or obsession, by fasting and prayer, to cast out any devil or devils, under pain of the imputation of imposture or cozenage and deposition from the ministry."[12] Since special permission was rarely, if ever, granted, in effect exorcism had been officially halted. But it proved easier to drive exorcism from the center to the periphery than to strip it entirely of its power. Exorcism had been a process of reintegration as well as a manifestation of authority; as the ethnographer Shirokogorov observed of the shamans of Siberia, exorcists could "master" harmful spirits and restore "psychic equilibrium" to whole communities as well as to individuals.[13] The pronouncements of English bishops could not suddenly banish from the land inner demons who stood, as Peter Brown puts it, "for the intangible emotional undertones of ambiguous situations and for the uncertain motives of refractory individuals."[14] The possessed gave voice to the rage, anxiety, and sexual frustration that built up easily in the authoritarian, patriarchal, impoverished, and plague-ridden world of early modern England. The Anglicans attempted to dismantle a corrupt and inadequate therapy without effecting a new and successful cure. In the absence of exorcism Harsnett could offer the possessed only the slender reed of Jacobean medicine; if the recently deciphered journal of the Buckinghamshire physician Richard Napier is at all representative, doctors in the period struggled to treat a significant number of cases of possession.[15]

But for Harsnett the problem does not really exist, for he argues that the great majority of cases of possession are either fraudulent or subtly called into existence by the ritual designed to treat them. Eliminate the cure and you eliminate the disease. He is forced to concede that at some distant time possession and exorcism were authentic, for Christ himself had driven a legion of unclean spirits out of a possessed man and into the Gadarene swine (Mark 5:1–19); but the age of miracles has passed, and corporeal possession by demons is no longer possible. The spirit abroad is "the spirit of illusion" (*Discovery*, p. A3). Whether they profess to be Catholics or Calvinists does not matter; all modern exorcists practice the same time-honored trade: "the feat of juggling and deluding the people by counterfeit miracles" (*Discovery*, p. A2). Exorcists sometimes contend, Harsnett acknowledges, that the casting out of devils is not a miracle but a wonder—"*mirandum & non miraculum*"—but "both terms spring from one root of wonder or marvel: an effect which a thing strangely done doth procure in the minds of the beholders, as being above the reach of nature and reason" (*Discovery*, p. A4[r–v]).

The significance of exorcism, then, lies not in any intrinsic quality of the ritual or in the character of the marks of possession but in the impression made upon the minds of the spectators. In *The Discovery of Witchcraft* (1584), a remarkable book that greatly influenced

Harsnett, Reginald Scot detailed some of the means used to shape this impression: the cunning manipulation of popular superstitions; the exploitation of grief, fear, and credulity; the skillful handling of illusionistic devices developed for the stage; the blending of spectacle and commentary; the deliberate arousal of anxiety coupled with the promise to allay it. Puritan exorcists throw themselves into histrionic paroxysms of prayer; Catholic exorcists deploy holy water, smoldering brimstone, and sacred relics. They seem utterly absorbed in the plight of the wretches who writhe in spectacular contortions, vomit pins, display uncanny strength, foam at the mouth, cry out in weird voices. But all of this apparent absorption in the supernatural crisis is an illusion; there is nothing real out there on the bed, in the chair, on the pulpit. The only serious action is transpiring in the minds of the audience.

Hence the exorcists take care, notes Harsnett, to practice their craft only when there is "a great assembly gathered together," and the ritual is then explicitly presented to this assembly with a formal prologue: "The company met, the *Exorcists* do tell them, *what a work of God they have in hand*, and after a long discourse, *how Sathan doth afflict the parties*, and *what strange things they shall see:* the said parties are brought forth, as it were a Bear to the stake, and being either bound in a chair, or otherwise held fast, they fall to their fits, and play their pranks point by point exactly, according as they have been instructed" (*Discovery*, p. 62).

What seems spontaneous is in fact carefully scripted, from the shaping of audience expectations to the rehearsal of the performers. Harsnett grants that to those who suspect no fraud the effect is extraordinarily powerful: "They are cast thereby into a wonderful astonishment" (*Discovery*, p. 70). Aroused by wonder to a heightened state of both attention and suggestibility, the beholders are led to see significance in the smallest gestures of the possessed and to apply that significance to their own lives. But the whole moving process is a dangerous fraud that should be exposed and punished in the courts.

. . . Exorcisms, Harsnett argues, are stage plays, most often tragicomedies, that cunningly conceal their theatrical inauthenticity and hence deprive the spectators of the rational disenchantment that frames the experience of a play. The audience in a theater knows that its misrecognition of reality is temporary, deliberate, and playful; the exorcist seeks to make the misrecognition permanent and invisible. Harsnett is determined to make the spectators see the theater around them, to make them understand that what seems spontaneous is rehearsed, what seems involuntary carefully crafted, what seems unpredictable scripted.

Not all of the participants themselves may fully realize that they are in a stage play. The account in *A Declaration of Egregious Popish*

*Impostures* presents the exorcists, Father Edmunds and his cohorts, as self-conscious professionals and the demoniacs (mostly impressionable young servingwomen and unstable, down-at-heels young gentlemen) as amateurs subtly drawn into the demonic stage business. Those selected to play the possessed in effect learn their roles without realizing at first that they are roles.

The priests begin by talking conspicuously about successful exorcisms abroad and describing in lurid detail the precise symptoms of the possessed. They then await occasions on which to improvise: a servingman "being pinched with penury, & hunger, did lie but a night, or two, abroad in the fields, and being a melancholic person, was scared with lightning, and thunder, that happened in the night, & lo, an evident sign, that the man was possessed" (24); a dissolute young gentleman "had a spice of the *Hysterica passio*" or, as it is popularly called, "the Mother" (25),[24] and that too is a sign of possession. An inflamed toe, a pain in the side, a fright taken from the sudden leaping of a cat, a fall in the kitchen, an intense depression following the loss of a beloved child—all are occasions for the priests to step forward and detect the awful presence of the demonic, whereupon the young "scholars," as Harsnett wryly terms the naive performers, "*frame* themselves jump and fit unto the Priests humors, to mop, mow, jest, rail, rave, roar, commend & discommend, and as the priests would have them, upon fitting occasions (according to the difference of times, places, and comers in) in all things to play the devils accordingly" (38).

To glimpse the designing clerical playwright behind the performance is to transform terrifying supernatural events into a human strategy. One may then glimpse the specific material and symbolic interests served by this particular strategy, above all by its clever disguising of the fact that it is a strategy.

The most obvious means by which the authorities of the English church and state could make manifest the theatricality of exorcism was the command performance: the ability to mime the symptoms at will would, it was argued, decisively prove the possession a counterfeit. Hence we find the performance test frequently applied in investigations of alleged supernatural visitations. In the 1590s, for example, Anne Kerke was accused of bewitching a child to death and casting the child's sister into a fit that closely resembled that of a demoniac: "her mouth being drawn aside like a purse, her teeth gnashing together, her mouth foaming, and her eyes staring."[25] The judge, Lord Anderson, ordered the sister to "show how she was tormented: she said she could not shew it, but when the fit was on her" (100). The reply was taken to he strong corroboration of the authenticity of the charge, and Anne Kerke was hanged.

A similar, if subtler, use of the performance test occurs in the early 1620s. Thomas Perry, known as the Boy of Bilson, would fall into fits upon hearing the opening verse from the gospel of John; other verses from Scriptures did not have the same effect. Three Catholic priests were called in to exorcise the evil spirit that possessed him. During the boy's fit—watched by a large crowd—one of the priests commanded the devil "to show by the sheet before him, how he would use one dying out of the Roman Catholic Church? who very unwillingly, yet at length obeyed, tossing, plucking, haling, and biting the sheet, that it did make many to weep and cry forth."[26] A similar but still fiercer demonstration was evoked in response to the names Luther, Calvin, and Fox. Then, predictably, the priest commanded the devil "to show what power he had on a good Catholic that died out of mortal sin? he thrust down his arms, trembled, holding down his head, and did no more" (51).[27] The Catholics triumphantly published an account of the case, *A Faithful Relation*.

English officials, understandably annoyed by such propaganda, remanded Perry to the custody of the bishop of Coventry and Lichfield. To test if the boy was authentically possessed or "an execrable wretch, who playest the devils part," the Bishop read aloud the verse that set off the symptoms; the boy fell into fits. When the boy recovered, the bishop told him that he would read the same verse in Greek; once again the boy fell into fits. But in fact the Bishop had not read the correct verse, and the boy had been tricked into performance. Since the Devil was "so ancient a scholar as of almost 6000 years standing" (59), he should have known Greek. The possession was proved to be a counterfeit, and the boy, it is said, confessed that he had been instructed by an old man who promised that he would no longer have to go to school.

The Protestants now produced their own account of the case, *The Boy of Bilson; or, A True Discovery of the Late Notorious Impostures of Certain Romish Priests in Their Pretended Exorcism*. "Although these and the like pranks have been often hissed of[f] the Stage, for stale and gross forgeries," the author declares, since the Catholics have ventured to publish their version, it is necessary to set the record straight. A reader of the Catholic account should understand "that he hath seen a *Comedy*, wherein the Actors, which present themselves, are these, A crafty *old man*, teaching the feats and pranks of counterfeiting a person *Demoniacal* and possessed of the *Devil*; the next, a most docible, subtle, and expert young *Boy*, far more dextrous in the Practique part, than his Master was in the Theory; after him appear three Romish *Priests*, the Authors of seducement, conjuring their only imaginary *Devils*, which they brought with them; and lastly, a *Chorus* of credulous people easily seduced, not so much by the subtlety of those *Priests*, as by their own sottishness" (9).

Performance kills belief; or rather acknowledging theatricality kills the credibility of the supernatural. Hence in the case of William Sommers the authorities not only took the demoniac's confession of fraud but also insisted that he perform his simulated convulsions before the mayor and three aldermen of Nottingham. If he could act his symptoms, then the possession would be decisively falsified. Darrel countered that "if he can act them all in such manner and form as is deposed, then he is, either still possessed, or more than a man: for no humans power can do the like."²⁸ But the officials denied that the original performances themselves, stripped of the awe that the spectators brought to them, were particularly impressive. Sommers's possession, Harsnett had said, was a "dumb show" that depended upon an interpretive supplement, a commentary designed at once to intensify and control the response of the audience by explicating both the significance and the relevance of each gesture. Now the state would in effect seize control of the commentary and thereby alter the spectators' perceptions. Sommers's audience would no longer see a demoniac; they would see someone playing a demoniac. Demonic possession would become theater.

## NOTES

8. Carlo Ginzburg, *I benandanti: Recerehe sulla stregoneria e sui culti agrari tra cinquecento e seicento* (Turin: Einaudi, 1966).

9. For Harsnett' s comments on witchcraft, see *Declaration*, pp. 135–36. The relation between demonic possession and witchcraft is complex. John Darrel evidently had frequent recourse, in the midst of his exorcisms, to accusations of witchcraft whose evidence was precisely the demonic possessions; Harsnett remarks wryly that "Of all the partes of the tragicall Comedie acted between him and *Somers*, there was no one Scene in it, wherein *M. Darrell* did with more courage and boldnes acte his part, then in this of the discouerie of witches" (*A Discovery of the Fraudulent Practises of J. Darrel . . . concerning the pretended possession and dispossession of W. Somers, etc.* [1599], p. 142). There is a helpful discussion of possession and witchcraft, along with an important account of Harsnett and Darrel, in Keith Thomas, *Religion and the Decline of Magic* (London: Weidenfeld and Nicolson, 1971).

10. I borrow the phrase "central zone" from Edward Shils, for whom it is coterminous with society's central value system, a system constituted by the general standards of judgment and action and affirmed by the society's elite (*Center and Periphery*, p. 3). At the heart of the central value system is an affirmative attitude toward authority,

which is endowed, however indirectly or remotely, with a measure of sacredness. "By their very possession of authority," Shils writes, elites "attribute to themselves an essential affinity with the sacred elements of their society, of which they regard themselves as the custodians" (5).

11. Brown, *Cult of the Saints*, pp. 109–11.

12. Thomas, *Religion and the Decline of Magic*, p. 485. "This effectively put an end to the practice," Thomas writes, "at least as far as conforming members of the Anglican Church were concerned."

13. S. M. Shirokogorov, *The Psycho-Mental Complex of the Tungus* (Peking: Routledge, 1935), p. 265.

14. Brown, *Cult of the Saints*, p. 110.

15. Michael MacDonald, *Mystical Bedlam* (Cambridge: Cambridge University Press, 1981). See also MacDonald's "Religion, Social Change, and Psychological Healing in England, 1600–1800," in *The Church and Healing*, ed. W. J. Shiels, Studies in Church History 19 (Oxford: Basil Blackwell, 1982); H. C. Erik Midelfort, "Madness and the Problems of Psychological History in the Sixteenth Century," *Sixteenth Century Journal* 12 (1981): 5–12.

16. *A Report Contayning a brief Narration of certain diuellish and wicked witcheries, practized by Olisse Barthram alias Doll Barthram in the Country of Suffolke*, bound with *The Triall of Maist. Dorrell, or A Collection of Defences against Allegations not yet suffered to receiue convenient answere* (1599), p. 94.

24. See Edmund Jorden, *A briefe discourse of a disease Called the Suffocation of the Mother* (London, 1603).

25. *A Report Contayning a brief Narration of certain diuellish and wicked witcheries*, pp. 99–100.

26. [Richard Baddeley,] *The Boy of Bilson, or A True Discovery of the Late Notorious Impostvres of Certaine Romish Priests in their pretended Exorcisme, or expulsion of the Diuell out of a young Boy, named William Perry, sonne of Thomas Perry of Bilson* (London: F. K., 1622), p. 51. Baddeley is quoting from the Catholic account of the events, which, in order to dispute, he reprints: *A Faithfull Relation of the Proceedings of the Catholicke Gentlemen with the Boy of Bilson; shewing how they found him, on what termes they meddled with him, how farre they proceeded with him, and in what case, and for what cause they left to deale further with him* (in Baddeley, pp. 45–54).

27. In both England and France the reliability of the devil's testimony was debated extensively. "We ought not to beleeue the Diuell," writes the exorcist and inquisitor Sebastian Michaelis, "yet when hee is compelled to discourse and relate a truth, then wee should feare and tremble, for it is a token of the wrath of God" (*Admirable Historie of the Possession and Conversion of a Penitent Woman*, p. C7v). Michaelis's long account of his triumph over a devil named Verrine was published, the translator claims, to show "that the Popish Priests,

in all Countries where men will beleeue them, are vniforme & like vnto themselues, since that which was done couertly in England, in the daies of Queene *Elizabeth*, by the Deuils of *Denham* in *Sara Williams* and her fellowes, is now publikely taken vp elsewhere by men of no small ranke" (A4r). This seems to me a disingenuous justification for publishing, without further annotation or qualification, over five hundred pages of Catholic apologetics, but obviously the Jacobean licensing authorities accepted the explanation.

28. [Darrel,] *A Briefe Narration of the possession, dispossession, and repossession of William Sommers*, p. Biiv.

[From Greenblatt, Stanley. *Negotiations of Social Energy in Renaissance England.* Berkeley: U of California P, 1988.] Copyright 1988 by University of California Press-Books. Reproduced with permission of University of California Press-Books.

# From *Hamlet versus Lear:*
## *Cultural Politics and Shakespeare's*
### *Art* (1993)
#### R. A. Foakes

THE RETURN of Edgar coincides with Lear's shift from self-pity to a concern with 'Poor naked wretches', and he comes in pat upon his cue. To the audience he is, of course Edgar in disguise placing madman, whose tears may spoil his 'counterfeiting' (3.6.61). Edgar displaces the Fool as nearest to Lear, and takes Lear's attention away from himself as he becomes the King's 'philosopher'. Edgar presents himself as a former 'servingman', perhaps a lover or court hanger-on, who has relished all the vices available to the fashionable gallant in Jacobean England. Now, reduced to penury, he is punished by the imaginary fiends that haunt him. He catalogues the corruptions of the courtier who is 'false of heart, light of ear; bloody of hand; hog in sloth, fox in stealth, wolf in greediness, dog in madness, lion in prey', and from this perspective the prince of darkness is indeed a 'gentleman'. So Edgar too reminds us of the larger context of the play, even as he prevokes Lear's attempt to strip off his clothing. Edgar's importance as a symbolic 'unaccommodated man' lies in stirring Lear here, and in 4.1 Gloucester, to a new awareness of what they neglected when in power, or simply failed to see; but for the audience, Edgar is not only a moral consciousness, a rebuke to the 'superfluous and lust-dieted man' (4.1.67), but also a witness from a younger generation to the sufferings of the old. In maintaining his disguise he always remains in control of himself, aloof from, and when necessary able to manipulate, the feelings of Lear and Gloucester, and so is able to become an agent of their recovery. Only by avoiding emotional commitment does Edgar remain clear-sighted and become a force for renewal and restitution; this is the main reason why Shakespeare does not permit him to reveal himself to his father until the very end.[12] The visual emblem of Poor Tom, the mad, leading the blind (''Tis the time's plague, when madmen lead the blind', 4.1. 46), recalls Lear with the Fool in the storm, a connection made for us by the addition of a few lines in F in Edgar's opening speech:

> Welcome then,
> Thou unsubstantial air that I embrace;
> The wretch that thou hast blown unto the worst
> Owes nothing to thy blasts.  [4.1.6–9 ~ *Evans Editor*]

Edgar's plaintive line a little later, 'Who is't can say, "I am at the worst"?' (line 25) thus in F again reminds us of Lear and anticipates worse to come, and yet this scene, also visually reunites the father with the son he cast out. F also omits Edgar's verbal flourish in which he names the five 'fiends' troubling him, so removing lines which distract from the pathos of the scene, and from Edgar's difficulty in maintaining his mask for Poor Tom.

Edmund returns to initiate the violence of the later part of the play by betraying his father, while Edgar returns as witness to the degredation of Gloucester and agent of his recovery. They set in motion contrasting movements, on the one hand towards conflict and disintegration and on the other towards reunion and order. The substantial changes made in Act 4 in F may be seen as intensifying the interaction between these movement. Before the death of Cornwall the division between him and Albany had extended into a quarrel between Goneril and Regan for the favours of Edmund, and Albany finds himself in 4.2 in the impossible position of siding with Gloucester and Lear while caught up in a war in which they, are the enemy. This scene is much abbreviated in F, losing thirty-four of its ninety-seven lines, including a reference by Goneril to a French force spreading its 'banners' in, England. One omission removes the dialogue in which Albany a second time depicts Goneril as a 'fiend' (he has already called her 'devil' and 'fiend' in lines found in both Q and F), and threatens to attack her (lines 63–8). The other large abridgment in the scene removes the dialogue in which Albany turns on Goneril and moralizes on what she and her sister, 'Tigers, not daughters', have done, in his speech beginning, 'Wisdom, and goodness, to the vile seem vile' (4.2.38–49). Here, as in 3.7, speeches that would coerce the viewer's, response are omitted from F, and the emphasis is on preparations for war, on Goneril's display of love for Edmund, on the split between her and Albany, and on the news of the blinding of Gloucester. F adds just one line, Goneril's ironic remark as Edmund leaves, and before Albany enters, 'Oh, the difference of man, and man', pointing for the audience beyond the contrast between her husband and Edmund to the differences and dissensions between other men in the play.

The threat of war escalates rapidly through Act 4, especially in the slimmed down Folio text, and to meet the forces of the army that has landed (from France, 4.2.4), the 'powers' of Albany are in the field by 4.5.

The quarrel between Goneril and Regan for the favours of Edmund also gathers pace. It is in this context that Cordelia returns in 4.4. She has been so long off stage that Shakespeare has been able to modify her character so that she now seems at first no longer the girl tough and bold enough to challenge her autocratic father-king and rebuke her older sisters, but rather in Q an almost holy figure, no longer measuring love according to her bond, but the very emblem of caring pity. F omits the elaborate establishment of a quasi-religious aura about this new Cordelia in the Gentleman's description of her 'holy' tears in 4.3. The brief image of her presented in the scene which follows in Q, and which is all we have in F, is enough to restore her as a figure of love and pity, notably in the echo of Christ's words (Luke 2.49) in her 'O dear father, / It is thy business that I go about'. The scene also starts with the news that Lear has been found, and so points to the reunion of another cast-off child with her father. At the same time, in F the opening stage direction calls for Cordelia to enter 'with Drum and Colours' (not in Q), and 'soldiers' ('others', Q), so making it clear that she is at the head of an army; and since here again Cordelia mentions the French connection,

> Therefore great France
> My mourning, and importun'd [important Q] tears hath pitied,
> (4.4.25–6)

the 'colours' presumably sufficiently indicated to the audience a French army opposed to the 'British powers' a Messenger reports as 'marching hitherward' (line 21). Her presence leading an army does relate to her boldness in the opening scene, as now Cordelia has made it her business, she says, to restore 'our ag'd father's right [rite F]'. Her use of the royal plural is notable, as is her concern for the 'right' of Lear; does she mean to restore her father to the power he has given away, to a, royalty he has relinquished? It would seem that there is after all, and in spite of her denial, some 'blown ambition' (line 27) in what she is doing; she is not merely rescuing Lear, but aiming to give him back the power he so abused. It seems that she is caught up in the horrible confusions caused by her father's initial act, for here she defends herself as acting out of pity and love, which merge with and at the same time paradoxically are alien to the image of the war she is seeking. Here the opposing impulses towards conflict and restoration of accord are poignantly dramatized.

When Cordelia translates her love for her father into a determination to restore him to power, she exercises power over him. When Edgar, who resurfaces as himself in 4.6, no longer playing Poor Tom, claims to be curing his father's despair, he is exercising power over Gloucester. The usual roles of father and child are reversed. The mime of Gloucester's 'death', staged by Edgar has an actor pretending to be blind fall over a 'cliff' he and we know isn't there, for the purpose Edgar says, of curing Gloucester's 'despair'; but though his recovery from his 'fall' leads him to acquire a measure of patience and renounce thoughts of suicide, the effect does not last, for Gloucester soon wishes for death at the hands of Oswald (line 230), and falls into 'ill thoughts again' (5.2.8) when we next see him. The mime of Gloucester throwing himself, as he supposses, over a cliff is the same in F as in Q, and seems to be there for its effect on the audience as much as for its uncertain effect on Gloucester. Critics, actors and directors do not agree on whether the episode is meant to be grotesque, tragic, absurd, or farcical, and argue about 'how much of an illusion his [Shakespeare's] audience might have been under about the presence of a cliff'.[13] As far as illusion is concerned, the audience is aware visually all the time that there is no cliff, and the point of the incident would be lost if they were under such an illusion. The sequence relates to a conventional device of having a character 'die' and return to life (like Bottom as Pyramus, Falstaff or Imogen) which is basically comic, both because we know the actor is not really dead, and because we and the characters are delighted to see them come to life again. But in *King Lear* Shakespeare transforms the convention: whatever other equalities may be detected in this scene, there is an element of gratuitous cruelty, about it, as Gloucester is drawn into a charade which raises his hopes for the one thing he wants, death, only to deprive him of what he calls 'that benefit' (line 61); if it helps him temporarily to 'bear / Affliction', it leaves him in the end still waiting for the death he has been offered and then denied ('a man may rot even here', 5.2.8). Peter Brook made his Gloucester faint as he fell, and come to convinced that he had died, and the more successful the actor is in conveying a sense of his illusion of suicide, the more cruel the effect seems to be, as he revives to cry 'Away, and let me die.'

This episode also brings the gods momentarily into the action, but they exist only as created and stage-managed by Edgar, so that the spectacle of Gloucester kneeling in prayer, 'O, you mighty gods! / This world I do renounce . . .', is at once pathetic and empty—there is no other world, except as Edgar produces it in his words, deceiving his father for the time being into believing his 'life's a miracle', and telling him what to think:

Think that the clearest gods, who make them [made their Q]
honours Of men's impossibilities, have preserved thee.

[4.6.73-4 ~ *Evans Editor*]

Gloucester may credit this for a little while, but we get no nearer to the gods in the play than as Edgar here creates them. It is an extraordinary contrast to *Hamlet*, where a Christian dispensation, a belief in God, in Providence and in another world are taken for granted in the action, if frequently questioned, and set against a sense of death as final, as mere oblivion. The action of *King Lear*, on the other hand, takes place in a present without a past, and in a secular world where the gods are verbal constructs, made present as Edgar produces them imaginatively for the dubious benefit of his father.[14] In relation to this, the single association of Cordelia with Christ in 4.4 merely helps to confirm her emblematic rehabilitation as a figure of pity, and does not have further reverberations in the play. . . .

The meeting of Gloucester and Lear is sandwiched between the 'death' and revival of Gloucester under Edgar's supervision, and the bringing back to consciousness of Lear under Cordelia's supervision. When Lear is brought on 'in a chair carried by Servants' (F; not in Q), and clothed in 'fresh garments' to be reunited once more with Cordelia, a dramatic point, of Gloucester's mimed suicide becomes clearer, for both men go through a symbolic death and an unwanted return to life. Lear's reconciliation with Cordelia, his kneeling to her when she asks his blessing, and his acceptance at last that he is 'a very foolish fond old man, / Fourscore and upward' (F adds, 'Not an hour more, nor less'), are very affecting. But the scene is double-edged, like that between Gloucester and Edgar at the beginning of 4.6, for again there is an element, unintended on Cordelia's part, of cruelty about it. We have seen Lear come to new perceptions in madness, exposing the corruptions of authority and making a mockery of kingship, perceptions that make it impossible for him to take on such authority again, and it is a further confusion that in her well-meaning love this 'kind and dear princess', as Kent calls her, is determined not only to restore her father to a life he would be glad to relinquish, but also to restore him to the power and majesty he can no longer command, and has given up. His first words are 'You do me wrong to take me out o'th'grave', so that her address to him, 'How does my Royal Lord? How fares your Majesty?', is doubly ironic in that she treats him as a monarch rather than as her father, and would give him back what he no longer wants (his life), and no longer has or can have (his power and status). In F the number of characters is reduced, as the Doctor who ministers to Lear (Q) vanishes, to be amalgamated with the 'Gentleman' who put fresh clothes on him, and eight lines are omitted from the dialogue of Cordelia and the Gentleman. F also leaves out the final sequence of twelve lines in Q, a conversation between Kent and the Gentleman about the latest news and rumours, and the expectation of battle, so that in F the scene ends with Lear's exit line, 'Pray [you F] now forget, and forgive, I am old and foolish.' This line gains extra weight in F, and its open syntax generalizes its meaning, allowing the possibility that Lear says not simply 'forgive me for my injustice to you', but 'forget and forgive all wrongs done in the past'. It is thus especially poignant that Cordelia cannot, as his words suggest he would do, forget or forgive her sisters, and in seeking to restore him to his 'right', his rule, by heading an army in battle against the British forces led by Albany and Edmund, she ends by inflicting on him yet more suffering. . . .

When Lear enters 'with Cordelia in his arms' (Q and F), the stage direction does not say she is dead, but the symbolism of the scene requires that she must be,[18] for Shakespeare has taken care to have the bodies of Goneril and Regan displayed on stage, so that for Lear too the wheel has come full circle, as the presence on stage of all three of his children dead strinkingly shows what he has brought upon himself by dividing the kingdom and casting out Cordelia. Lear, preoccupied with himself and Cordelia, wants to believe she is alive ('This feather stirs, she lives'), but chorus-like, Kent, Albany and Edgar see his entrance carrying her as an image of horror, as if it were the 'promis'd end', the end of the world, for they and we know she is dead, and can see the bodies of Goneril and Regan, as Kent reminds us by trying to tell Lear 'Your eldest daughters have fordone [foredoome Q] themselves, / And desperately are dead.' Lear, it seem, is spared an awareness of their deaths; when Kent speaks, Lear does not appear to listen:

> ALBANY He knows not what he says, and vain is it. [it is Q]
> That we present us to him.                    (5.3.294–5)

Lear is absorbed in himself and his burden, so much that he does not really communicate with Albany or Edgar or Kent, except in the brief momentary recognition of Kent, until just before he dies, when he turns, probably to Edgar, to ask, 'Pray you undo this button'. Edgar, attending to him, cries, 'He faints', and Lear comes to only to wish for death, saying, 'Break heart, I prithee break;' In F Kent speaks this last line, and Lear's last words are an addition,

> Do you see this? Look on her? Look her lips,
> Look there, look there!          [5.3.311–12 ~ Evans Editor]

What he sees or thinks he sees has been much debated; to some it seems a final cruel delusion if he imagines Cordelia to be alive, to others a blessed release for him in a moment of imagined reunion. Lear has lost his power and all he had, he has destroyed his world, and outlived all his children, and the final scene stretches out his suffering beyond the point at which to have died would have been fitting ('You do me wrong to take me out o' th' grave'), as Gloucester died at the moment of recognition of his lost child. And yet at the end the only thing to wish for him is a gentle death, and in F this is what he gets. His ending is, indeed, both cruel and gentle, and full of irony in relation to his aim in dividing the kingdom so that he could 'Unburthen'd crawl toward death' (1.1.140, F only). For at the last he enters burdened, carrying in Cordelia, and if Albany had his way, would be further weighed down by the return of his power:

> for us, we will resign
> During the life of this old majesty
> To him our absolute power, you [i.e., Kent and Edgar] to your rights
> With boot, and such addition as your, honours [honour Q]
> Have more than merited. All friends shall taste
> The wages of their virtue, and all-foes
> The cup of their deservings.
>
> (5.3.299–305)

Albany's words have been seen as simply inadequate, and as refuted by the death of Lear,[19] since virtue does not have its reward in the case of Cordelia. Albany, however, reminds us here of a central concern of the play, rule and power; after all that Lear has done to abuse his power, it would be sentimental in the extreme to give it back to him, but Albany is making a fitting gesture to an aged man, 'this [great F] decay', for whom death is very near. Albany is concerned about the future of the realm, and in the 'general woe' of the moment, offers after the death of Lear to hand over power to Edgar and Kent. F gives the last speech to Edgar ('Duke', i.e., Albany, Q), so that it becomes a reminder that Albany is saying what he feels, not what he ought to say; but at least we can imagine that things will not be the same now Lear has gone, and under Albany and Edgar the 'gor'd state' will be renewed and better ruled. . . .

The later part of the action moves simultaneously towards conflict and reconciliation. Edgar leads his father to safety, yet fails to reveal himself, and is at once cruel and kind in practising on him by letting him experience a mock-death and return to life again. So too, Cordelia lovingly helps to restore her father to his senses, yet insists on leading him into battle to recover for him a power he no longer wants or can wield. Both Gloucester and Lear undergo a symbolic death and restoration, and both are denied the release they desire from suffering; both might say, as Lear does, 'You do me wrong to take me out o' th' grave', since the play offers no hint of a life beyond death, and to prolong their, life, in this world is only, to test their endurance further. The end is thus full of paradoxes, as, Gloucester is left almost to the last in ignorance that Edgar lives, and Lear is not allowed to forget or forgive, but is marched by Cordelia; into a battle which brings her death, destroying the one thing that now matters to him. Lear is ironically offered his kingdom again when he no longer cares about it, and when he is visually linked to the dead bodies of all three, of his children, whose destruction is the outcome of his initial division of the kingdom. Lear's, death, like that of Gloucester, is thus a defeat in victory, both cruel and kind, a necessary release and a stretching out of him still further on, the cruel rack of the world he has made. And it is a world *he* has made—he begins the play as a despot locked inside his role, unable to see the consequences of his actions, because he has lost ordinary human contact with others. In the last act we are not shown the battle in which Lear and Cordelia are defeated, in spite of the build-up towards it and the display of soldiers and colours; the fight we do see, shown ar length, is that between Edgar and Edmund, which symbolizes in the victory of Edgar the restoration of a better order, one 'pregnant to good pity'—a restoration confirmed in the final speeches of the play, when Edgar and Albany are left to pick up the pieces and sustain the 'gor'd state', and it does not much matter which of them has the closing lines. At the same time there is a powerful sense of closure, of the end of an era, of reaching a point of rest; it is a moment for taking stock, and for looking to a future that will be different because of what has happened in the play—that is to say, because of now past events:

> The oldest hath [have Q] borne most; we that are young
> Shall never see so much, nor live so long.
>
> [5.3.326–7 ~ *Evans Editor*]

The lines sound almost trite, but in F they refer explicitly to Lear, and they mark the huge gap between the beginning of the play, where there is no past to influence his actions, and a new condition, in which awareness of past suffering, it is hinted, will make for a better-world.[24]

As the two old men become the focus of suffering in the play, so in their reunion when mad or blind in 4.6 they act out a parody of the power relations once so important to them, Lear 'every inch a king', Gloucester anxious to kiss Lear's hand in submission, and it is only by this reduction of them to political insignificance that recovery can come. The great curve of the action takes them from security and immense power out into the storm, and into what seems an endless renewal of suffering: 'Who is't can say we are at the worst?' Yet it also restores to them the love of their lost children, and brings them to an acceptance of the mortality and humanity they have to learn they share with others. Their deaths are at once painful and a blessing, the fulfilment of a long process that makes them aware of the wrongs they have done, and that enables them as a consequence to find release through suffering at the end. The Folio text strengthens this design by making the later action more direct and less cluttered by moralizing, so sharpening the sense of cruelty in kindness, of suffering in reconciliation, of victory in defeat and defeat in victory, of love as selfish and as selfless, and of the inadequacy of moralizing and of ordinary notions of justice to account for what the play has shown us. The reason for the addition in F at the end of Lear's final speech becomes clearer:

> Do you see this? Look on her? Look her lips,
> Look there, look there!           [5.3.311–12 ~ Evans Editor]

These words, together with the transfer in F of 'Break heart, I prithee break' to Kent, round out the design of the play and the paradoxes of the ending by allowing Lear the momentary joy of imagining Cordelia may be alive, a joy which is heart-breaking because it recalls an earlier moment when he hoped she would speak and her lips said nothing, and because it is delusory, so that, with Kent, we know there is nothing left to wish for Lear except the oblivion of death.

## NOTES

12. In *Disowning Knowledge*, Stanley Cavell assumes that Edgar wants to avoid being recognized: 'There are no lengths to which we may not go in order to avoid being revealed, even to those we love and are loved by' (pp. 55–6).

13. *King Lear*, ed. Bratton, p. 175. [Reference is to *King Lear*. Plays in Performance series, eds. Julie Hankey and J.S. Bratton. Bristol: Bristol Classical Press, 1987. ~ Evans Editor]

14. The whole play is, of course, in one sense a verbal construct; but as represented on the stage, Edgar here appears within Shakespeare's construct as the author of his own fiction in the layered illusions of reality in the play.

16. Stanley Cavell thinks Lear's love for Cordelia is not the 'plain love of a daughter for father', and is 'incompatible with the idea of her having any (other) lover', *Disowning Knowledge*, p. 70.

17. *King Lear*, ed. Bratton, p. 197.

18. E.A.J. Honigmann argues that Cordelia could be alive here, and opens her eyes but is unable to speak in this final scene; see *Myriad-Minded Shakespeare* (London: Macmillan, 1989), pp. 90–2.

19. See, for example, N. S. Brooke, *King Lear* (London: Arnold, 1963), pp. 54–5.

20. But it does not change him so completely as Stephen Urkowitz claims in arguing that Albany has 'moral elevation' in Q, and espouses 'no positively defined ethical standards' in F; he produces a reading 'utterly and irreconcilably at odds with the conventional view'; see

*Shakespeare's Revision of King Lear* (Princeton: Princeton University Press, 1980), pp. 92–3 and 126.

21. Belsey, *The Subject of Tragedy*, p. 33. [Methuen: London, 1985. ~*Evans Editor*]

22. Patterson, *Shakespeare and the Popular Voice*, p. 116. [Cambridge, USA: Blackwell, 1990. ~ *Evans Editor*].

23. McLuskie, 'The Patriarchal Bard', pp. 98–9. [Excerpts from McLuskie's fine essay appear in "Critical Essays: Modern" in this Evans Edition. The entire commentary is in *Political Shakespeare: Essays in Cultural Materialism*. 2nd edition, eds. Jonathan Dollimer and Alan Sinfield. Ithaca, New York: Cornell UP. ~ *Evans Editor*]

24. Philip C. Maguire argues ingeniously in *Speechless Dialect: Shakespeare's Open Silences* (Berkeley and Los Angeles: University of California Press, 1985) that the play ends with the silence of either Edgar (in Q) or Albany (in F), which can be interpreted in various ways; Edgar's and Albany's 'silence' may show their refusal to take on power after Lear dies. This argument is another way of destabilizing the play, and the silences of Edgar and Albany here are invented by the critic: the absence of a speech becomes a presence, pregnant with meanings.

[From *Hamlet versus Lear: Cultural Politics and Shakespeare's Art*. Cambridge, U.K.: Cambridge UP, 1993.] Reprinted with the permission of Cambridge University.

# From "*KING LEAR* AND THE PSYCHOLOGY OF DYING" (1982)

Susan Snyder

IN A sense, all tragedy addresses the necessity of dying. That is, regardless of whether or not the tragic hero is dead at the end (Shakespeare's always are), tragedy's peculiar blend of dignity and defeat expresses our deeply paradoxical reaction to our own mortality. What that mortality means is that the highest human potential cannot be infinite, that death will inevitably undo our treasured, all-absorbing construction—the self. From one point of view, dying feels right. Man is a part of nature, governed, as our vulnerable bodies remind us, by nature's laws of growth and decay. Man is also a moral being with convictions of guilt and unworthiness, a far cry from the God he venerates. At the same time, it is impossibly *wrong* that the precious ego must submit like any oblivious beast to death's impersonal blotting-out. We cannot really imagine our own non-being, as Freud observed: "at bottom no one believes in his own death, or to put the same thing in another way, in the unconscious every one of us is convinced of his own immortality."[1] Tragedy provides an objective correlative for this basic ambivalence of ours. Its inevitable downward course toward destruction embodies one reaction: death is right, death comes from inside us. Against this arc of tragic action develops that special dimension of the protagonist we call heroic, which by asserting the ever-expanding human capability protests implicitly mat death is wrong, a disaster unfairly imposed by some outside enemy on "else immortal us." Tragic events themselves generate heroic expansion. Oedipus becomes wiser in his searching and suffering than was the confident ruler who opened the play. Macbeth in his agony of conscience and his full experience of despair has explored more of the human condition than the admired military man whom we first meet. It may be that our pleasure in tragedy is owing in part to its power of bringing together what in our psyches simply coexist unrelated, these two reactions of recognition and resistance—bringing them together, not in resolution, which is impossible, but in energizing interaction.[2]

1. "Thoughts for the Time on War and Death," *Collected* Papers, 4, p. 305.   2. I have explored this view of tragedy at more length in the Introduction to *The Comic Matrix of Shakespeare's Tragedies* (Princeton: Princeton Univ. Press, 1979).

Of course, to say that tragedy enacts our ambivalent response to death and to what death makes absolute, the failure of power and the end of hope, is not at all to say that all tragedies are "about" death. If *King Lear* in fact corresponds to the rhythm of dying, as Freud suggests, it is a special sort of tragedy; and its undeniable special potency may derive from this direct appeal to the very springs of tragic power. No tragedy of Shakespeare moves us more deeply, *involves* us, so that like Dr. Johnson we can hardly bear to look at the final catastrophe. Yet on the surface *Lear* seems remote in both matter and manner from our lives. Lear himself is no Everyman but an autocratic king. He begins the play by abdicating, but even in the act of giving up power he clings to "the name, and all th' addition to a king,"[3] retaining a train of one hundred knights and conducting a bizarre inquest of his three heirs to find out which of them pays him most tribute of love. Goneril and Regan soon reveal themselves as totally selfish, destructive to the point of denying Lear even shelter, so that he must endure the fury of the elements unprotected on a desolate heath. The rejected Cordelia, on the other hand, is so good that she "redeems nature from the general curse / Which twain have brought her to" (4.6.206–7). Eventually she seeks out this rejecting father, rescues him, forgives him, and in a way dies for him. Amid these all-or-nothing characters and situations, Lear's sufferings are correspondingly hyperbolical. They push him into complete mental breakdown before he returns to sanity, is reconciled with Cordelia, and in response to her death himself expires in exhaustion. These improbable events are made even more improbable by duplication. Gloucester's children are as archetypal in their moral sets as Lear's and behave with parallel exaggeration. Allowing full impact for Shakespeare's extraordinary language, which ranges in this play from the richly complex to the shockingly simple, we may still ask if there is not something special in this highly stylized dramatic pattern to tap such deep springs of recognition and emotional response.

Can it be that what we recognize in *Lear* is the process of dying? Each of us in that sense is a king who must eventually give up his kingdom. The loss of power and autonomy can be bitter, and the takeover generation will naturally look heartless and ungrateful to the loser. Culture's niceties and abstract concerns are stripped away as death draws closer, yielding to the demands of the ailing body. Mind as well as body may go out of control—a humiliation, but also

---

3. 1.1. 136. All Shakespeare quotations are from *The Riverside Shakespeare*, ed. G. Blakemore Evans (Boston: Houghton Mifflin, 1974).

perhaps a release. Or, under the stress of this fearful new experience, the mind may need to wrestle with the meaning of past life, call into question the principles never before examined. We may hope to win through before the end to peace with ourselves, to make friends at last with the necessity of dying. Lear's career from that reluctant abdication through struggle and pain to his reconciliation with Cordelia parallels the course of many dying patients observed by Elisabeth Kübler-Ross and other students of death and dying, from initial denial to acceptance. Indeed, the stages of response Kübler-Ross outlines in her study all have their correspondences, naturalistic and symbolic, in the action of the play. [See Elizabeth Kübler-Ross. *On Death and Dying*. New York: Macmillan, 1969. According to Kübler-Ross, there are five stages in the process of dying, all of which have parallels in *King Lear*—in the life of the king and that of Gloucester as well: (1) denial, discussed in the excerpt below, (2) anger, especially in Lear's curses and in the storm scene, (3) bargaining, as in the love-test and discussion about the number of knights to be retained, (4) depression (seen throughout the play) and (5) acceptance, especially when both Lear and Gloucester become resigned to their respective fates. ~ *Evans Editor*]

. . .

The intense *physicality* of this play also links it with the process of dying. Action and metaphor both are preoccupied with the body, its demands and vulnerabilities. The plot of *King Lear* has its share of physical violence, perhaps more than its share. There is nothing in the other plays so savage as the scene in which Cornwall and Regan, partners in sadism as well as marriage, put out Gloucester's eyes. Cornwall's servant stabs him and is immediately run through by Regan's sword. Oswald takes a beating from Kent and later a fatal one from Edgar, who also kills his brother in a duel. Goneril stabs herself after poisoning Regan. Cordelia is hanged. Lear is quick in his choler to threaten violence. Others, like Albany, helplessly anticipate it: "It will come, / Humanity must perforce prey upon itself, / Like monsters of the deep" (4.2.48–50). Unlike most of Shakespeare's tragic heroes, Lear and Gloucester are made to suffer physically as well as mentally. The audience must register, along with Gloucester's despair, his grotesque mutilated face with wounds where the eyes should be. And in Lear's spiritual ordeal on the heath we are not allowed to forget his physical exposure. "The tyranny of the open night's too rough / For nature to endure. . . . this contentious storm / Invades us to the skin. . . . In such a night / To shut me out? Pour on, I will endure. . . . the pelting of this pitiless storm. . . . this cold night. . . .

this extremity of skies. . . . this tyrannous night."[4] All through the storm-scene runs the insistent leitmotiv—cold, cold, COLD, eight times in the space of 184 lines.

These evocations of physical suffering cluster in the middle of the play, although retrospective references continue to remind us of the body's pains and frailties.[5] But the blows, stabs, and buffetings of *Lear* are not confined to dramatic action and situation. They are woven all through the language, so that physical violence dominates the metaphoric world of the play. Caroline Spurgeon found that the imagery of *Lear* keeps in our consciousness "a human body in anguished movement, tugged, wrenched, beaten, pierced, stung, scourged, dislocated, flayed, gashed, scalded, tortured and finally broken on the rack." What is more, evils of the mind or emotions are typically expressed as physical ones.[6]

. . .

The play's "story" is not, of course, of two old men coping with terminal cancer. Lear and Gloucester do not face death overtly until the action is far advanced, and Shakespeare does not dwell on their reactions when the time comes. What the two do face from the beginning is the loss of power—which is, after all, what dying is about: increasing helplessness, dependence on others with the accompanying indignities, autonomy waning until the self has no more function. Gloucester's power is wrested from him. By the middle of the play he has lost his title and lands, and he never regains them. The plot requires that Lear as king initiate his own transfer of power, but two aspects of the abdication are striking. First, the decision seems to have been imposed on him by age and weariness:

> 'tis our fast intent
> To shake all cares and business from our age,
> Conferring them on younger strengths, while we
> Unburthen'd crawl toward death.
>
> (1.1.38–41)

For all the King's vigor and authority, he is clearly entering a terminal phase.[7] Second, Lear is by no means psychologically ready to yield

---

**4.** 3.4.2–3, 6–7, 17–18, 29, 78, 102, 151.  **5.** Cordelia broods on Lear's ordeal in 4.3 and 7. Lear himself recalls it in 4.6. Any time the eyeless Gloucester is onstage, of course, such verbal reminders are unnecessary.  **6.** Caroline Spurgeon, *Shakespeare's Imagery and What it Tells Us* (New York: Macmillan, 1936), pp. 339 and 342–43. **7.** Freud observed in "The Theme of the Three Caskets" (p. 255) that when one considers Lear as not only old but soon to die, "the extraordinary project of dividing the inheritance . . . loses its strangeness."

up power, whatever he says. Denial, the first stage in Kubler-Ross's rhythm, begins immediately. When he banishes Kent for defending Cordelia, he is exercising automatically, unconsciously, the royal authority he has just supposedly handed over to others. There is a stagy quality to this scene—Lear formally dividing his lands among his daughters in response to their ritual protestations of love—that underlines its unreality for Lear himself. What rings true is his rage at being crossed, both here by Cordelia and Kent and later when Goneril and Regan try to get rid of his retinue of knights. Those hundred knights, as director Grigori Kozintsev realized when he was filming *Lear*, are not separate individuals but a collective representation of Lear's royal way of life.[8] In defending his knights—"My train are men of choice and rarest parts /. . .And in the most exact regard support / The worships of their name"[9]—he asserts his own worth as a person. When his daughters chip away at that worth, the worship of his name, by reducing his retinue, Lear reacts with the curses and commands of angry majesty. He ignores the new realities of power, just as he often fails to hear the Fool's jibing reminders that a king with no kingdom is nothing.[10] Another denial sequence occurs when Lear refuses to believe what he sees—that Regan and Cornwall have exercised their new power to put *his* servant in the stocks.

LEAR  No.
KENT  Yes.
LEAR  No, I say.
KENT  I say yea.
LEAR  No, no, they would not.
KENT  Yes, they have.
LEAR  By Jupiter, I swear no.

(2.4.15–21)

The self, convinced at the deepest level of its own immortality, rejects even the most direct evidence to the contrary.

. . .

By now many readers are probably objecting that I have fallen into an old trap for *Lear* critics, that of ignoring or refusing to face fully the play's agonizing last scene. Lear's last trauma is not his own death but Cordelia's; and he does *not* go gentle into his good night. True,

---

8. Kozintsev, "*Hamlet* and *King Lear*: Stage and Film," *Shakespeare 1971*, ed. Clifford Leech and J.M.R. Margeson (Toronto: Univ. of Toronto Press, 1972), p. 197. 9. 1.4.263–66. 10. On the communication blocks that dying patients may erect as aids to denial, see Edwin S. 1955), pp. 53–55.

and in both cases it could not be otherwise, because Shakespeare was writing a tragedy. Whatever psychiatrists may see as desirable adjustment, tragedy's business has always been to assert the self in the face of annihilation, to protest even while bowing to the inevitable. . . .

Together Cordelia's death and Lear's act out the paradox of mortality as both unnatural and inevitable. Hers is senseless and violent. Edmund has ordered the nameless captain to do away with her, but he repents and sends a countermand. He is, for no good dramatic or moral reason, too late. "I might have sav'd her," says Lear (5.3.271), and we do in fact feel that *someone* easily might have. Cut off young against all expectation and justice, Cordelia embodies our sense of death as wrong, outrageous. The hanging, the attack from without, expresses our unconscious conviction that, since death cannot be natural to us, it must come as "a malicious intervention from the outside by someone else."[11] Lear, on the other hand, is old and exhausted. As he collapses over Cordelia's body, those looking on see nothing unnatural, only the inevitable end of aging and decay. "The wonder is he hath endur'd so long" (5.3.317). No outside assassin here, but an internal process of wearing out, experience taking its toll. The enemy is he who would try to interfere with that process:

> he hates him
> That would upon the rack of this tough world
> Stretch him out longer.
> (5.3.314–16)

"*Ein alter Mann ist stets ein König Lear.*" ['An old man is always a King Lear'] Goethe's epigram is about the loneliness of the old, missing their contemporaries and cut off from the next generation. But in the light of recent work in the psychology of dying, it may be true in a deeper way that every old man is a King Lear. Now that death is at last being discussed openly, we find as so often that Shakespeare has been there before us.

11. *On Death and Dying*, p.2.

[From Snyder, Susan, "*King Lear and the Psychology of Dying.*" *Shakespeare Quarterly* 33 (1982): 449–60.] © 1982 The Folger Shakespeare Library. Reprinted with permission of The Johns Hopkins University Press.

# From "KING LEAR
## AND THE
## BEDLAM BEGGAR" (1996)

### William C. Carroll

> The winds and persecutions of the sky.
> The country gives me proof and precedent
> Of Bedlam beggars who with roaring voices
> Strike in their numbed and mortified arms
> Pins, wooden pricks, nails, sprigs of rosemary;
> And with this horrible object, from low farms,
> Poor pelting villages, sheepcotes, and mills,
> Sometimes with lunatic bans, sometimes with prayers,
> Enforce their charity. Poor Turlygod! Poor Tom!
> That's something yet. Edgar I nothing am.
>
> (*King Lear* 2.3.5–21)

Edgar's self-description follows the [Bedlam beggar] tradition closely, as he takes on the part with all its theatrical implications—grimed face, presented nakedness, roaring voice—and disappears into "nothing," into Tom's body. The gap between Tom's "basest and most poorest shape" (1.7) and Edmund's "shape as true, / As honest madam's issue" (1.2.8–9) seems absolute.

During the heath scene, Lear says to, or of, Tom, "Thou wert better in a grave than to answer with thy uncovered body this extremity of the skies" (3.4.100–102). For Lear, though not for those aware of who Tom is, the beggar's shivering, near-naked body is "the thing itself; unaccommodated man is no more but such a poor, bare, forked animal as thou art" (3.4.105–7). Lear's vision is powerful but incomplete: when he asks of Tom, "Is man no more than this?" (lines 101–2), we want to reply "Yes, much more," for the entire role of Poor Tom, as we have seen, is a complicated fiction. Tom is *always* "more than this," because he is always Edgar-as-Tom, and Edgar-as-Tom's suffering is in part a *performance* of marginality, exclusion, and dispossession. What seems to be the basest shape of nature is also seen by the audience to be a social construct: a stereotypical beggar's role fantastically performed by an Edgar who far out-tops even his brother's histrionic genius.

Yet "sophisticated" as he is, Edgar nevertheless still feels, in all its real pain, the role he performs. The burden of both playing and being such a creature as Poor Tom is very heavy for Edgar, the more so because Edgar's impersonation of Poor Tom is a particularly graphic and horrifying instance. "What are you there?" Gloucester asks, and Edgar tells him, with a vengeance:

> Poor Tom, that eats the swimming frog, the toad, the tadpole, the wall newt and the water; that in the fury of his heart, when the foul fiend rages, eats cow dung for salads, swallows the old rat and the ditch-dog, drinks the green mantle of the standing pool; who is whipped from tithing to tithing and stock-punished, and imprisoned; who hath had three suits to his back, six shirts to his body,
>> Horse to ride, and weapon to wear;
>> But mice and rats and such small deer
>> Have been Tom's food for seven long year.
>
> (3.4.128–38)[1]

Tom seems little more than an embodied mouth here, a paradigm of mere appetite which eats and drinks the scum of nature. This relentless emphasis on the physical body—what it ingests, how it is punished, what it wears—marks Tom's complete fall to the bottom of the lake of darkness, making Lear's belief that "our basest beggars / Are in the poorest thing superfluous" (2.4.266–67) seem optimistic by comparison. To be Tom at all is to feign *and* to endure grotesque physical torment.

The play's insistence on the suffering of the body is not confined to the Gloucester plot, to be sure, but it is represented most intensely there. Certainly Lear, Kent, and Cordelia endure their own physical tortures. As terrible as it is to shut an old man out in a storm, however, Lear's greatest punishments, in keeping with the nature of his transgression, are suffered in the heart. "We are not ourselves," he says, "when nature, being oppressed, commands the mind / To suffer with the body" (2.4.105–7). When an image of bodily torture is used with respect to Lear, such as the "rack," it is the rack "of this tough world" (5.3.320), but it is Gloucester who is physically bound, tormented, and blinded. When Lear feels as if he is "bound / Upon a wheel of fire, that mine own tears / Do scald like molten lead" (4.7.47–49), his suffering is internalized, the image figurative, though no less powerful or "real." And when Lear is cut, he is "cut to th' brains" (4.6.193), in an exquisite agony of suffering and despair, but it is Poor Tom who would actually lacerate his "numbed and mortified arms," and Edmund who will

1. The verbal links to other characters in the play—Kent is also "stock-punished" in 2.2, Oswald is called "three-suited" at 2.2.15—again make Edgar's experience refract that of others.

enact the "queasy question" (2.1.17) by cutting his own arm while claiming that Edgar "with his prepared sword he charges home / My unprovided body, latched mine arm" (2.1.50–51). For Edgar, Lear's insight that "when the mind's free, / The body's delicate" (3.4.11–12) is transformed into overwhelming bodily pain as a cause, consequence, and sign of mental suffering.

The great irony of the figure of Poor Tom is that while it is his body that endures mutilation and deprivation, it is Edgar's spirit that is trapped within, and Edgar—who would "the pain of death . . . hourly die / Rather than die at once" (5.3.189–90)—suffers spiritually. Many readers have always seen Tom as the embodiment of Edgar's suffering even as he is also a way of escaping it, but we should also recognize how Poor Tom is in a sense the *cause* of Edgar's suffering. Edgar's suffering is both released and caused by his performance of Tom's suffering.

To be Poor Tom is Edgar's trial. And in becoming as it were all body, subjected to nature, Edgar is forced to live out a grotesque version of what it must be like to be Edmund. Poor Tom's sufferings are therefore not only Edgar's—it is clear how his own personal pain is transmitted through this hideous disguise—but they are Edmund's as well. Displacement links them together, as does their fate to be nothing more than natural bodies, forbidden by law or culture from any place in the social hierarchy; Edmund's bastardy and Edgar's vagrancy are mirrored forms of arbitrary social exclusion. The link between. Edmund and Poor Tom is thus both implicit—Poor Tom appears only when Edmund has displaced Edgar and disappears when the son and heir is reunited with his father—and explicit, since Edmund first performs the voice of Poor Tom. Facing yet another banishment by his father—"He hath been out nine years, and away he shall again" (1.1.32–33)—Edmund has carefully engineered his plot so that he and his brother will be forced to exchange places: the category of "sonne and heir" and social outcast will be reversed; "the base / Shall top th'legitimate" (1.2.20–21) only to replace it. Edgar has not chosen this enforced role—no explicit motive is articulated for him—but it fits him perfectly.

The place where Edgar is freed and Poor Tom vanishes is Dover Cliff. Poor Tom of Bedlam is both "some fiend," as Edgar says (4.6.72), and "a poor unfortunate beggar" (line 68), as Gloucester says, and in 4.6 Edgar is released from the "fiend." The process begins with Gloucester's unexpected tenderness, when he asks the Old Man leading him to "bring some covering for this naked soul, / "Which I'll entreat to lead me" (4.1.44–45).

[From Carroll, William C. *Fat King, Lean Beggar: Representations of Poverty in the Age of Shakespeare*. Ithaca, New York: Cornell UP, 1996.] Reprinted by permission of Cornell University Press.

# FOR FURTHER READING, VIEWING, AND LISTENING

## READING

Aebischer, Pascale. *Shakespeare's Violated Bodies: Stage and Screen Performance*. Cambridge, UK: Cambridge UP, 2004.

Bate, Jonathan. *Soul of the Age: A Biography of the Mind of Shakespeare*. New York: Random House, 2009.

Bell, Millicent. *Shakespeare's Tragic Skepticism*. New Haven: Yale UP, 2002.

Bratton, J.S., ed., *King Lear*. Plays in Performance series, eds. Julie Hankey and J.S. Bratton. Bristol: Bristol Classical Press, 1987.

Brayton, Dan. "Angling in the Lake of Darkness: Possession, Dispossession, and the Politics of Discovery in *King Lear*." *ELH* 70 (2003): 399-426.

Calabritto, Monica. "Distracted Subjects and Gender in Shakespeare and Early Modern Culture, and Separate Theaters: Bethlem ("Bedlam") Hospital and the Shakespearean Stage." *Shakespeare Quarterly* 56 (2005): 484–87.

Charney, Maurice. *Wrinkled Deep in Time: Aging in Shakespeare*. New York: Columbia UP, 2009.

Colie, Rosalie L. and F. T. Flahiff, eds. *Some Facets of* King Lear: *Essays in Prismatic Criticism*. Toronto: U of Toronto P, 1974.

Cooke, Katharine. *A. C. Bradley and His Influence in Twentieth-Century Shakespeare Criticism*. Oxford: Oxford UP, 1972.

Crowl, Samuel. *Shakespeare Observed: Studies in Performance on Stage and Screen*. Athens: Ohio UP, 1992.

Davies, Anthony. *Filming Shakespeare's Plays*. Cambridge, UK: Cambridge UP, 1988.

Garber, Marjorie. *Shakespeare after All*. New York: Pantheon, 2004.

———. *Shakespeare and Modern Culture*. New York: Pantheon/Random House, 2008.

Gibbons, Brian. *Shakespeare and Multiplicity*. 1993. Cambridge, UK: Cambridge UP, digital printing, 1998.

Goodman, Russell, ed. *Contending with Stanley Cavell*. Oxford: Oxford UP, 2005.

Greer, Germaine. *Shakespeare*. Oxford, Oxford UP, 1986.

Greenblatt, Stanley. *Will in the World: How Shakespeare Became Shakespeare*. New York: Norton, 2004.

Hapgood, Robert. "Shakespeare on Film and Television." In *The Cambridge Companion to Shakespeare Studies*, ed. Stanley Wells. Cambridge, UK: Cambridge UP, 1986.

Harwood, Ronald. *Sir Donald Wolfit, C.B.E.: His Life and Work in the Unfashionable Theater.* New York: St. Martin's P, 1971.

——. *The Dresser.* New York: Grove, 1980.

Hatchuel, Sarah. *Shakespeare from Stage to Screen.* Cambridge, UK: Cambridge UP, 2004.

Honigmann, E. A. J. *Shakespeare: Seven Tragedies Revisited: The Dramatist's Manipulation of Response.* 1976; rev. New York: Palgrave, 2002.

Jackson, Russell, ed. *The Cambridge Companion to Shakespeare on Film.* Cambridge, UK: Cambridge UP, 2000.

Jones, Emrys. *Scenic Form in Shakespeare.* Oxford: Clarendon P, 1971.

Kastan, David Scott, ed. *A Companion to Shakespeare.* 1999. Oxford: Blackwell, 2006.

Kermode, Frank. *The Age of Shakespeare.* New York: Modern Library, 2003.

——*Shakespeare's Language.* New York: Farrar, Straus, Giroux, 2000.

Knutson, Rosalyn. *The Repertory of Shakespeare's Company, 1594–1603* Fayetteville: U of Arkansas Press. 1991

Kozintsev. Grigori. *King Lear: The Space of Tragedy: The Diary of a Film Director.* Trans. Mary Mackintosh. Foreword by Peter Brook. Berkeley: U of California P, 1977.

Kronenfeld, Judy. *King Lear and the Naked Truth.* Durham: Duke UP, 1998.

Lusardi, James and June Schlueter. *Reading Shakespeare in Performance: King Lear.* Cranbury, NJ: Associated U Presses, 1991.

Lynch, Stephen. "Introduction: Rethinking Shakespeare's Sources." In *Shakespearean Intertextuality: Studies in Selected Sources and Plays.* Westport, CT: Greenwood, 1997: 1–122.

MacDonald, Michael, ed. *Witchcraft and Hysteria in Elizabethan London: Edward Jorden and the Mary Glover Case.* London: Tavistock/Routledge, 1991.

Maquire, Philip C. *Speechless Dialect: Shakespeare's Open Silences.* Berkeley and Los Angeles: U of California P, 1985.

McGrath, Alister. *In the Beginning: The Story of the King James Bible.* New York: Doubleday, 2001.

Miola, Robert S. *Shakespeare's Reading.* Oxford: Oxford UP, 2000.

Moisan, Thomas and Douglas Bruster, eds. *In the Company of Shakespeare: Essays in English Renaissance Literature in Honor of G. Blakemore Evans.* Madison: Fairleigh Dickinson UP, 2002.

Murphy, John L. *Darkness and Devils: Exorcism and "King Lear."* Athens, Ohio: U of Ohio P., 1984.

Nuttall, A. D. *Shakespeare the Thinker.* New Haven: Yale UP, 2006.

Peterson, Kaara L. "*Historica Passio*: Early Modern Medicine, *King Lear,* and Editorial Practice." *Shakespeare Quarterly* 57 (2006): 1–22.

Petronella, Vincent F. "An Eclectic Critical Approach: Sources, Language, Imagery, Character, and Themes." *Approaches to Teaching Shakespeare's King Lear,* ed. Robert H. Ray. New York: Modern Language Association, 1986: 38–49.

Rollins, Hyder, ed. *The Letters of John Keats*, 1814-1821. 2 vols. Cambridge, USA: Harvard UP, 1958.

Skura, Meredith. "Dragon Fathers and Unnatural Children: Warring Generations in *King Lear* and Its Sources." *Comparative Drama* 42 (2008): 121–48.

Spivack, Bernard. *Shakespeare and the Allegory of Evil: The History of a Metaphor in Relation to His Major Villains.* New York: Columbia UP, 1958.

Walker, D. P. *Unclean Spirits: Possession and Exorcism in France and England in the Late Sixteenth and Early Seventeenth Centuries.* Philadelphia: U of Pennsylvania P, 1981.

Warren, Michael. *The Complete King Lear: 1608–23.* In 4 Parts. Berkeley: U of California P, 1989.

Weis, René, ed. King Lear: *A Parallel Text Edition.* 1993. 2$^{nd}$ ed. London: Longman, 2010.

## VIEWING

An Annotated International Database of Shakespeare on Film, Television, and Radio. British Universities Film & Video Council. bufvc. ac.uk/shakspeare/

Harwood, Sir Ronald. *The Dresser.* Dir. Peter Yates. Perf. Albert Finney as "Sir" [i.e., Sir Donald Wolfit], Tom Courtney, Eileen Atkins, Edward Fox, Michael Gough, Zena Walker. Columbia Pictures. 1983. Film, VHS, and DVD.

*Re Lear [King Lear].* Silent Film. Dir. Gerolamo Lo Savio. Perf. Ermete Novelli, Francesca Bertini, Olga Giannini Novelli, Giannina Chiantoni. Film d'Arte Italiana, 1910. DVD.

*The Yiddish King Lear [Der Yidisher Kenig Lir].* With English Subtitles. Dir. Harry Thomashefsky. Perf. Maurice Krohner, Esther Adler, Jeanette Paskewish, Jacob Bergreen Miriam Grossman. Lear Pictures, Inc. 1935. Film and VHS.

Shakespeare. *King Lear.* Dir. Peter Brook. Perf. Orson Welles, Micheál MacLiammóir, Alan Badel, Natasha Parry, Margaret Phillips. Omnibus/CBS-TV, 1953. DVD and VHS.

——*King Lear/Korol Lir* (Russian text by Boris Pasternak; sub-titles). Dir. Grigori Kozintsev. Perf. Juri Jarvet , Oleg Dal, Valentina Shendrikova. Lenfilm Studio, 1969. Film, VHS and DVD.

——*King Lear.* Dir. Peter Brook. Perf. Paul Scofield, Irene Worth, Cyril Cusack, Susan Engel, Alan Webb. Columbia Tristar GB, 1971. Film, VHS, and DVD.

——*King Lear.* Dir. Tony Davenall. Perf. Patrick Magee, Peter Jeffrey, Wendy Allnutt, Beth Harris, Ann Lynn, Patrick Mower. Thames Television, 1976. DVD.

——*King Lear.* Dir. Jonathan Miller. Perf. Michael Hordern, Frank
Middlemass, Anton Lesser, Penelope Wilton, Brenda Blethyn, John
Schrapnel. BBC/Time-Life, 1982. VHS and DVD.

——*King Lear.* Dir. Michael Elliott. Perf. Sir Laurence Olivier, John
Hurt, Dorothy Tutin, Diana Rigg, Leo McKern. Granada Television,
1983. DVD.

——*King Lear.* Dir. Richard Eyre. Perf. Ian Holm, Timothy West,
Amanda Redman, David Burke, Victoria Hamilton. BBC-Television,
1992. DVD.

_____*King Lear.* Dir. Brian Blessed. Perf. Brian Blessed, Hildegarde Neil (as
Fool), Jason Riddington, Phillipa Peak, Clare Laurie, Caroline Lennon.
Cromwell Productions and La Mancha Productions, 1999. DVD.

——*Great Performances: King Lear.* Dir. Trevor Nunn, Chris Hunt. Perf.
Ian McKellen, Romola Garai, Frances Barber. PBS Home Video,
2009. DVD.

### LISTENING

——*King Lear.* Dir. George Rylands. Perf. William Devlin, Prunella
Scales, Peter Orr, Michael Blakewell. Argo, 1961. Audiocassette.

——*King Lear.* Dir. Howard Sackler. Perf. Paul Scofield, Pamela Brown,
Rachel Roberts. Caedmon Audio Books, 1965. Audiocassette and CD.

——*King Lear.* Dir John Tydeman. Perf. Paul Scofield, Emilia Fox,
Kenneth Branagh. Naxos, 2002. CD.

——*King Lear.* Dir. Glyn Dearman. Perf. Sir John Gielgud, Kenneth
Branagh, Judi Dench, Eileen Atkins, Robert Stephens, Bob Hoskins,
Emma Thompson, Simon Russell Beale, Derek Jacobi. BBC Radio 3,
1994. Audiocassette and CD.

——*King Lear.* Dir. Clive Brill. Perf. Trevor Peacock, Samantha Bond,
Anton Lesser. Arkangel Shakespeare, 2005. CD.